Rosario + Vampire

Season II

10

AKIHISA IKEDA

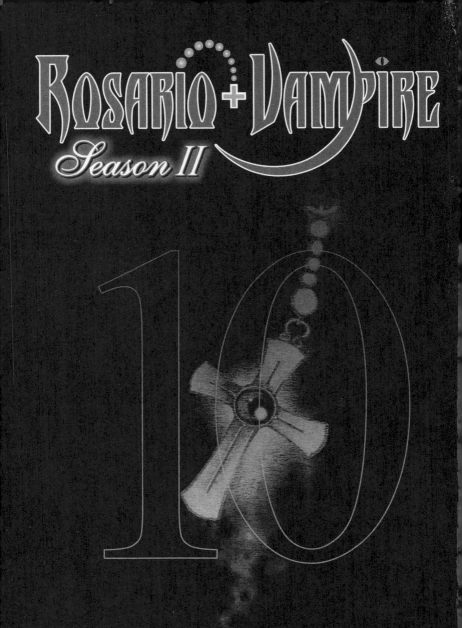

Horror Story Thus Far

Tsukune Aono accidentally enrolls in Yokai Academy, a high school for monsters! After befriending the school's cutest girl, Moka Akashiya, he decides to stay...even though Yokai has a zero-tolerance policy towards humans. (A fatal policy.) Tsukune has to hide his true identity while fending off attacks by monster gangs. He survives with the help of his News Club friends—Moka, Kurumu, Yukari, and Mizore. When Moka's Rosario seal begins to weaken, our friends travel to the Huang's home in Hong Kong to get it fixed. Unfortunately, when the great sorceror Tohofuhai attempts to repair it, Tsukune, Mizore and Tohofuhai are transported into Moka's mind, where they witness traumatic memories from her past and learn of Alucard, the True Ancestor of the vampires, who seeks to destroy the world. Then Moka is kidnapped by her sister Aqua, an operative of the evil organization Fairy Tale, which plans to resurrect Alucard! Tsukune and his friends begin training in earnest to save Moka from their clutches. While enduring the agony of master Tohofuhai's Body Alteration Spell, which will enable him to wield magic, Tsukune begins to transform into his out-of-control ghoul form. But Kurumu saves him...

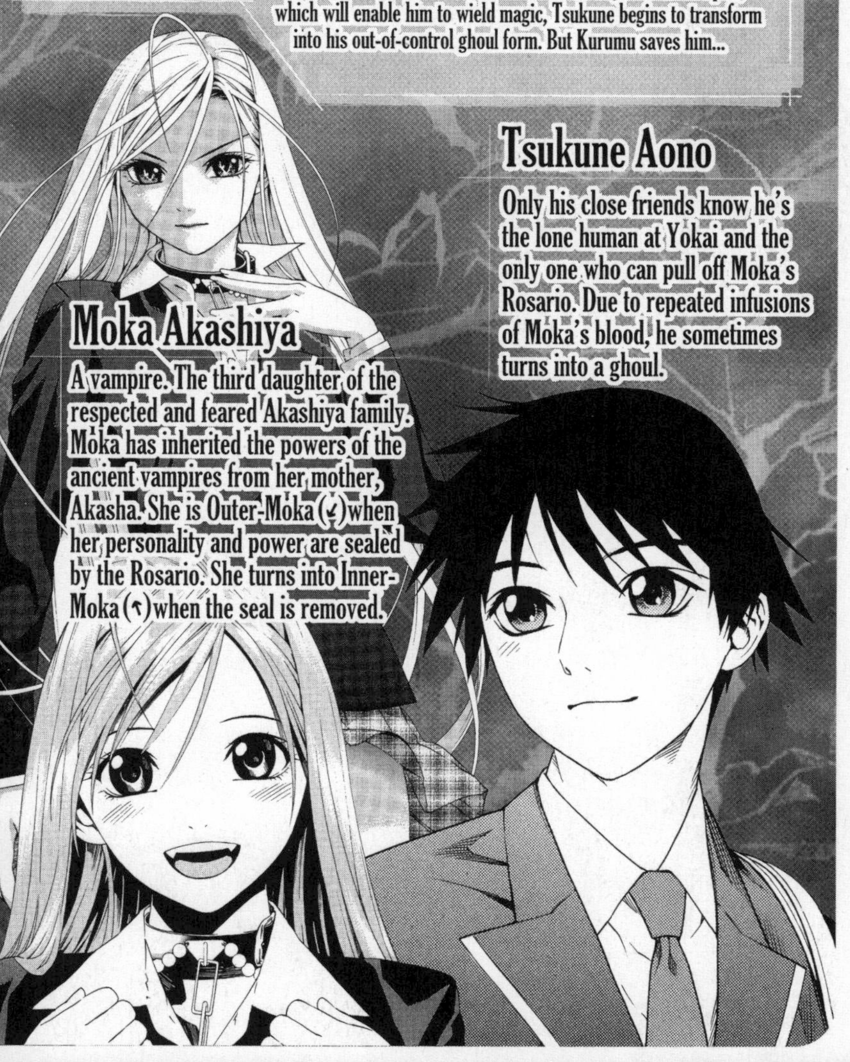

Tsukune Aono

Only his close friends know he's the lone human at Yokai and the only one who can pull off Moka's Rosario. Due to repeated infusions of Moka's blood, he sometimes turns into a ghoul.

Moka Akashiya

A vampire. The third daughter of the respected and feared Akashiya family. Moka has inherited the powers of the ancient vampires from her mother, Akasha. She is Outer-Moka (↙) when her personality and power are sealed by the Rosario. She turns into Inner-Moka (↑) when the seal is removed.

Kurumu Kurono

A succubus. Also adored by all the boys—for two obvious reasons. Fights with Moka over Tsukune.

Yukari Sendo

A mischievous witch. Much younger than the others. A genius who skipped several grades. Cute, but has a sharp tongue.

Mizore Shirayuki

A snow fairy who manipulat ice. She fell in love with Tsukune after reading his newspaper articles. ♡ It see her parents have accepted h love for outsider Tsukune!

Ruby Tojo

A witch who only learned to trust humans after meeting Tsukune. Now employed as Yokai's headmaster's assistant. A bit of a masochist.

Aqua Shuzen

Moka's elder sister and the eldest daughter. Having lost her mother as a child, she was raised by relatives in China. A master of Chinese martial arts.

Koko Shuzen

Moka's stubborn little sister. Koko worships Moka's inner vampiric self but hates her sweet exterior. Koko's pet bat transforms into a weapon.

Fangfang Huang

Freshman at Yokai Academy, the only son of a Chinese Mafia family that controls China's most dangerous monsters. Also a "Yasha," a Chinese demon who excels at transformation and sorcery. In awe of Tsukune.

Tohofuhai

Founder of the Huang Family, one of the three Dark Lords, and said to be the greatest sorcerer in the world—but now just a hardcore otaku?!

Hokuto Kaneshiro

A charismatic figure at Yokai Academy, despite being human. Betrayed Tsukune. Now a member of Fairy Tale's 1st branch office.

Miyabi Fujisaki

An executive at Fairy Tale, a sinister group based in the human world.

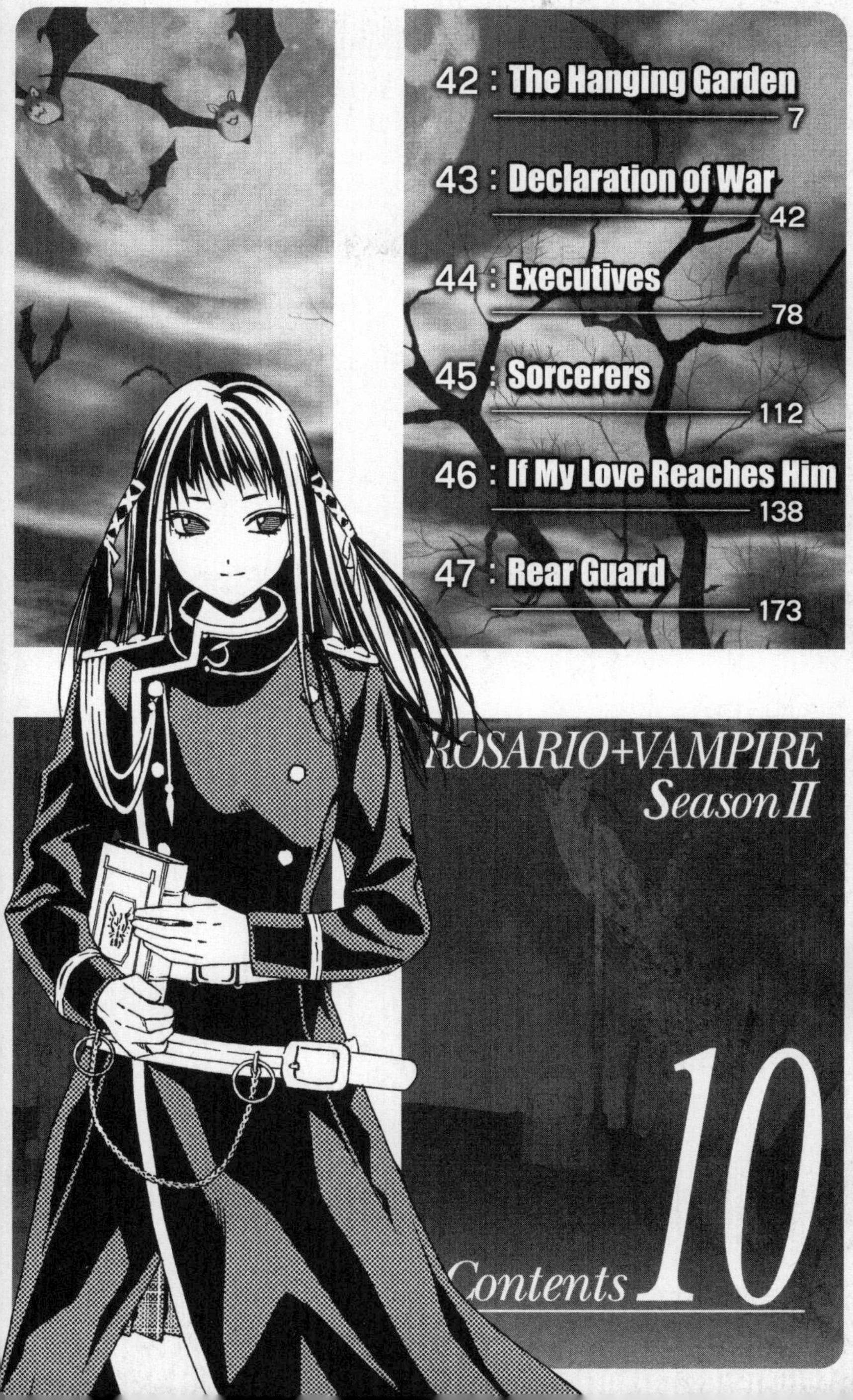

ROSARIO+VAMPIRE
Season II

Contents 10

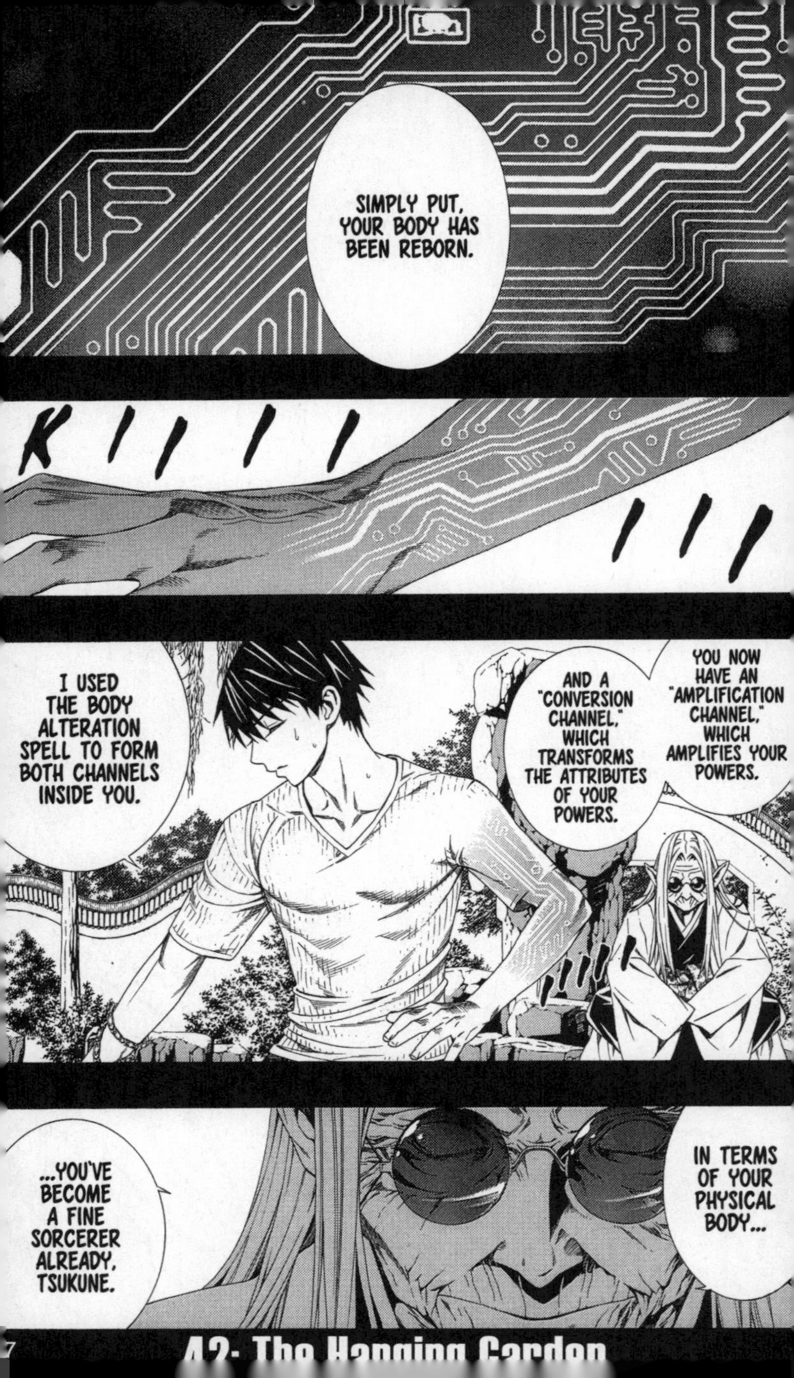
SIMPLY PUT, YOUR BODY HAS BEEN REBORN.
KIIII
III
YOU NOW HAVE AN "AMPLIFICATION CHANNEL," WHICH AMPLIFIES YOUR POWERS.
AND A "CONVERSION CHANNEL," WHICH TRANSFORMS THE ATTRIBUTES OF YOUR POWERS.
I USED THE BODY ALTERATION SPELL TO FORM BOTH CHANNELS INSIDE YOU.
IN TERMS OF YOUR PHYSICAL BODY...
...YOU'VE BECOME A FINE SORCERER ALREADY, TSUKUNE.

42: The Hanging Garden

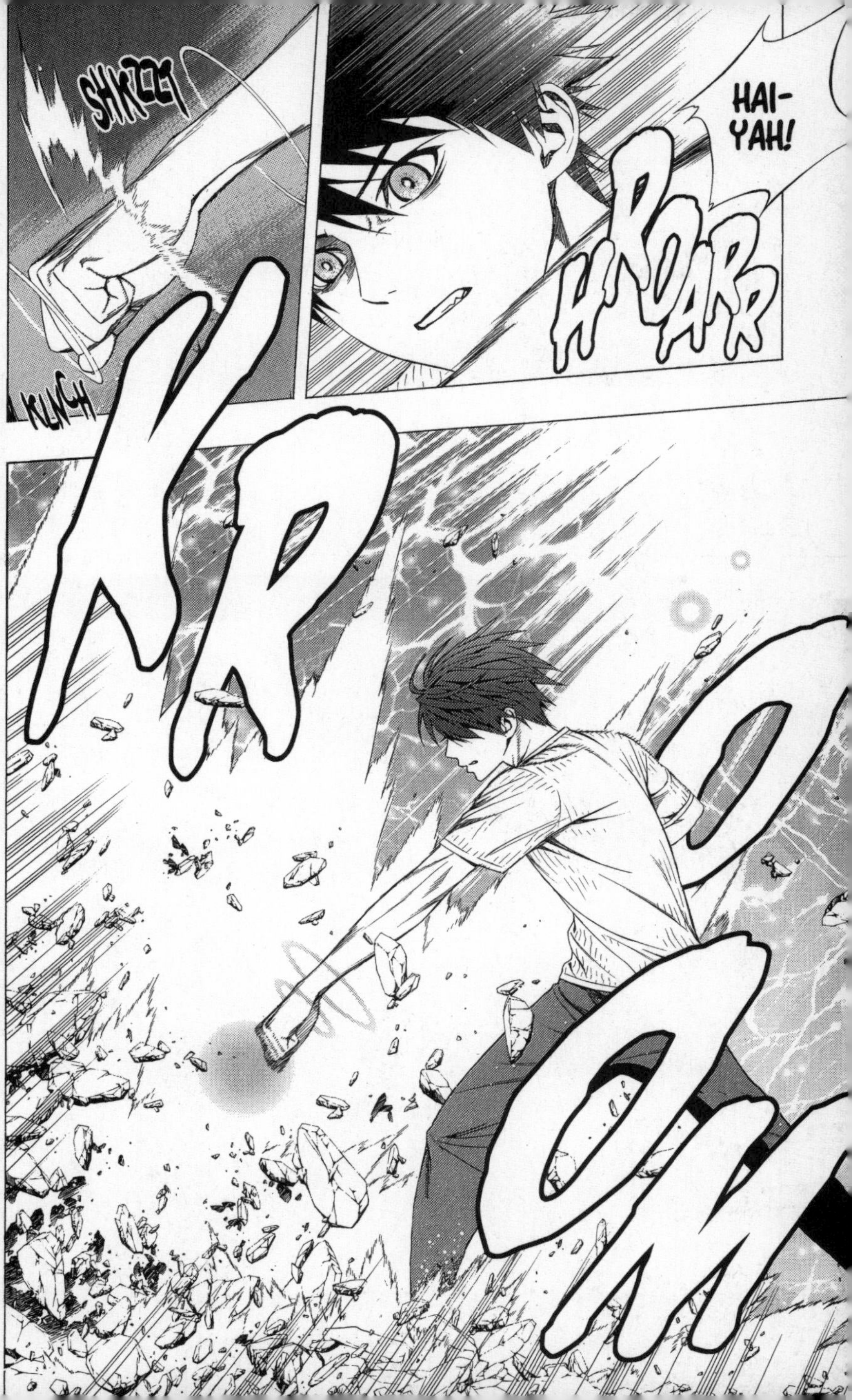
HAI-YAH!
HROARR
SHKZZT
KLNCH
KROOM

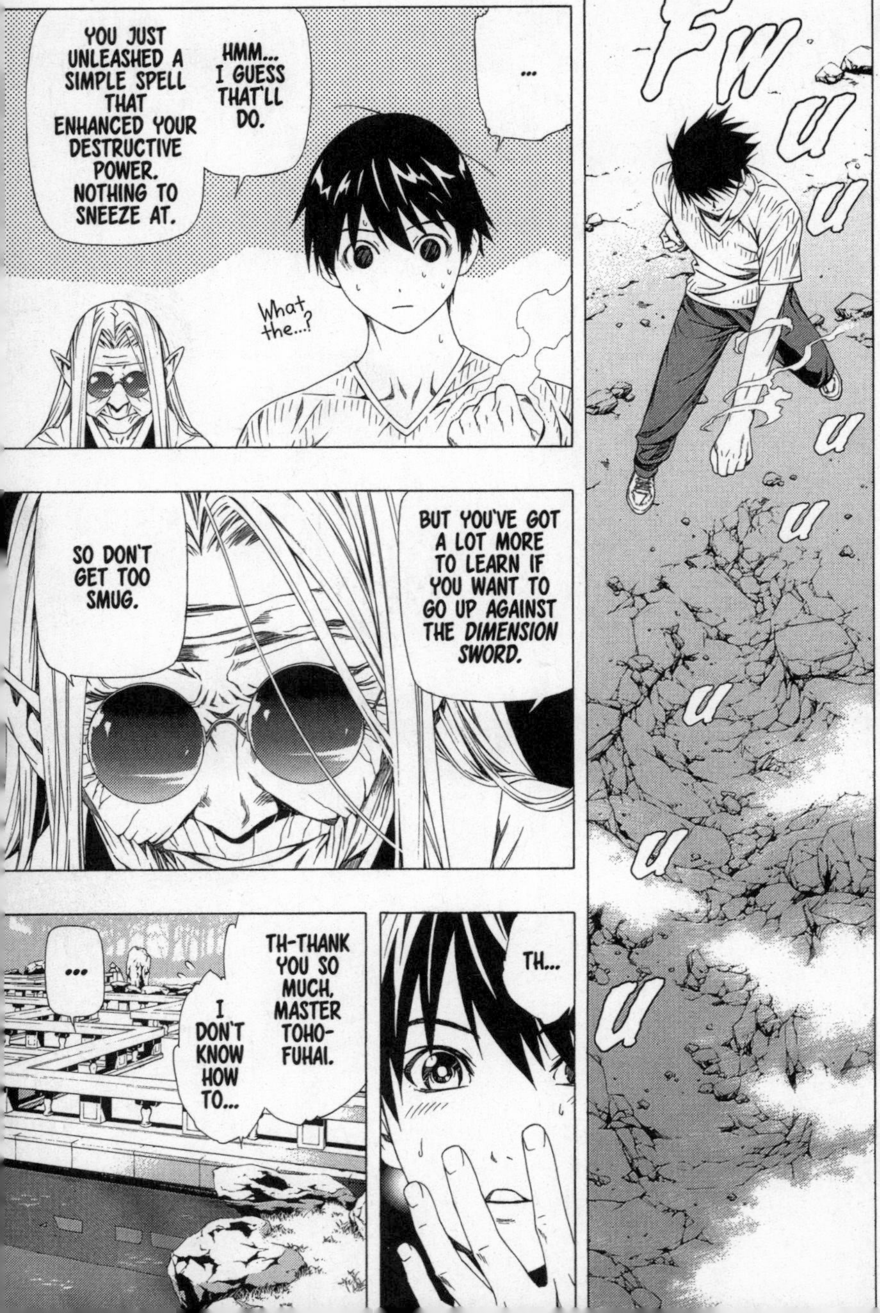
FWuuuuuuu
...
HMM... I GUESS THAT'LL DO.
YOU JUST UNLEASHED A SIMPLE SPELL THAT ENHANCED YOUR DESTRUCTIVE POWER. NOTHING TO SNEEZE AT.
What the...?
BUT YOU'VE GOT A LOT MORE TO LEARN IF YOU WANT TO GO UP AGAINST THE *DIMENSION SWORD.*
SO DON'T GET TOO SMUG.
TH...
TH-THANK YOU SO MUCH, MASTER TOHO-FUHAI.
I DON'T KNOW HOW TO...
...

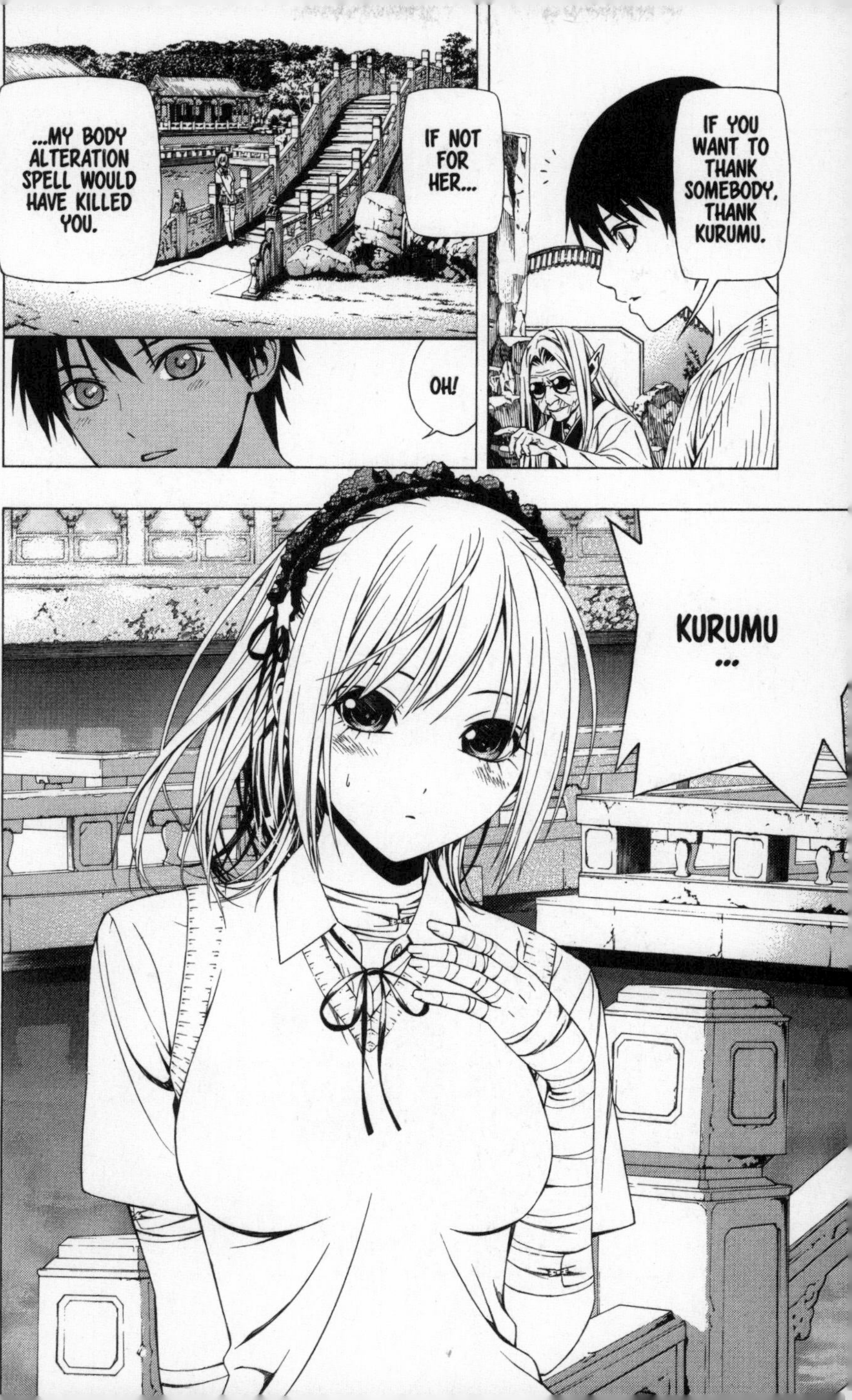
IF YOU WANT TO THANK SOMEBODY, THANK KURUMU.
IF NOT FOR HER...
...MY BODY ALTERATION SPELL WOULD HAVE KILLED YOU.
OH!
KURUMU ...

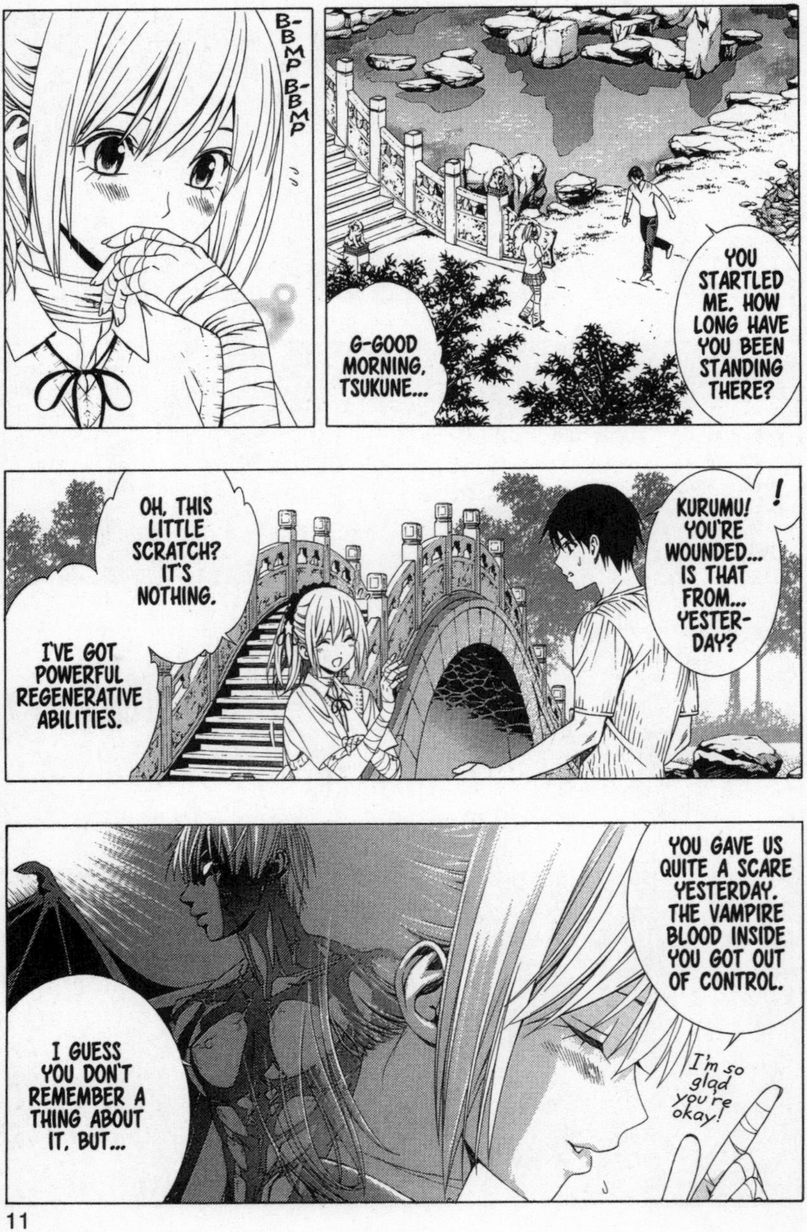
YOU STARTLED ME. HOW LONG HAVE YOU BEEN STANDING THERE?
G-GOOD MORNING, TSUKUNE...
B-BBMP B-BBMP
!
KURUMU! YOU'RE WOUNDED... IS THAT FROM... YESTER-DAY?
OH, THIS LITTLE SCRATCH? IT'S NOTHING.
I'VE GOT POWERFUL REGENERATIVE ABILITIES.
YOU GAVE US QUITE A SCARE YESTERDAY. THE VAMPIRE BLOOD INSIDE YOU GOT OUT OF CONTROL.
I'm so glad you're okay!
I GUESS YOU DON'T REMEMBER A THING ABOUT IT, BUT...

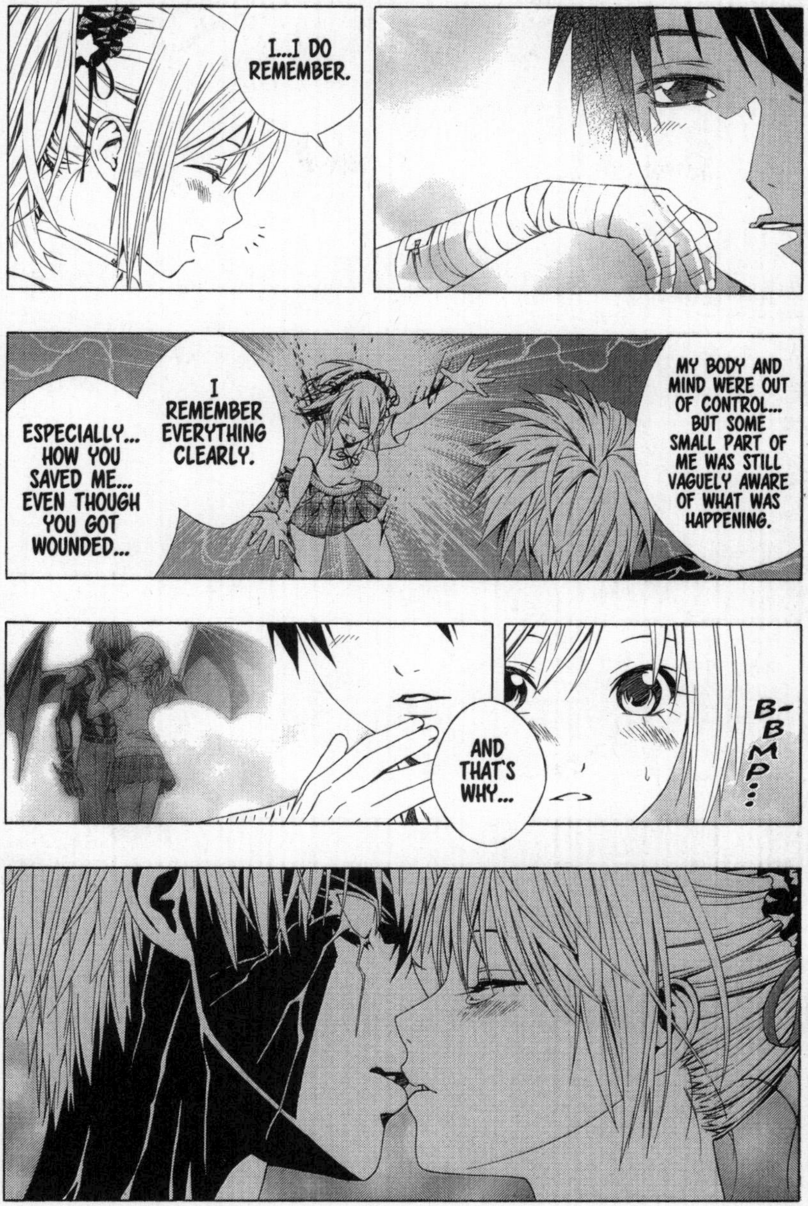
I...I DO REMEMBER.
MY BODY AND MIND WERE OUT OF CONTROL... BUT SOME SMALL PART OF ME WAS STILL VAGUELY AWARE OF WHAT WAS HAPPENING.
I REMEMBER EVERYTHING CLEARLY.
ESPECIALLY... HOW YOU SAVED ME... EVEN THOUGH YOU GOT WOUNDED...
B-BMP...
AND THAT'S WHY...

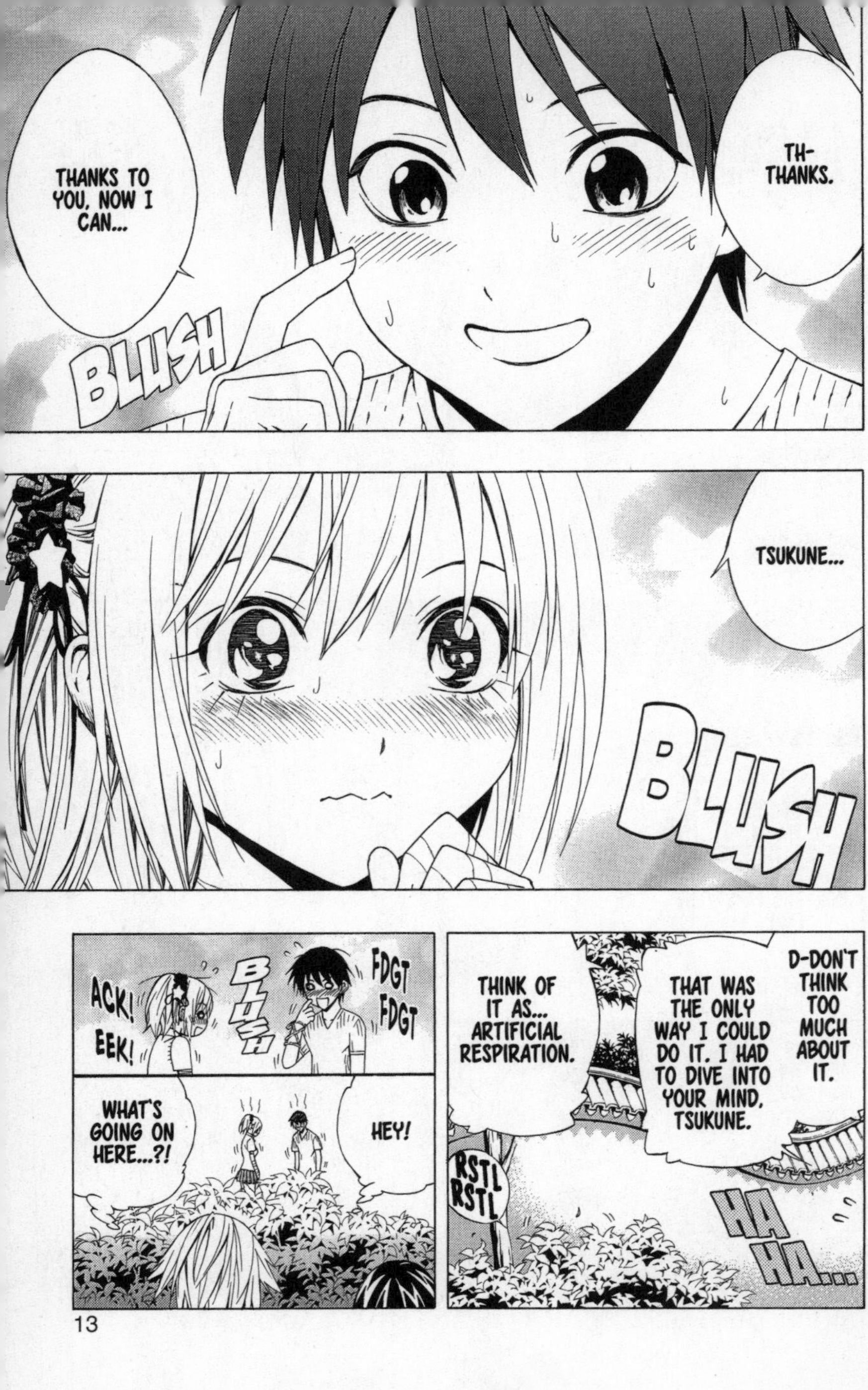
TH- THANKS.
THANKS TO YOU, NOW I CAN...
BLUSH
TSUKUNE...
BLUSH
D-DON'T THINK TOO MUCH ABOUT IT.
THAT WAS THE ONLY WAY I COULD DO IT. I HAD TO DIVE INTO YOUR MIND, TSUKUNE.
THINK OF IT AS... ARTIFICIAL RESPIRATION.
HA HA...
RSTL RSTL
FDGT FDGT
BLUSH
ACK! EEK!
HEY!
WHAT'S GOING ON HERE...?!

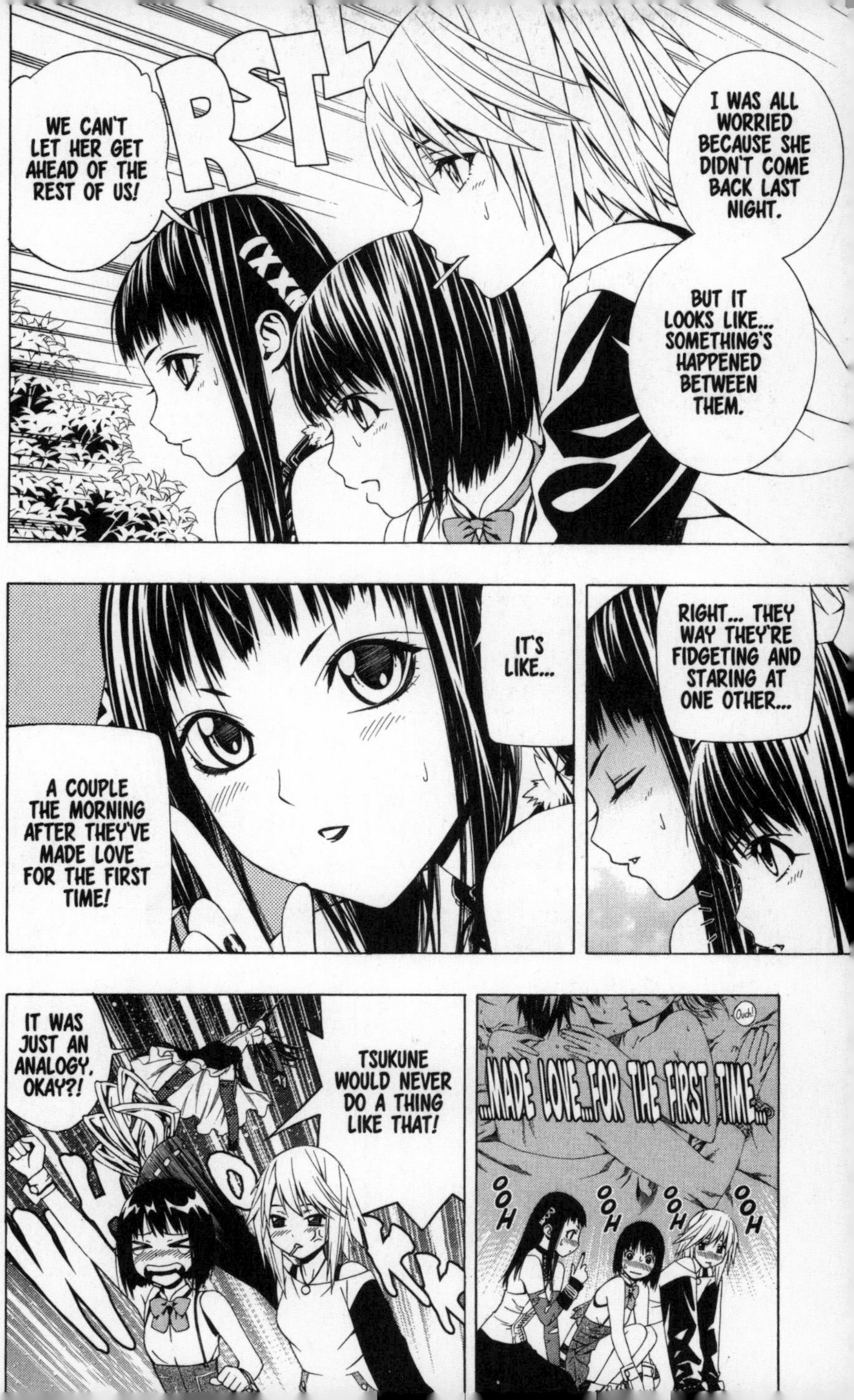
I WAS ALL WORRIED BECAUSE SHE DIDN'T COME BACK LAST NIGHT.
BUT IT LOOKS LIKE... SOMETHING'S HAPPENED BETWEEN THEM.
RSTL
WE CAN'T LET HER GET AHEAD OF THE REST OF US!
RIGHT... THEY WAY THEY'RE FIDGETING AND STARING AT ONE OTHER...
IT'S LIKE...
A COUPLE THE MORNING AFTER THEY'VE MADE LOVE FOR THE FIRST TIME!
Ouch!
...MADE LOVE...FOR THE FIRST TIME...
OOH
OOH
OOH
OOH
TSUKUNE WOULD NEVER DO A THING LIKE THAT!
IT WAS JUST AN ANALOGY, OKAY?!

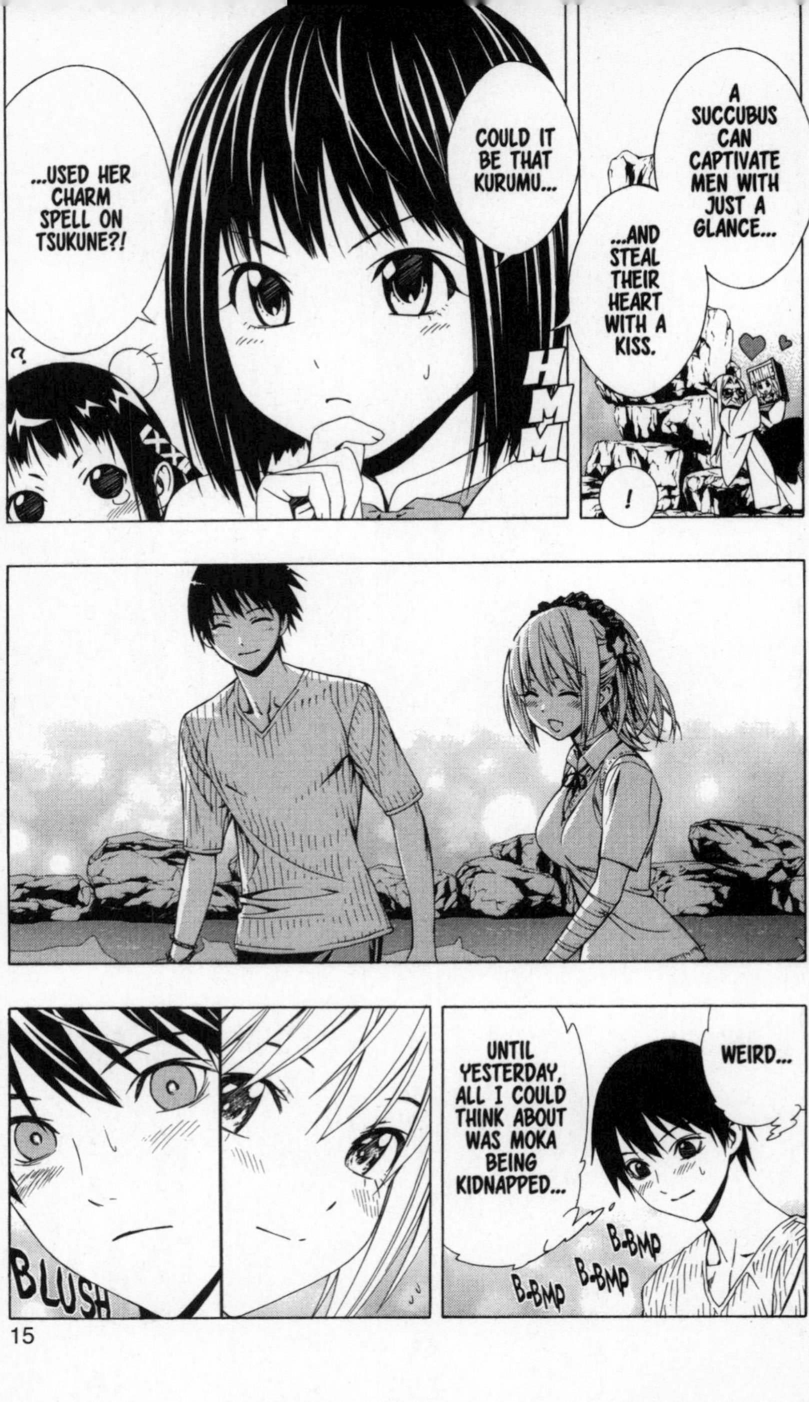
A SUCCUBUS CAN CAPTIVATE MEN WITH JUST A GLANCE...
...AND STEAL THEIR HEART WITH A KISS.
!
COULD IT BE THAT KURUMU...
...USED HER CHARM SPELL ON TSUKUNE?!
HMMM
?
WEIRD...
UNTIL YESTERDAY, ALL I COULD THINK ABOUT WAS MOKA BEING KIDNAPPED...
B-BMP
B-BMP
B-BMP
BLUSH

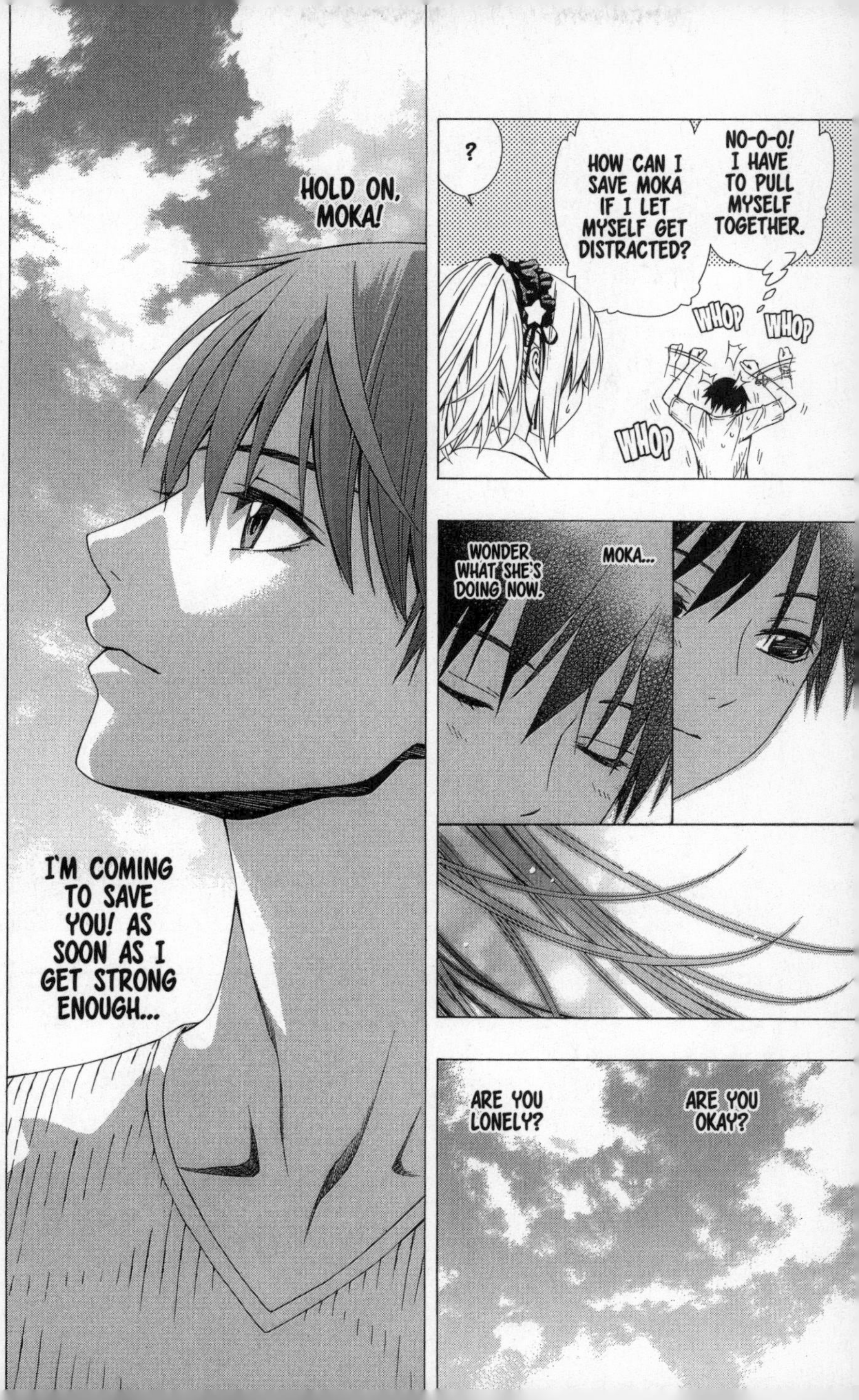
NO-O-O! I HAVE TO PULL MYSELF TOGETHER.
HOW CAN I SAVE MOKA IF I LET MYSELF GET DISTRACTED?
?
WHOP
WHOP
WHOP
MOKA...
WONDER WHAT SHE'S DOING NOW.
ARE YOU OKAY?
ARE YOU LONELY?
HOLD ON, MOKA!
I'M COMING TO SAVE YOU! AS SOON AS I GET STRONG ENOUGH...

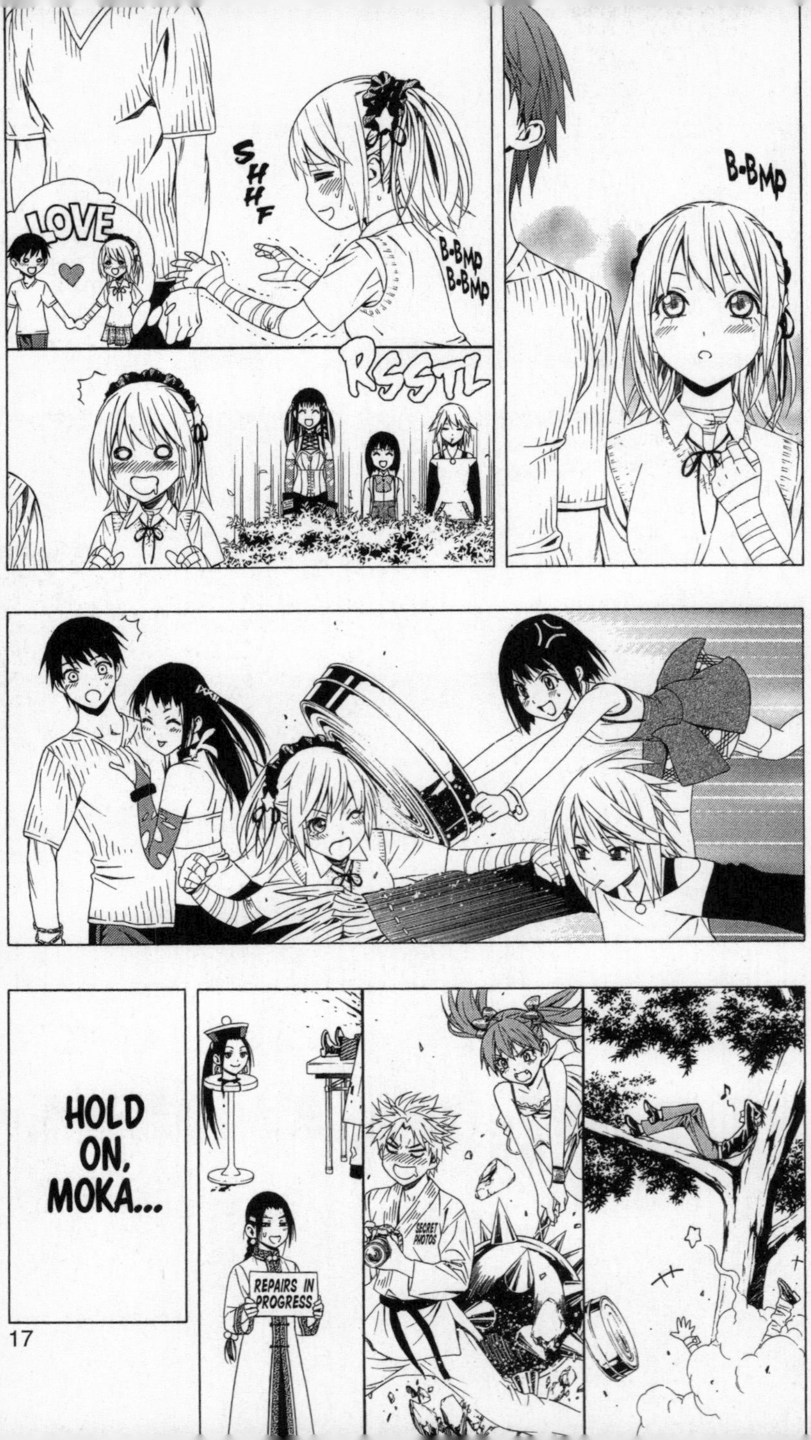
B-BMP
B-BMP
B-BMP
SHHF
LOVE
RSSTL
SECRET PHOTOS
REPAIRS IN PROGRESS
HOLD ON, MOKA...

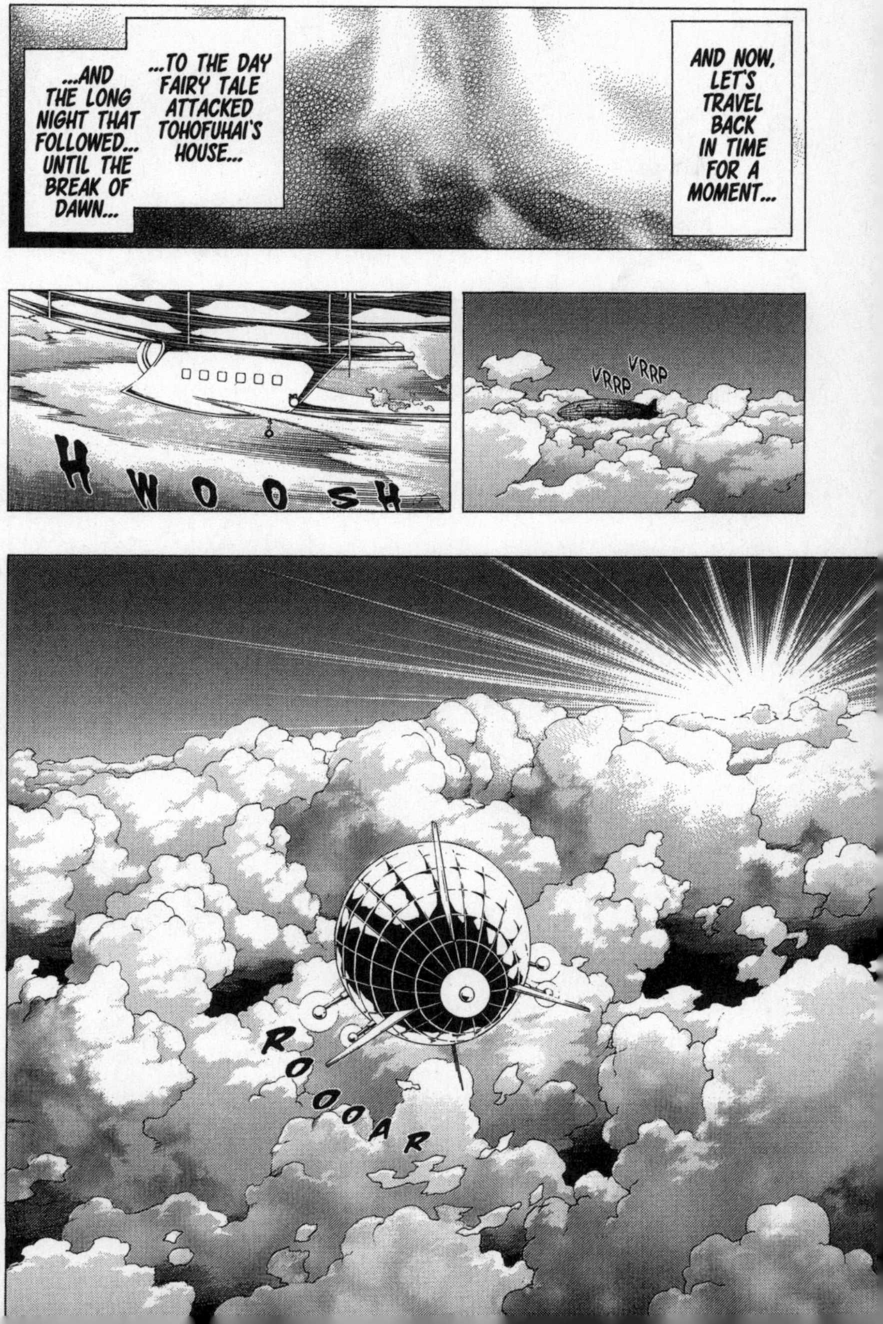
AND NOW, LET'S TRAVEL BACK IN TIME FOR A MOMENT...
...TO THE DAY FAIRY TALE ATTACKED TOHOFUHAI'S HOUSE...
...AND THE LONG NIGHT THAT FOLLOWED... UNTIL THE BREAK OF DAWN...
VRRP
VRRP
HWOOSH
ROOOAR

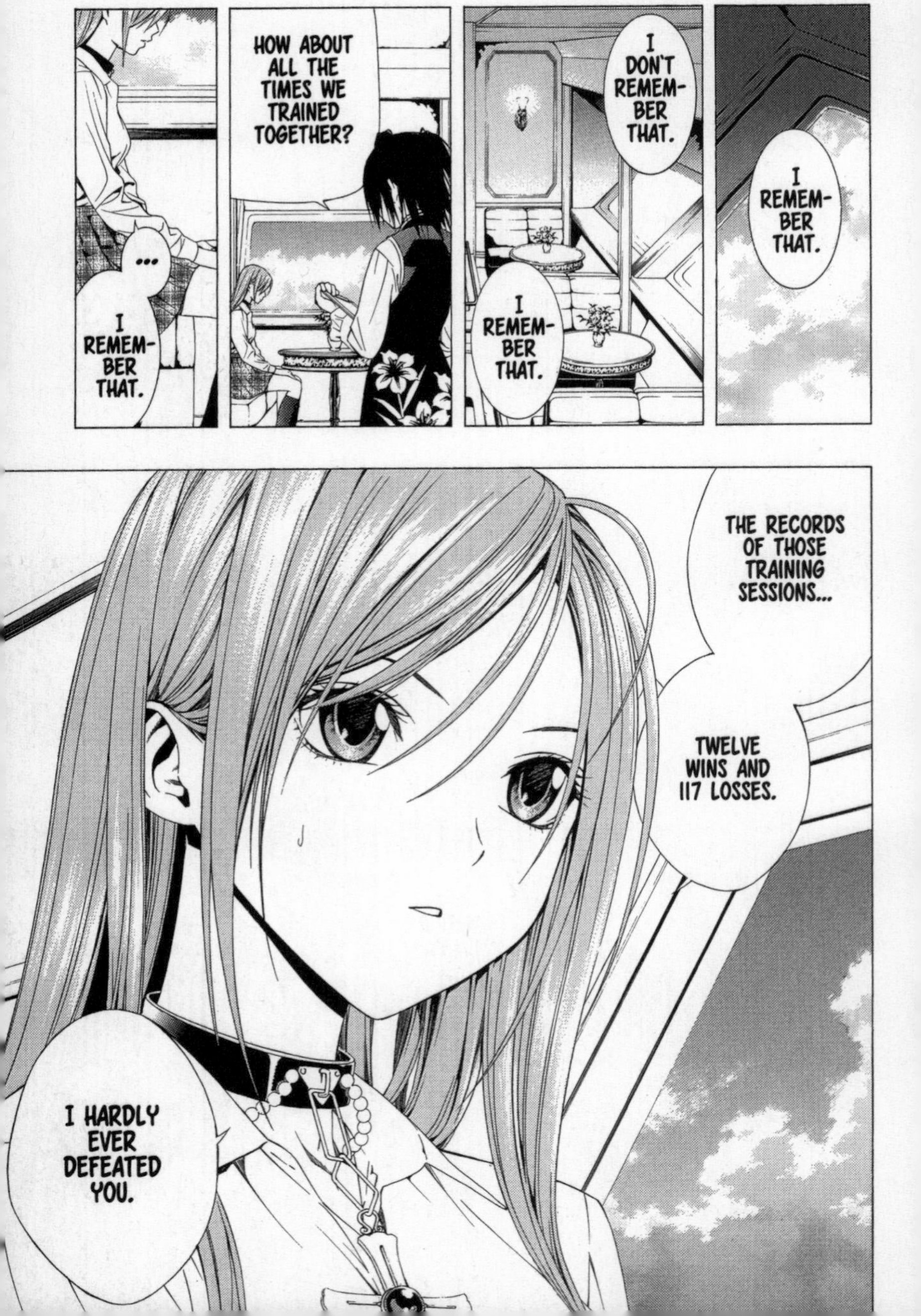

I REMEMBER THAT.
I DON'T REMEMBER THAT.
I REMEMBER THAT.
HOW ABOUT ALL THE TIMES WE TRAINED TOGETHER?
...
I REMEMBER THAT.
THE RECORDS OF THOSE TRAINING SESSIONS...
TWELVE WINS AND 117 LOSSES.
I HARDLY EVER DEFEATED YOU.

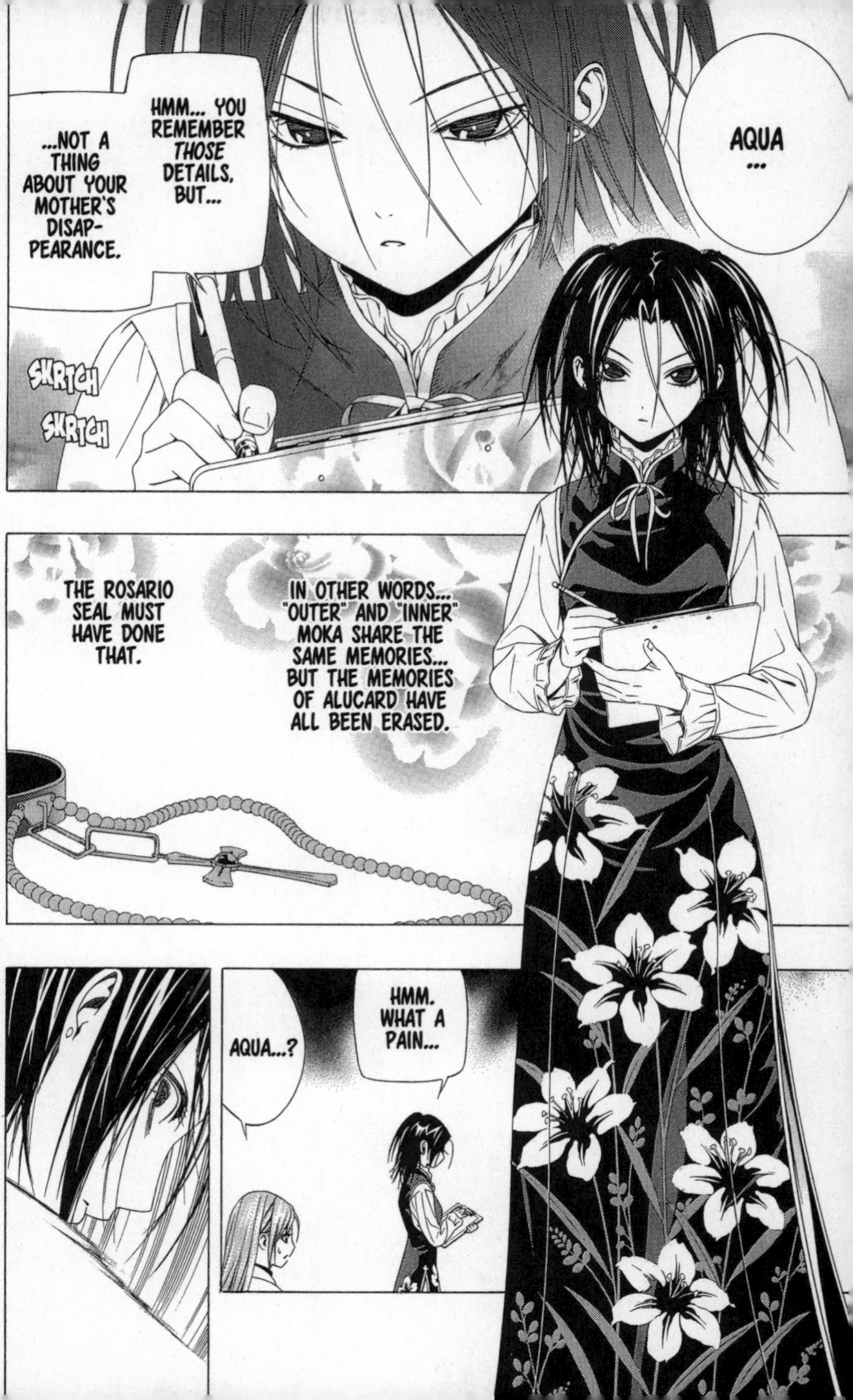
AQUA...
HMM... YOU REMEMBER THOSE DETAILS, BUT...
...NOT A THING ABOUT YOUR MOTHER'S DISAP-PEARANCE.
SKRTCH
SKRTCH
IN OTHER WORDS... "OUTER" AND "INNER" MOKA SHARE THE SAME MEMORIES... BUT THE MEMORIES OF ALUCARD HAVE ALL BEEN ERASED.
THE ROSARIO SEAL MUST HAVE DONE THAT.
HMM. WHAT A PAIN...
AQUA...?

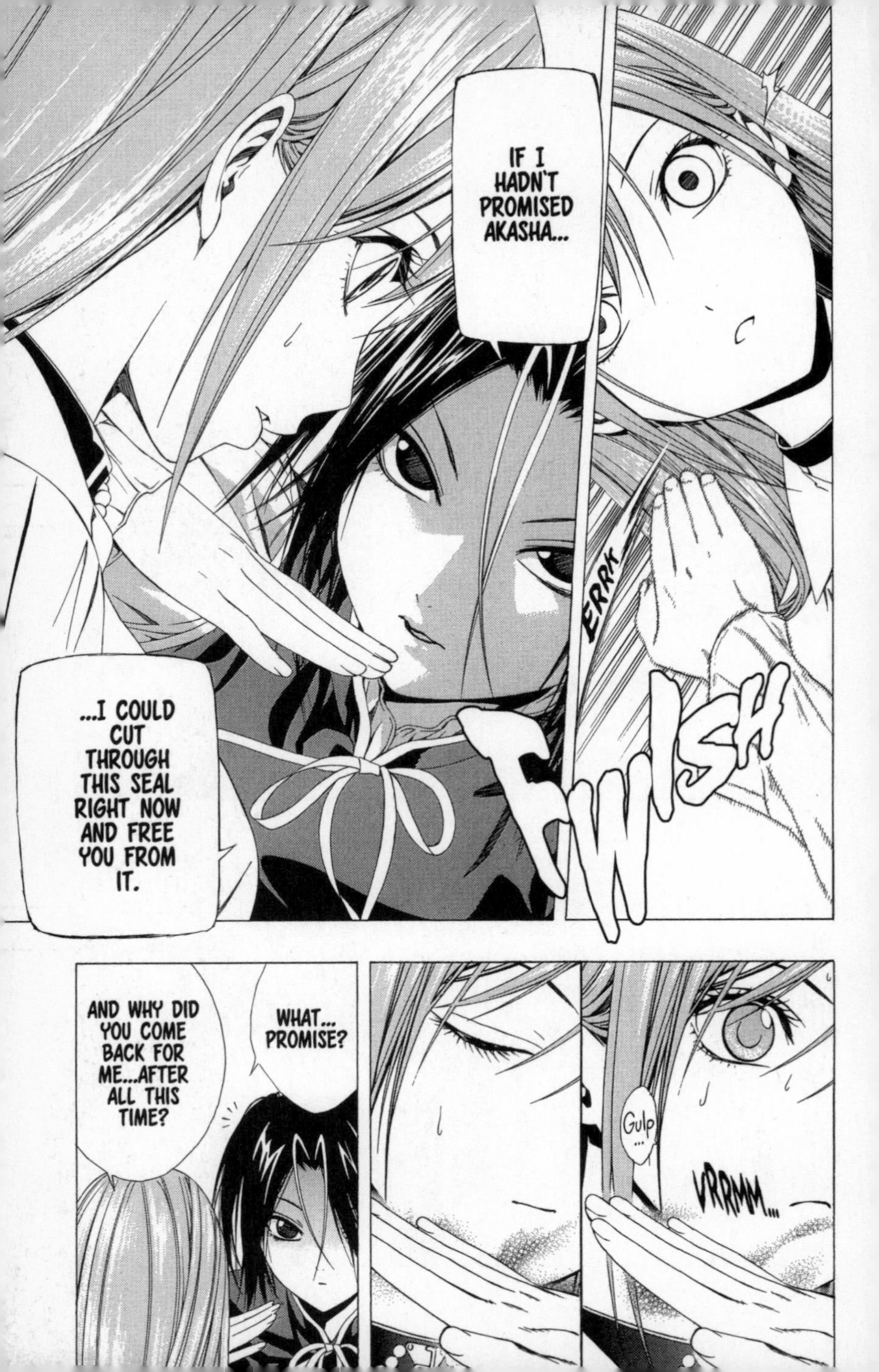
IF I HADN'T PROMISED AKASHA...
ERRK
FWISH
...I COULD CUT THROUGH THIS SEAL RIGHT NOW AND FREE YOU FROM IT.
Gulp...
VRRMM...
WHAT... PROMISE?
AND WHY DID YOU COME BACK FOR ME...AFTER ALL THIS TIME?

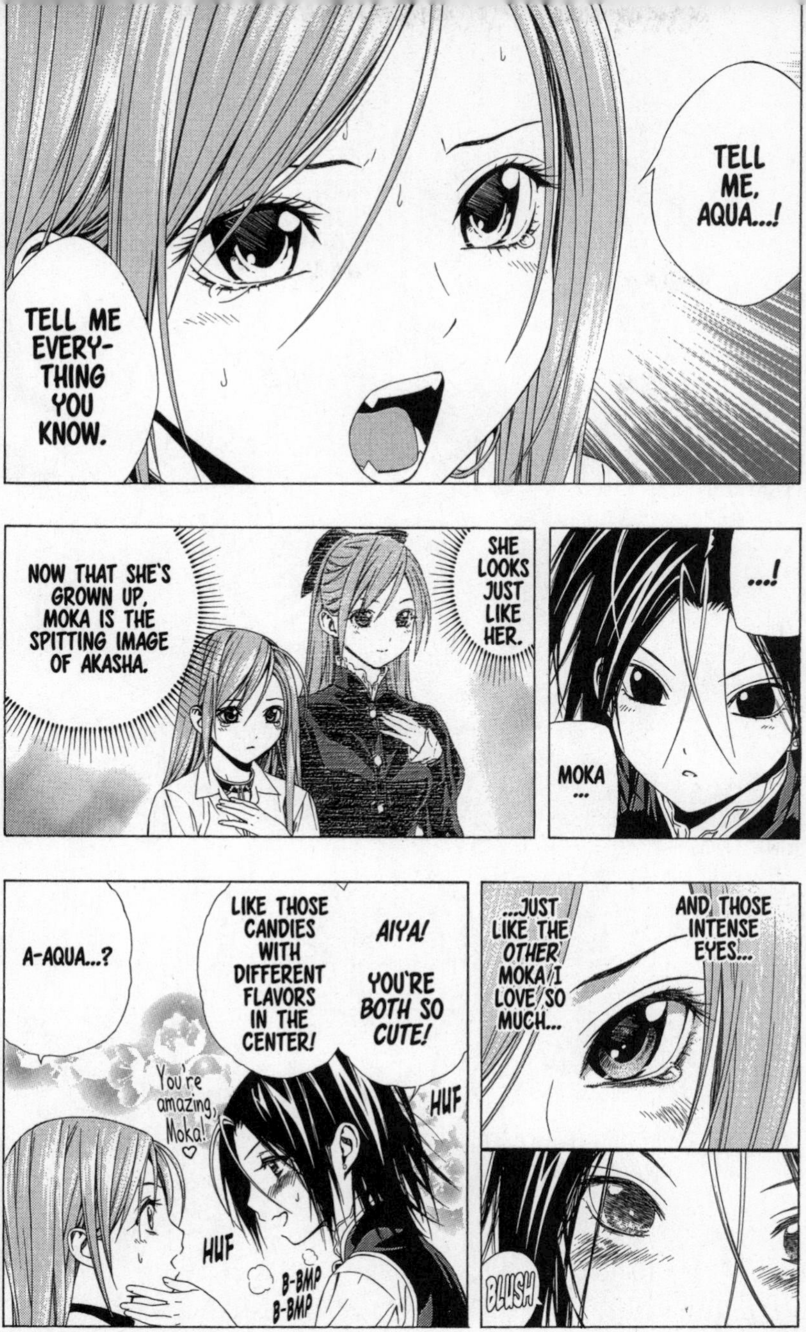
TELL ME, AQUA...!
TELL ME EVERY-THING YOU KNOW.
...!
MOKA...
SHE LOOKS JUST LIKE HER.
NOW THAT SHE'S GROWN UP, MOKA IS THE SPITTING IMAGE OF AKASHA.
AND THOSE INTENSE EYES...
...JUST LIKE THE OTHER MOKA I LOVE SO MUCH...
BLUSH
AIYA! YOU'RE BOTH SO CUTE!
LIKE THOSE CANDIES WITH DIFFERENT FLAVORS IN THE CENTER!
HUF
A-AQUA...?
You're amazing, Moka! ♡
HUF
B-BMP B-BMP

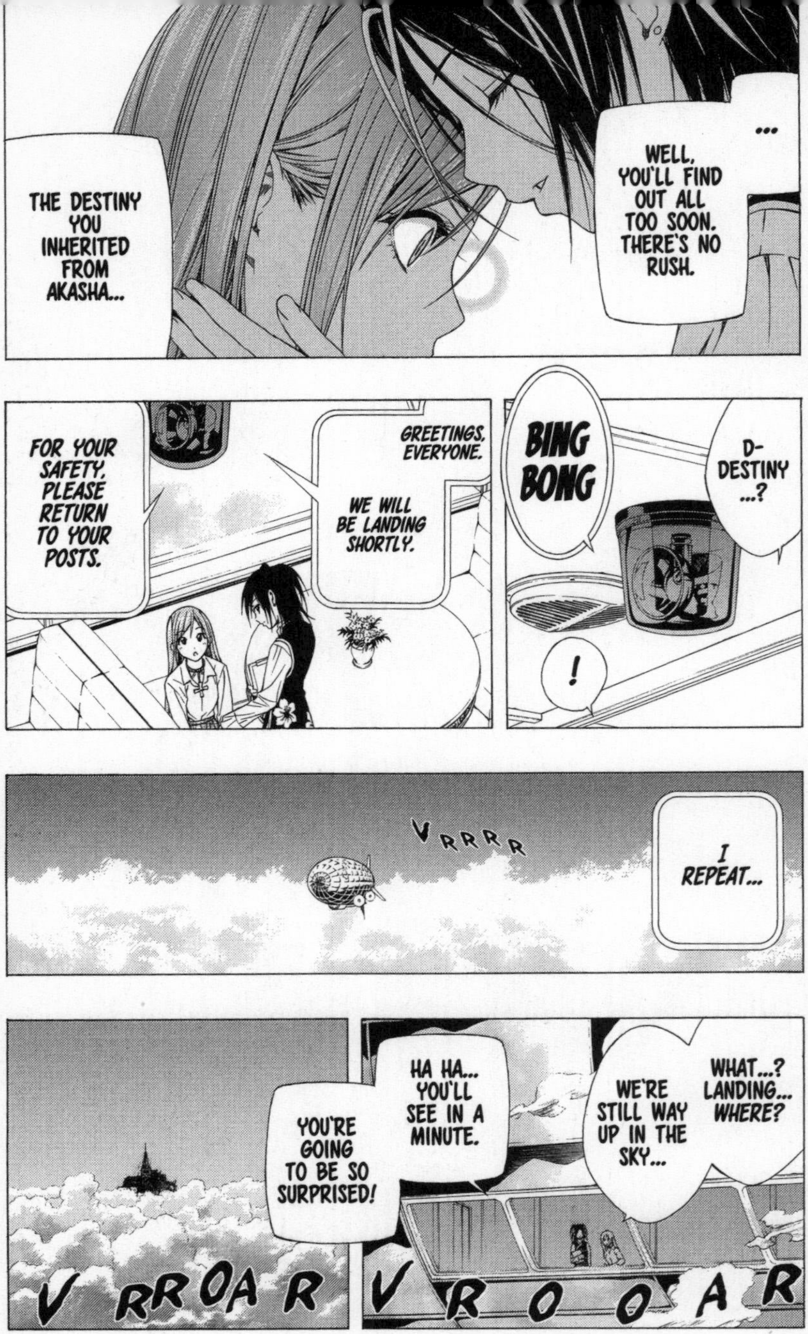
...
WELL, YOU'LL FIND OUT ALL TOO SOON. THERE'S NO RUSH.
THE DESTINY YOU INHERITED FROM AKASHA...
D-DESTINY ...?
BING BONG
!
GREETINGS, EVERYONE.
WE WILL BE LANDING SHORTLY.
FOR YOUR SAFETY, PLEASE RETURN TO YOUR POSTS.
I REPEAT...
VRRRR
WHAT...? LANDING... WHERE?
WE'RE STILL WAY UP IN THE SKY...
HA HA... YOU'LL SEE IN A MINUTE.
YOU'RE GOING TO BE SO SURPRISED!
VROOOAR
VRROAR

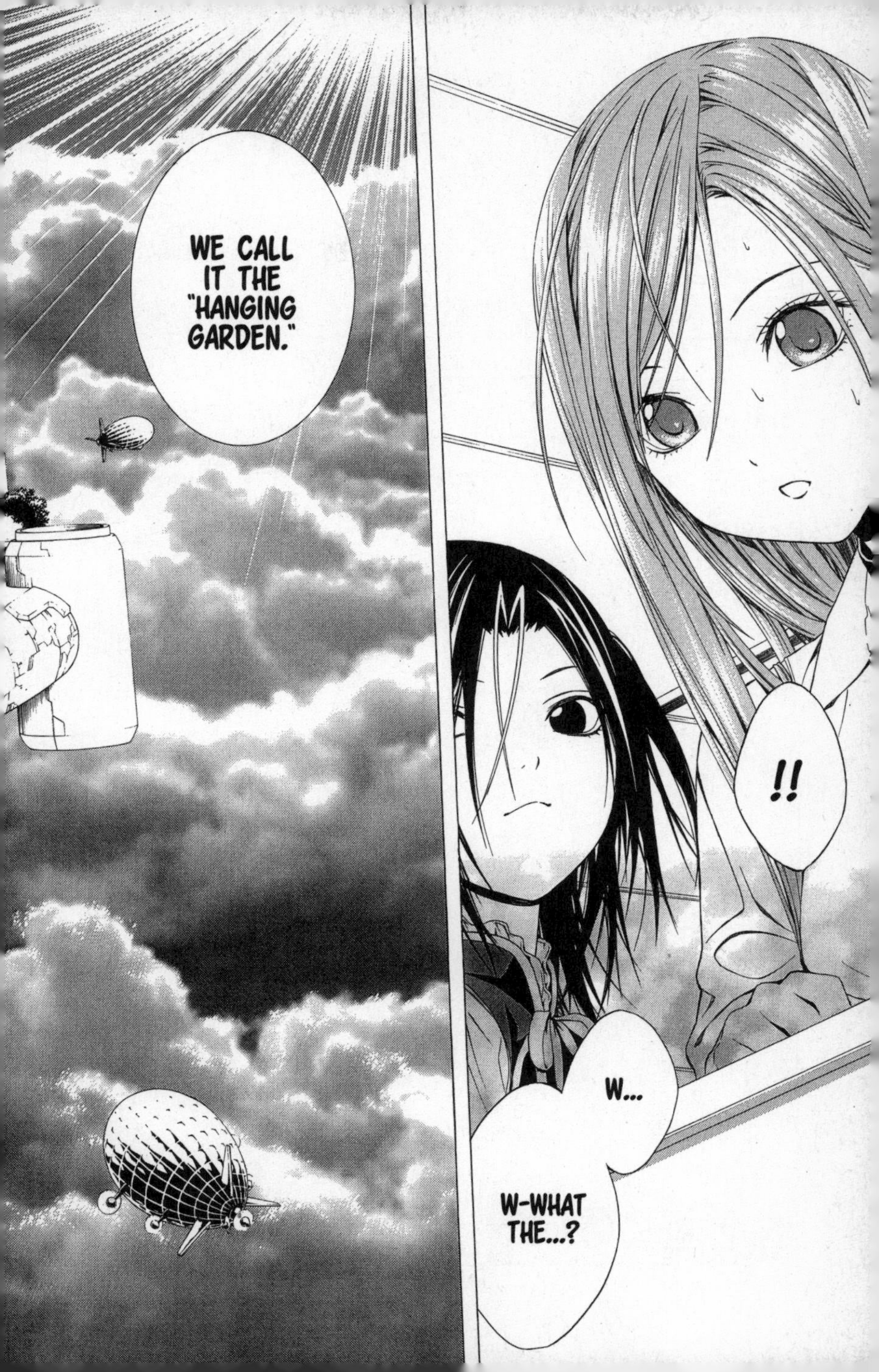
!!
W...
W-WHAT THE...?
WE CALL IT THE "HANGING GARDEN."

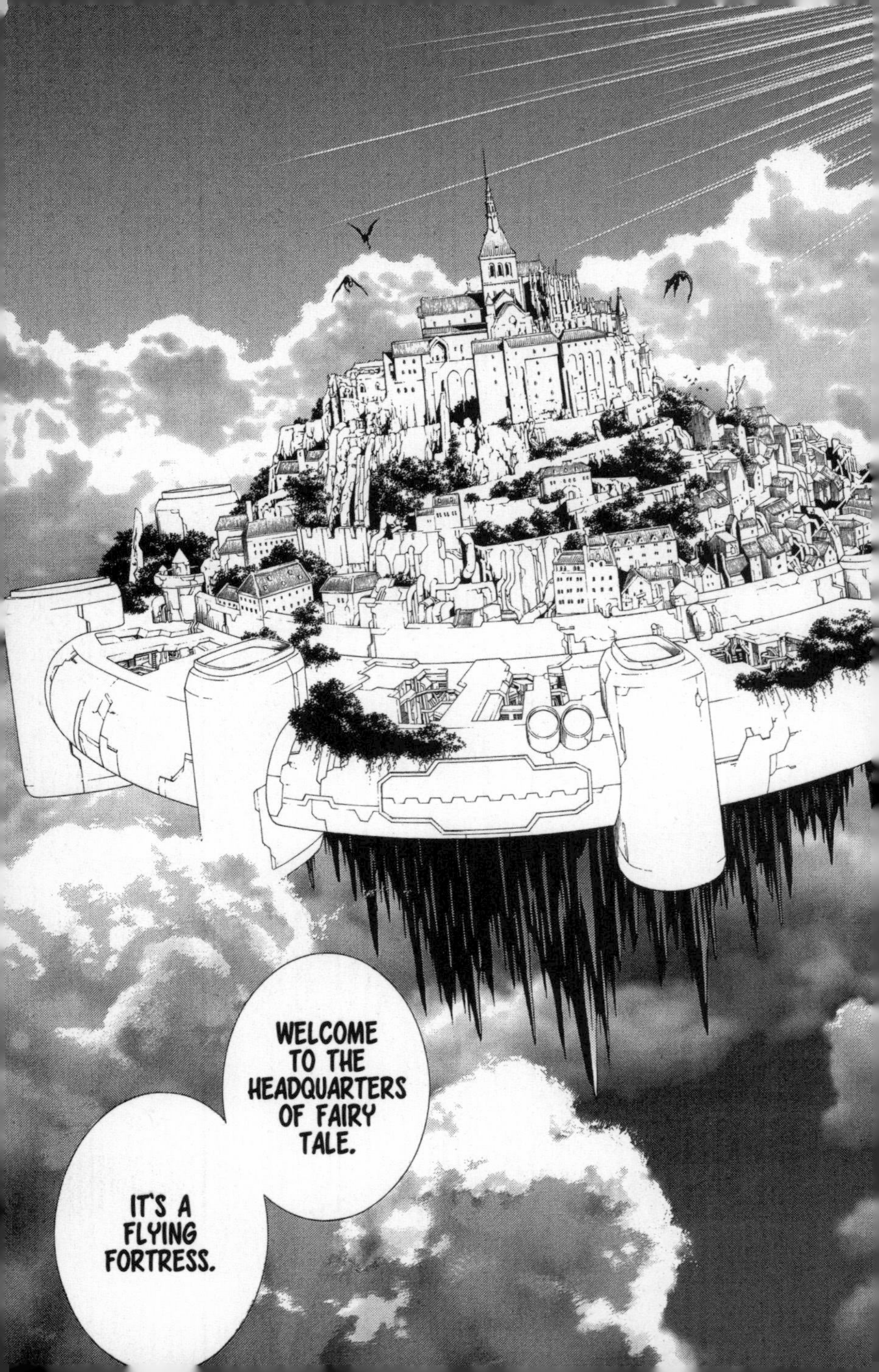
WELCOME TO THE HEADQUARTERS OF FAIRY TALE.
IT'S A FLYING FORTRESS.

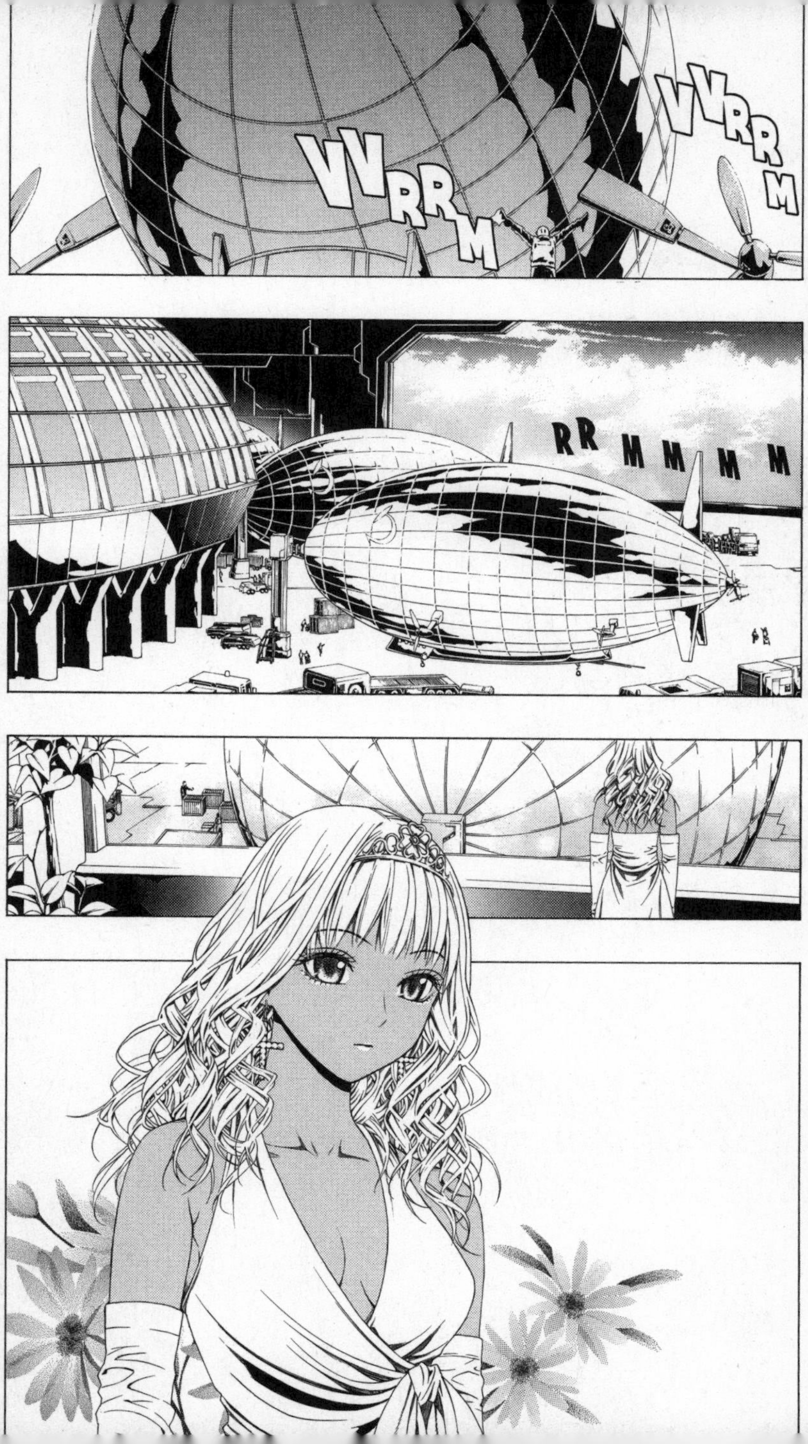
VVRRM
VVRRM
RRMMMM

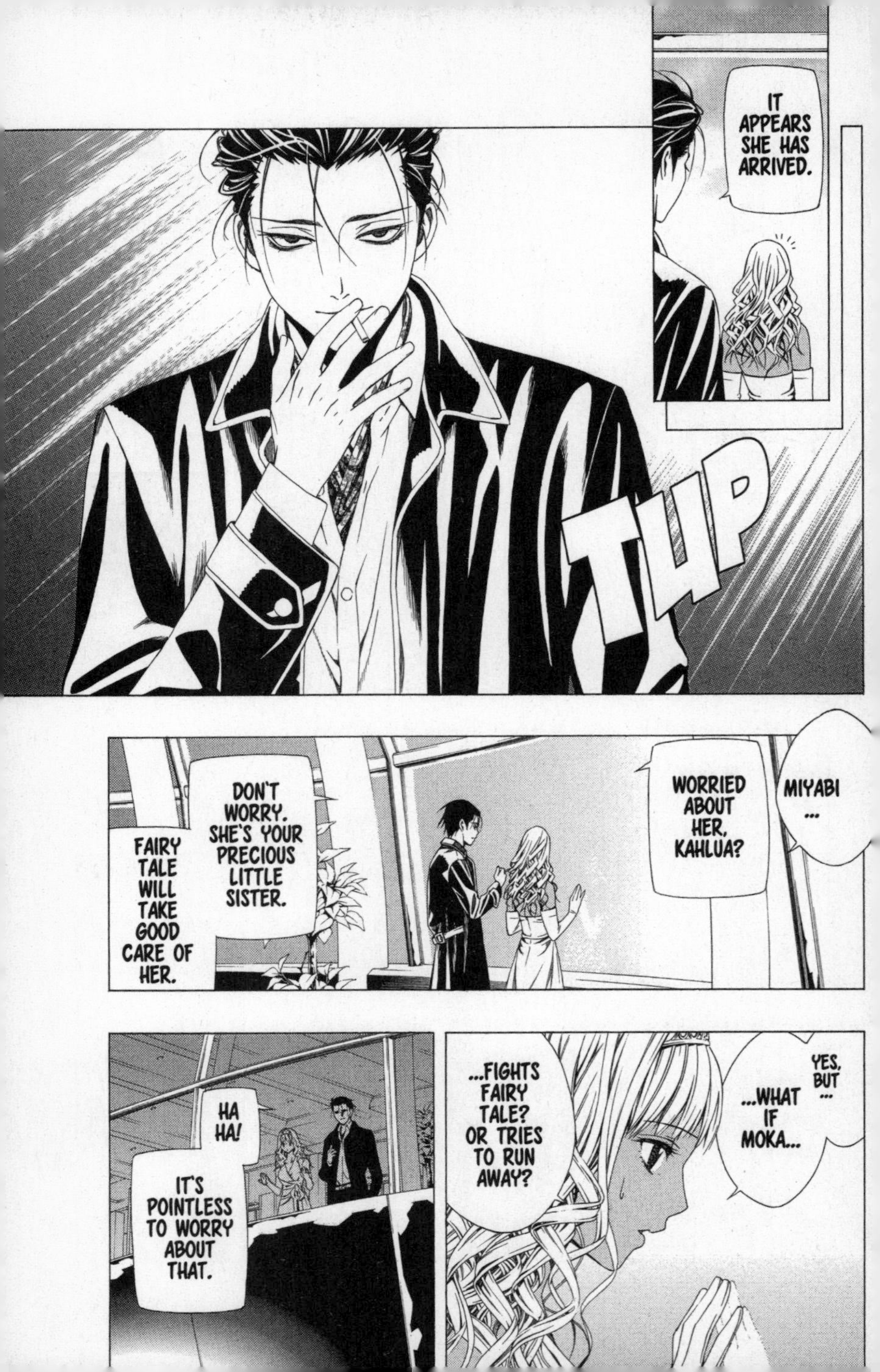
IT APPEARS SHE HAS ARRIVED.
TUP
MIYABI...
WORRIED ABOUT HER, KAHLUA?
DON'T WORRY. SHE'S YOUR PRECIOUS LITTLE SISTER.
FAIRY TALE WILL TAKE GOOD CARE OF HER.
YES, BUT...
...WHAT IF MOKA...
...FIGHTS FAIRY TALE? OR TRIES TO RUN AWAY?
HA HA!
IT'S POINTLESS TO WORRY ABOUT THAT.

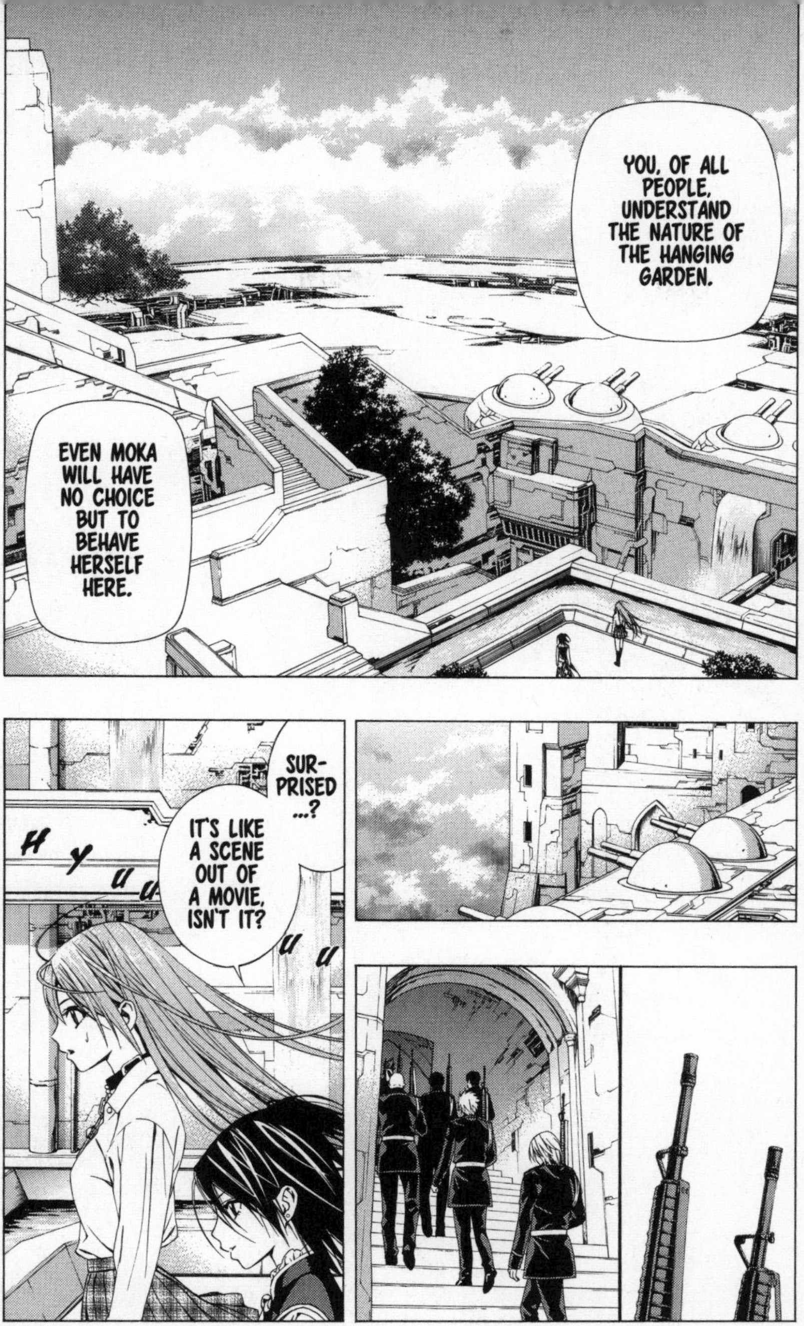
YOU, OF ALL PEOPLE, UNDERSTAND THE NATURE OF THE HANGING GARDEN.
EVEN MOKA WILL HAVE NO CHOICE BUT TO BEHAVE HERSELF HERE.
SUR-PRISED ...?
IT'S LIKE A SCENE OUT OF A MOVIE, ISN'T IT?
HyuuUUU

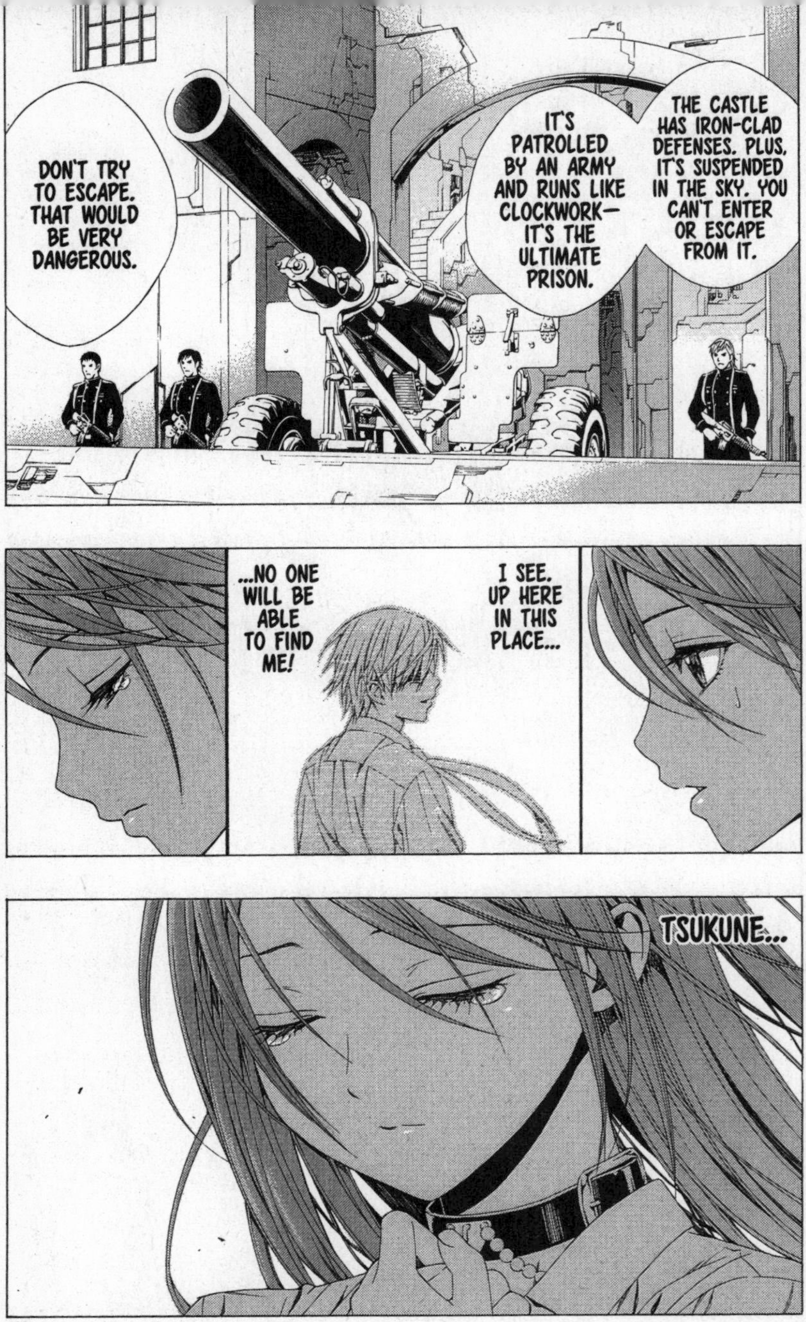
THE CASTLE HAS IRON-CLAD DEFENSES. PLUS, IT'S SUSPENDED IN THE SKY. YOU CAN'T ENTER OR ESCAPE FROM IT.
IT'S PATROLLED BY AN ARMY AND RUNS LIKE CLOCKWORK—IT'S THE ULTIMATE PRISON.
DON'T TRY TO ESCAPE. THAT WOULD BE VERY DANGEROUS.
I SEE. UP HERE IN THIS PLACE...
...NO ONE WILL BE ABLE TO FIND ME!
TSUKUNE...

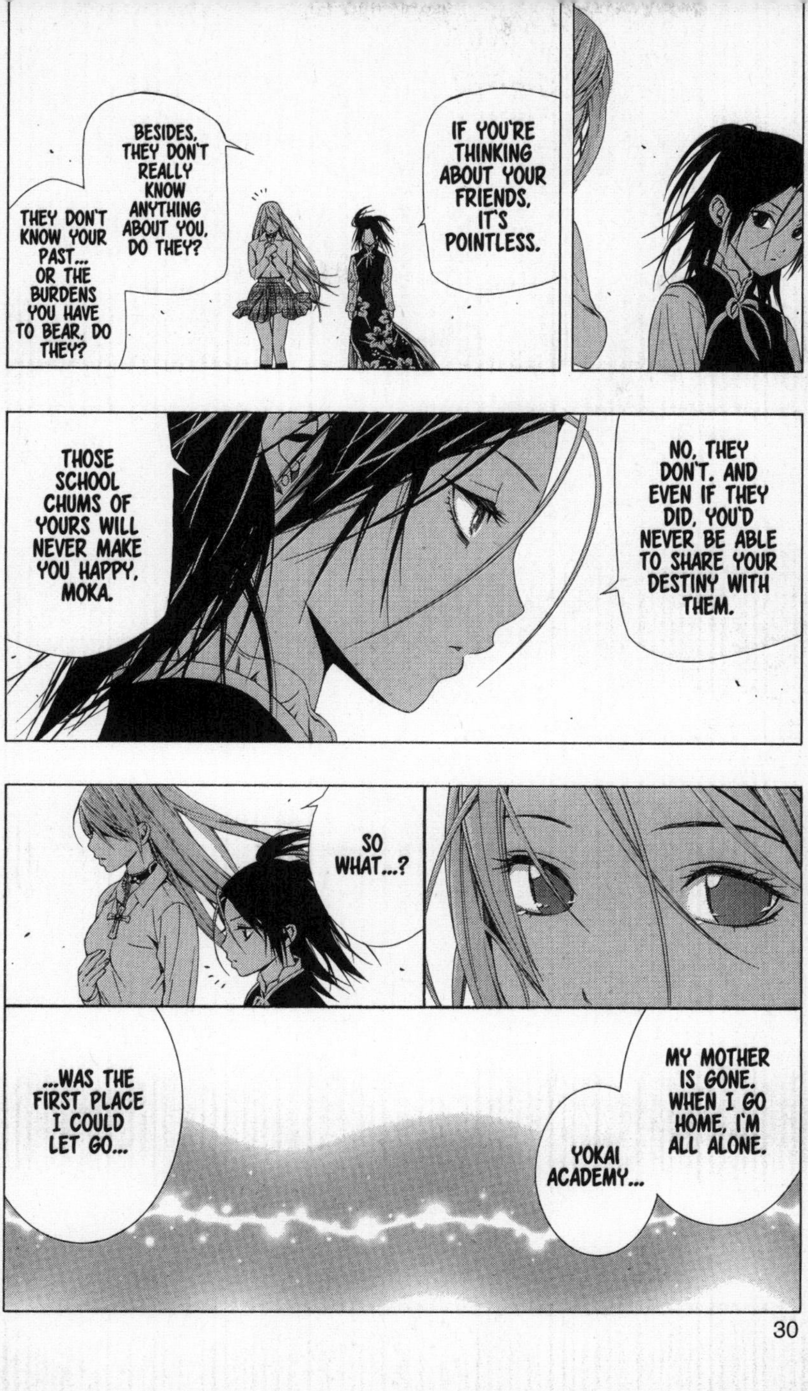
IF YOU'RE THINKING ABOUT YOUR FRIENDS, IT'S POINTLESS.
BESIDES, THEY DON'T REALLY KNOW ANYTHING ABOUT YOU, DO THEY?
THEY DON'T KNOW YOUR PAST... OR THE BURDENS YOU HAVE TO BEAR, DO THEY?
NO, THEY DON'T. AND EVEN IF THEY DID, YOU'D NEVER BE ABLE TO SHARE YOUR DESTINY WITH THEM.
THOSE SCHOOL CHUMS OF YOURS WILL NEVER MAKE YOU HAPPY, MOKA.
SO WHAT...?
MY MOTHER IS GONE. WHEN I GO HOME, I'M ALL ALONE.
YOKAI ACADEMY...
...WAS THE FIRST PLACE I COULD LET GO...

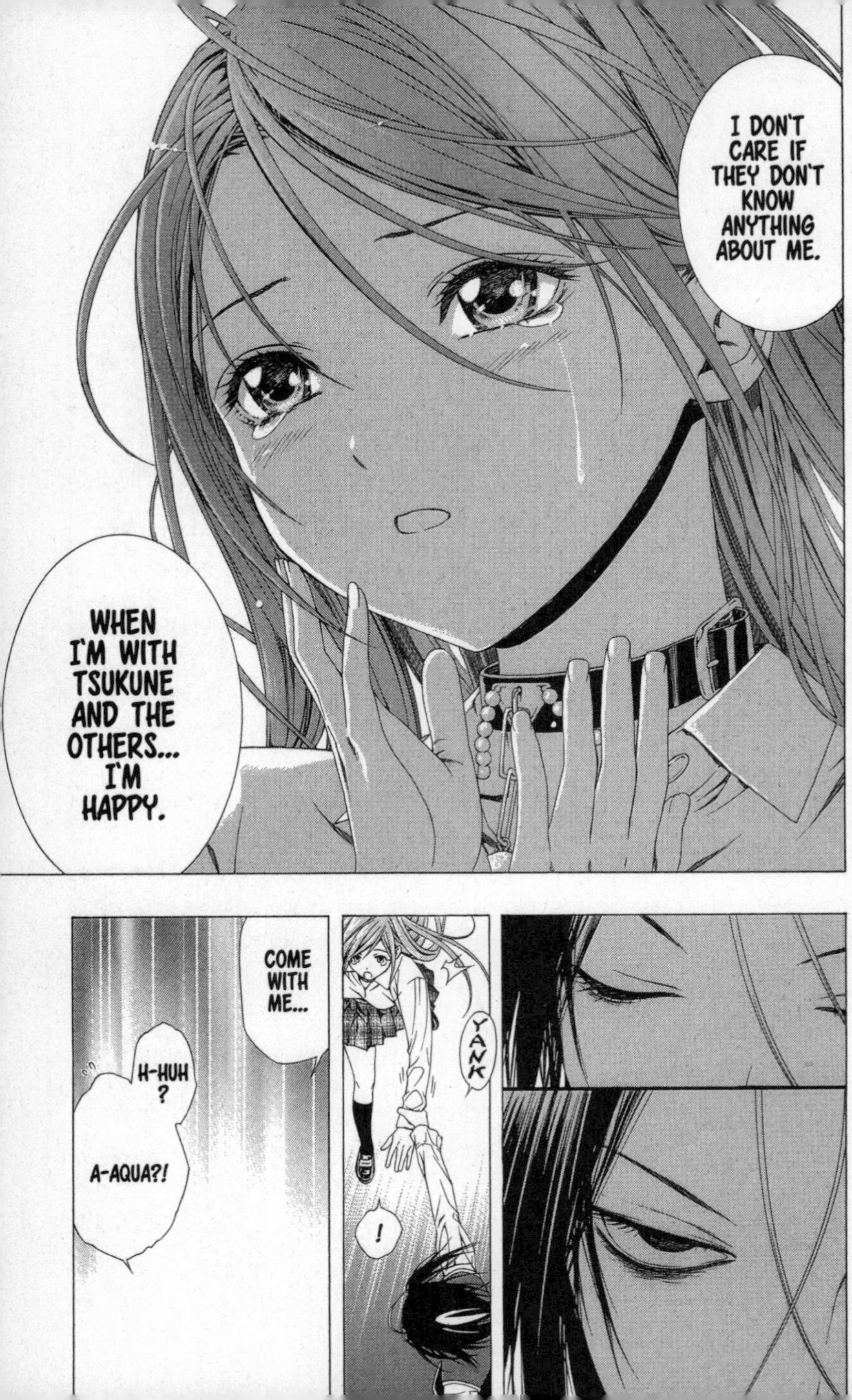
I DON'T CARE IF THEY DON'T KNOW ANYTHING ABOUT ME.
WHEN I'M WITH TSUKUNE AND THE OTHERS... I'M HAPPY.
COME WITH ME...
YANK
!
H-HUH?
A-AQUA?!

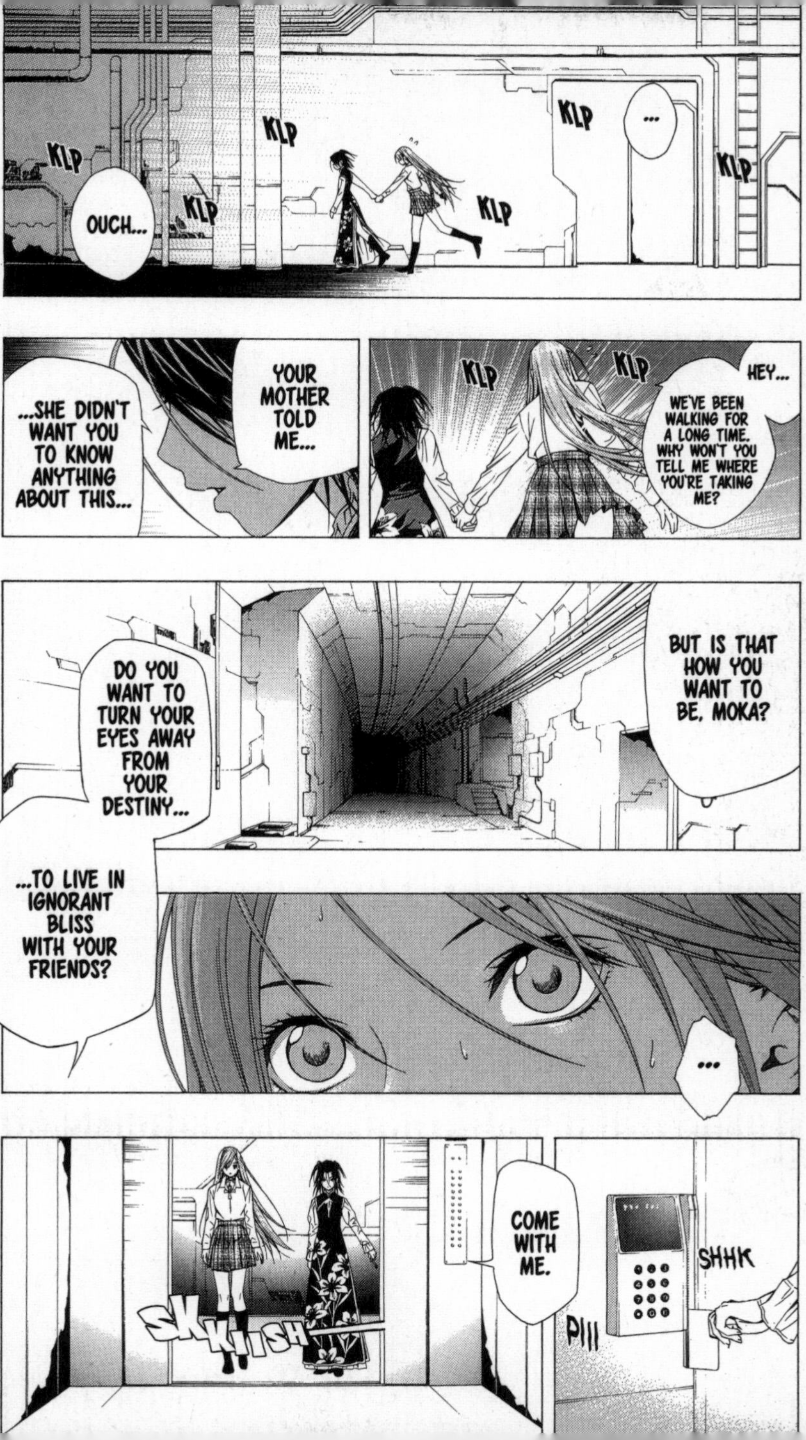
...
KLP
KLP
KLP
KLP
KLP
KLP
OUCH...
HEY...
WE'VE BEEN WALKING FOR A LONG TIME. WHY WON'T YOU TELL ME WHERE YOU'RE TAKING ME?
KLP
KLP
YOUR MOTHER TOLD ME...
...SHE DIDN'T WANT YOU TO KNOW ANYTHING ABOUT THIS...
BUT IS THAT HOW YOU WANT TO BE, MOKA?
DO YOU WANT TO TURN YOUR EYES AWAY FROM YOUR DESTINY...
...TO LIVE IN IGNORANT BLISS WITH YOUR FRIENDS?
...
SHHK
PIII
COME WITH ME.
SKKIISH

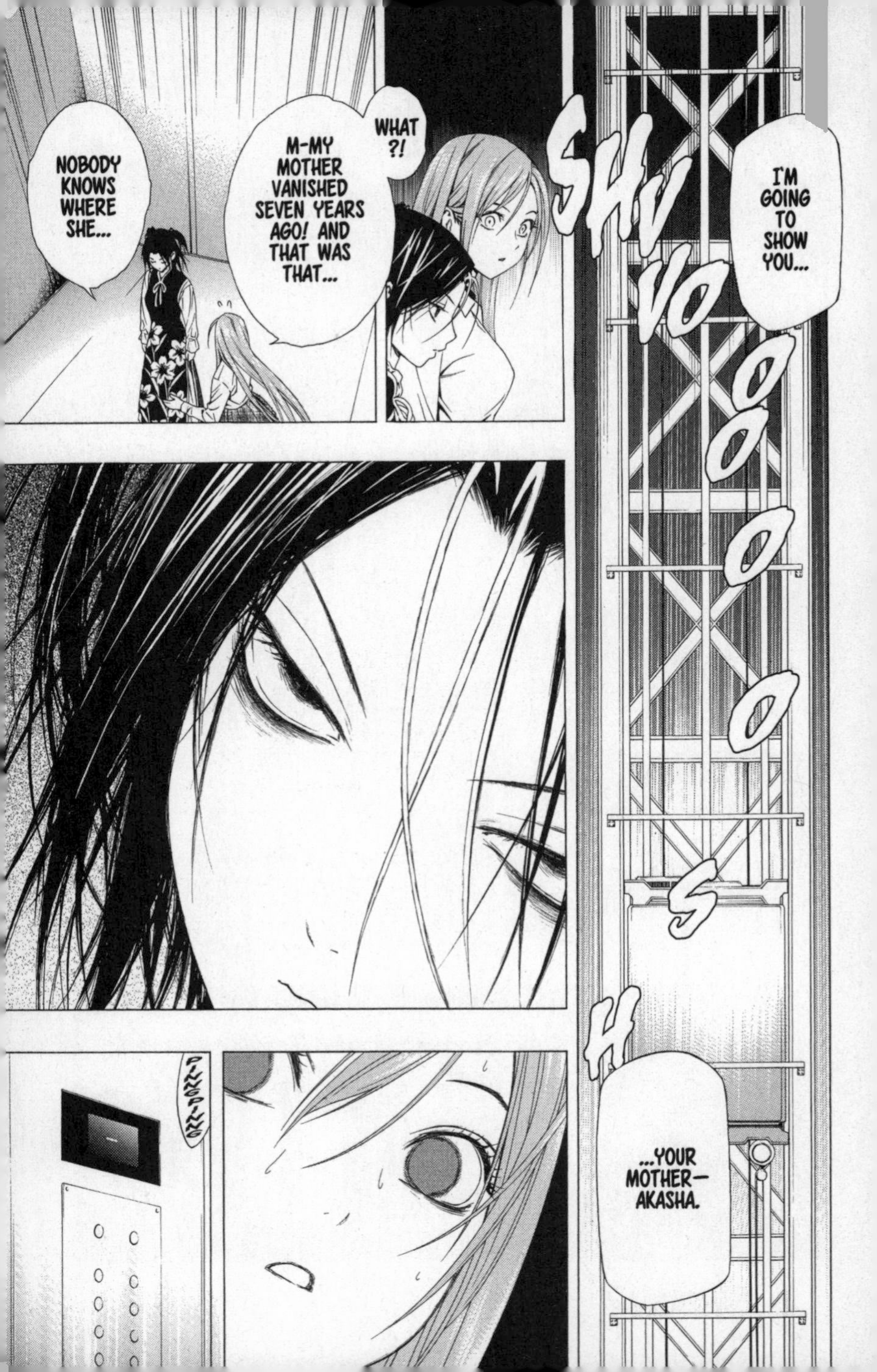

I'M GOING TO SHOW YOU...
SHVOOOOOOSH
...YOUR MOTHER—AKASHA.
WHAT ?!
M-MY MOTHER VANISHED SEVEN YEARS AGO! AND THAT WAS THAT...
NOBODY KNOWS WHERE SHE...
PINNGPING

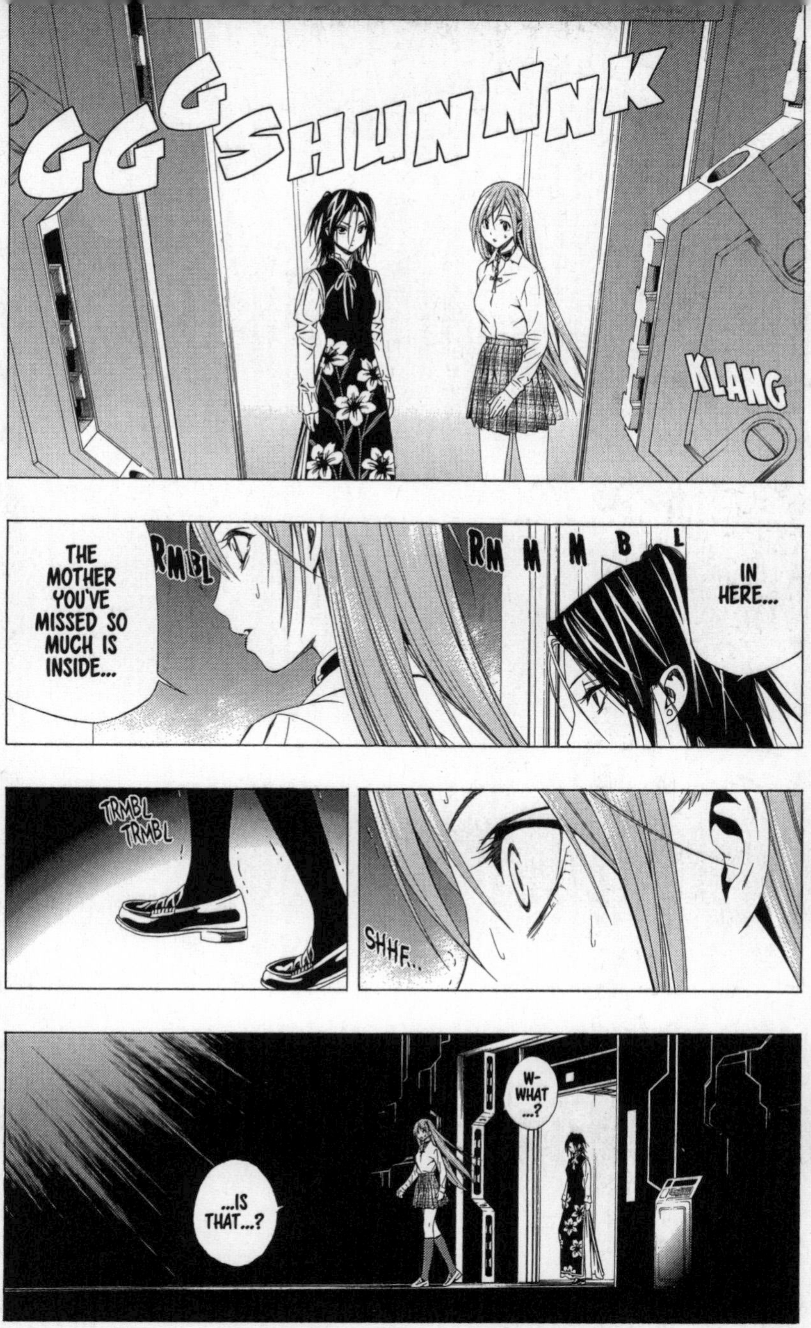
GGGSHUNNNK
KLANG
RMMMBL
IN HERE...
RMBL
THE MOTHER YOU'VE MISSED SO MUCH IS INSIDE...
SHHF...
TRMBL TRMBL
W-WHAT...?
...IS THAT...?

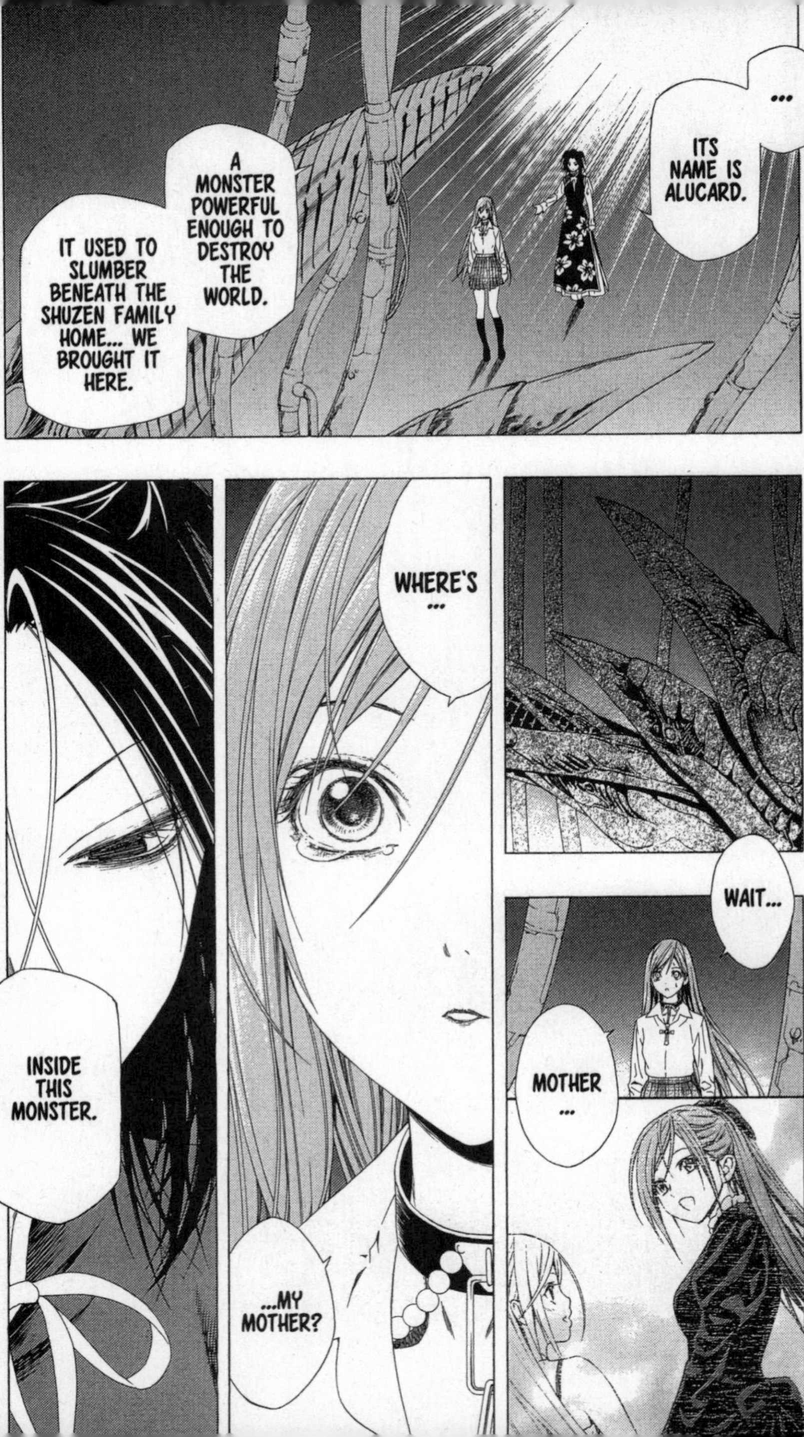
...
ITS NAME IS ALUCARD.
A MONSTER POWERFUL ENOUGH TO DESTROY THE WORLD.
IT USED TO SLUMBER BENEATH THE SHUZEN FAMILY HOME... WE BROUGHT IT HERE.
WAIT...
MOTHER...
WHERE'S...
...MY MOTHER?
INSIDE THIS MONSTER.

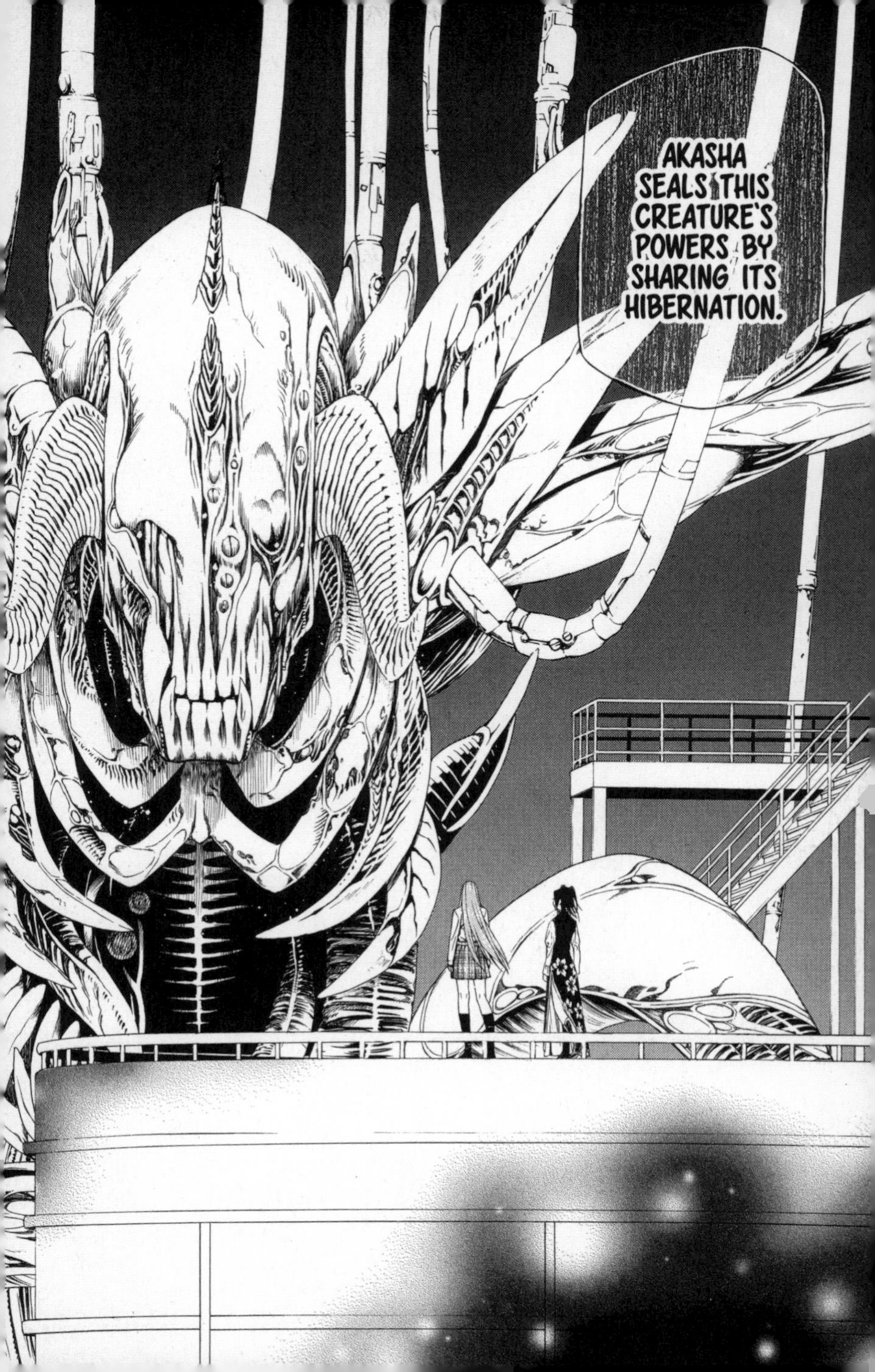
AKASHA SEALS THIS CREATURE'S POWERS BY SHARING ITS HIBERNATION.

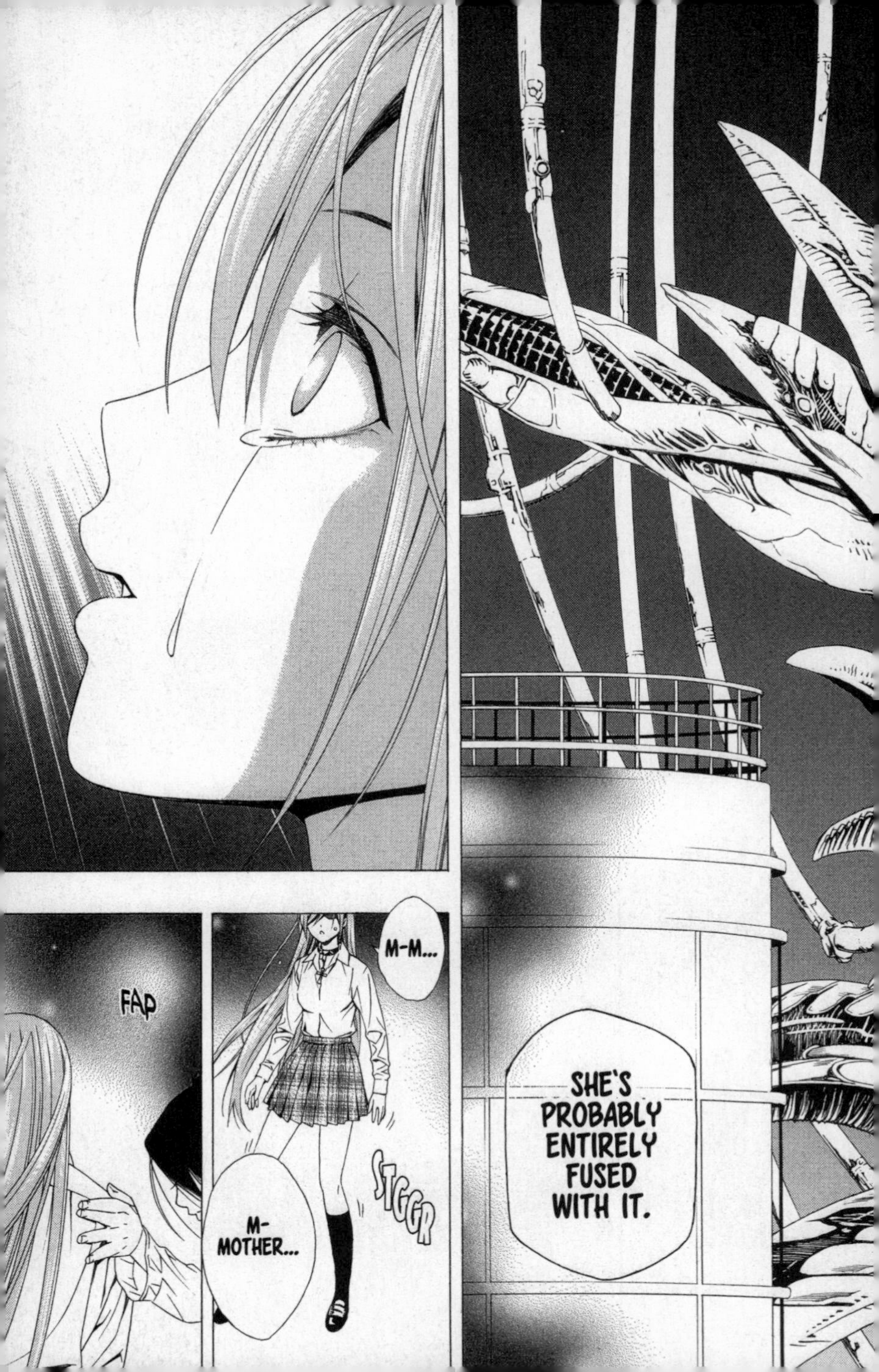
SHE'S PROBABLY ENTIRELY FUSED WITH IT.
M-M...
STGGR
M-MOTHER...
FAP

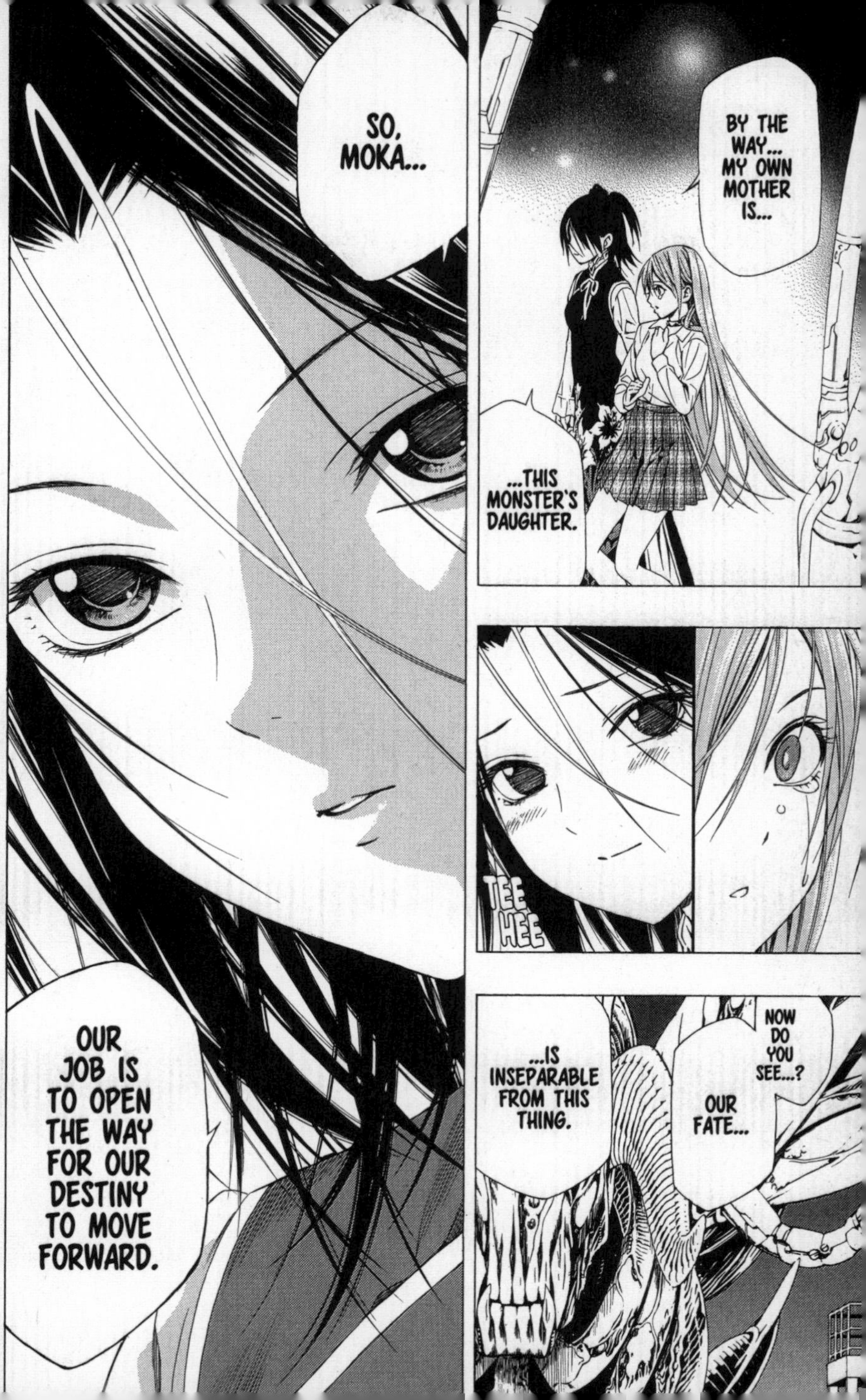
BY THE WAY... MY OWN MOTHER IS...
...THIS MONSTER'S DAUGHTER.
TEE HEE
NOW DO YOU SEE...?
OUR FATE...
...IS INSEPARABLE FROM THIS THING.
SO, MOKA...
OUR JOB IS TO OPEN THE WAY FOR OUR DESTINY TO MOVE FORWARD.

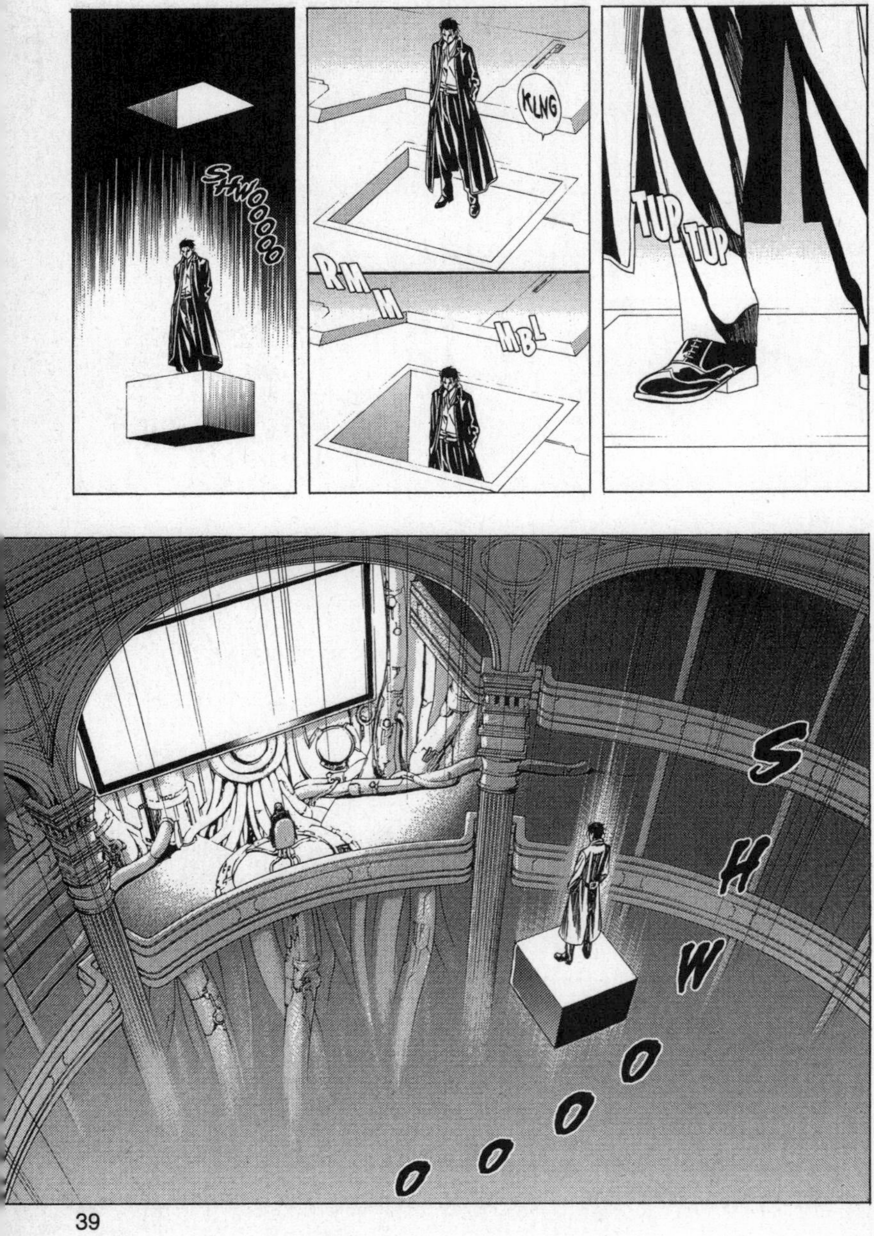
TUP TUP
KLNG
RMMMBL
SHWOOOOO
SHWOOOO

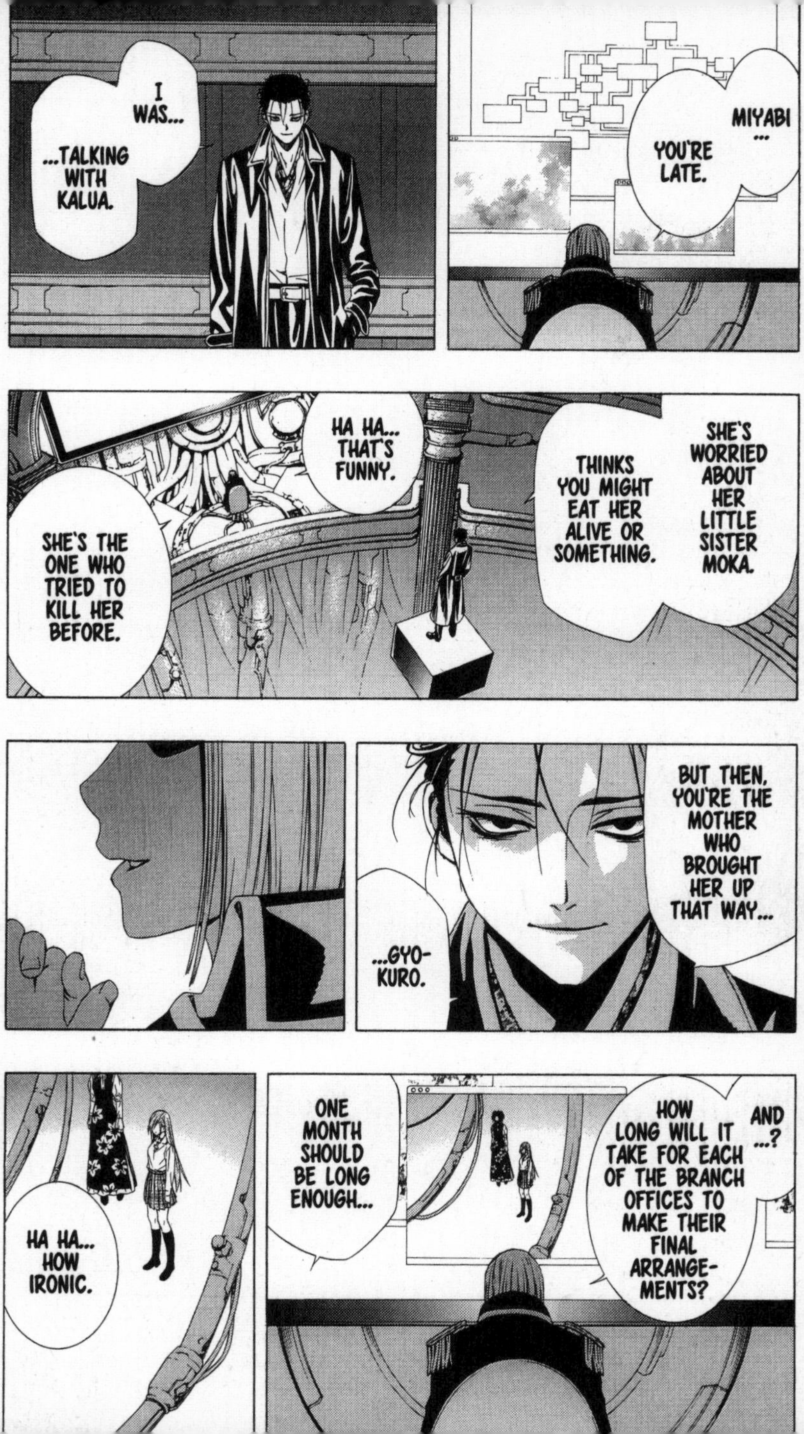
MIYABI...
YOU'RE LATE.
I WAS...
...TALKING WITH KALUA.
SHE'S WORRIED ABOUT HER LITTLE SISTER MOKA.
THINKS YOU MIGHT EAT HER ALIVE OR SOMETHING.
HA HA... THAT'S FUNNY.
SHE'S THE ONE WHO TRIED TO KILL HER BEFORE.
BUT THEN, YOU'RE THE MOTHER WHO BROUGHT HER UP THAT WAY...
...GYO-KURO.
AND...?
HOW LONG WILL IT TAKE FOR EACH OF THE BRANCH OFFICES TO MAKE THEIR FINAL ARRANGE-MENTS?
ONE MONTH SHOULD BE LONG ENOUGH...
HA HA... HOW IRONIC.

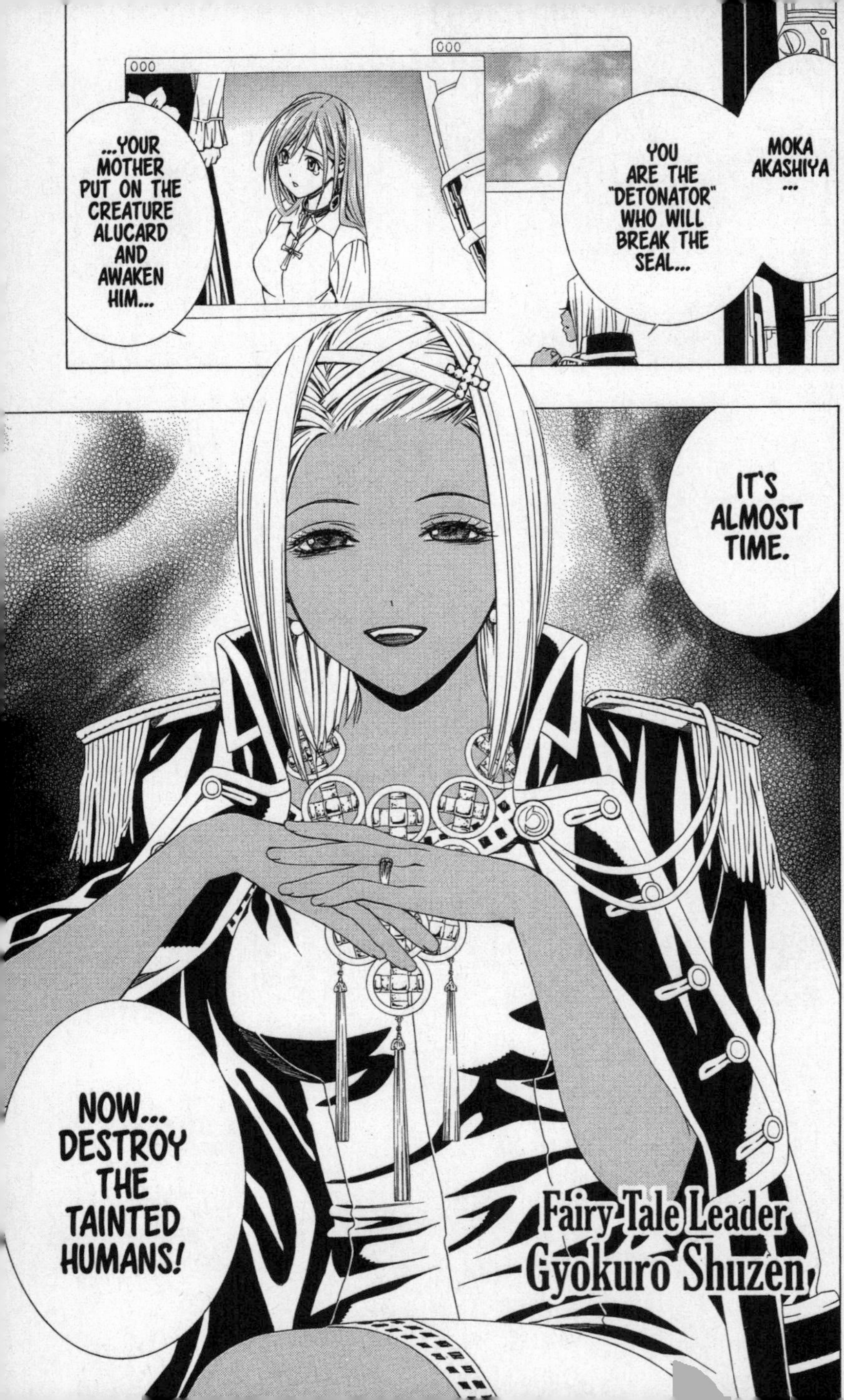
MOKA AKASHIYA ...
YOU ARE THE "DETONATOR" WHO WILL BREAK THE SEAL...
...YOUR MOTHER PUT ON THE CREATURE ALUCARD AND AWAKEN HIM...
IT'S ALMOST TIME.
NOW... DESTROY THE TAINTED HUMANS!
Fairy Tale Leader
Gyokuro Shuzen

43: Declaration of War

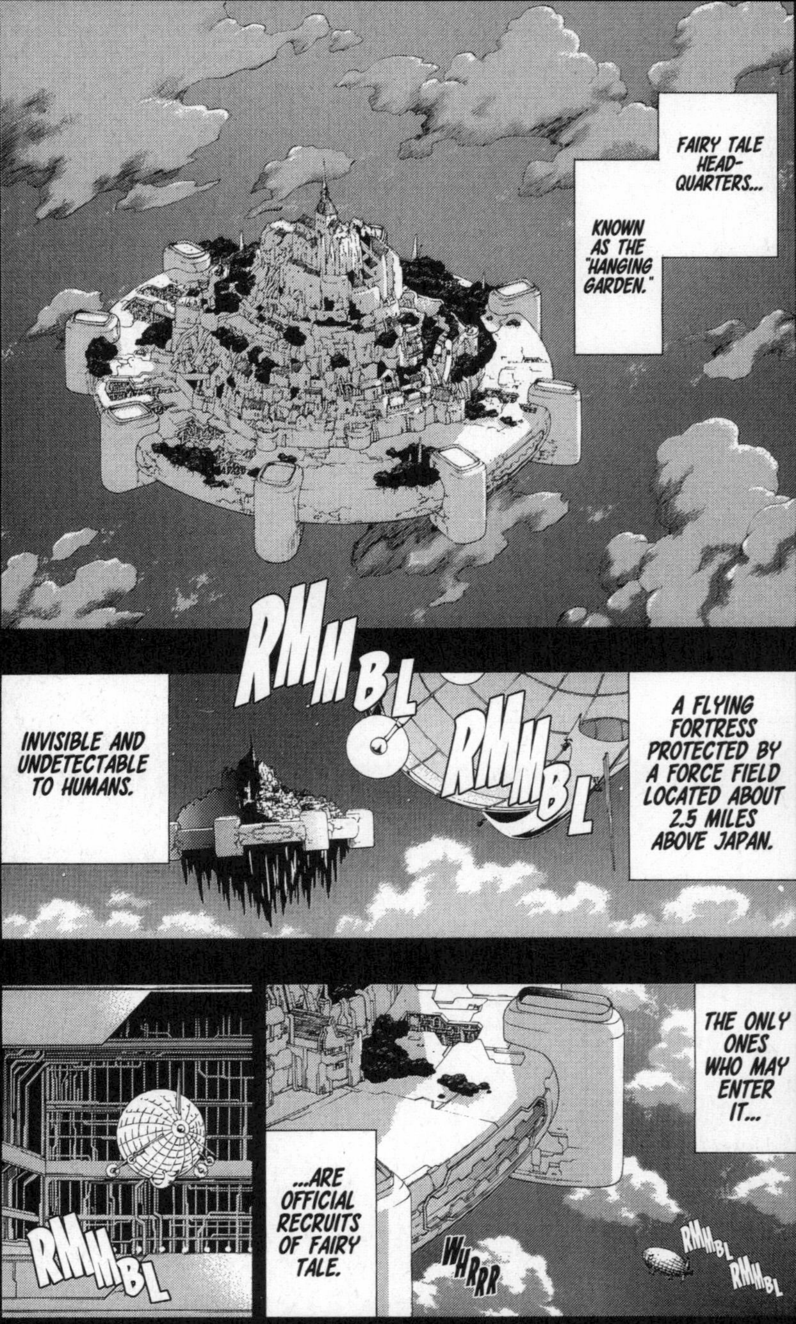
FAIRY TALE HEAD-QUARTERS...
KNOWN AS THE "HANGING GARDEN."
RMMBL
A FLYING FORTRESS PROTECTED BY A FORCE FIELD LOCATED ABOUT 2.5 MILES ABOVE JAPAN.
RMMBL
INVISIBLE AND UNDETECTABLE TO HUMANS.
THE ONLY ONES WHO MAY ENTER IT...
...ARE OFFICIAL RECRUITS OF FAIRY TALE.
RMMBL
RMMBL
WHRRR
RMMBL

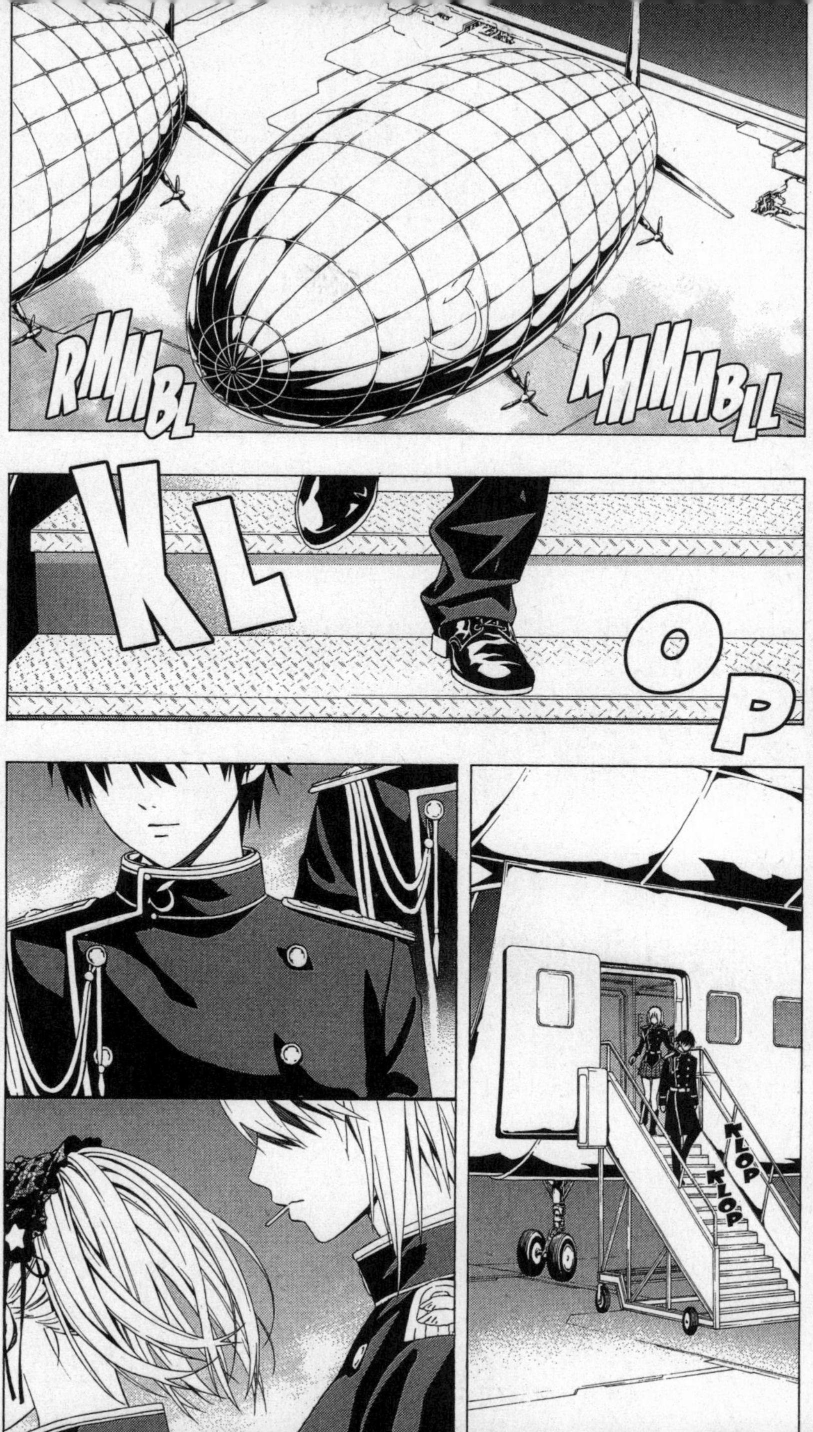
RMMMBLL
RMMBL
KLOP
KLOP
KLOP

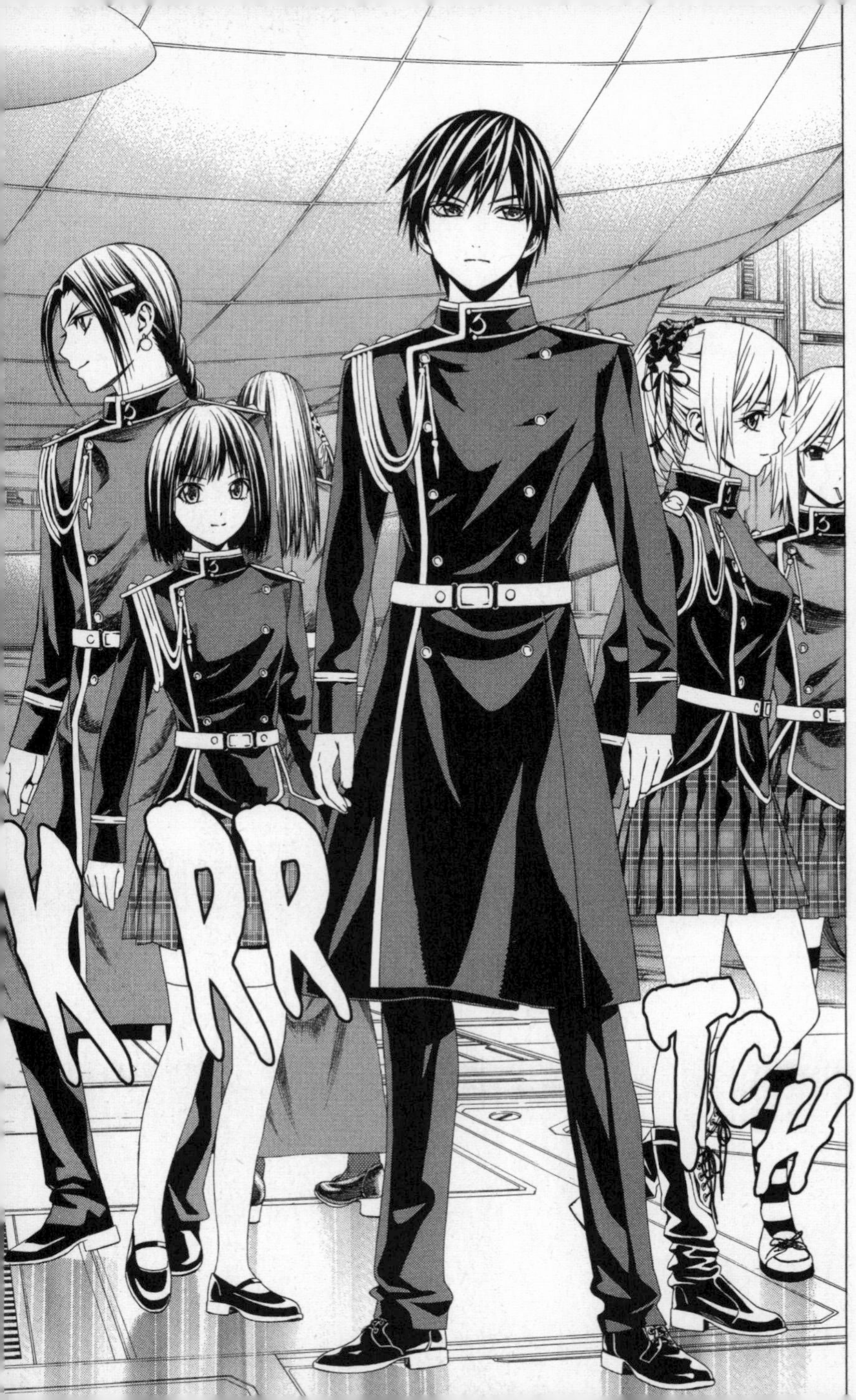

TCH
WRR

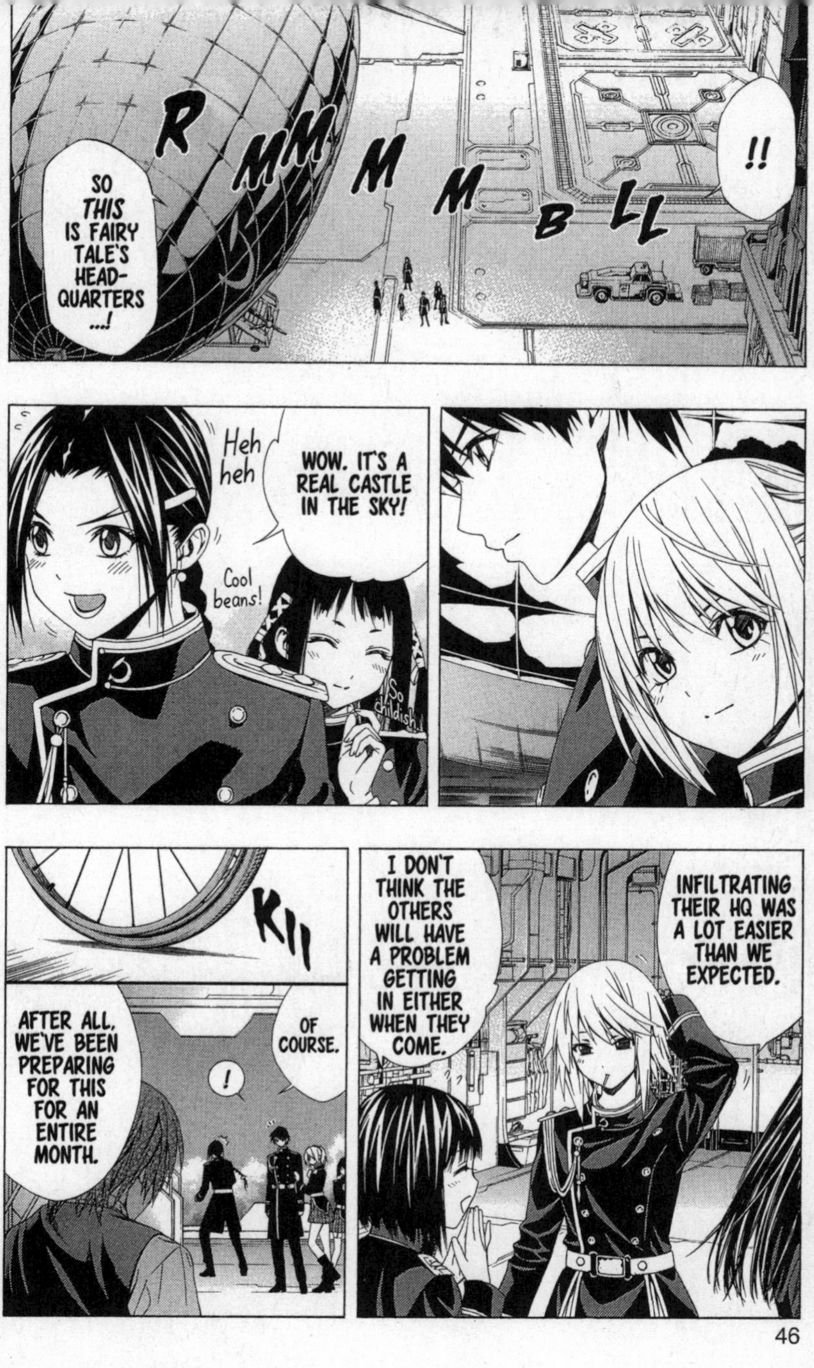
!!
RMMMMBLL
SO THIS IS FAIRY TALE'S HEADQUARTERS...!
WOW. IT'S A REAL CASTLE IN THE SKY!
Heh heh
Cool beans!
So childish
INFILTRATING THEIR HQ WAS A LOT EASIER THAN WE EXPECTED.
I DON'T THINK THE OTHERS WILL HAVE A PROBLEM GETTING IN EITHER WHEN THEY COME.
KII
OF COURSE.
!
AFTER ALL, WE'VE BEEN PREPARING FOR THIS FOR AN ENTIRE MONTH.

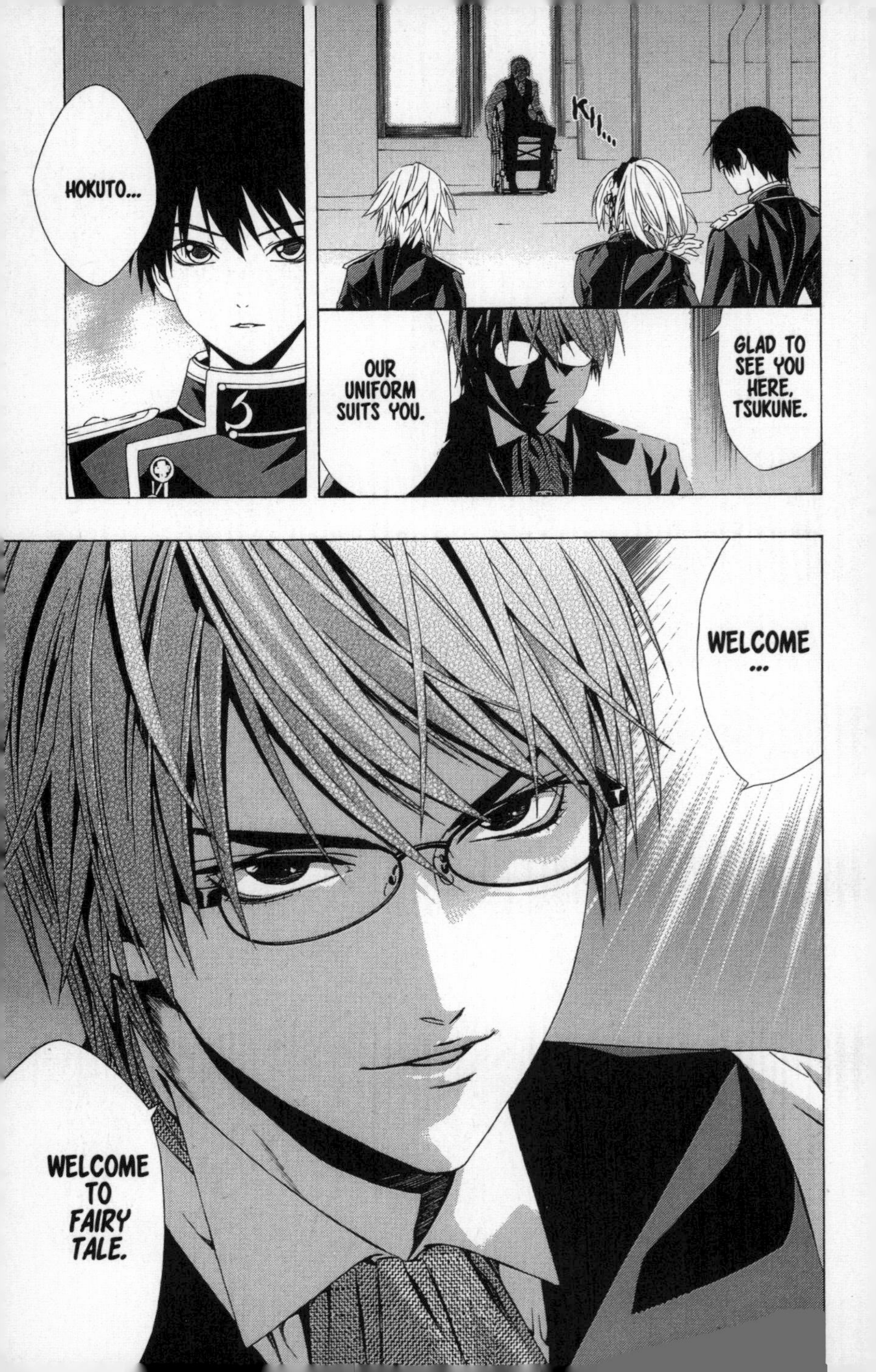
KII...
GLAD TO SEE YOU HERE, TSUKUNE.
OUR UNIFORM SUITS YOU.
HOKUTO...
WELCOME...
WELCOME TO FAIRY TALE.

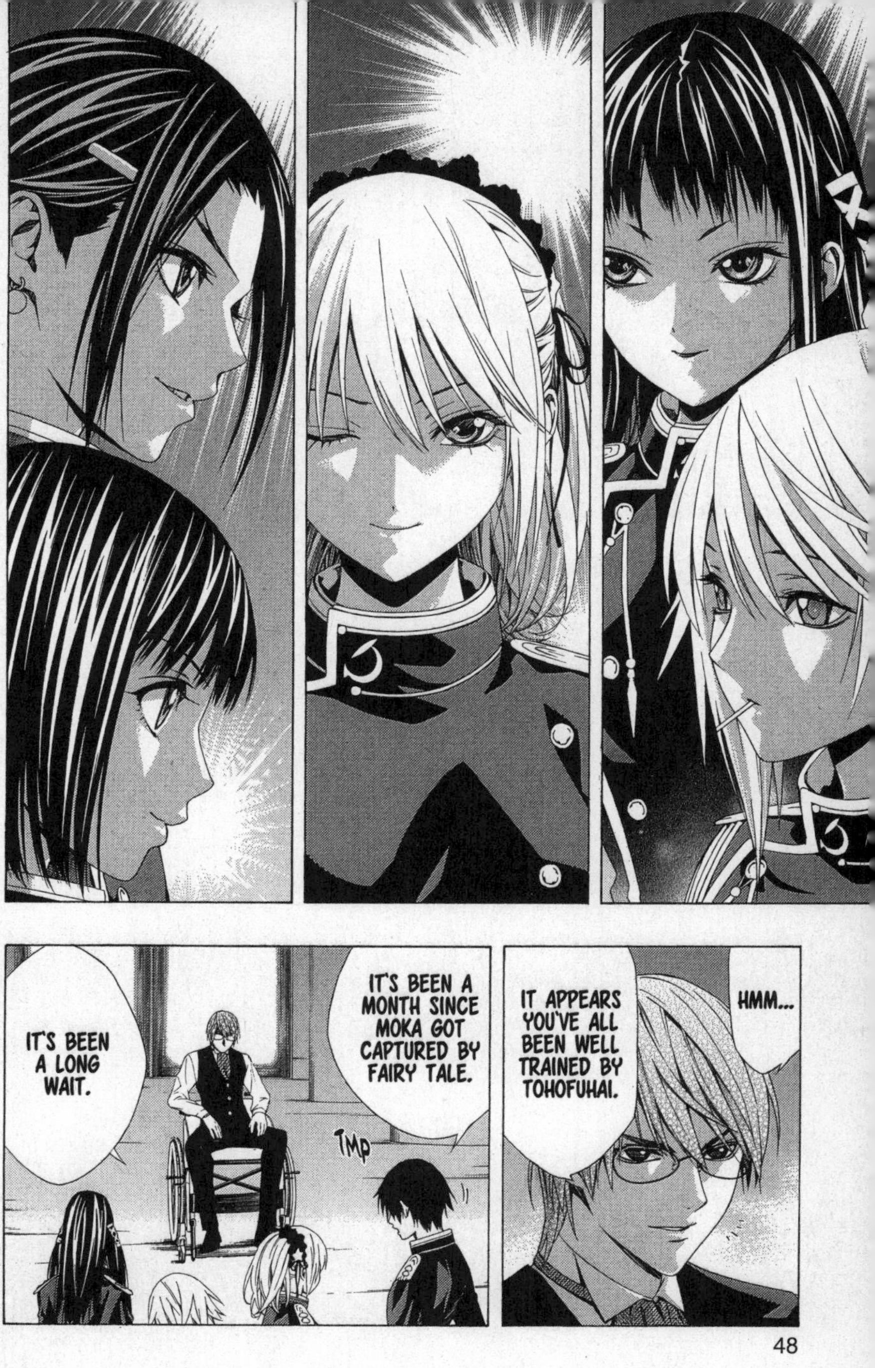
HMM...
IT APPEARS YOU'VE ALL BEEN WELL TRAINED BY TOHOFUHAI.
IT'S BEEN A MONTH SINCE MOKA GOT CAPTURED BY FAIRY TALE.
TMP
IT'S BEEN A LONG WAIT.

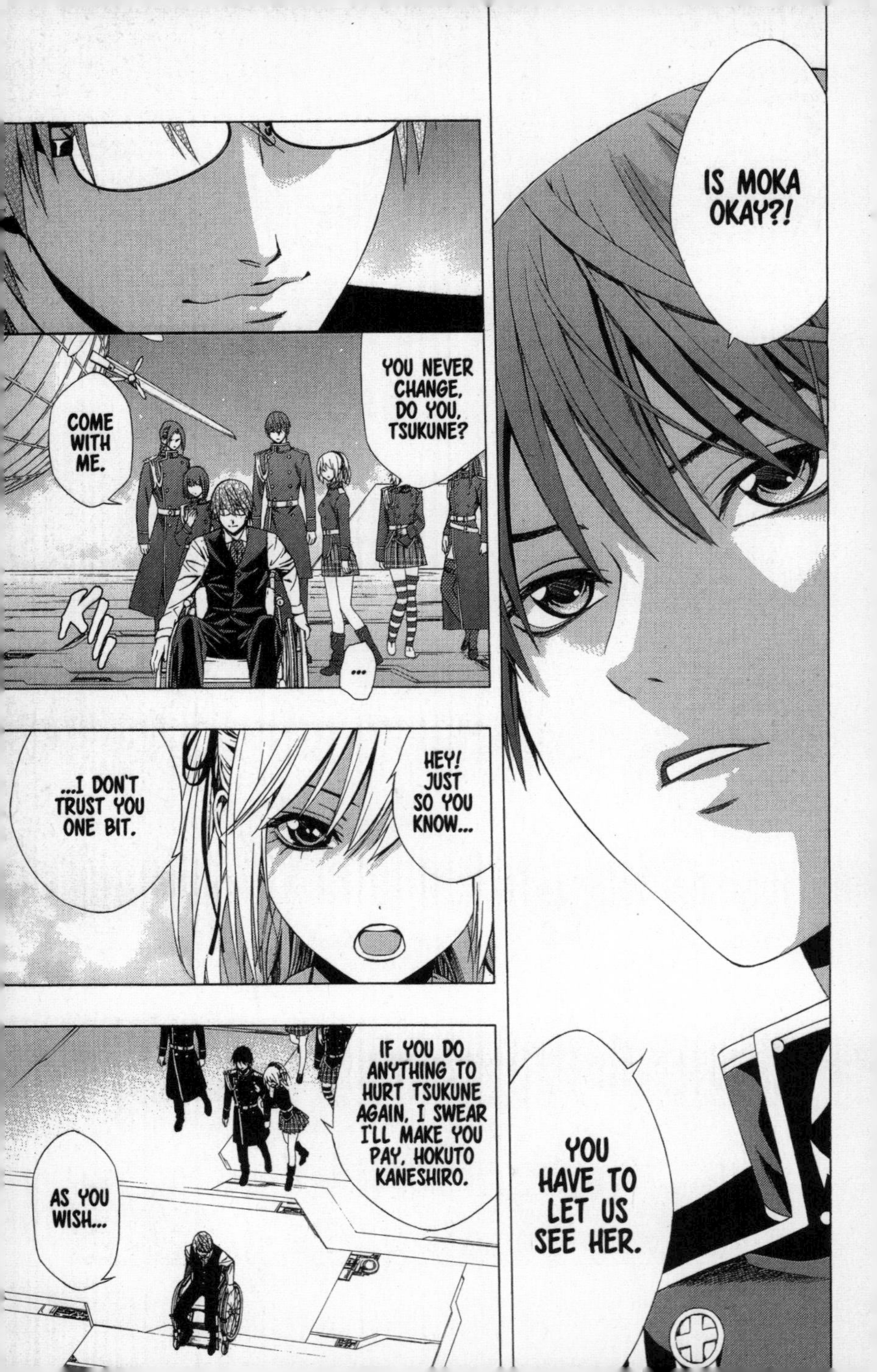
IS MOKA OKAY?!
YOU HAVE TO LET US SEE HER.
YOU NEVER CHANGE, DO YOU, TSUKUNE?
COME WITH ME.
...
HEY! JUST SO YOU KNOW...
...I DON'T TRUST YOU ONE BIT.
IF YOU DO ANYTHING TO HURT TSUKUNE AGAIN, I SWEAR I'LL MAKE YOU PAY, HOKUTO KANESHIRO.
AS YOU WISH...

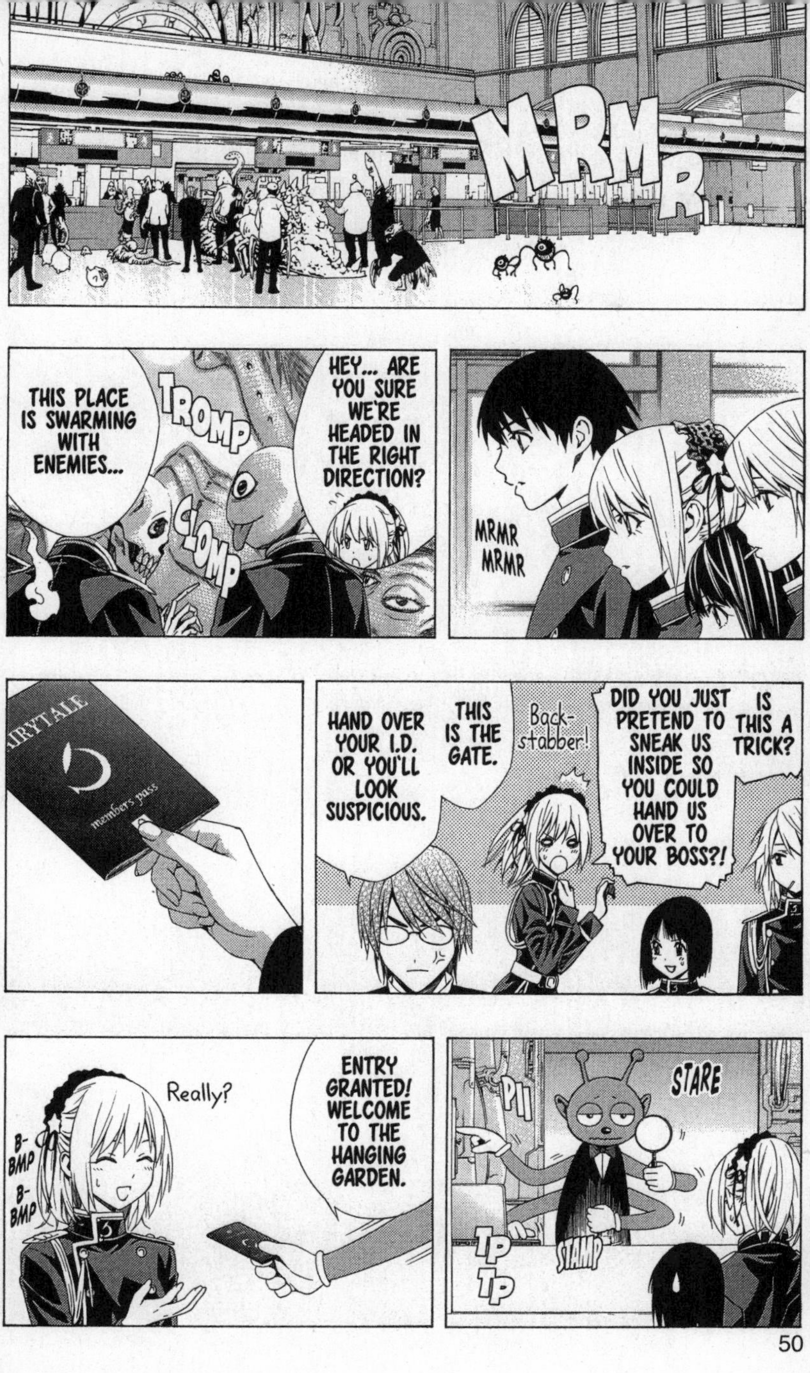
MRMR
MRMR MRMR
HEY... ARE YOU SURE WE'RE HEADED IN THE RIGHT DIRECTION?
TROMP
THIS PLACE IS SWARMING WITH ENEMIES...
CLOMP
IS THIS A TRICK?
DID YOU JUST PRETEND TO SNEAK US INSIDE SO YOU COULD HAND US OVER TO YOUR BOSS?!
Back-stabber!
THIS IS THE GATE.
HAND OVER YOUR I.D. OR YOU'LL LOOK SUSPICIOUS.
members pass
STARE
PII
STAMP
TP TP
ENTRY GRANTED! WELCOME TO THE HANGING GARDEN.
Really?
B-BMP B-BMP

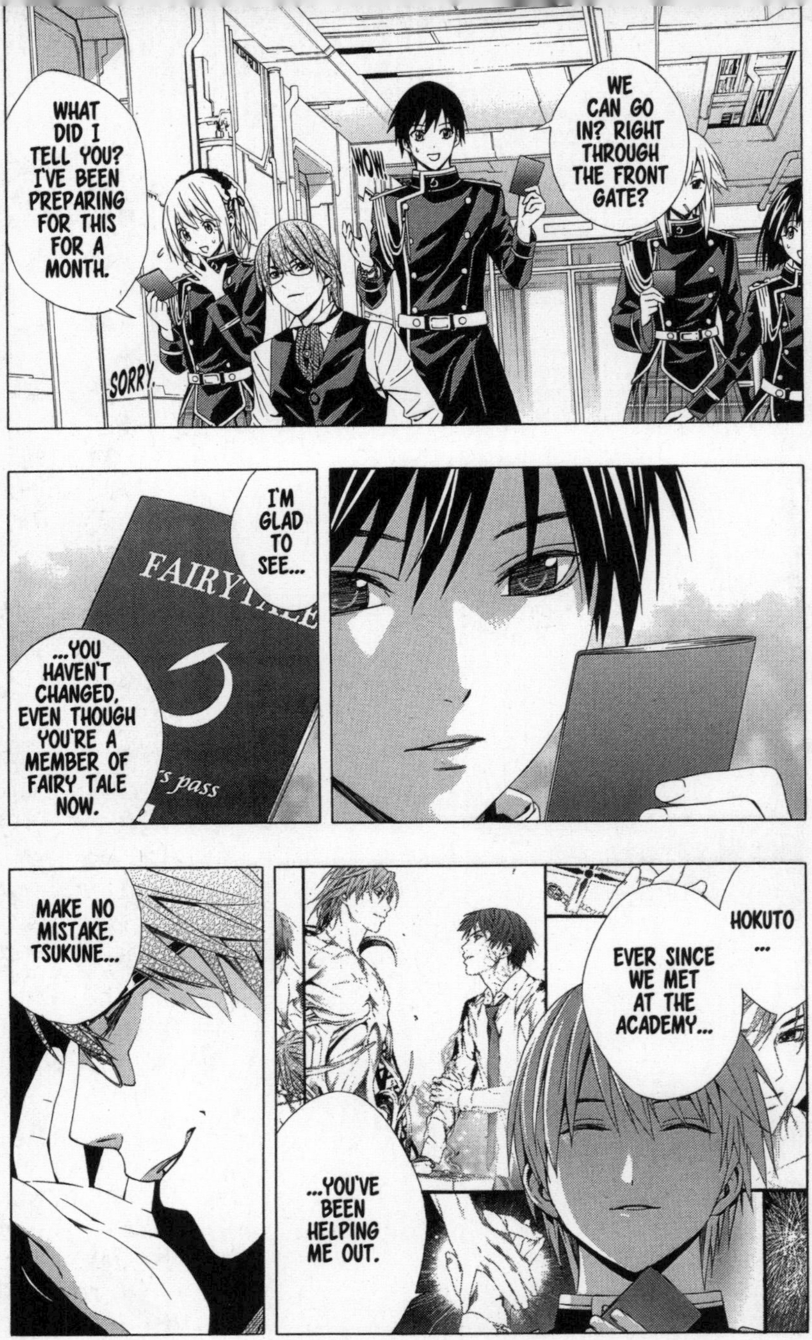
WE CAN GO IN? RIGHT THROUGH THE FRONT GATE?
WOW!
WHAT DID I TELL YOU? I'VE BEEN PREPARING FOR THIS FOR A MONTH.
SORRY.
I'M GLAD TO SEE...
FAIRYTALE
...YOU HAVEN'T CHANGED, EVEN THOUGH YOU'RE A MEMBER OF FAIRY TALE NOW.
HOKUTO...
EVER SINCE WE MET AT THE ACADEMY...
...YOU'VE BEEN HELPING ME OUT.
MAKE NO MISTAKE, TSUKUNE...

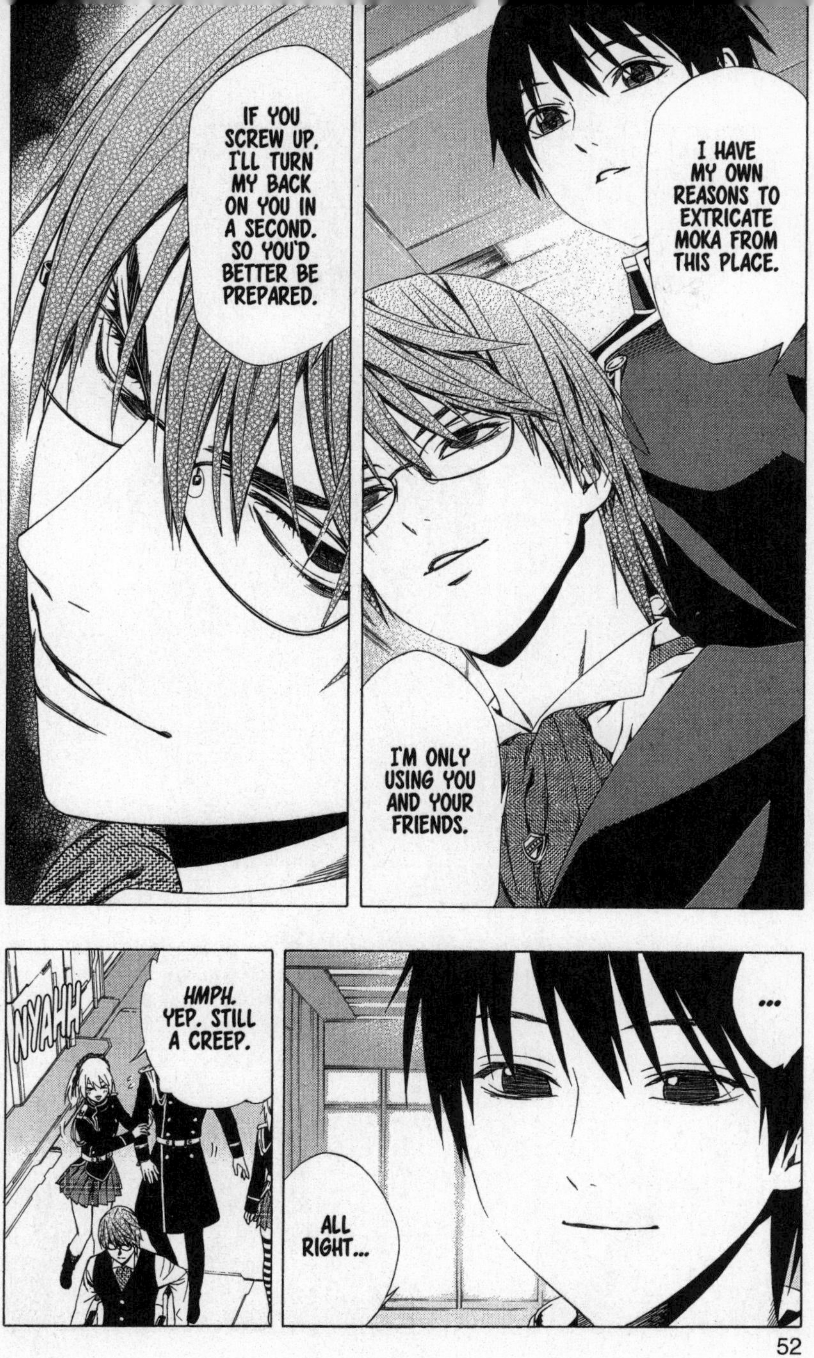
I HAVE MY OWN REASONS TO EXTRICATE MOKA FROM THIS PLACE.
I'M ONLY USING YOU AND YOUR FRIENDS.
IF YOU SCREW UP, I'LL TURN MY BACK ON YOU IN A SECOND. SO YOU'D BETTER BE PREPARED.
...
ALL RIGHT...
NYAHH
HMPH. YEP. STILL A CREEP.

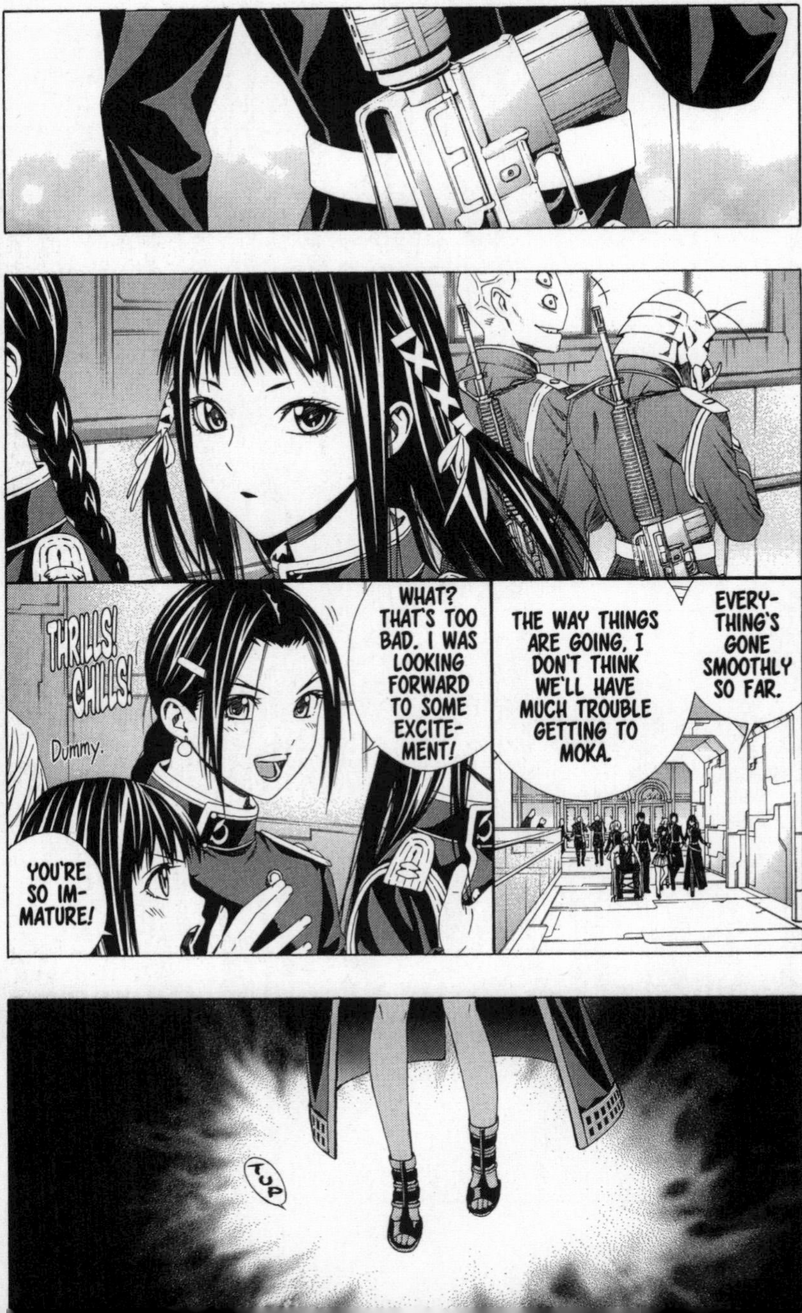
EVERY-THING'S GONE SMOOTHLY SO FAR.
THE WAY THINGS ARE GOING, I DON'T THINK WE'LL HAVE MUCH TROUBLE GETTING TO MOKA.
WHAT? THAT'S TOO BAD. I WAS LOOKING FORWARD TO SOME EXCITE-MENT!
THRILLS! CHILLS!
Dummy.
YOU'RE SO IM-MATURE!
TUP

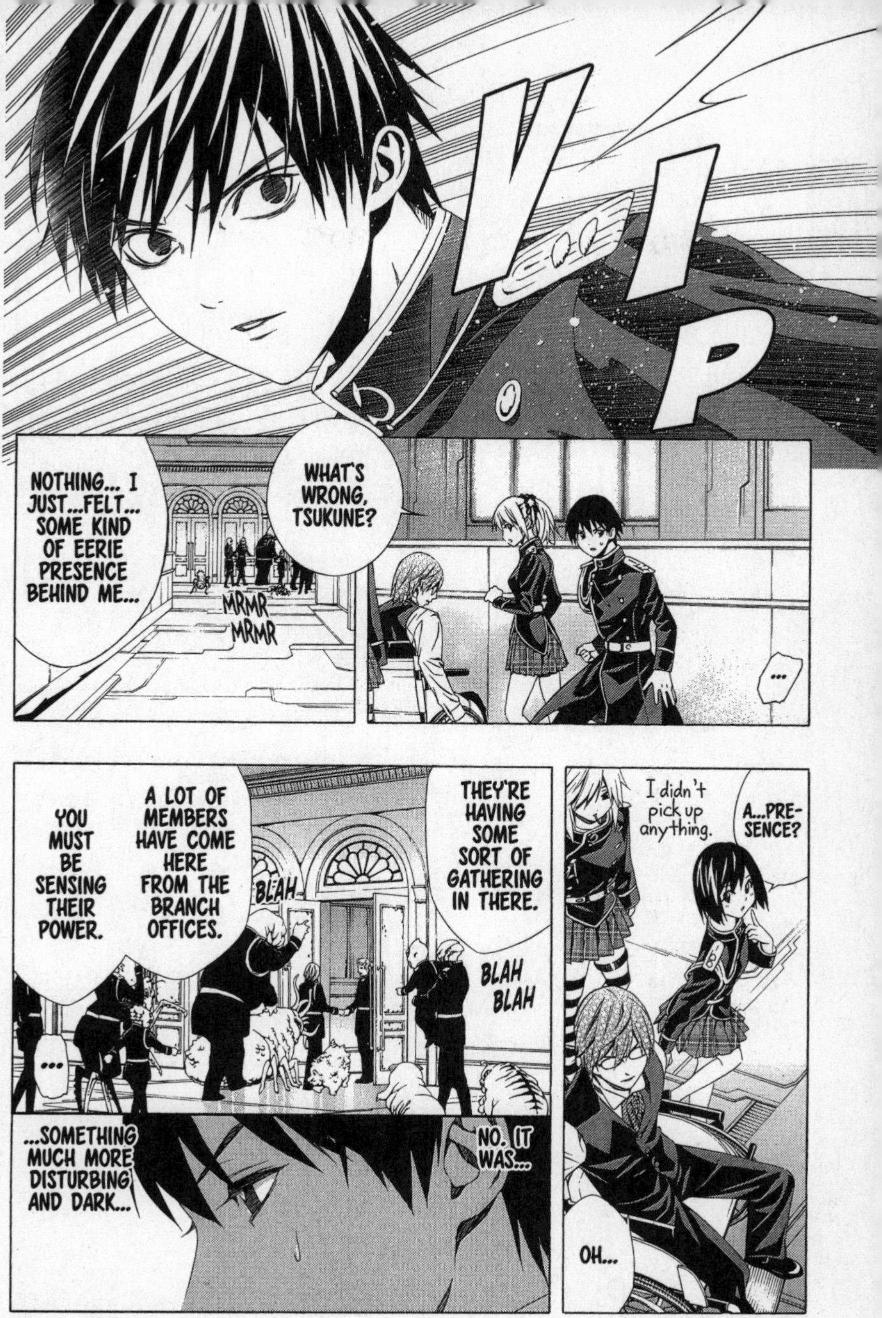
VIIP
WHAT'S WRONG, TSUKUNE?
...
NOTHING... I JUST...FELT... SOME KIND OF EERIE PRESENCE BEHIND ME...
MRMR MRMR
A...PRE-SENCE?
I didn't pick up anything.
OH...
THEY'RE HAVING SOME SORT OF GATHERING IN THERE.
BLAH BLAH
BLAH
A LOT OF MEMBERS HAVE COME HERE FROM THE BRANCH OFFICES.
YOU MUST BE SENSING THEIR POWER.
...
NO. IT WAS...
...SOMETHING MUCH MORE DISTURBING AND DARK...

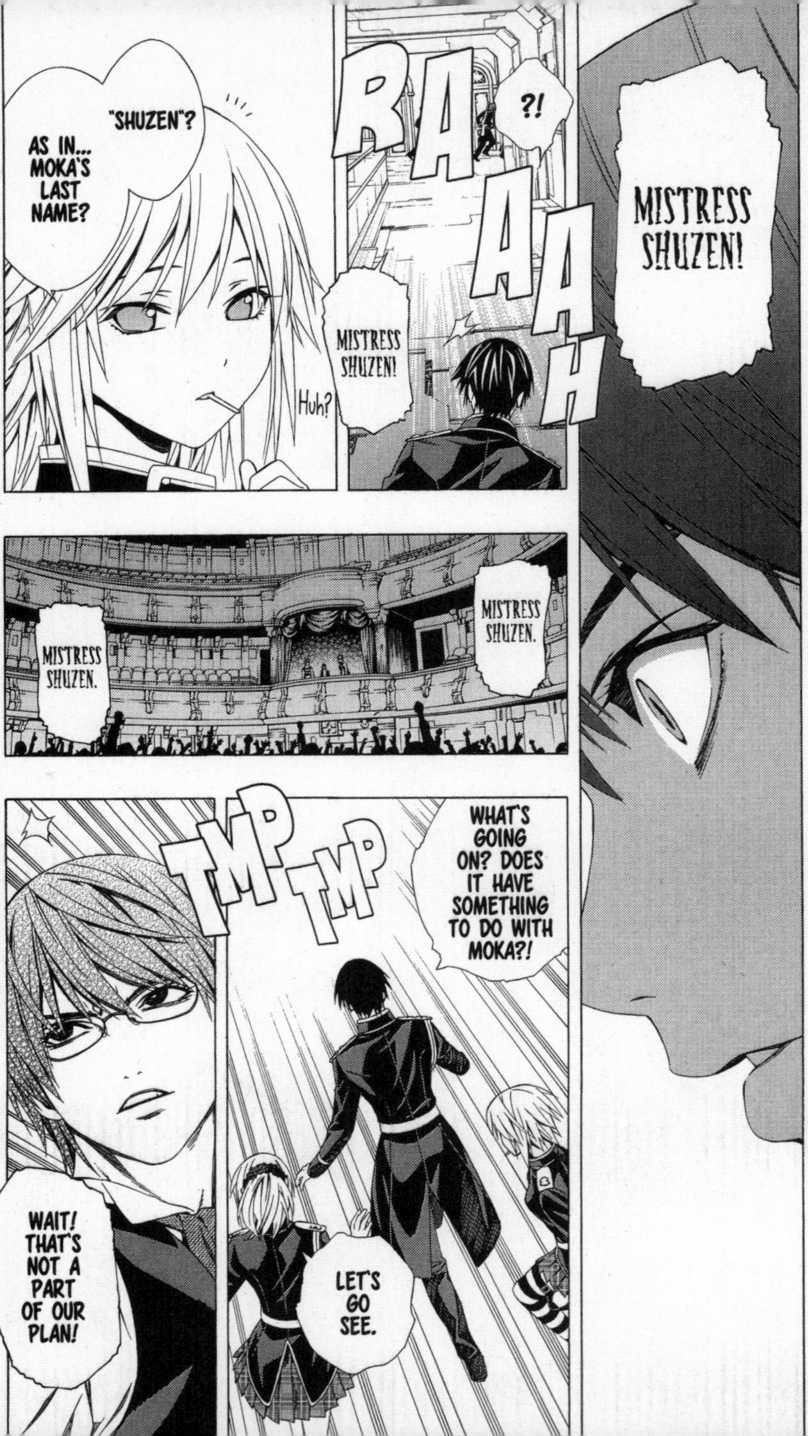
MISTRESS SHUZEN!
?!
RAAAAH
MISTRESS SHUZEN!
"SHUZEN"?
AS IN... MOKA'S LAST NAME?
Huh?
MISTRESS SHUZEN.
MISTRESS SHUZEN.
TMP TMP
WHAT'S GOING ON? DOES IT HAVE SOMETHING TO DO WITH MOKA?!
LET'S GO SEE.
WAIT! THAT'S NOT A PART OF OUR PLAN!

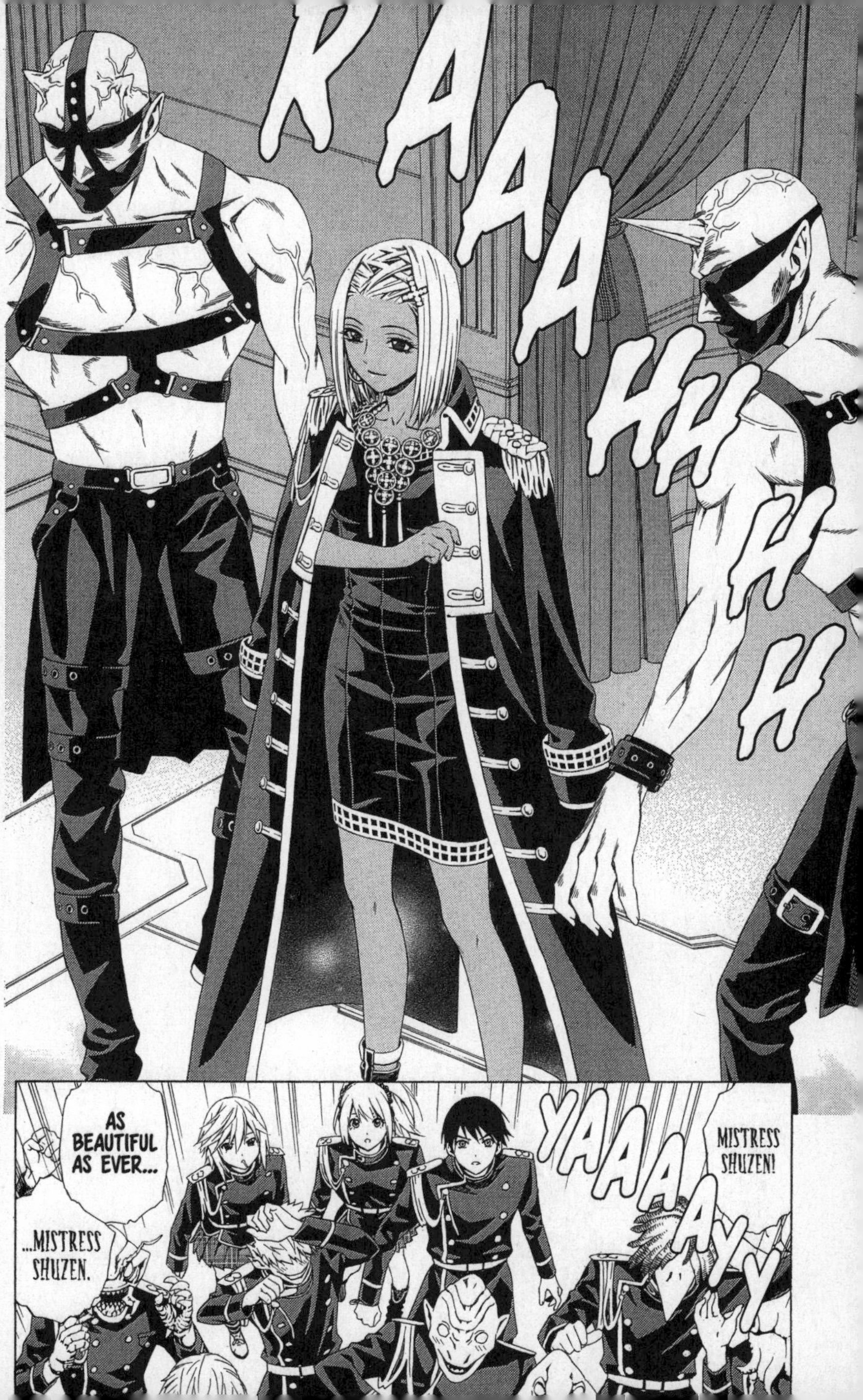
RAAAAHHHH
MISTRESS SHUZEN!
YAAAAAYY
AS BEAUTIFUL AS EVER...
...MISTRESS SHUZEN.

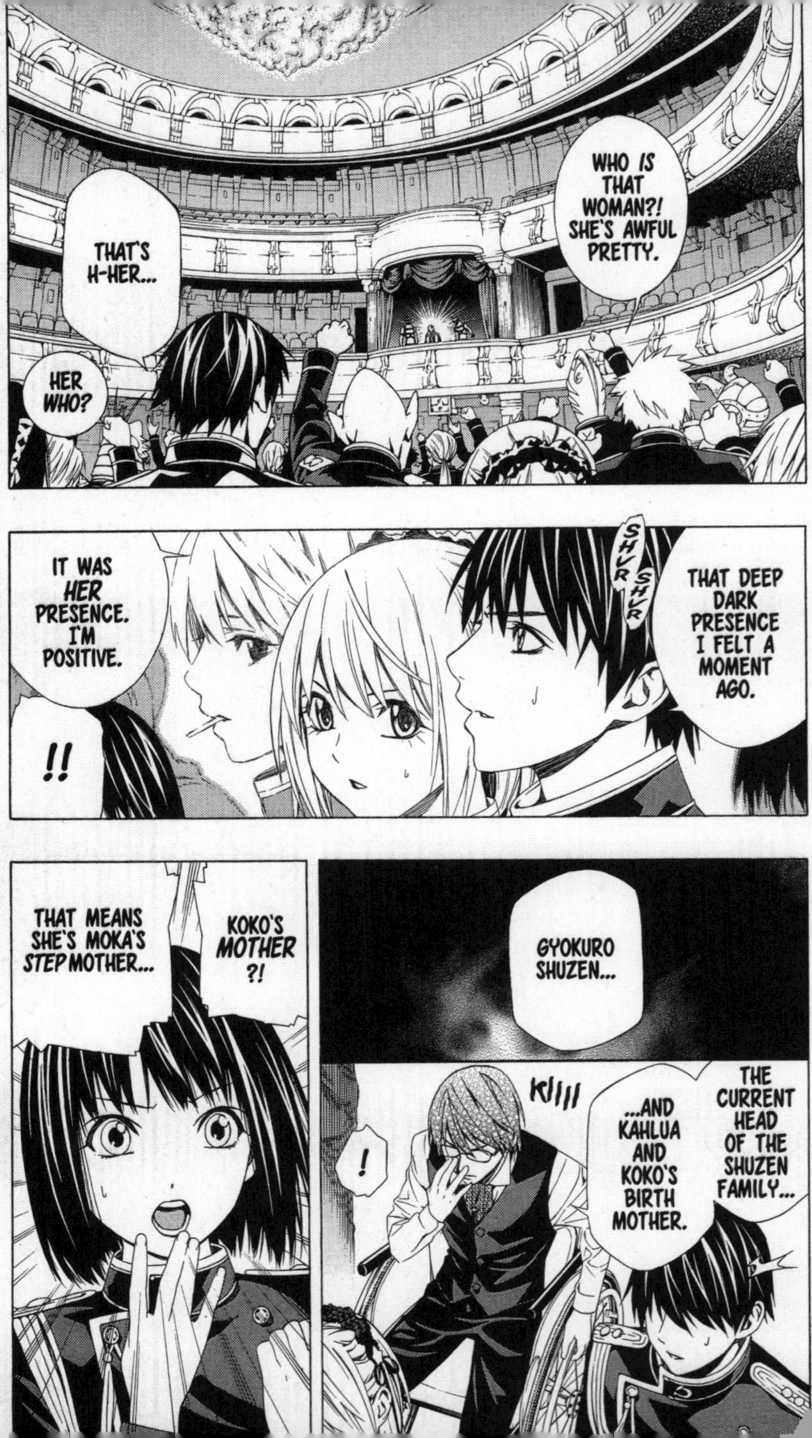
WHO IS THAT WOMAN?! SHE'S AWFUL PRETTY.
THAT'S H-HER...
HER WHO?
SHUR SHUR
THAT DEEP DARK PRESENCE I FELT A MOMENT AGO.
IT WAS HER PRESENCE. I'M POSITIVE.
!!
GYOKURO SHUZEN...
THE CURRENT HEAD OF THE SHUZEN FAMILY...
...AND KAHLUA AND KOKO'S BIRTH MOTHER.
KIIII
!
KOKO'S MOTHER ?!
THAT MEANS SHE'S MOKA'S STEPMOTHER...

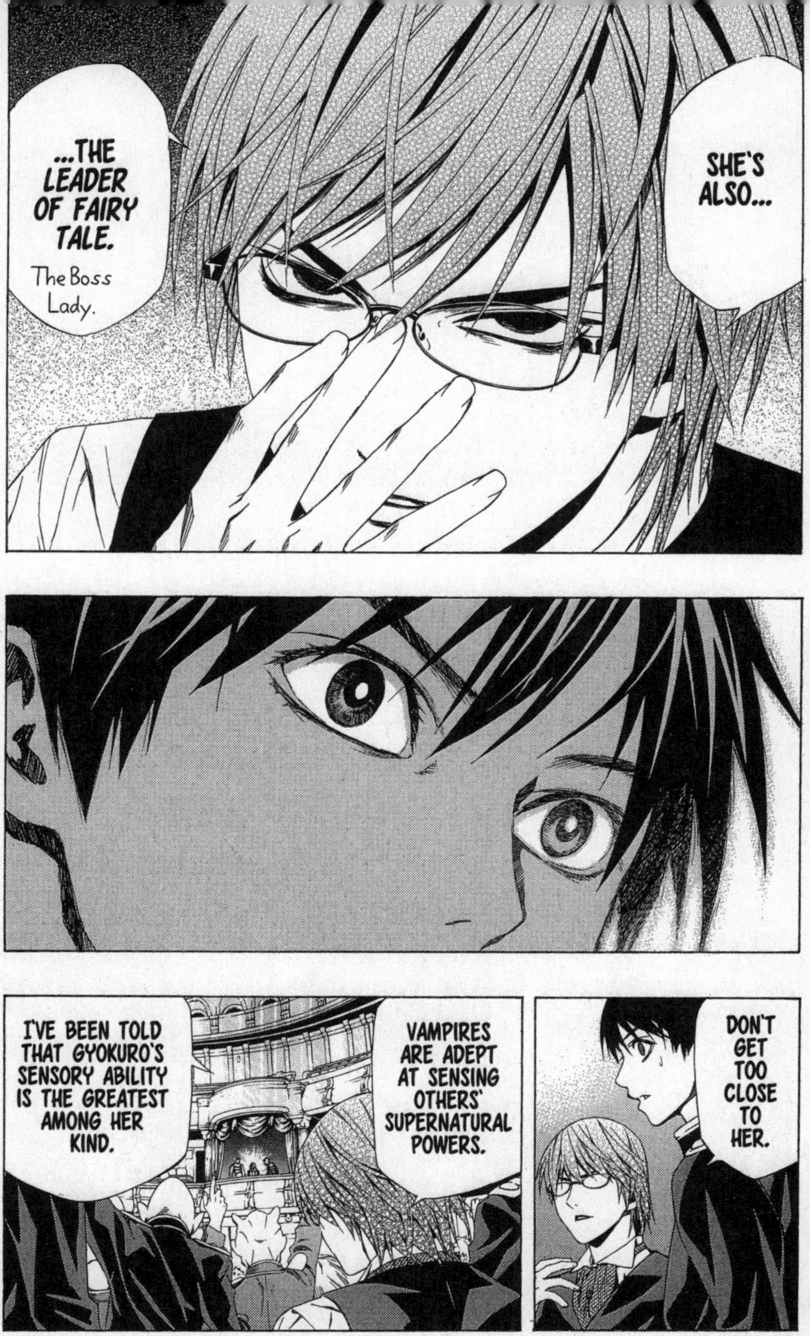
SHE'S ALSO...
...THE LEADER OF FAIRY TALE.
The Boss Lady.
DON'T GET TOO CLOSE TO HER.
VAMPIRES ARE ADEPT AT SENSING OTHERS' SUPERNATURAL POWERS.
I'VE BEEN TOLD THAT GYOKURO'S SENSORY ABILITY IS THE GREATEST AMONG HER KIND.

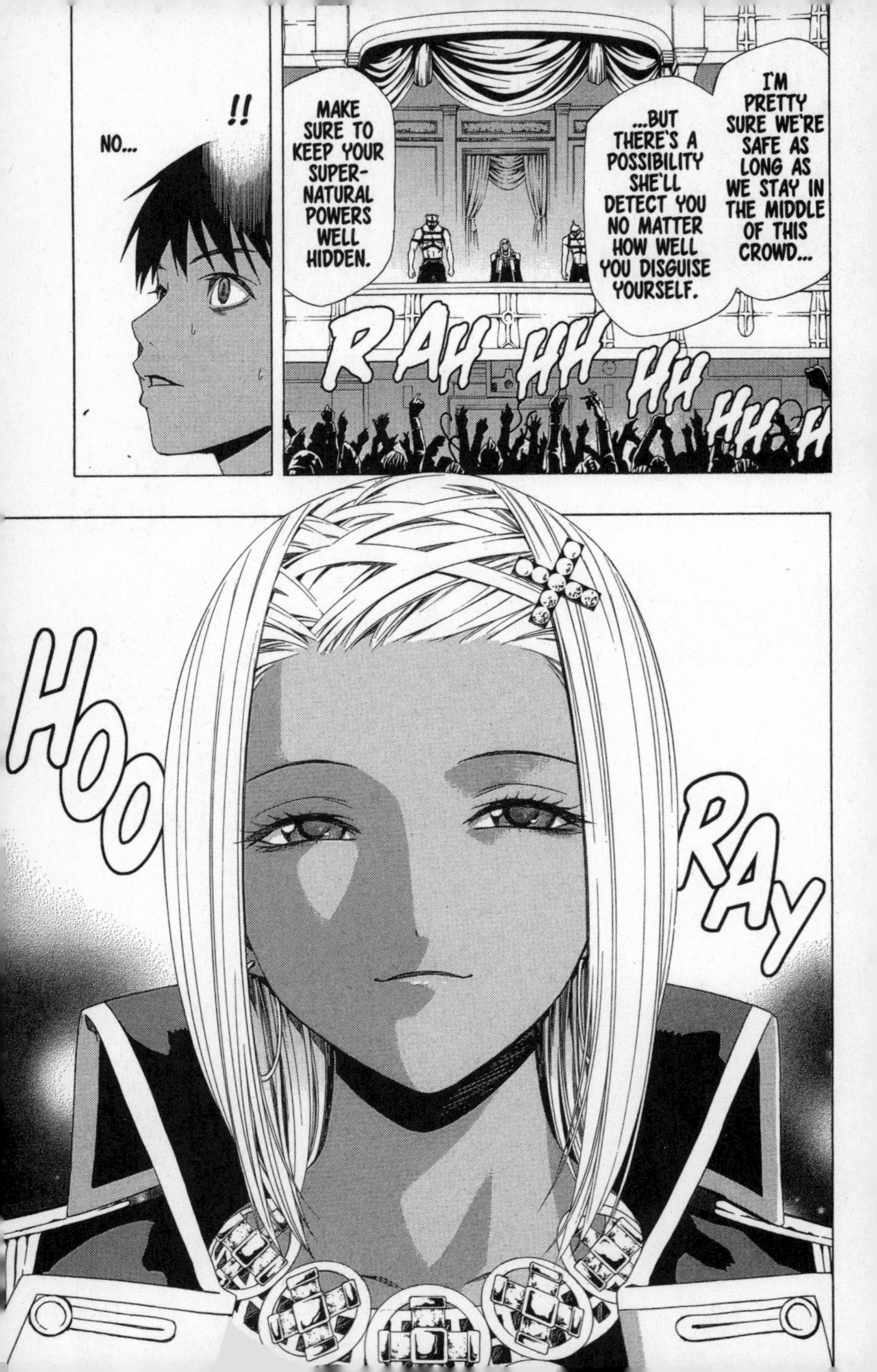
I'M PRETTY SURE WE'RE SAFE AS LONG AS WE STAY IN THE MIDDLE OF THIS CROWD...
...BUT THERE'S A POSSIBILITY SHE'LL DETECT YOU NO MATTER HOW WELL YOU DISGUISE YOURSELF.
MAKE SURE TO KEEP YOUR SUPER-NATURAL POWERS WELL HIDDEN.
RAHHHHHHHH
!!
NO...
HOORAY

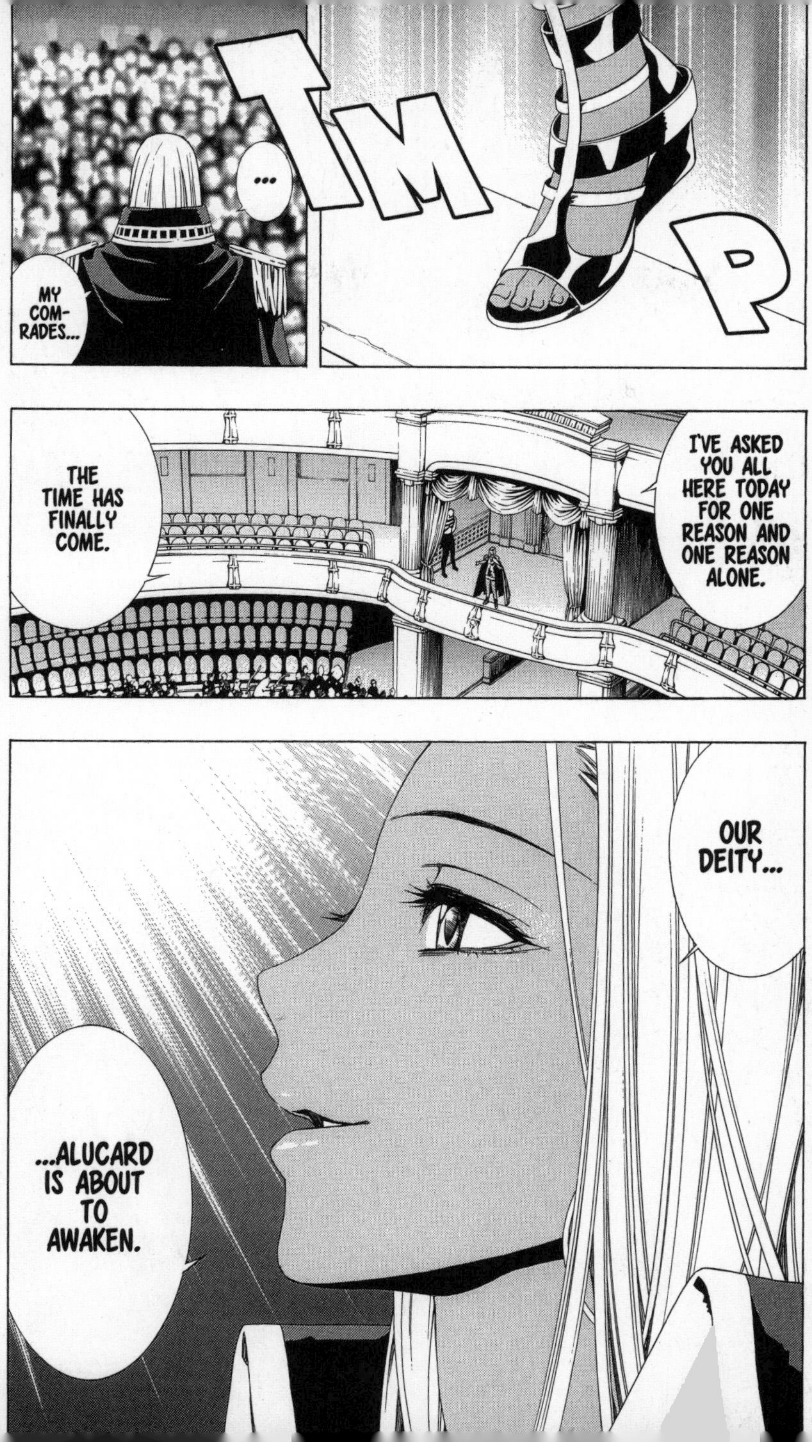
TMP
...
MY COM-RADES...
I'VE ASKED YOU ALL HERE TODAY FOR ONE REASON AND ONE REASON ALONE.
THE TIME HAS FINALLY COME.
OUR DEITY...
...ALUCARD IS ABOUT TO AWAKEN.

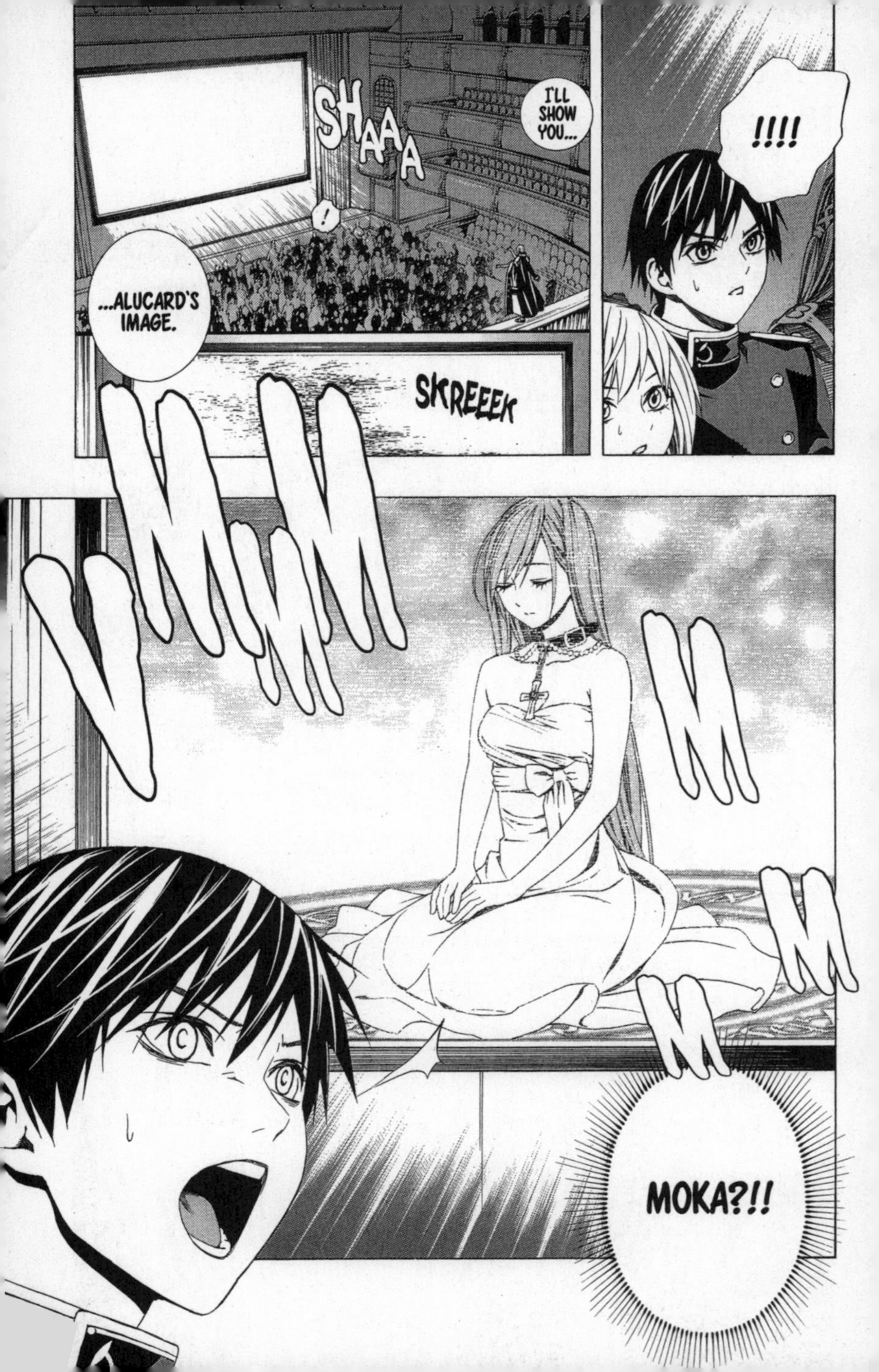
!!!!
I'LL SHOW YOU...
SHAAA
!
...ALUCARD'S IMAGE.
SKREEEK
VMMM
MMM
MOKA?!!

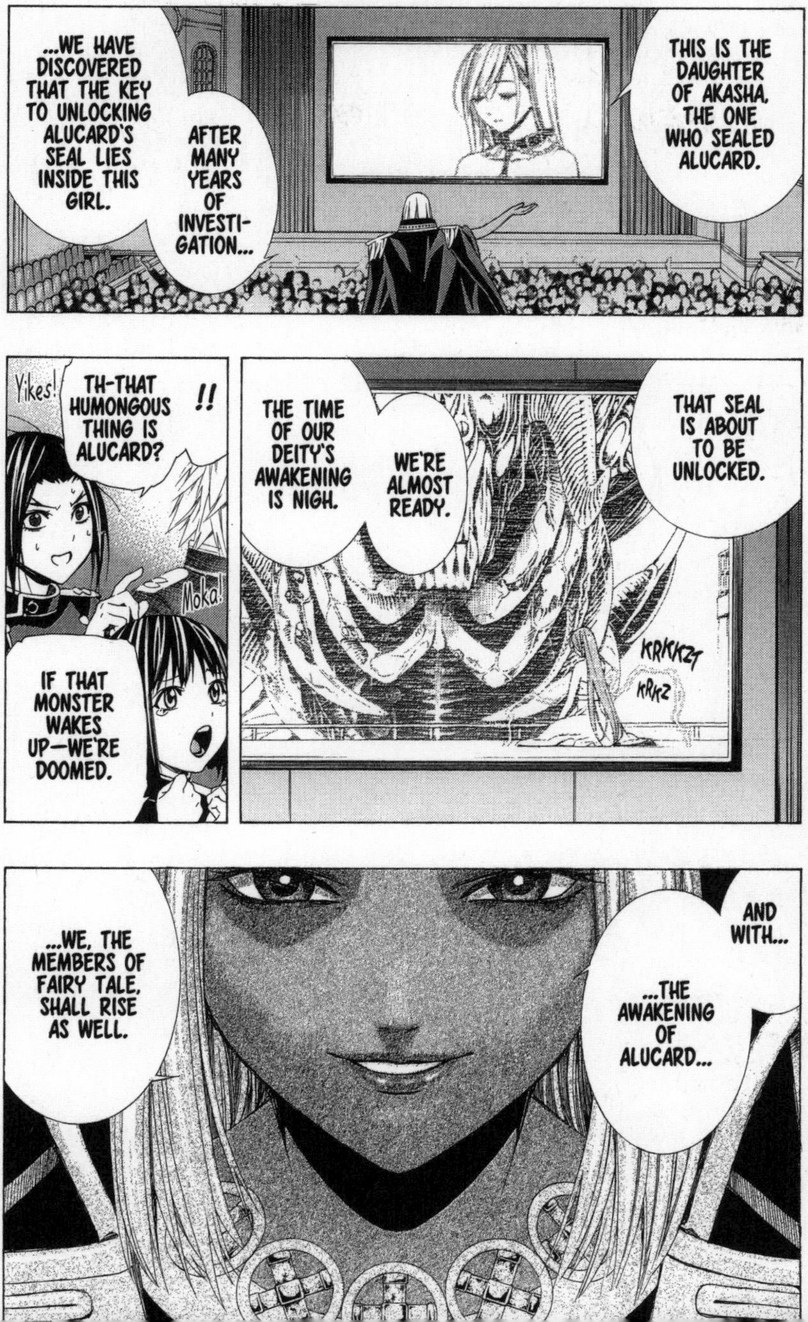
THIS IS THE DAUGHTER OF AKASHA, THE ONE WHO SEALED ALUCARD.
AFTER MANY YEARS OF INVESTI-GATION...
...WE HAVE DISCOVERED THAT THE KEY TO UNLOCKING ALUCARD'S SEAL LIES INSIDE THIS GIRL.
THAT SEAL IS ABOUT TO BE UNLOCKED.
WE'RE ALMOST READY.
THE TIME OF OUR DEITY'S AWAKENING IS NIGH.
KRKKZT
KRKZ
!!
TH-THAT HUMONGOUS THING IS ALUCARD?
Yikes!
Moka!
IF THAT MONSTER WAKES UP—WE'RE DOOMED.
AND WITH...
...THE AWAKENING OF ALUCARD...
...WE, THE MEMBERS OF FAIRY TALE, SHALL RISE AS WELL.

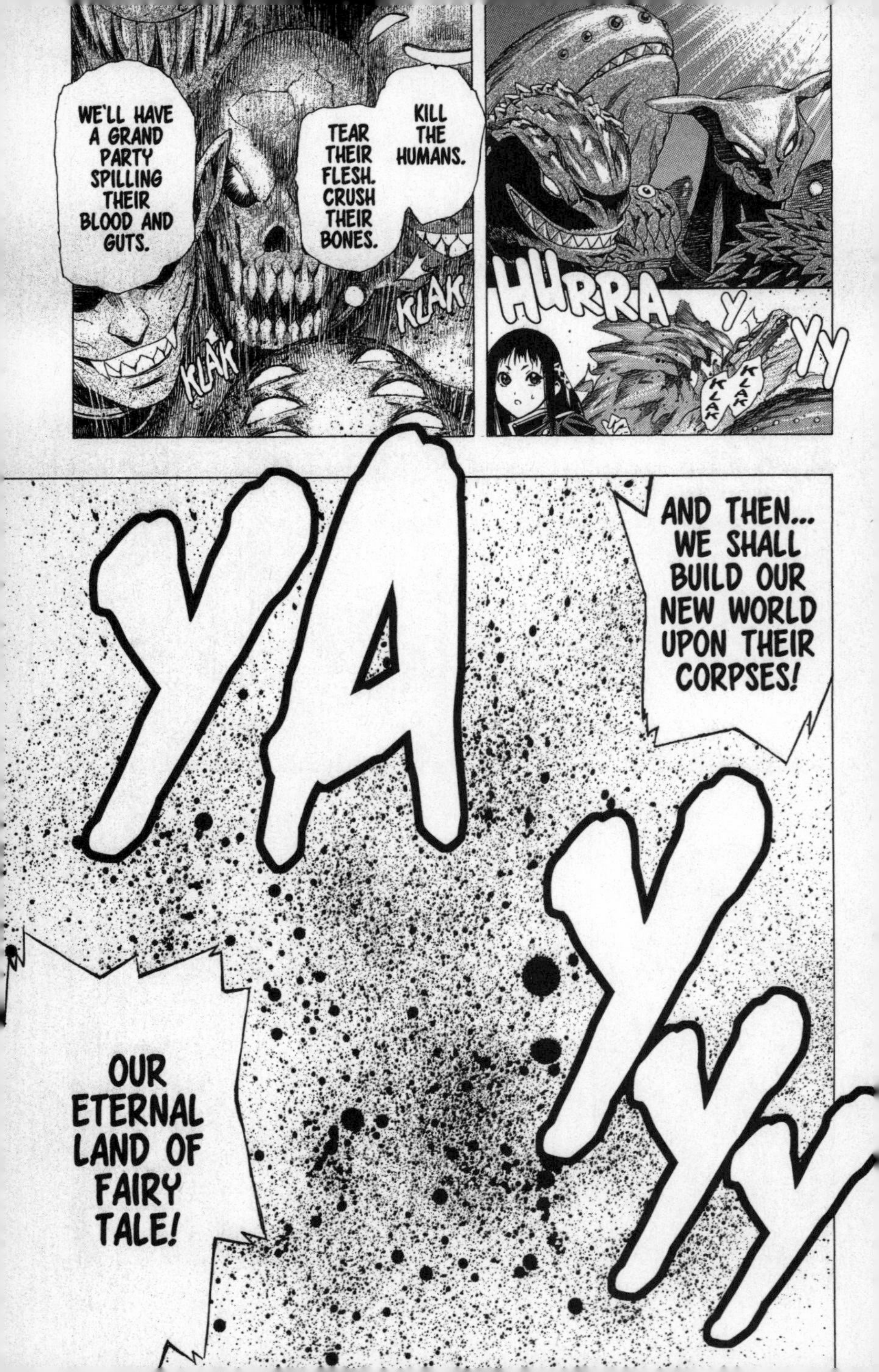
HURRA Y YY
KLAK
KLAK
KILL THE HUMANS.
TEAR THEIR FLESH. CRUSH THEIR BONES.
WE'LL HAVE A GRAND PARTY SPILLING THEIR BLOOD AND GUTS.
KLAK
KLAK
AND THEN... WE SHALL BUILD OUR NEW WORLD UPON THEIR CORPSES!
YA YYY
OUR ETERNAL LAND OF FAIRY TALE!

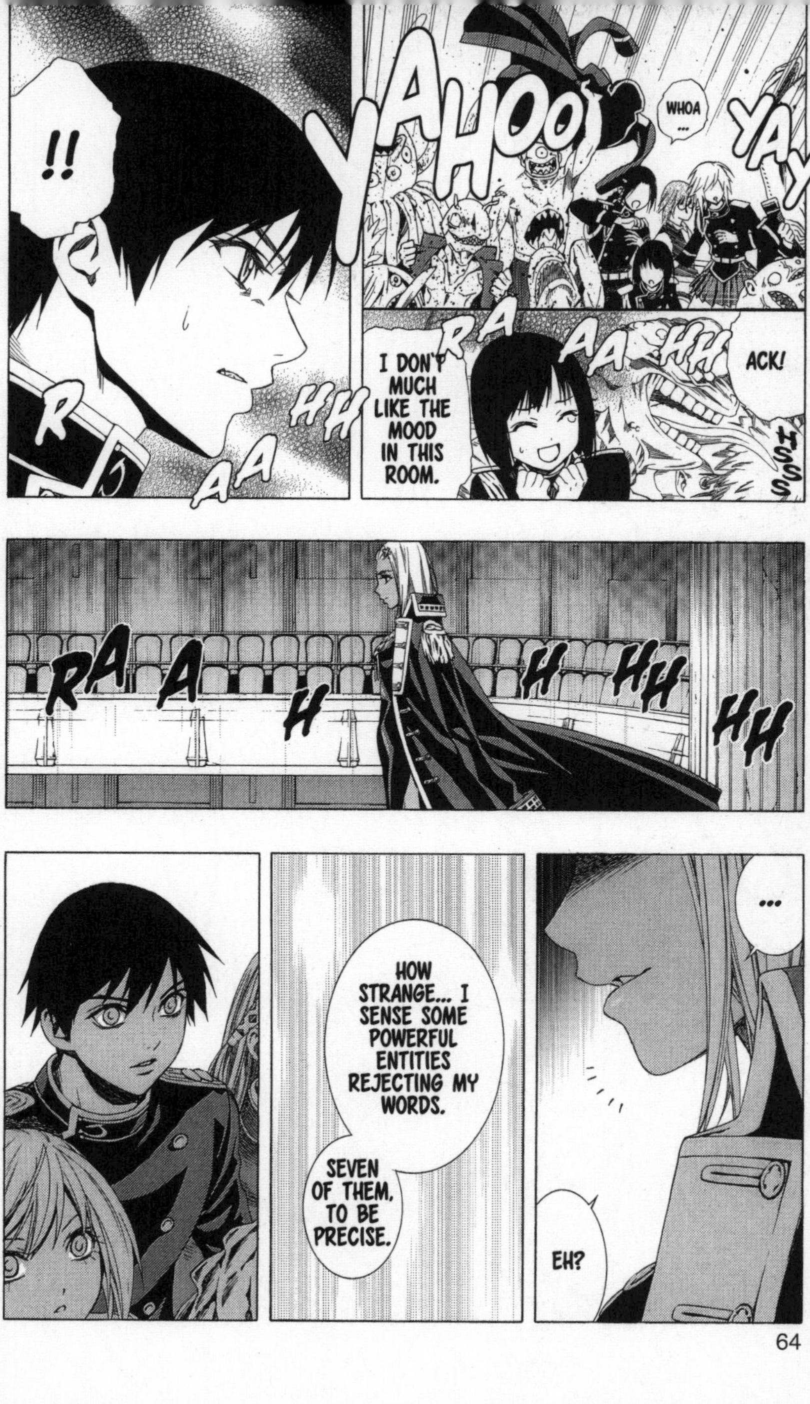
YAHOO
WHOA ...
YAY
I DON'T MUCH LIKE THE MOOD IN THIS ROOM.
RAAAHH
ACK!
HSSS
!!
RHHAA
RAAHHHHHH
...
EH?
HOW STRANGE... I SENSE SOME POWERFUL ENTITIES REJECTING MY WORDS.
SEVEN OF THEM, TO BE PRECISE.

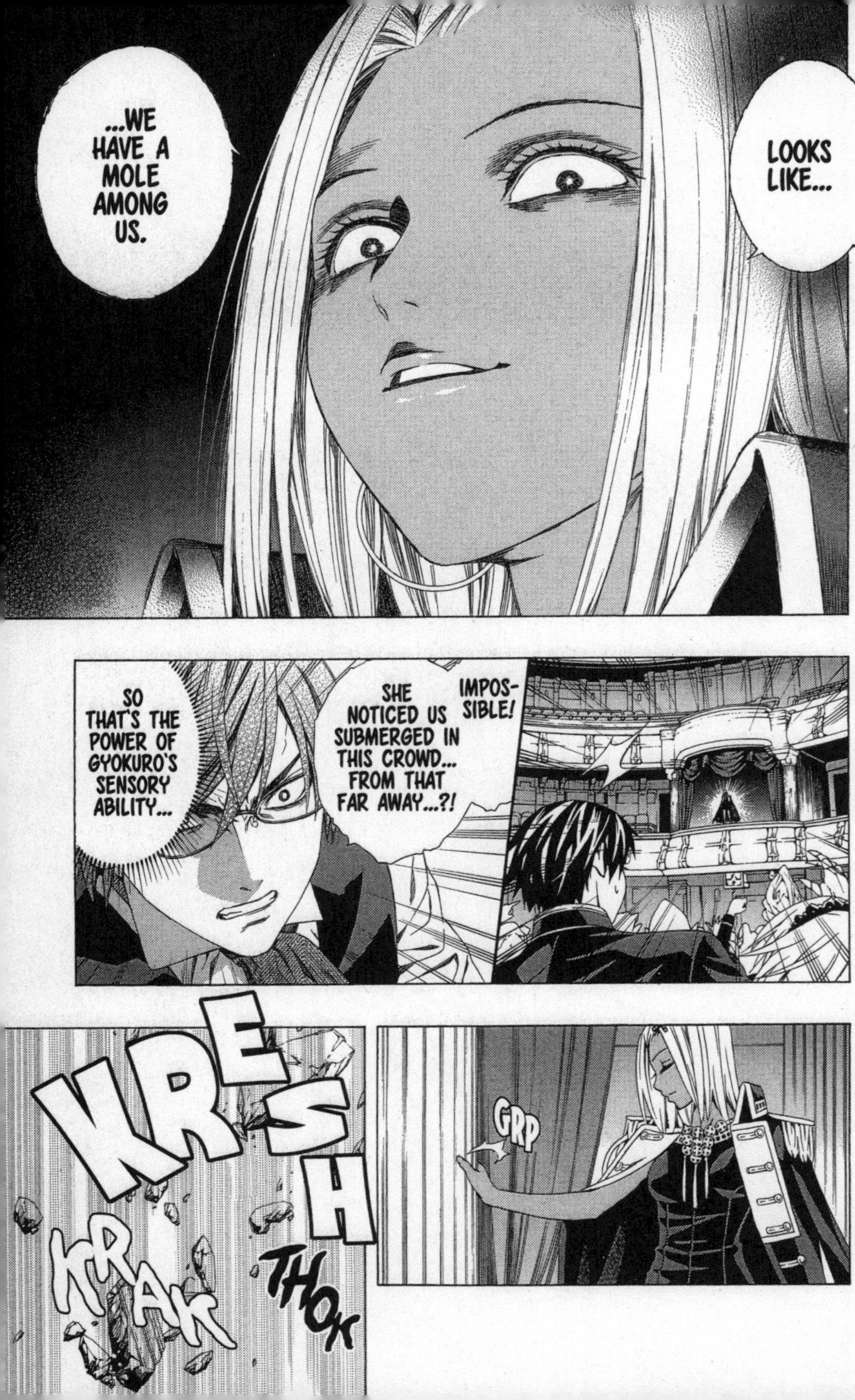
LOOKS LIKE...
...WE HAVE A MOLE AMONG US.
IMPOS-SIBLE!
SHE NOTICED US SUBMERGED IN THIS CROWD... FROM THAT FAR AWAY...?!
SO THAT'S THE POWER OF GYOKURO'S SENSORY ABILITY...
GRP
KRESH
KRAK
THOK

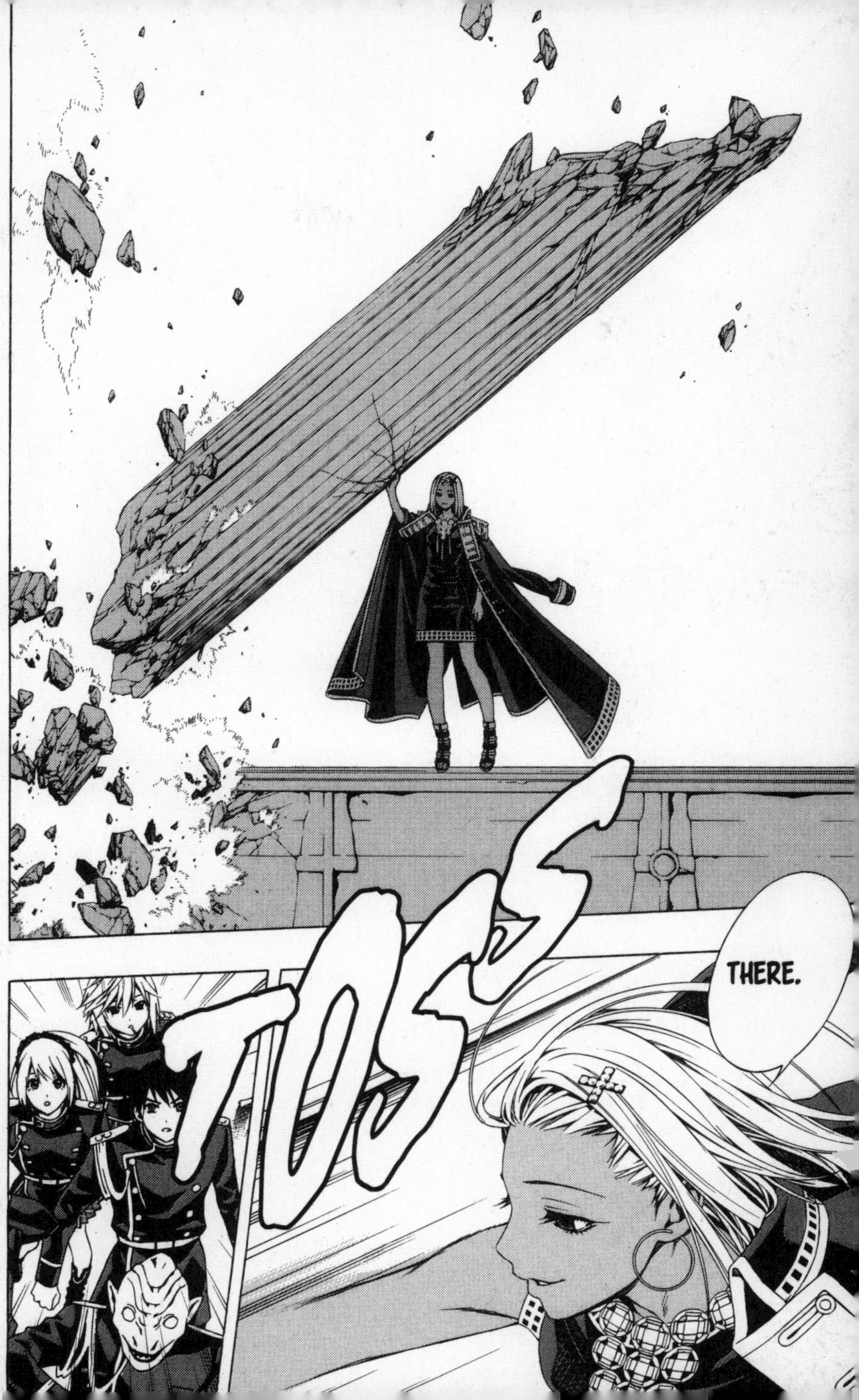
THERE.
TOSS

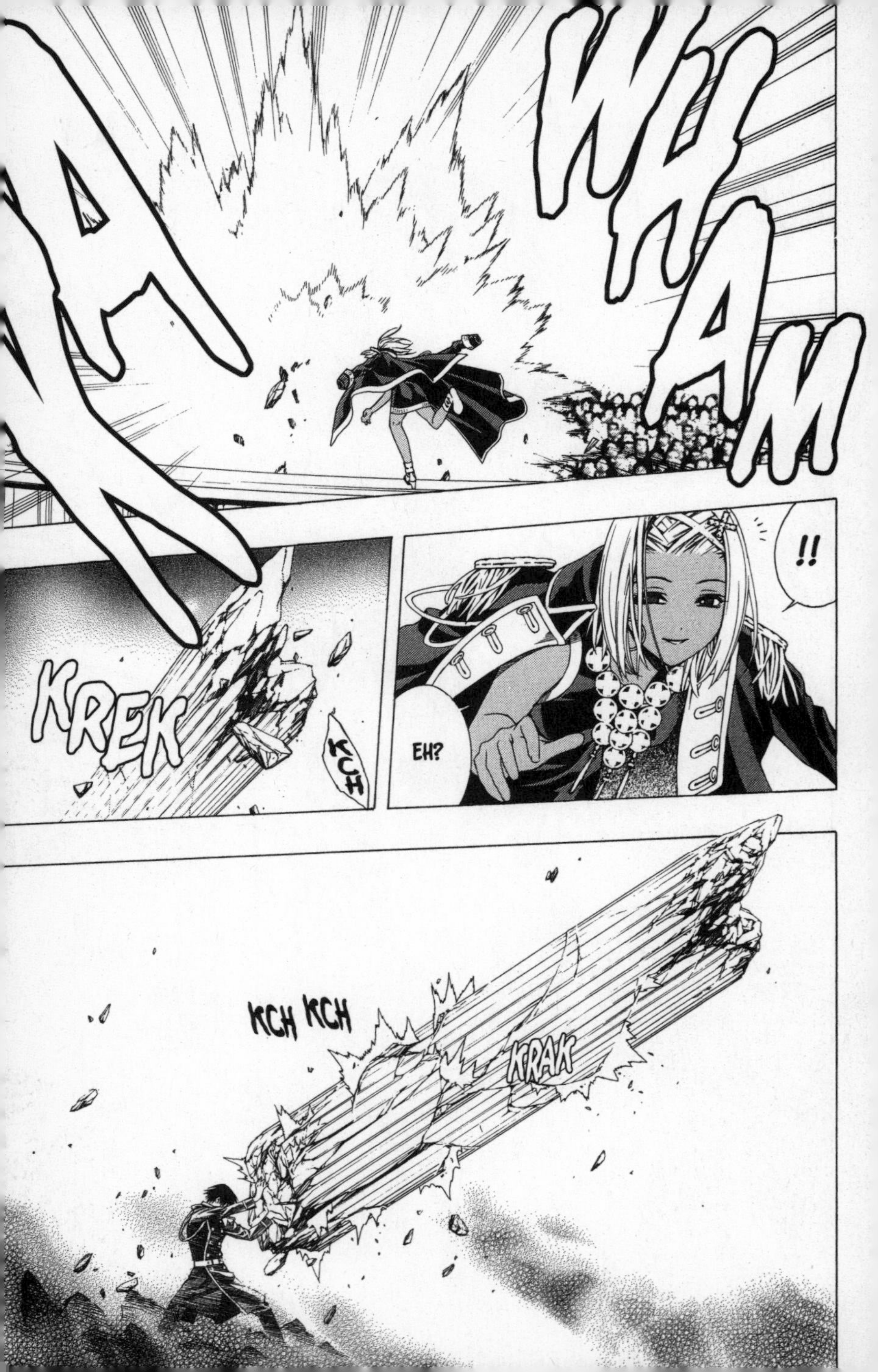
WHAM
!!
EH?
KREK
KCH
KRAK
KCH KCH

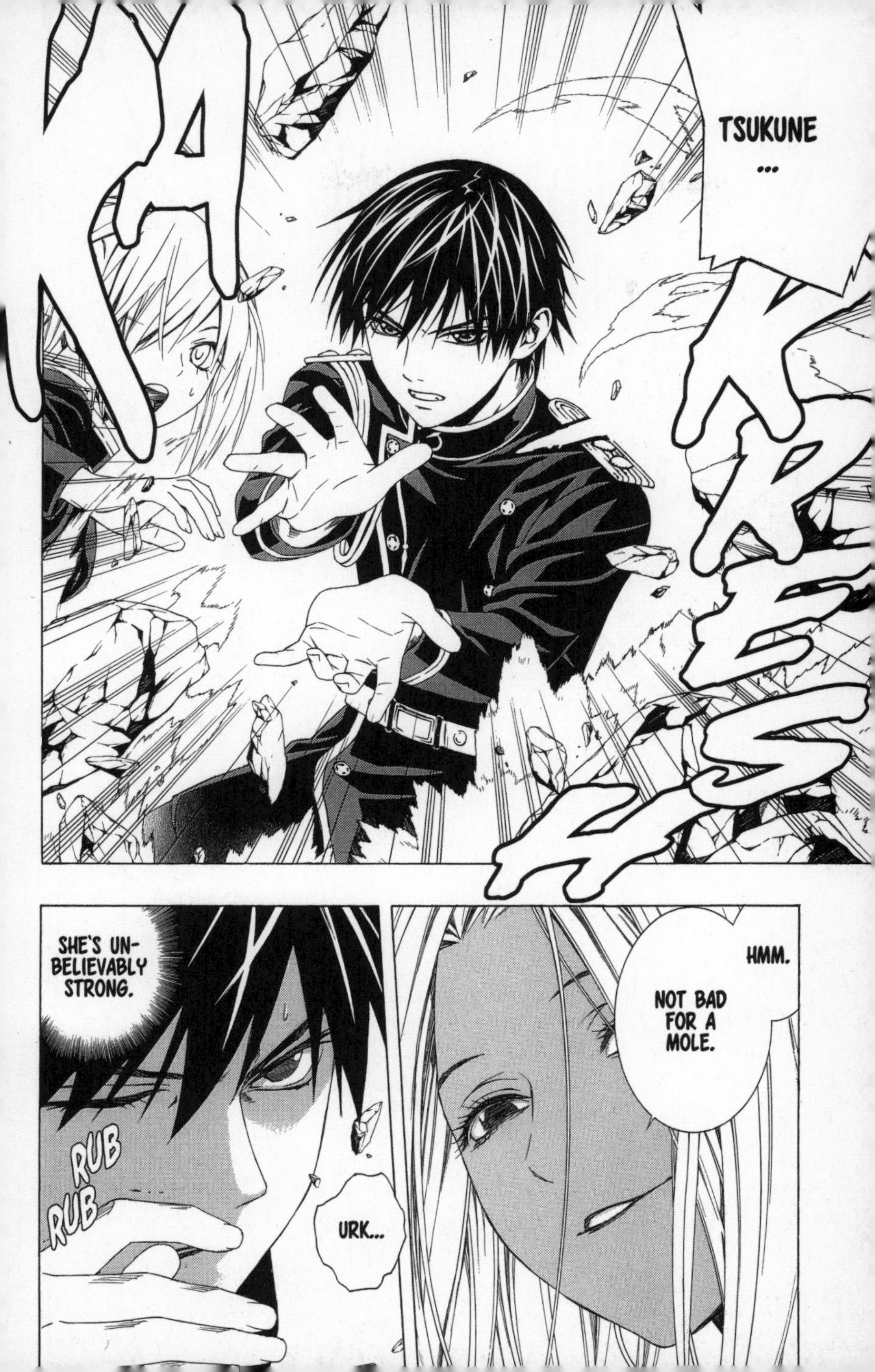
TSUKUNE ...
HMM.
NOT BAD FOR A MOLE.
SHE'S UN-BELIEVABLY STRONG.
URK...
RUB RUB

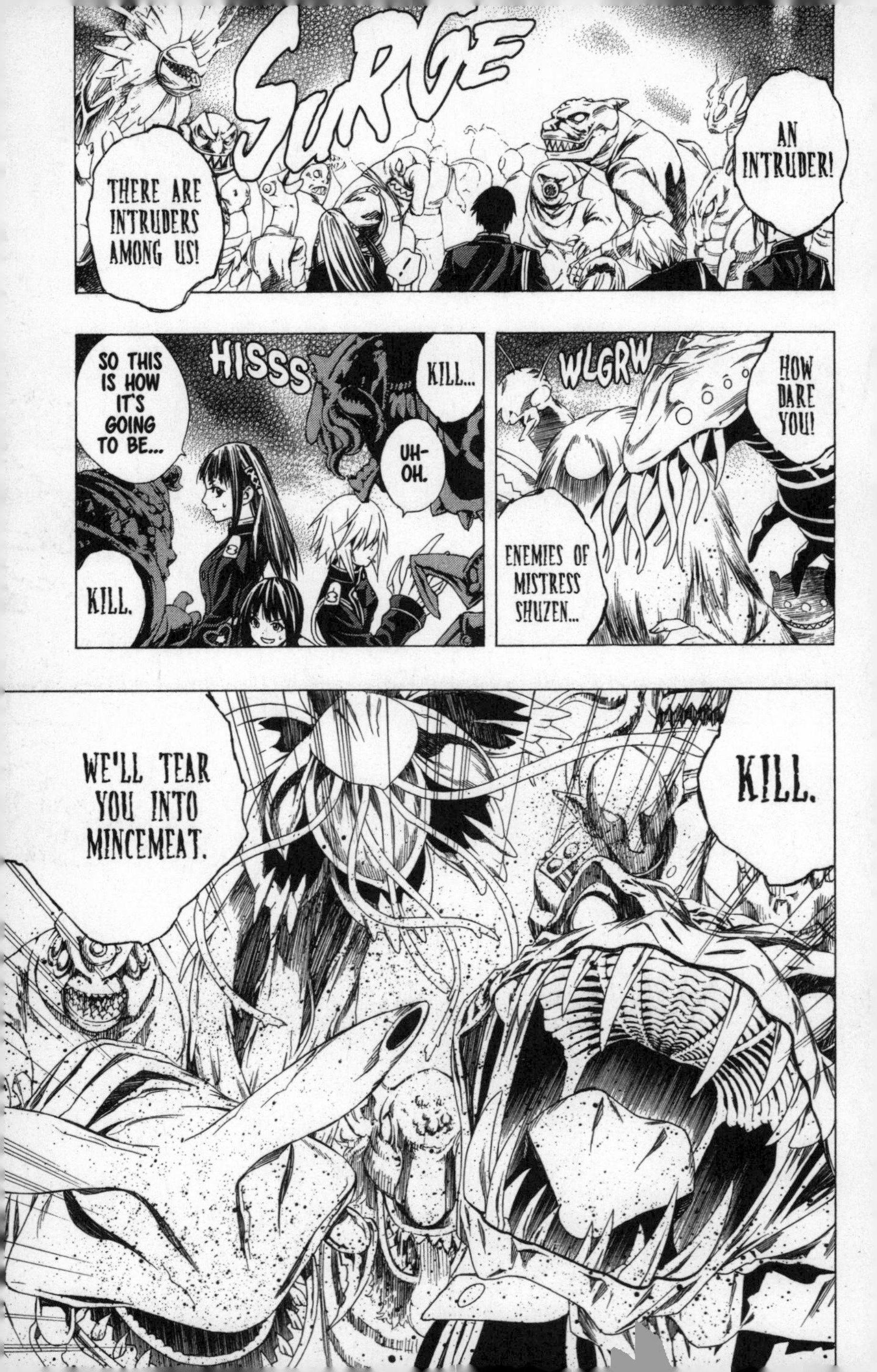
AN INTRUDER!
SURGE
THERE ARE INTRUDERS AMONG US!
HOW DARE YOU!
WLGRW
ENEMIES OF MISTRESS SHUZEN...
KILL...
HISSS
SO THIS IS HOW IT'S GOING TO BE...
UH-OH.
KILL.
KILL.
WE'LL TEAR YOU INTO MINCEMEAT.

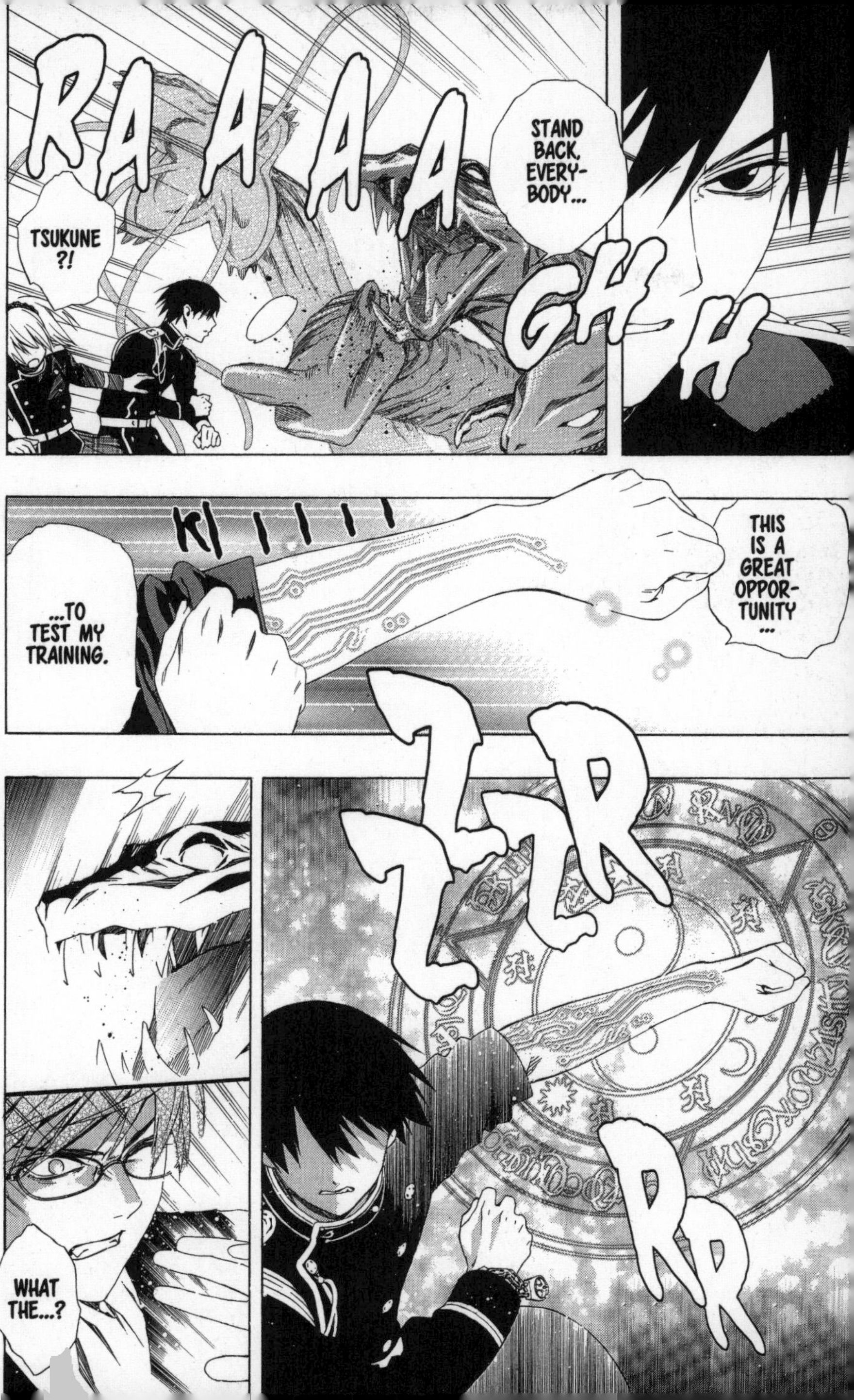
STAND BACK, EVERYBODY...
RAAAAGHH
TSUKUNE ?!
THIS IS A GREAT OPPORTUNITY ...
KIIIII
...TO TEST MY TRAINING.
ZZZRRRR
WHAT THE...?

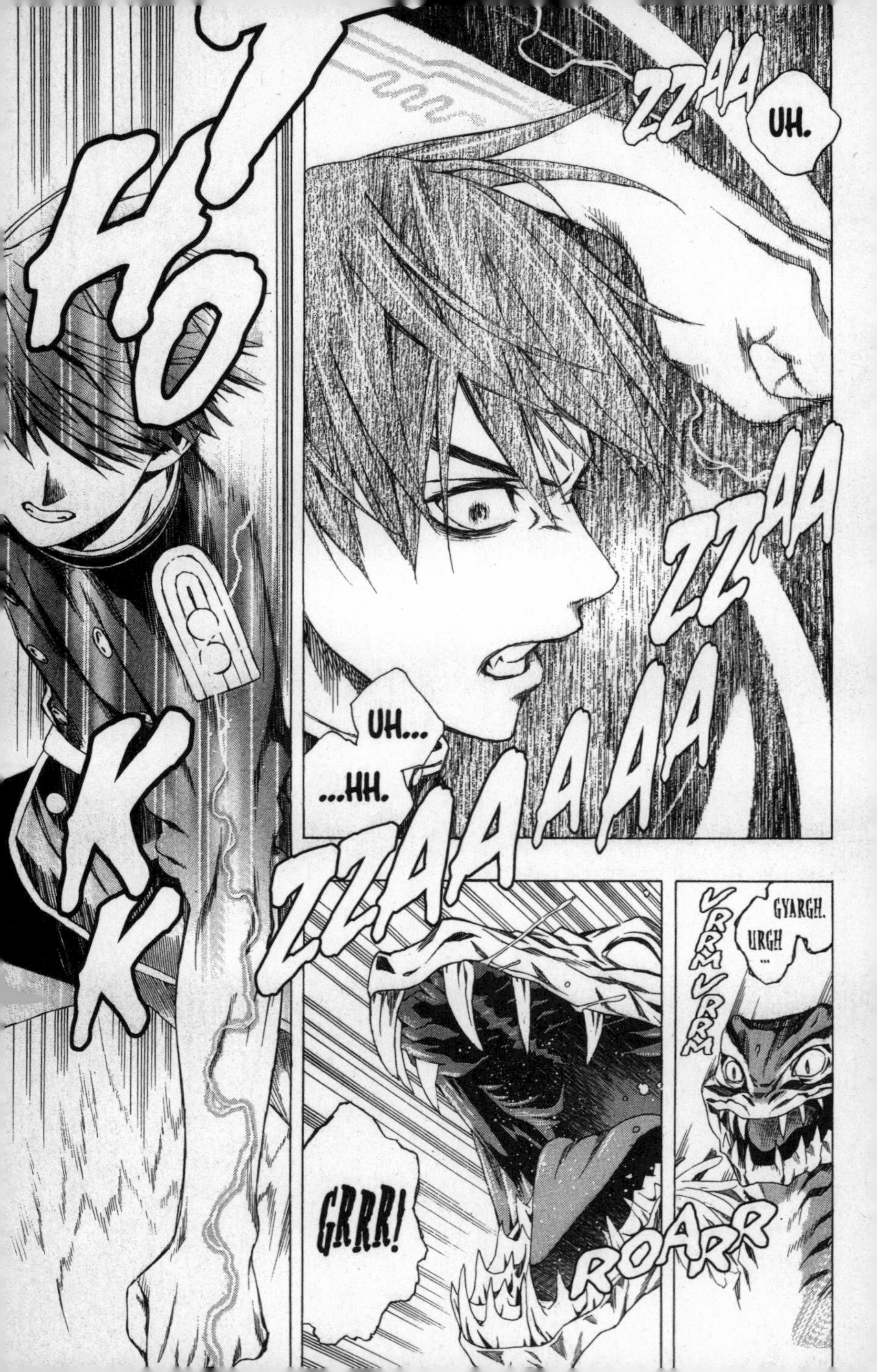
ZZAA
UH.
ZZAA
UH...
...HH.
ZZAAAAAAA
VRRMVRRM
GYARGH.
URGH...
ROARR
GRRR!

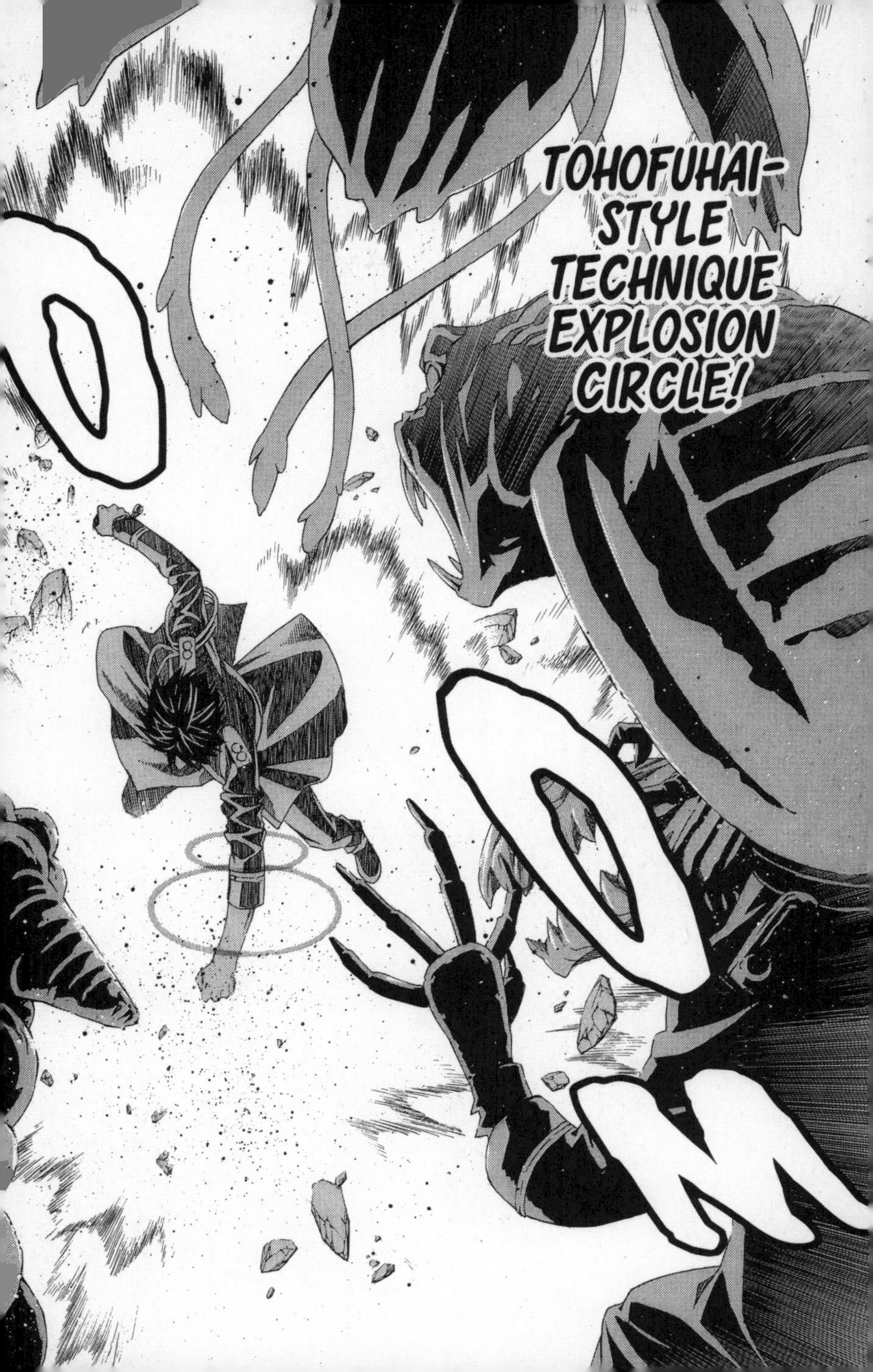
TOHOFUHAI-STYLE TECHNIQUE EXPLOSION CIRCLE!

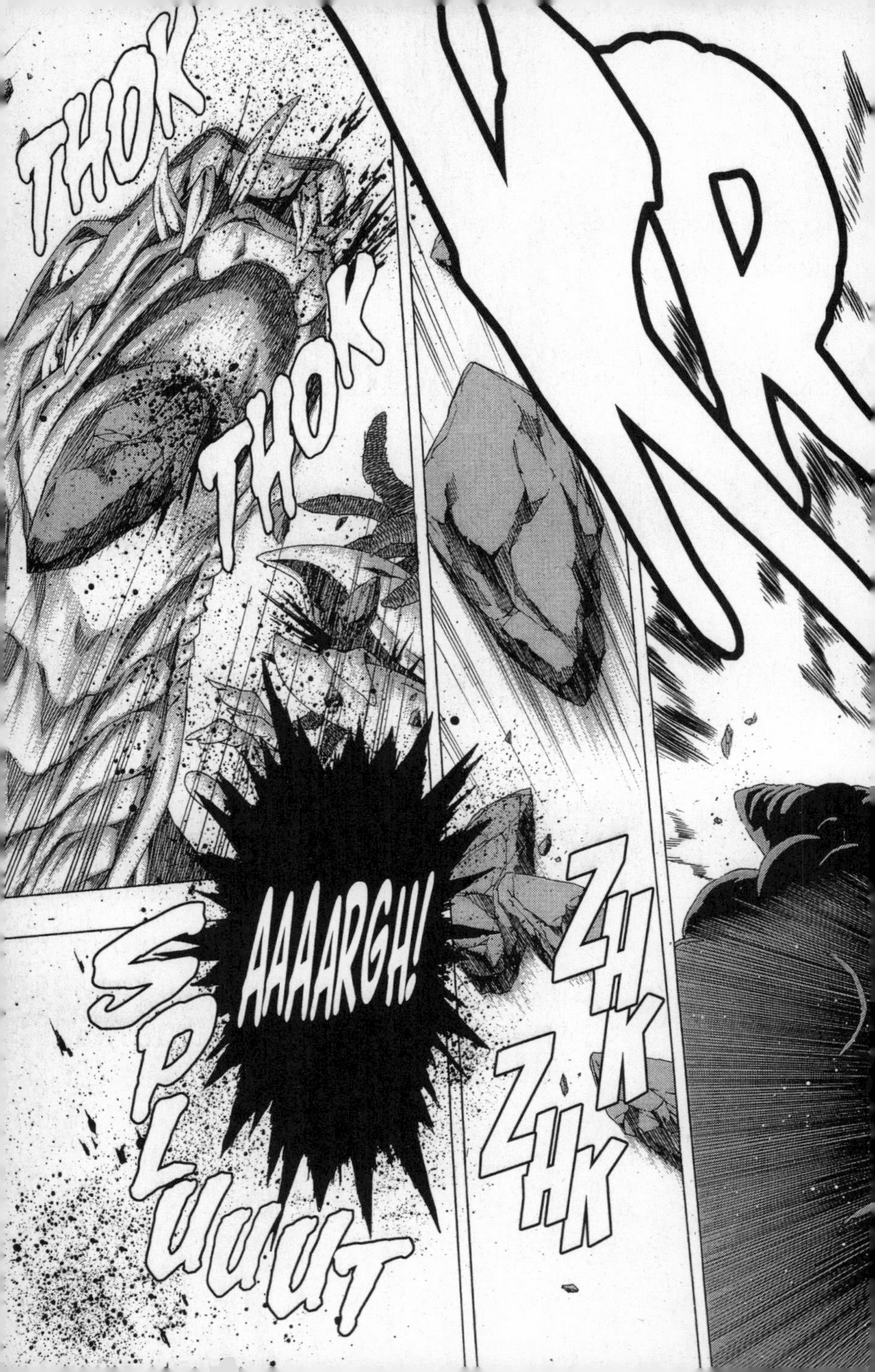
THOK
THOK
ZHK
ZHK
AAAARGH!
SPLUUUT

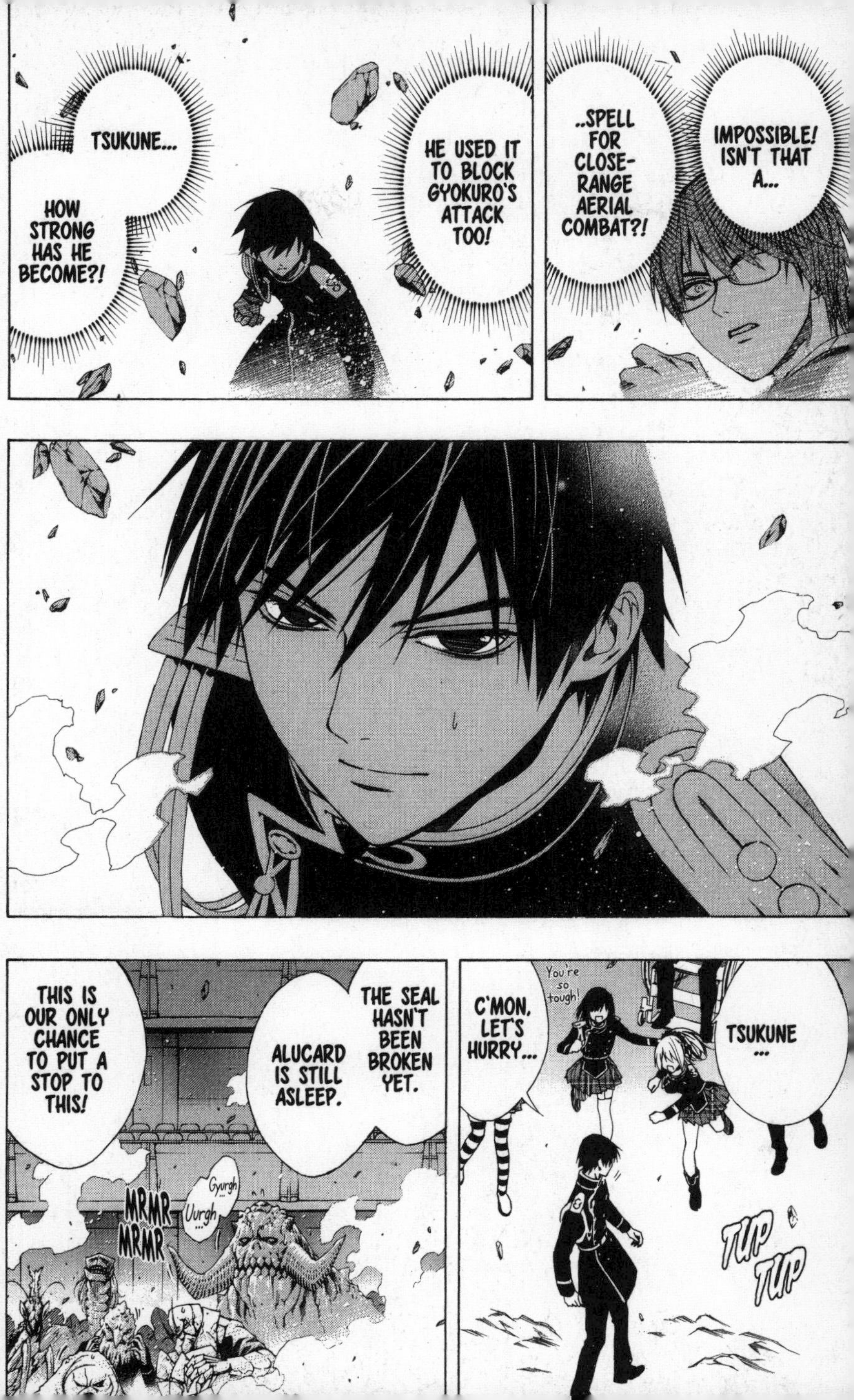
IMPOSSIBLE! ISN'T THAT A...
..SPELL FOR CLOSE-RANGE AERIAL COMBAT?!
HE USED IT TO BLOCK GYOKURO'S ATTACK TOO!
TSUKUNE...
HOW STRONG HAS HE BECOME?!
TSUKUNE ...
You're so tough!
C'MON, LET'S HURRY...
TUP TUP
THE SEAL HASN'T BEEN BROKEN YET.
ALUCARD IS STILL ASLEEP.
THIS IS OUR ONLY CHANCE TO PUT A STOP TO THIS!
Gyurgh ...
Uurgh ...
MRMR MRMR

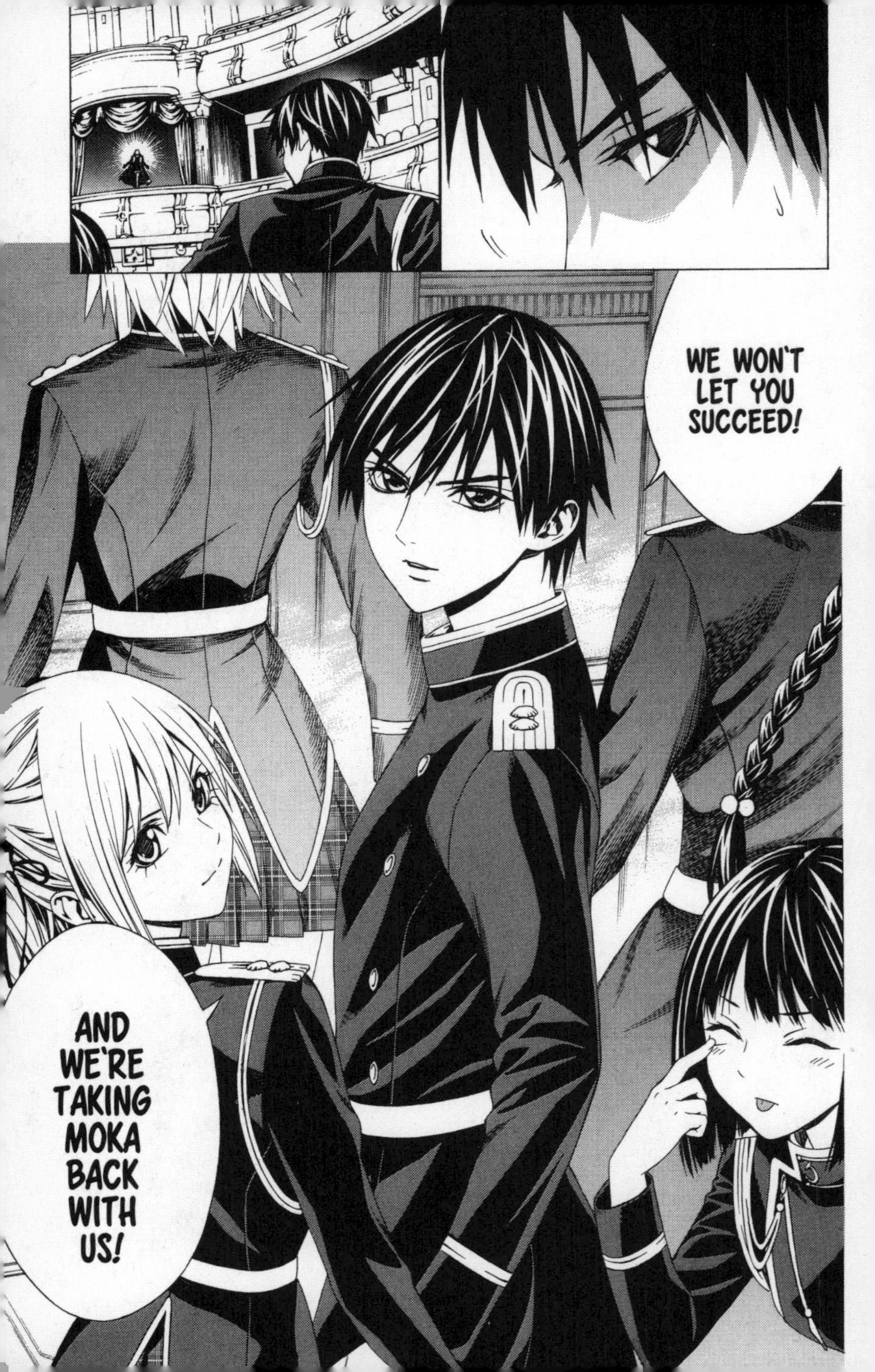
WE WON'T LET YOU SUCCEED!
AND WE'RE TAKING MOKA BACK WITH US!

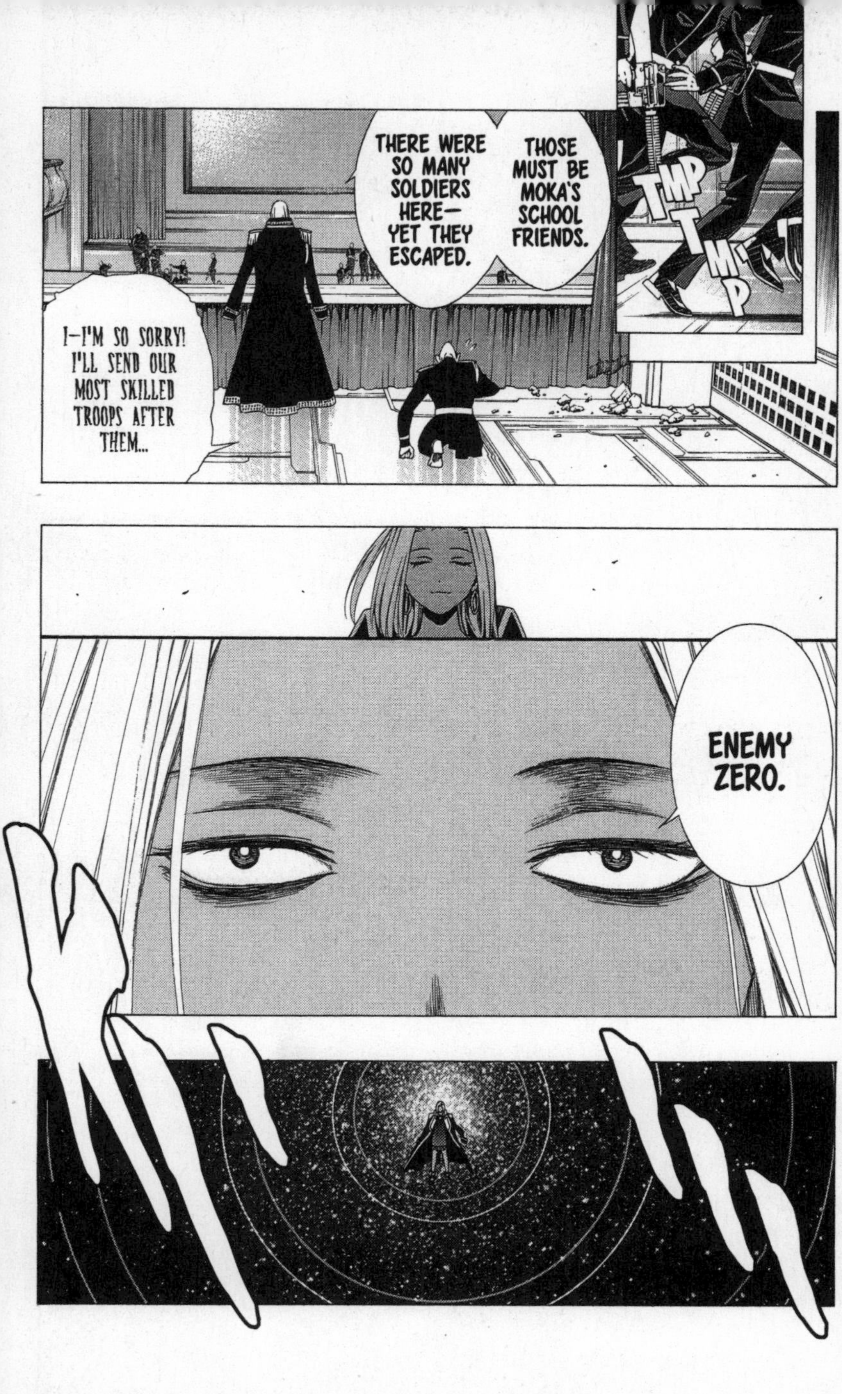
TMP
TMP
THOSE MUST BE MOKA'S SCHOOL FRIENDS.
THERE WERE SO MANY SOLDIERS HERE— YET THEY ESCAPED.
I—I'M SO SORRY! I'LL SEND OUR MOST SKILLED TROOPS AFTER THEM...
ENEMY ZERO.

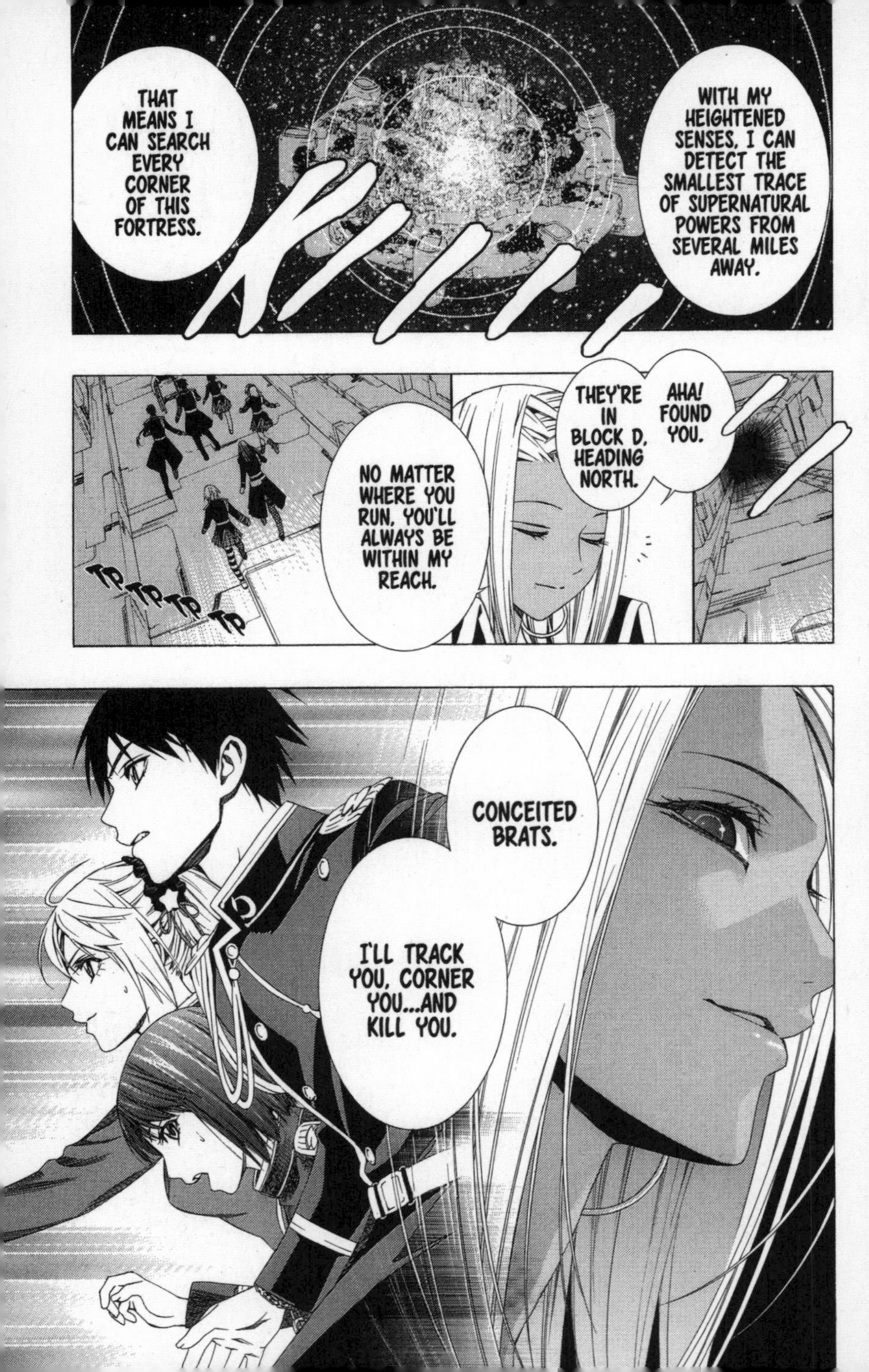
WITH MY HEIGHTENED SENSES, I CAN DETECT THE SMALLEST TRACE OF SUPERNATURAL POWERS FROM SEVERAL MILES AWAY.
THAT MEANS I CAN SEARCH EVERY CORNER OF THIS FORTRESS.
AHA! FOUND YOU.
THEY'RE IN BLOCK D, HEADING NORTH.
NO MATTER WHERE YOU RUN, YOU'LL ALWAYS BE WITHIN MY REACH.
TP TP TP TP TP
CONCEITED BRATS.
I'LL TRACK YOU, CORNER YOU...AND KILL YOU.

44: Executives

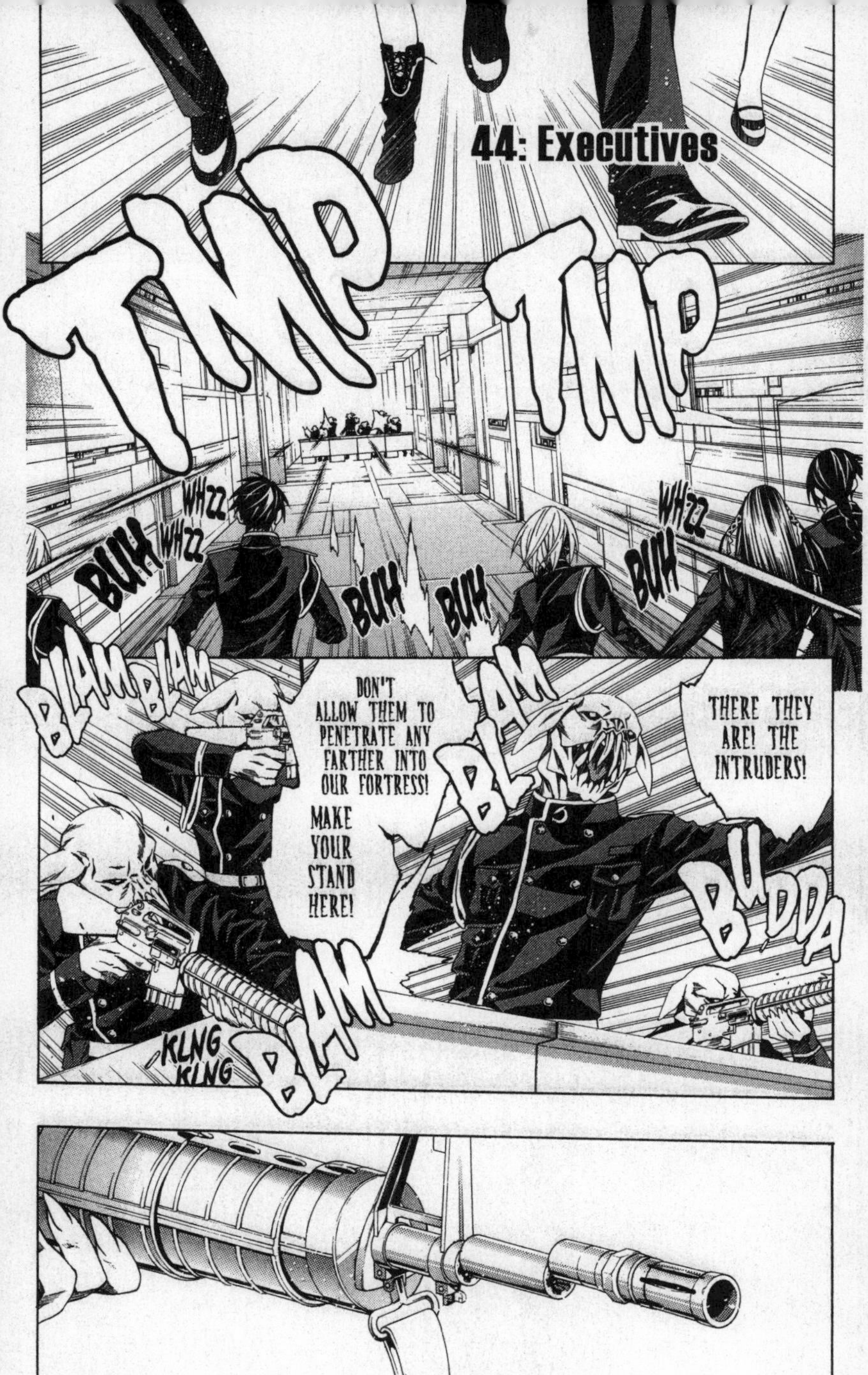
TMP TMP
WHZZ WHZZ
BUH
BUH BUH
WHZZ
BUH
THERE THEY ARE! THE INTRUDERS!
BUDDA
BLAM BLAM
DON'T ALLOW THEM TO PENETRATE ANY FARTHER INTO OUR FORTRESS!
MAKE YOUR STAND HERE!
BLAM BLAM
BLAM BLAM
KLNG KLNG

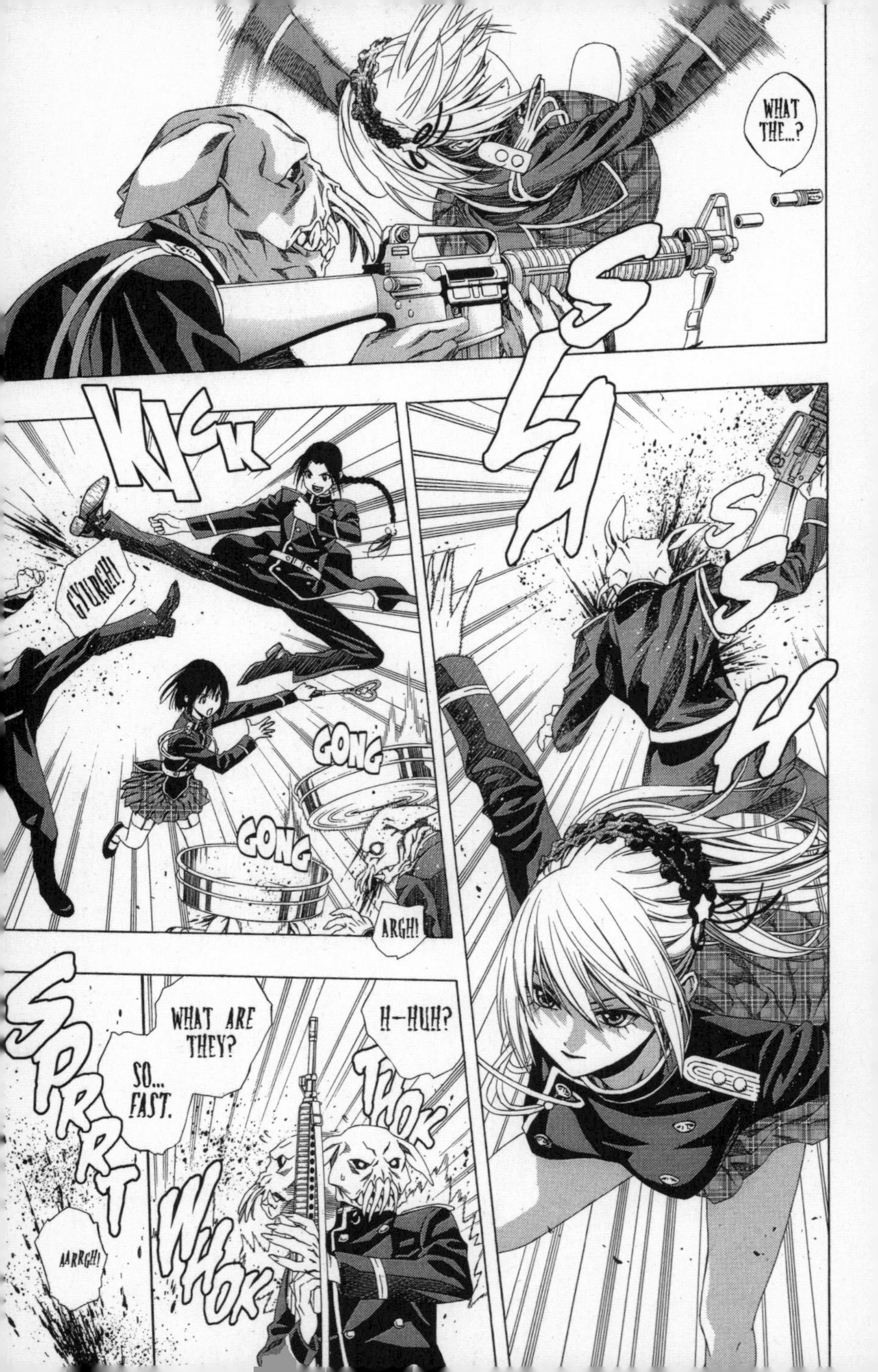
WHAT THE...?
SLASSSH
KICK
GYURGH!
GONG
GONG
ARGH!
H-HUH?
WHAT ARE THEY?
SO... FAST.
THOK
WHOK
SPRRT
AARRGH!

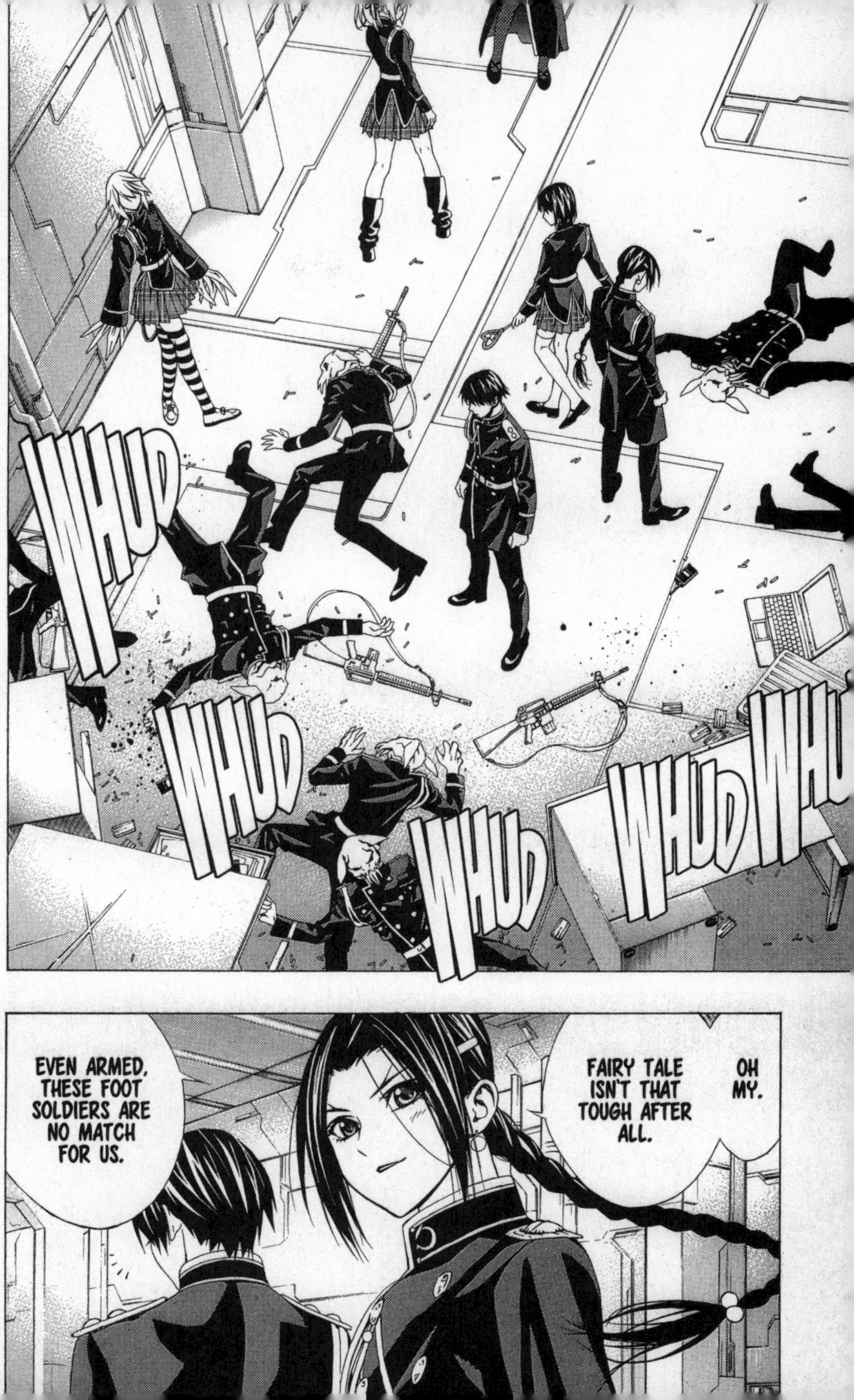
WHU
WHUD
WHUD
WHUD
WHUD
OH MY.
FAIRY TALE ISN'T THAT TOUGH AFTER ALL.
EVEN ARMED, THESE FOOT SOLDIERS ARE NO MATCH FOR US.

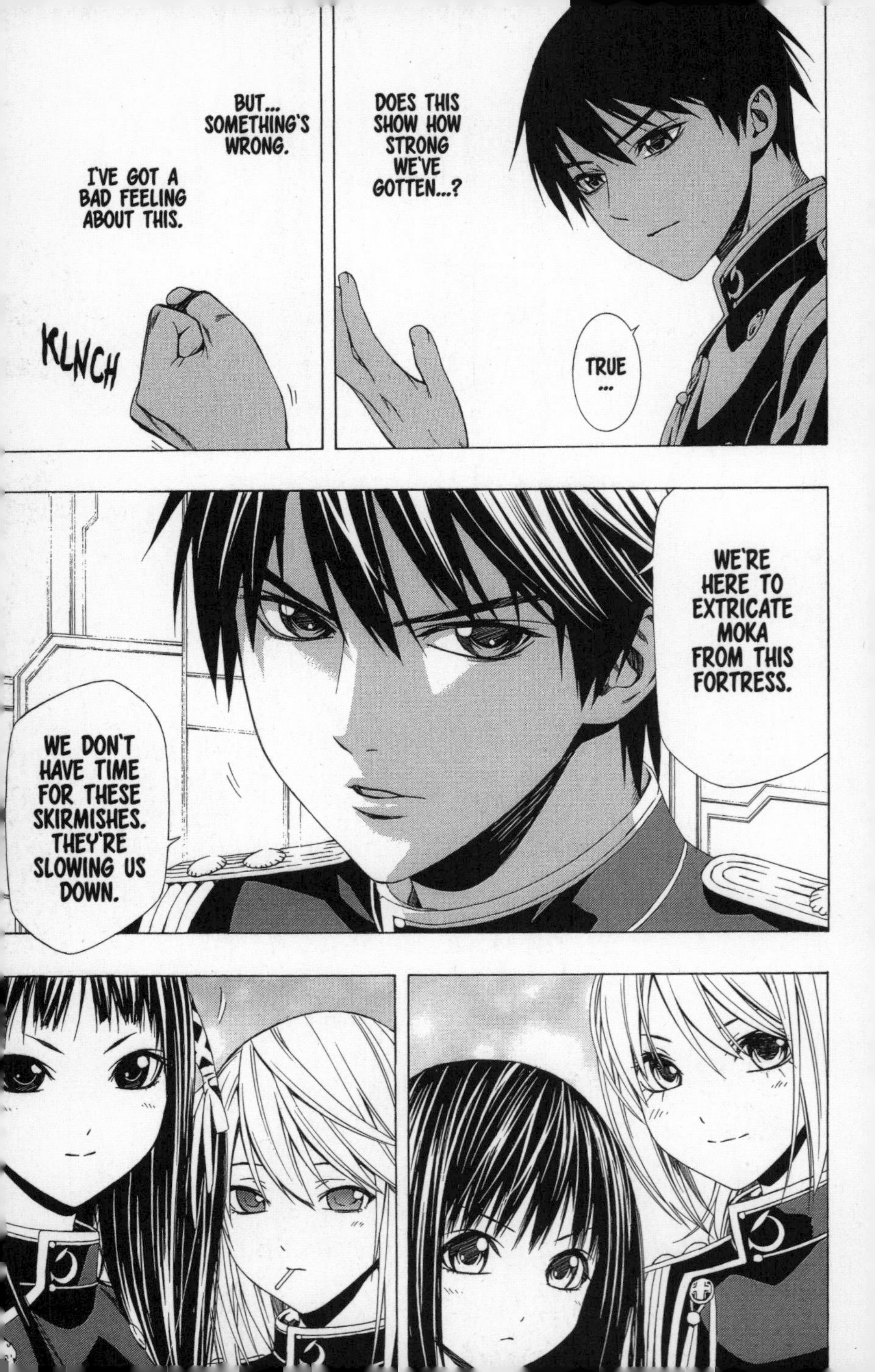
DOES THIS SHOW HOW STRONG WE'VE GOTTEN...?
TRUE ...
BUT... SOMETHING'S WRONG.
I'VE GOT A BAD FEELING ABOUT THIS.
KLNCH
WE'RE HERE TO EXTRICATE MOKA FROM THIS FORTRESS.
WE DON'T HAVE TIME FOR THESE SKIRMISHES. THEY'RE SLOWING US DOWN.

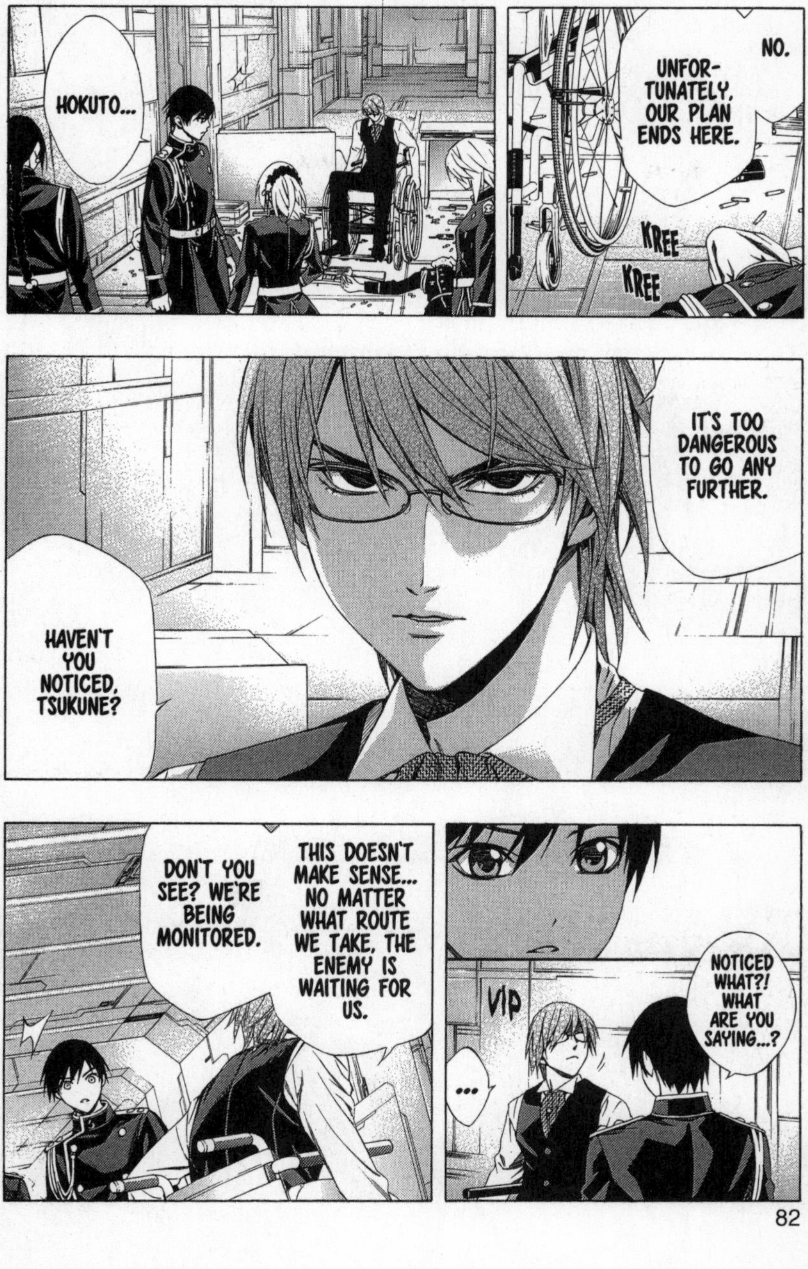
NO.
UNFOR-TUNATELY, OUR PLAN ENDS HERE.
KREE
KREE
HOKUTO...
IT'S TOO DANGEROUS TO GO ANY FURTHER.
HAVEN'T YOU NOTICED, TSUKUNE?
NOTICED WHAT?! WHAT ARE YOU SAYING...?
VIP
...
THIS DOESN'T MAKE SENSE... NO MATTER WHAT ROUTE WE TAKE, THE ENEMY IS WAITING FOR US.
DON'T YOU SEE? WE'RE BEING MONITORED.

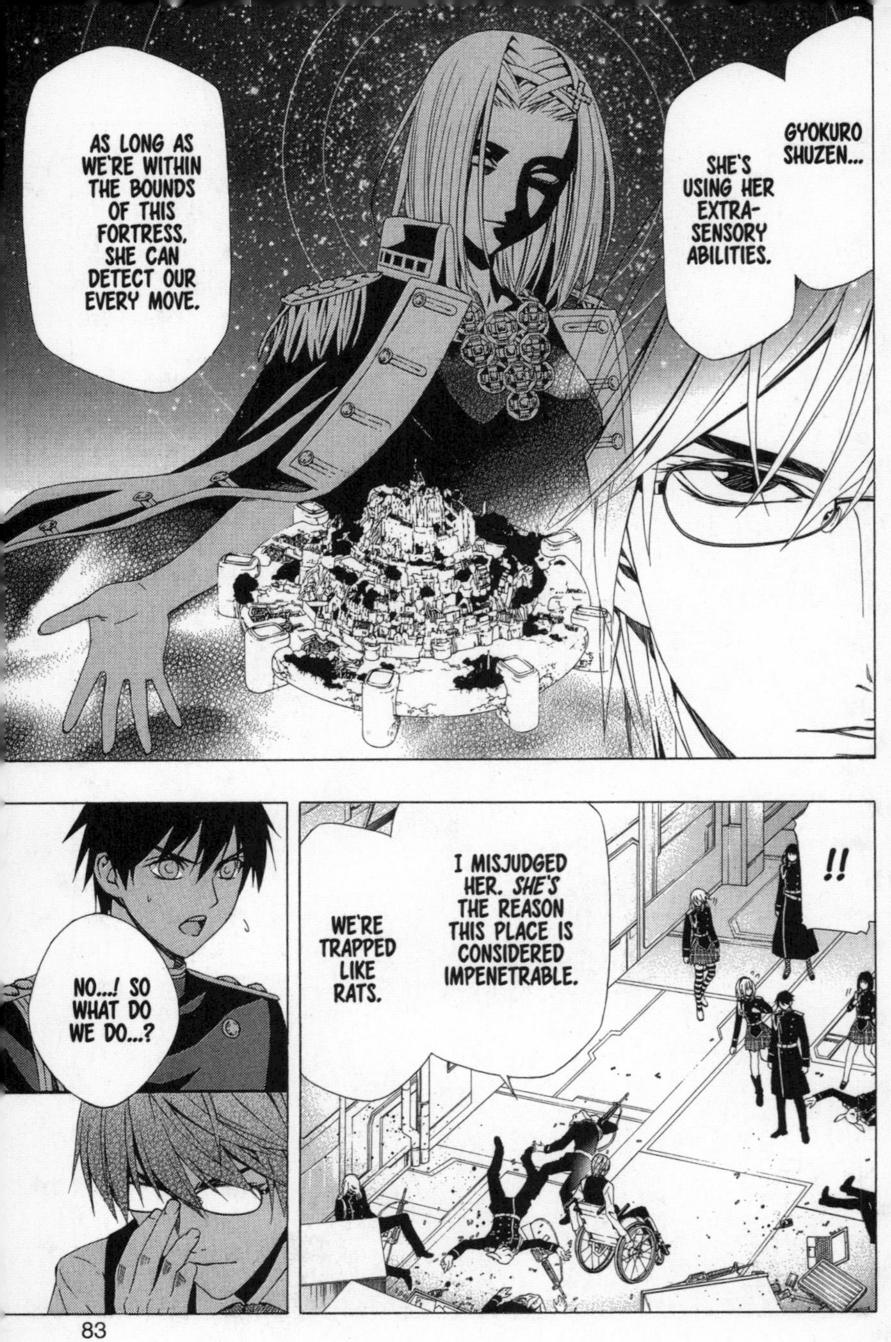
GYOKURO SHUZEN...
SHE'S USING HER EXTRA-SENSORY ABILITIES.
AS LONG AS WE'RE WITHIN THE BOUNDS OF THIS FORTRESS, SHE CAN DETECT OUR EVERY MOVE.
!!
I MISJUDGED HER. *SHE'S* THE REASON THIS PLACE IS CONSIDERED IMPENETRABLE.
WE'RE TRAPPED LIKE RATS.
NO...! SO WHAT DO WE DO...?

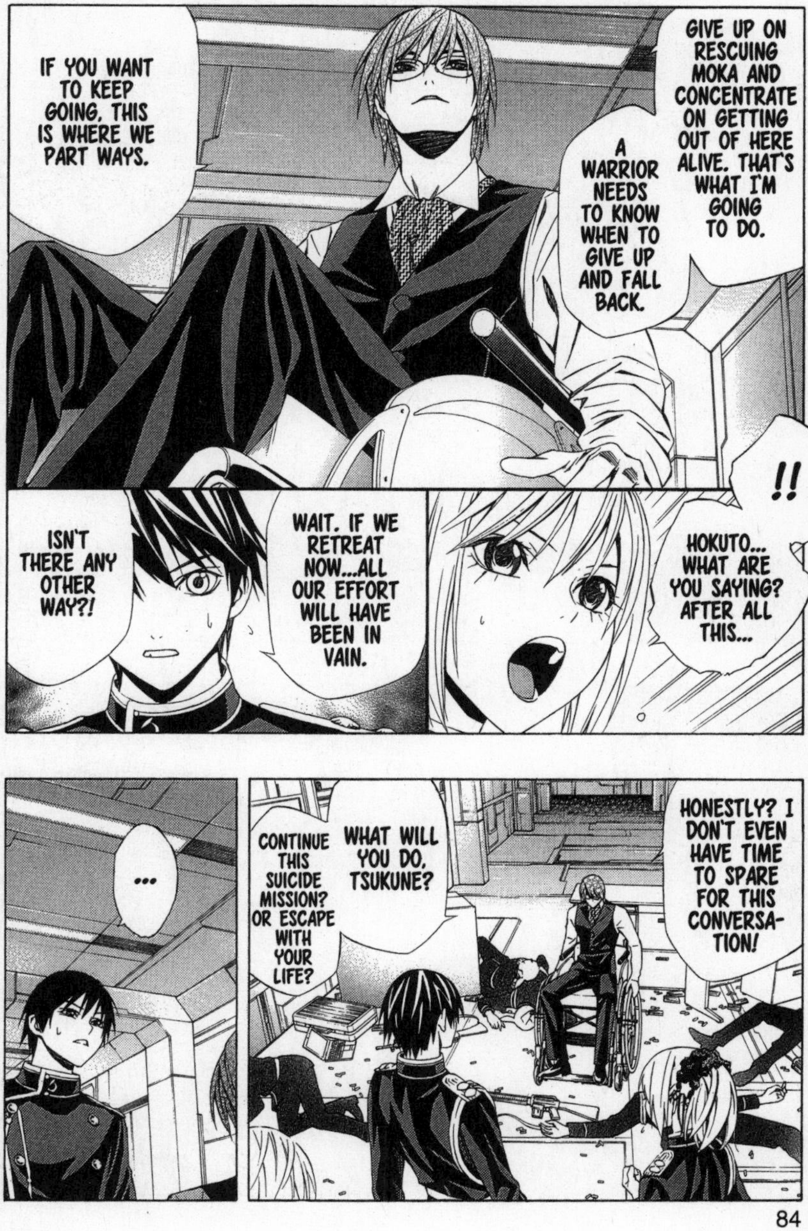
GIVE UP ON RESCUING MOKA AND CONCENTRATE ON GETTING OUT OF HERE ALIVE. THAT'S WHAT I'M GOING TO DO.
A WARRIOR NEEDS TO KNOW WHEN TO GIVE UP AND FALL BACK.
IF YOU WANT TO KEEP GOING, THIS IS WHERE WE PART WAYS.
!!
HOKUTO... WHAT ARE YOU SAYING? AFTER ALL THIS...
WAIT. IF WE RETREAT NOW...ALL OUR EFFORT WILL HAVE BEEN IN VAIN.
ISN'T THERE ANY OTHER WAY?!
HONESTLY? I DON'T EVEN HAVE TIME TO SPARE FOR THIS CONVERSATION!
WHAT WILL YOU DO, TSUKUNE?
CONTINUE THIS SUICIDE MISSION? OR ESCAPE WITH YOUR LIFE?
...

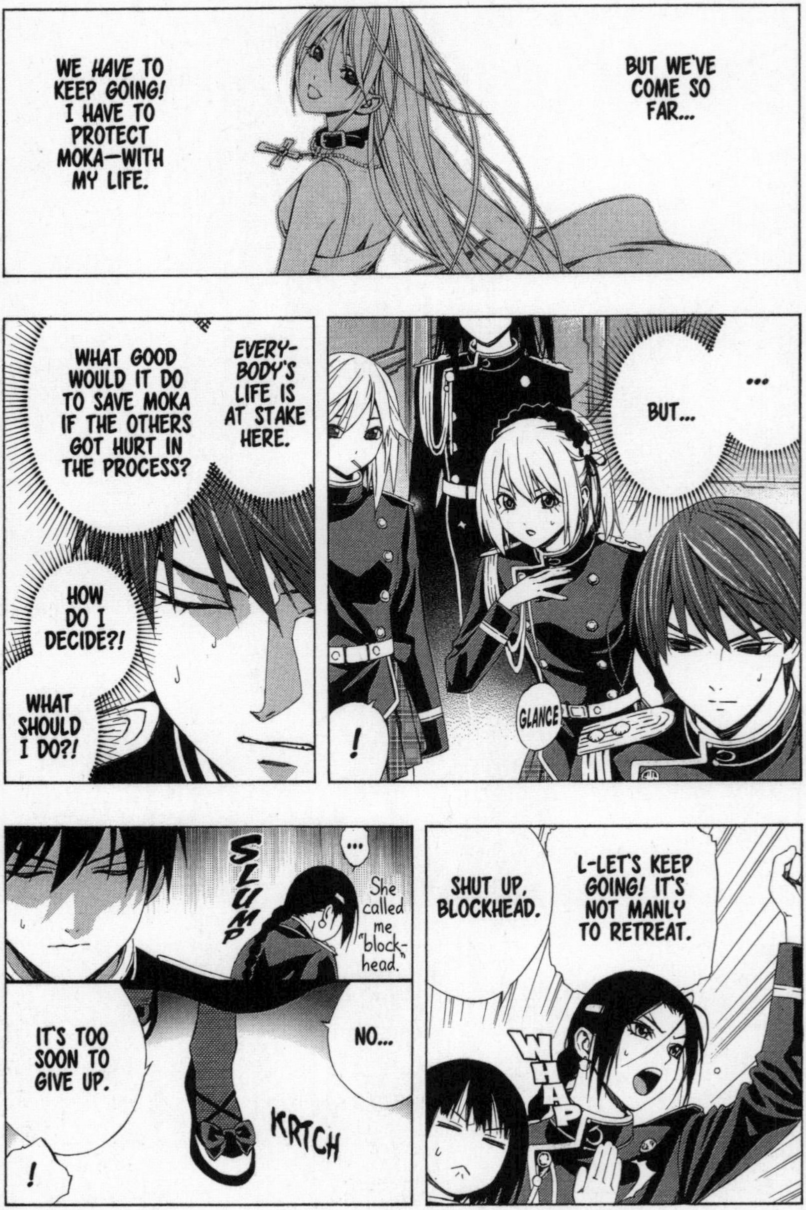
BUT WE'VE COME SO FAR...
WE *HAVE* TO KEEP GOING! I HAVE TO PROTECT MOKA—WITH MY LIFE.
...
BUT...
GLANCE
!
EVERYBODY'S LIFE IS AT STAKE HERE.
WHAT GOOD WOULD IT DO TO SAVE MOKA IF THE OTHERS GOT HURT IN THE PROCESS?
HOW DO I DECIDE?!
WHAT SHOULD I DO?!
L-LET'S KEEP GOING! IT'S NOT MANLY TO RETREAT.
SHUT UP, BLOCKHEAD.
WHAP
...
SLUMP
She called me "blockhead."
NO...
KRTCH
IT'S TOO SOON TO GIVE UP.
!

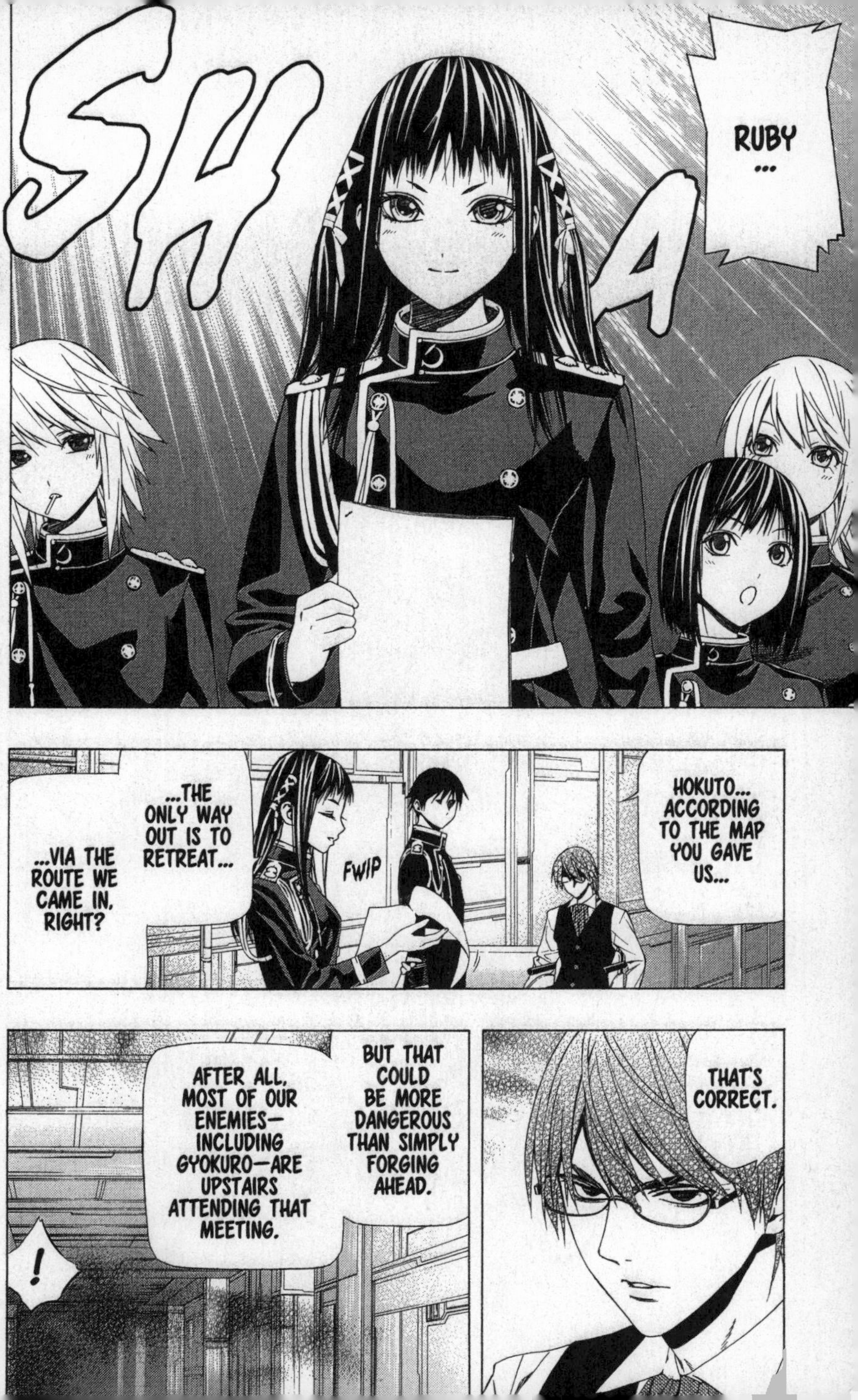
RUBY...
SHA
HOKUTO... ACCORDING TO THE MAP YOU GAVE US...
FWIP
...THE ONLY WAY OUT IS TO RETREAT...
...VIA THE ROUTE WE CAME IN, RIGHT?
THAT'S CORRECT.
BUT THAT COULD BE MORE DANGEROUS THAN SIMPLY FORGING AHEAD.
AFTER ALL, MOST OF OUR ENEMIES—INCLUDING GYOKURO—ARE UPSTAIRS ATTENDING THAT MEETING.
!

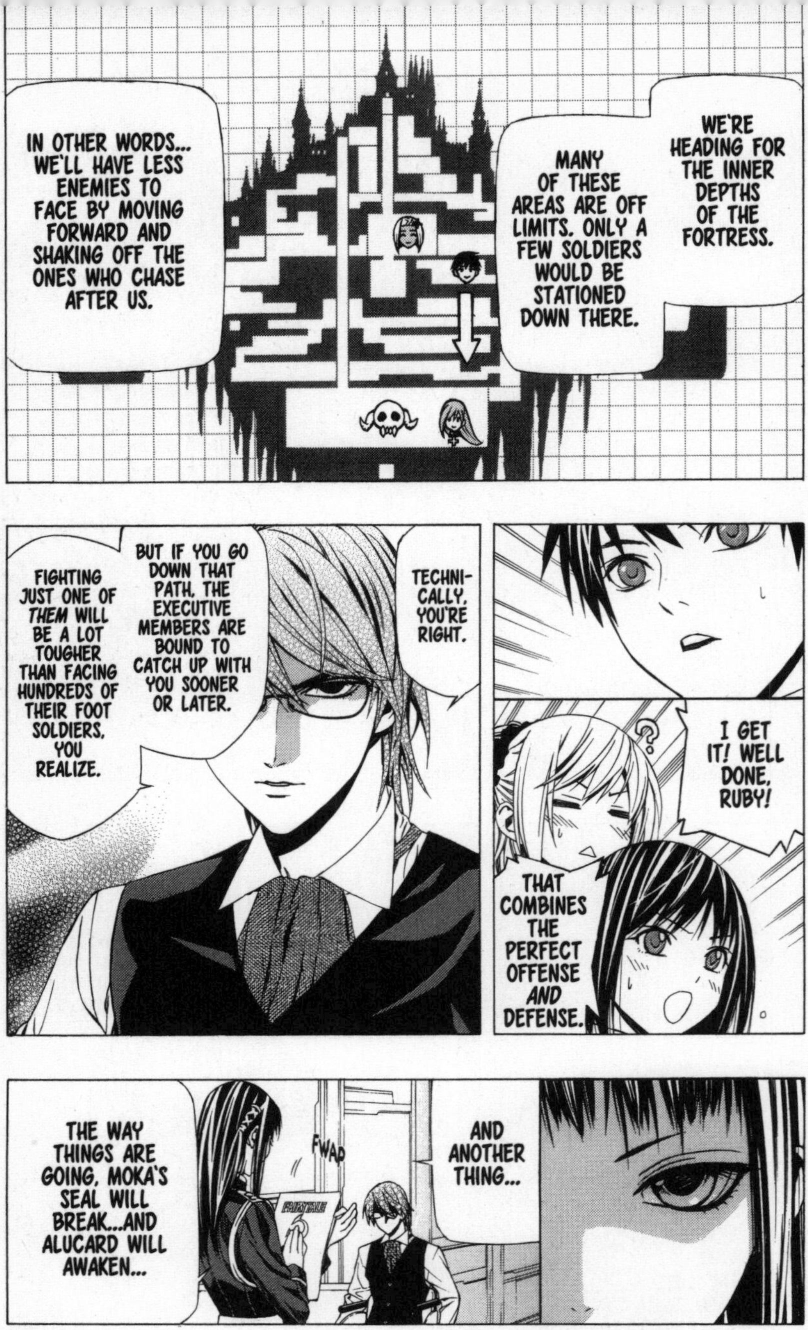
WE'RE HEADING FOR THE INNER DEPTHS OF THE FORTRESS.
MANY OF THESE AREAS ARE OFF LIMITS. ONLY A FEW SOLDIERS WOULD BE STATIONED DOWN THERE.
IN OTHER WORDS... WE'LL HAVE LESS ENEMIES TO FACE BY MOVING FORWARD AND SHAKING OFF THE ONES WHO CHASE AFTER US.
I GET IT! WELL DONE, RUBY!
THAT COMBINES THE PERFECT OFFENSE *AND* DEFENSE.
TECHNICALLY, YOU'RE RIGHT.
BUT IF YOU GO DOWN THAT PATH, THE EXECUTIVE MEMBERS ARE BOUND TO CATCH UP WITH YOU SOONER OR LATER.
FIGHTING JUST ONE OF *THEM* WILL BE A LOT TOUGHER THAN FACING HUNDREDS OF THEIR FOOT SOLDIERS, YOU REALIZE.
AND ANOTHER THING...
FWAP
THE WAY THINGS ARE GOING, MOKA'S SEAL WILL BREAK...AND ALUCARD WILL AWAKEN...

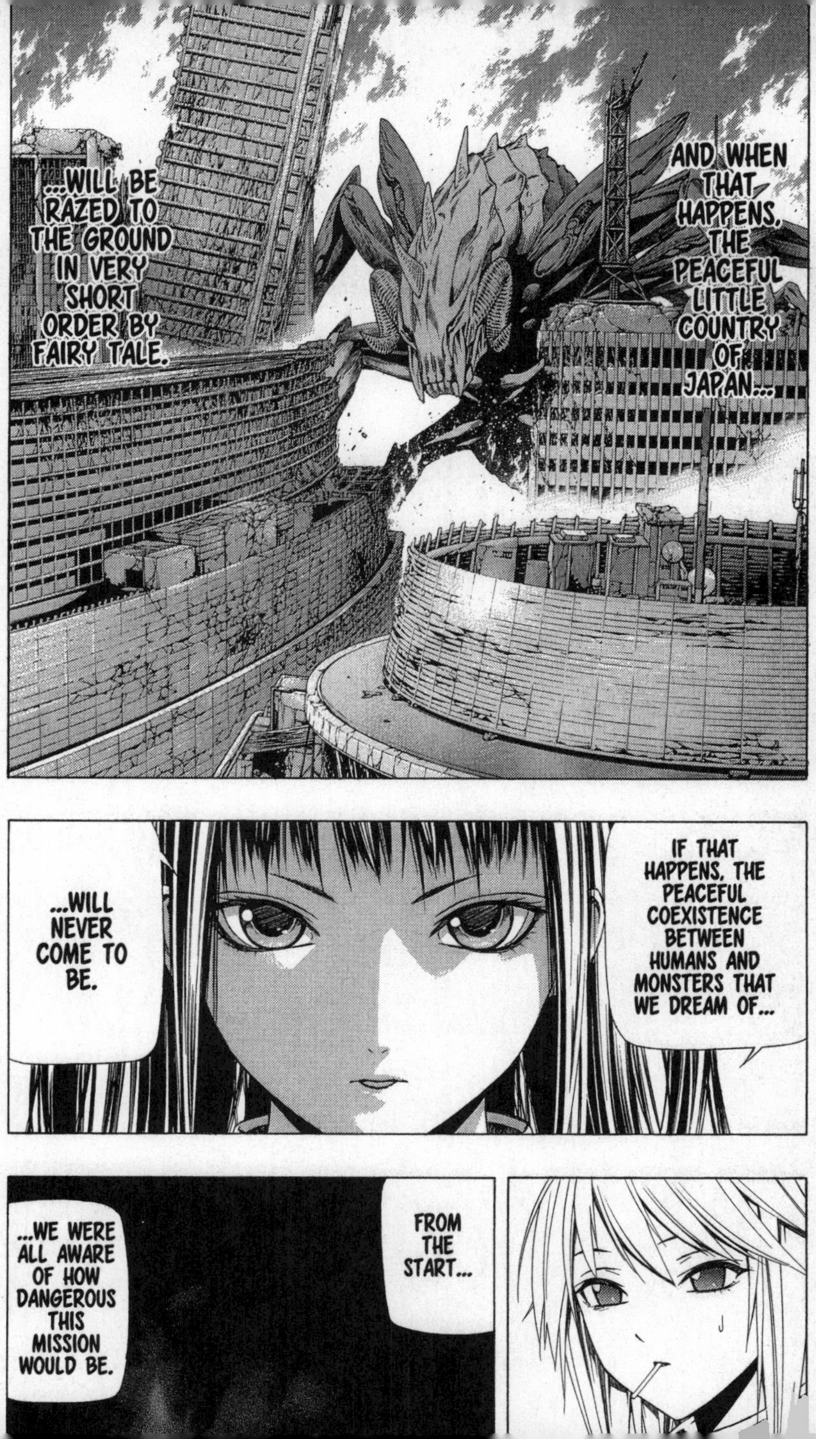
AND WHEN THAT HAPPENS, THE PEACEFUL LITTLE COUNTRY OF JAPAN...
...WILL BE RAZED TO THE GROUND IN VERY SHORT ORDER BY FAIRY TALE.
IF THAT HAPPENS, THE PEACEFUL COEXISTENCE BETWEEN HUMANS AND MONSTERS THAT WE DREAM OF...
...WILL NEVER COME TO BE.
FROM THE START...
...WE WERE ALL AWARE OF HOW DANGEROUS THIS MISSION WOULD BE.

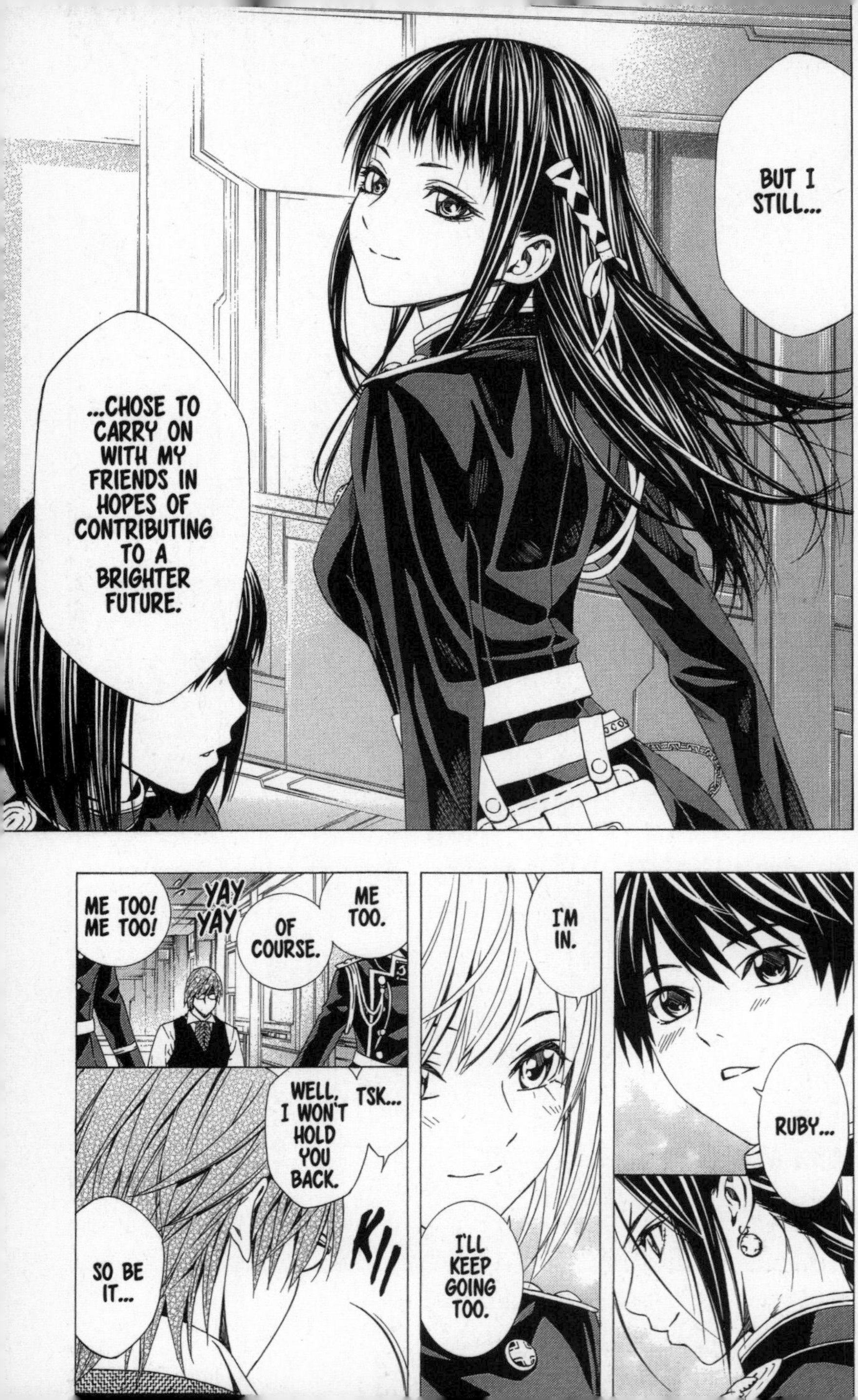
BUT I STILL...
...CHOSE TO CARRY ON WITH MY FRIENDS IN HOPES OF CONTRIBUTING TO A BRIGHTER FUTURE.
RUBY...
I'M IN.
I'LL KEEP GOING TOO.
ME TOO.
OF COURSE.
YAY YAY
ME TOO! ME TOO!
TSK...
WELL, I WON'T HOLD YOU BACK.
KII
SO BE IT...

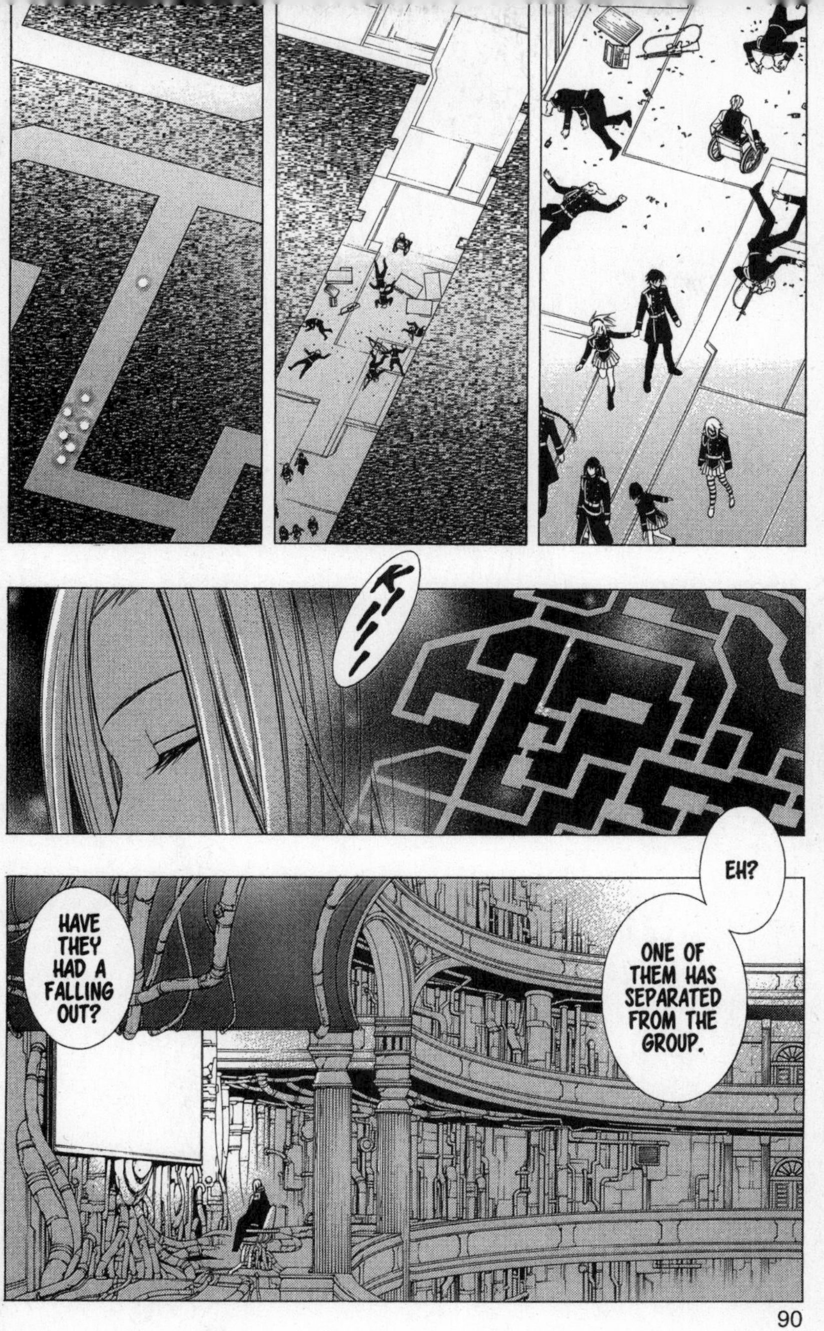
KI-I-I-
EH?
ONE OF THEM HAS SEPARATED FROM THE GROUP.
HAVE THEY HAD A FALLING OUT?

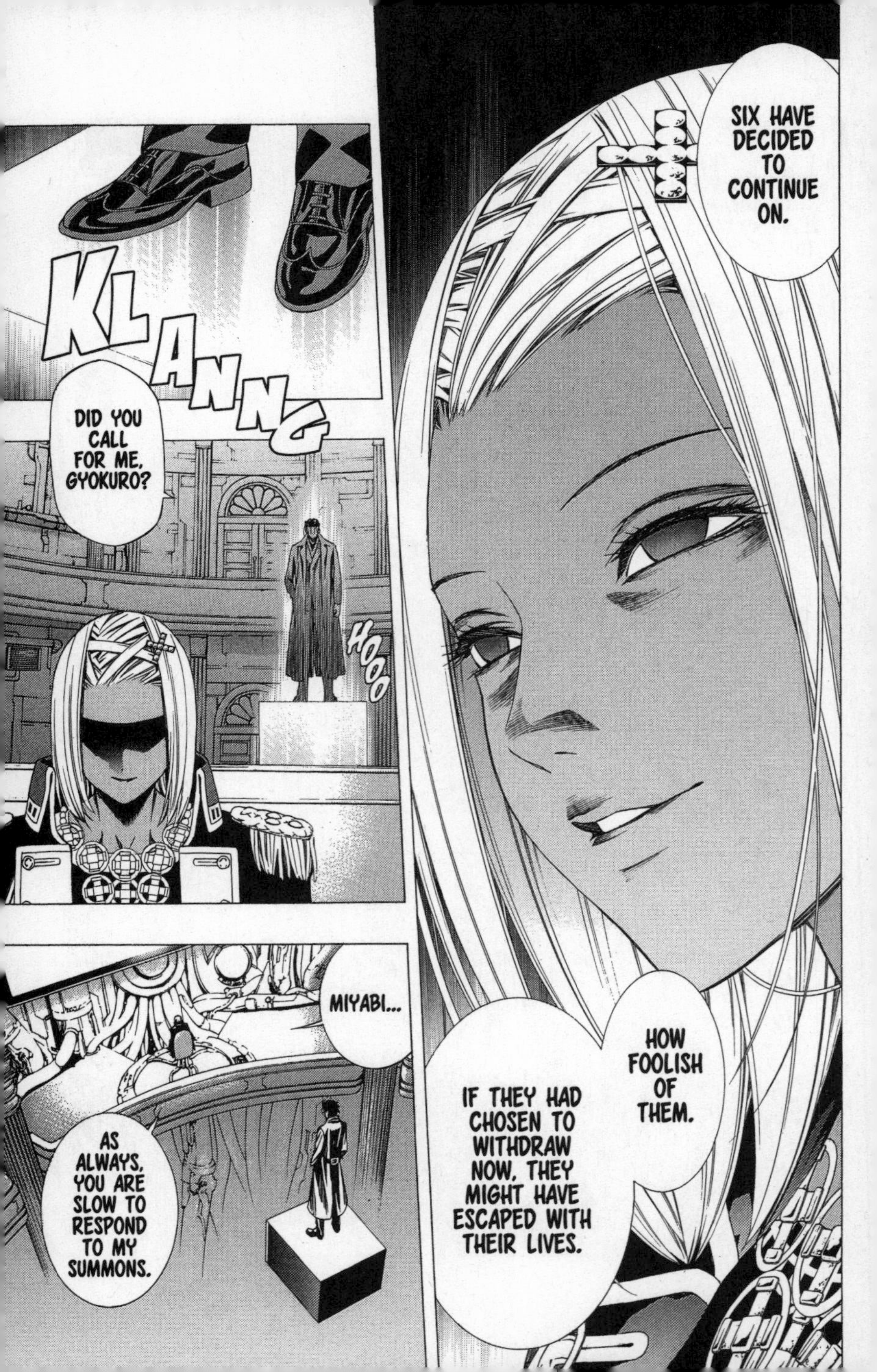
SIX HAVE DECIDED TO CONTINUE ON.
HOW FOOLISH OF THEM.
IF THEY HAD CHOSEN TO WITHDRAW NOW, THEY MIGHT HAVE ESCAPED WITH THEIR LIVES.
KLANNG
DID YOU CALL FOR ME, GYOKURO?
HOOO
MIYABI...
AS ALWAYS, YOU ARE SLOW TO RESPOND TO MY SUMMONS.

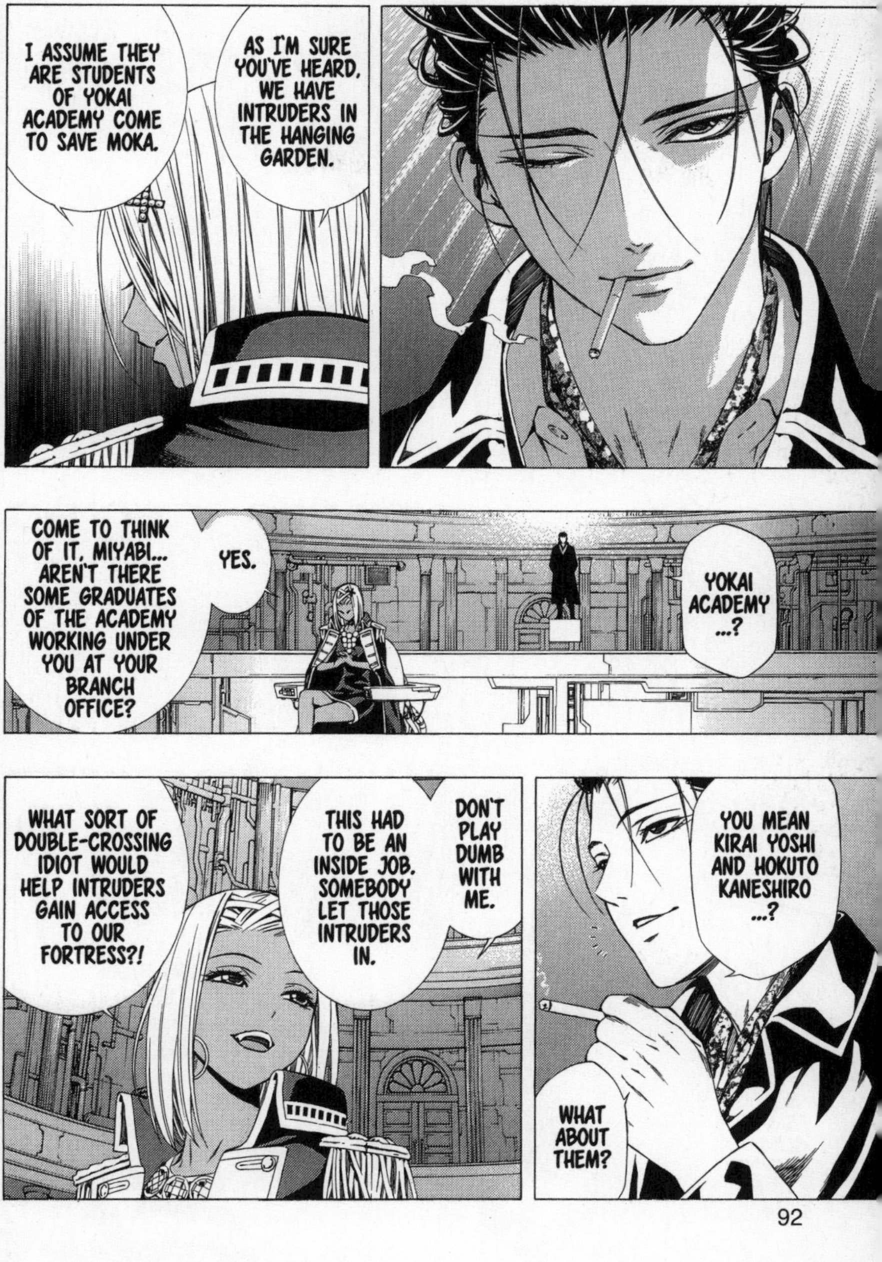
AS I'M SURE YOU'VE HEARD, WE HAVE INTRUDERS IN THE HANGING GARDEN.
I ASSUME THEY ARE STUDENTS OF YOKAI ACADEMY COME TO SAVE MOKA.
YOKAI ACADEMY ...?
YES.
COME TO THINK OF IT, MIYABI... AREN'T THERE SOME GRADUATES OF THE ACADEMY WORKING UNDER YOU AT YOUR BRANCH OFFICE?
YOU MEAN KIRAI YOSHI AND HOKUTO KANESHIRO ...?
WHAT ABOUT THEM?
DON'T PLAY DUMB WITH ME.
THIS HAD TO BE AN INSIDE JOB. SOMEBODY LET THOSE INTRUDERS IN.
WHAT SORT OF DOUBLE-CROSSING IDIOT WOULD HELP INTRUDERS GAIN ACCESS TO OUR FORTRESS?!

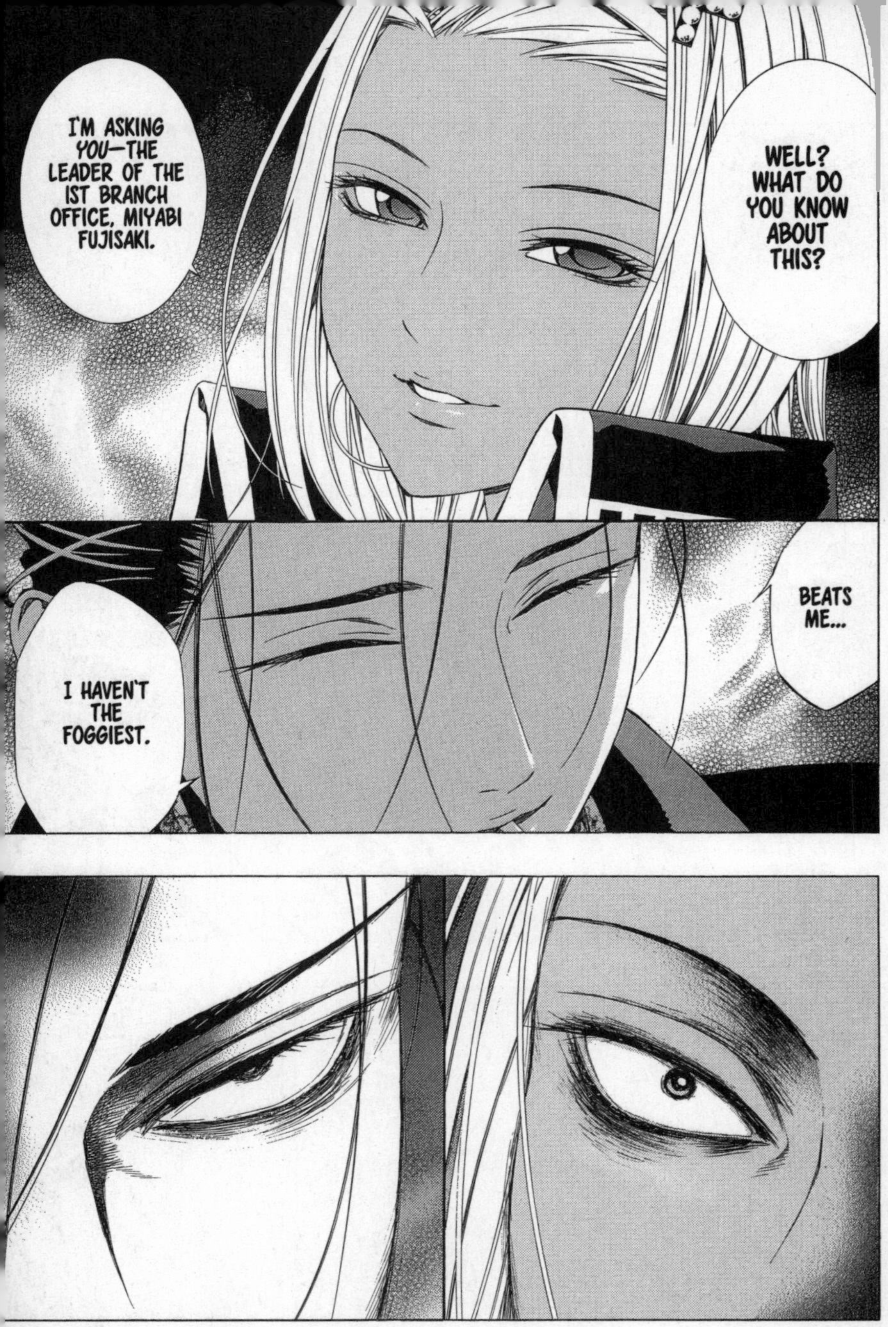
WELL? WHAT DO YOU KNOW ABOUT THIS?
I'M ASKING *YOU*—THE LEADER OF THE 1ST BRANCH OFFICE, MIYABI FUJISAKI.
BEATS ME...
I HAVEN'T THE FOGGIEST.

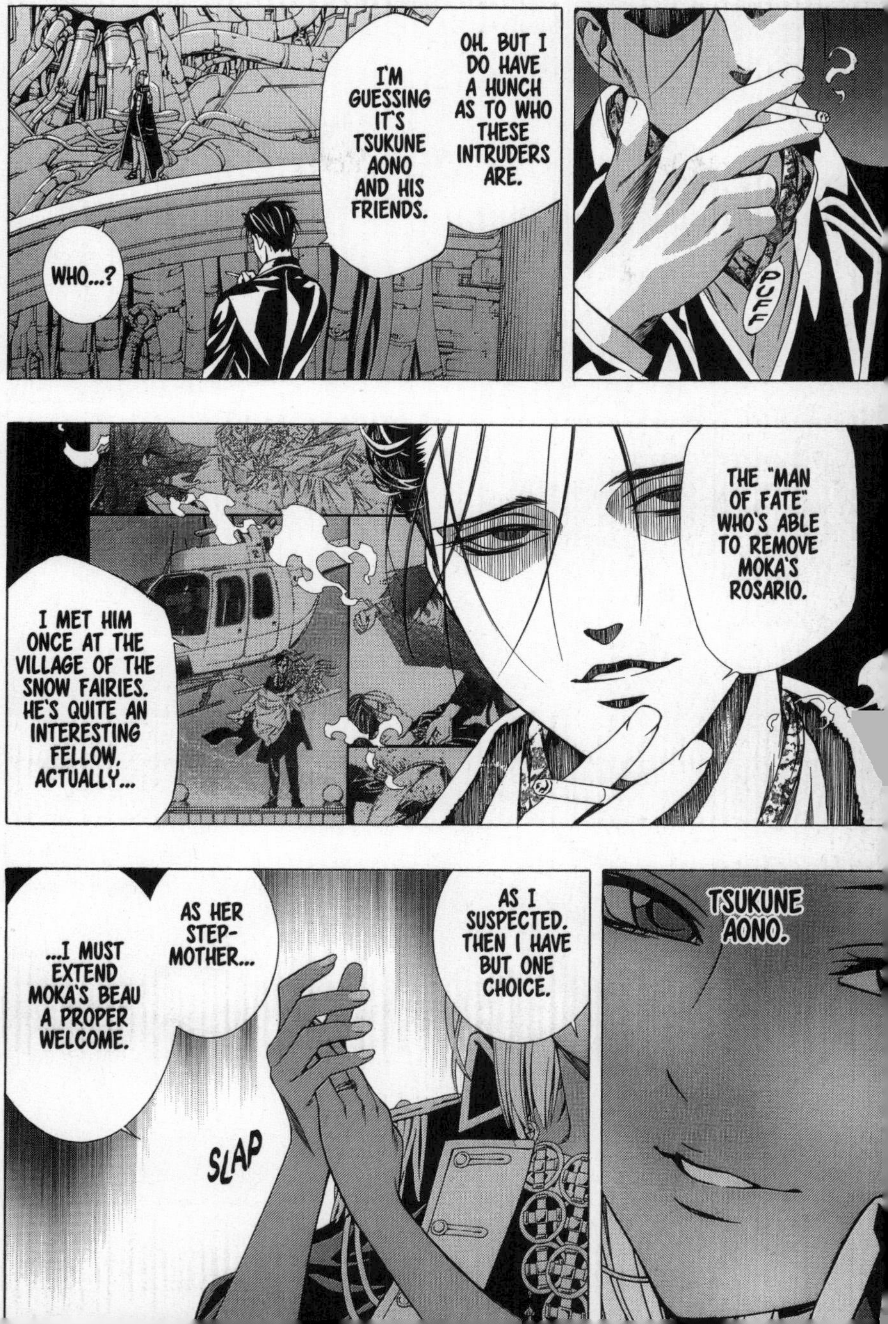
PUFF
OH. BUT I DO HAVE A HUNCH AS TO WHO THESE INTRUDERS ARE.
I'M GUESSING IT'S TSUKUNE AONO AND HIS FRIENDS.
WHO...?
THE "MAN OF FATE" WHO'S ABLE TO REMOVE MOKA'S ROSARIO.
I MET HIM ONCE AT THE VILLAGE OF THE SNOW FAIRIES. HE'S QUITE AN INTERESTING FELLOW, ACTUALLY...
TSUKUNE AONO.
AS I SUSPECTED. THEN I HAVE BUT ONE CHOICE.
AS HER STEP-MOTHER...
...I MUST EXTEND MOKA'S BEAU A PROPER WELCOME.
SLAP

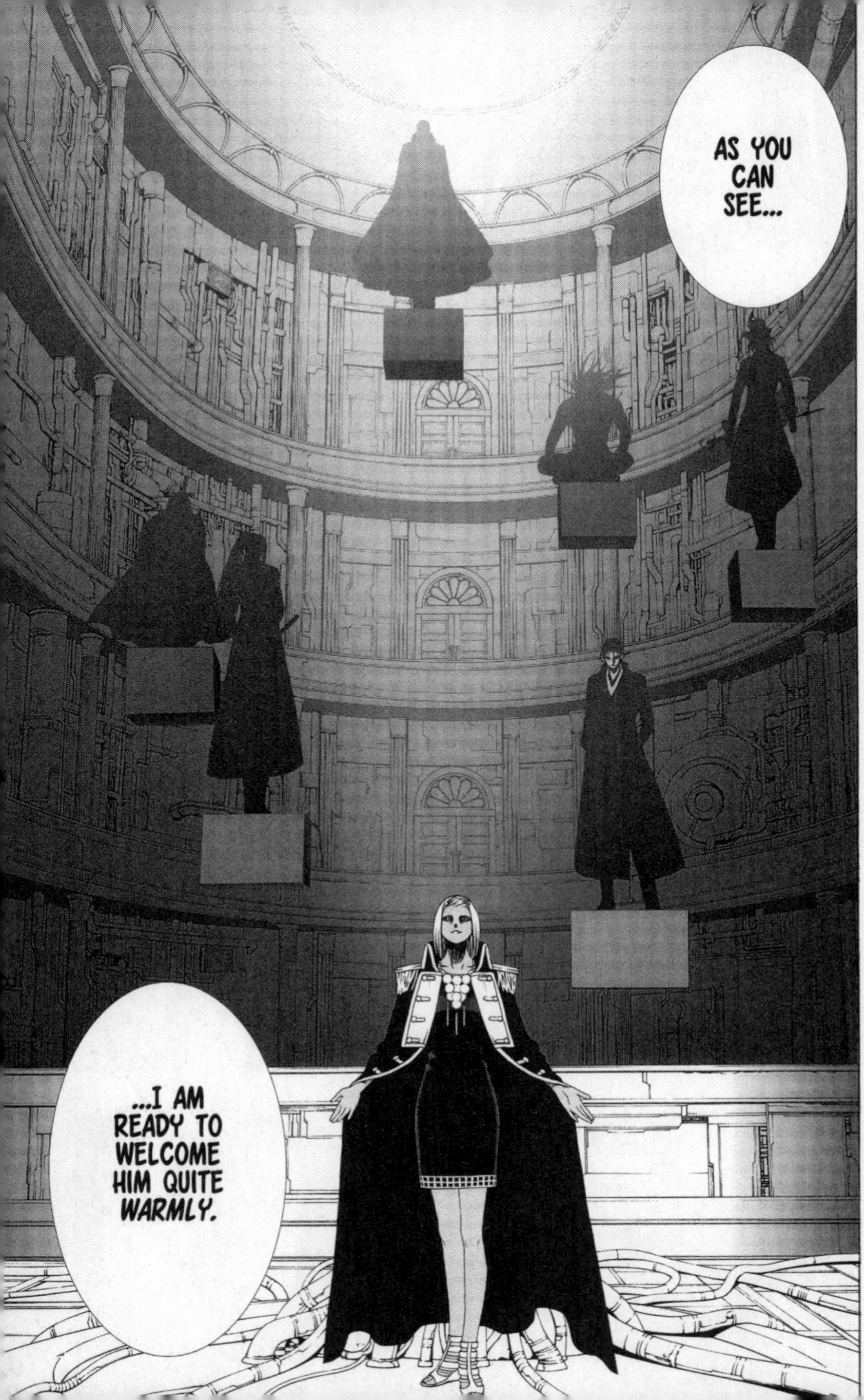
AS YOU CAN SEE...
...I AM READY TO WELCOME HIM QUITE *WARMLY.*

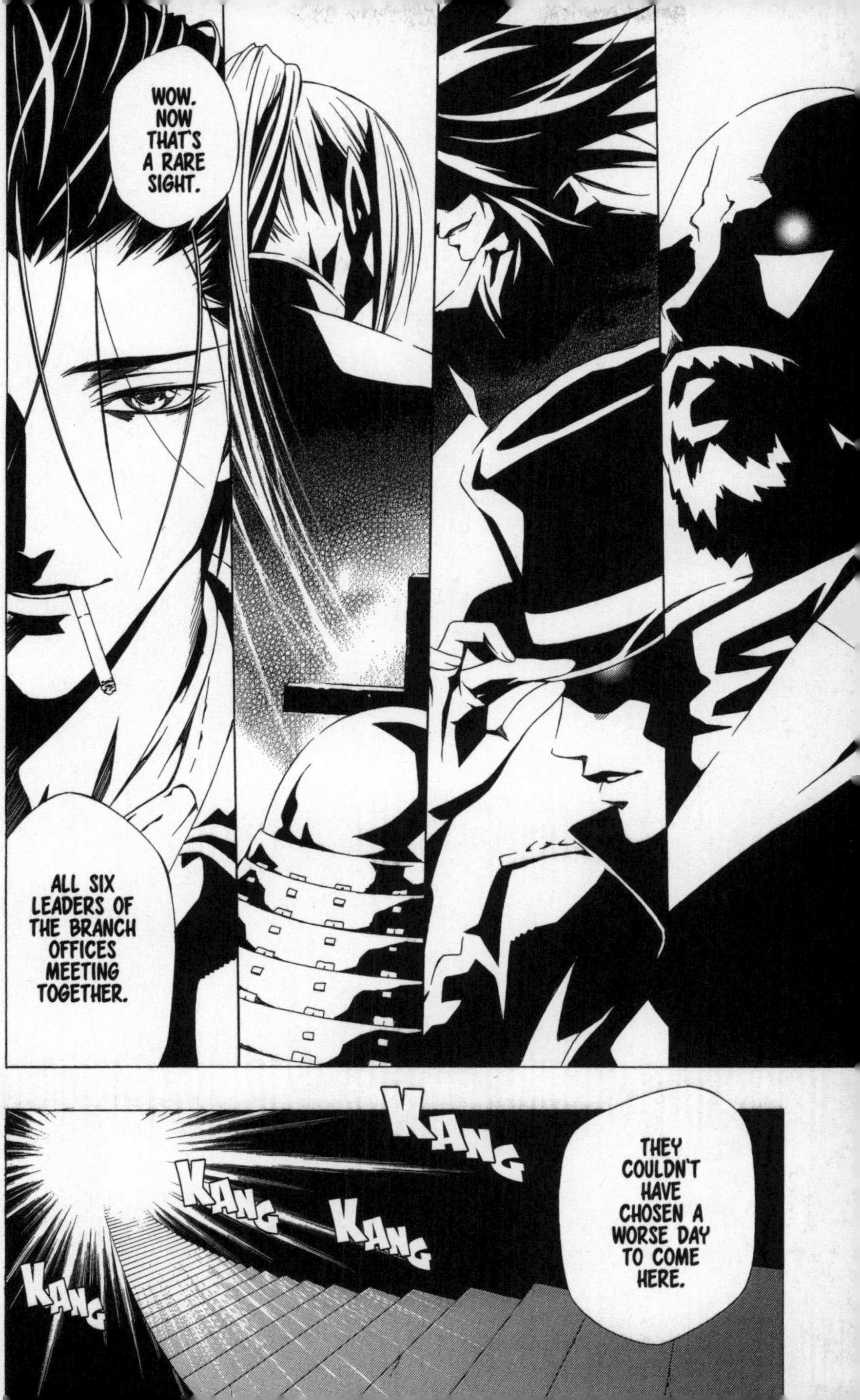
WOW. NOW THAT'S A RARE SIGHT.
ALL SIX LEADERS OF THE BRANCH OFFICES MEETING TOGETHER.
THEY COULDN'T HAVE CHOSEN A WORSE DAY TO COME HERE.
KANG
KANG
KANG
KANG

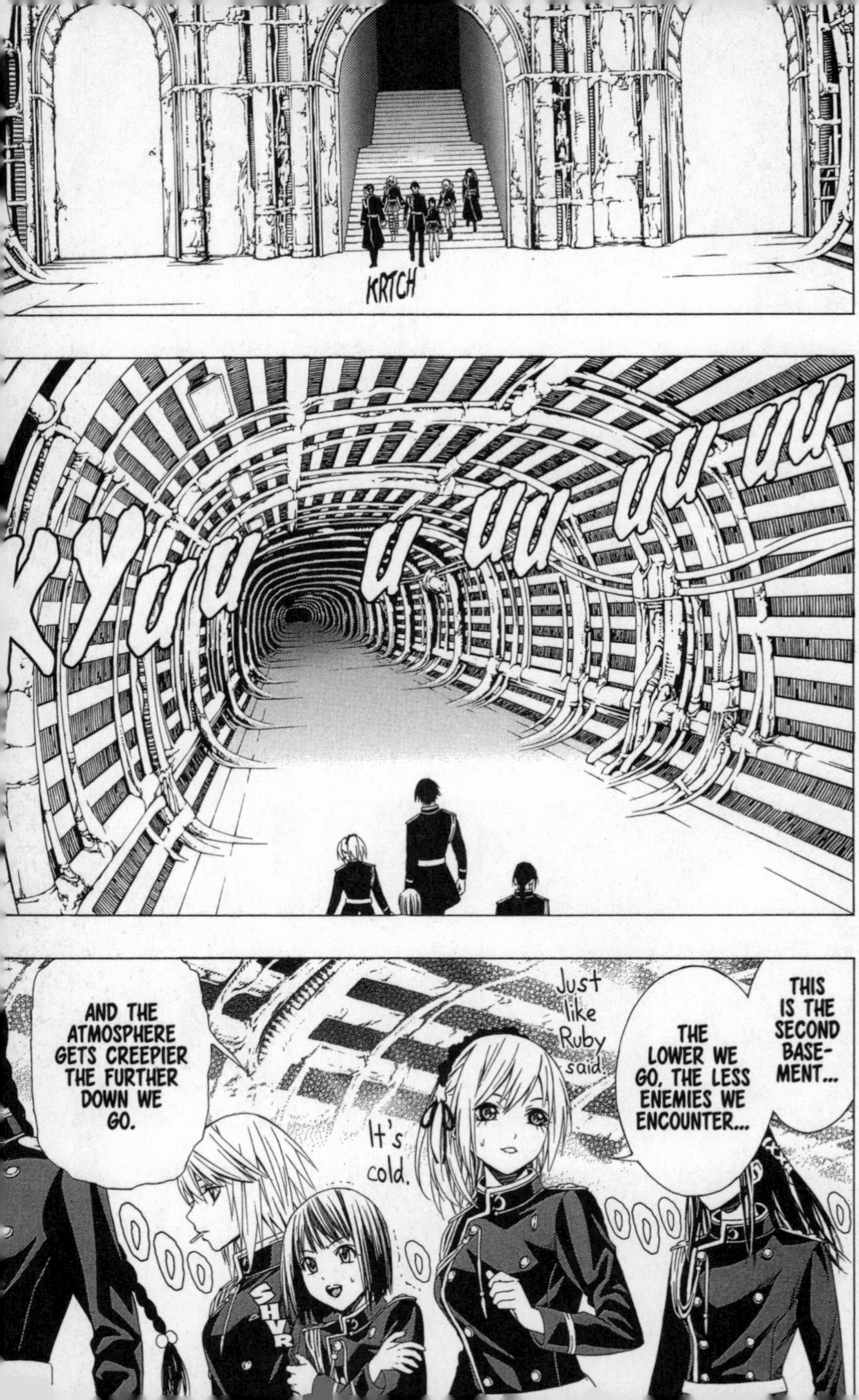
KRTCH
KYUU U UU UU UU
THIS IS THE SECOND BASE-MENT...
THE LOWER WE GO, THE LESS ENEMIES WE ENCOUNTER...
Just like Ruby said.
It's cold.
AND THE ATMOSPHERE GETS CREEPIER THE FURTHER DOWN WE GO.
SHVR

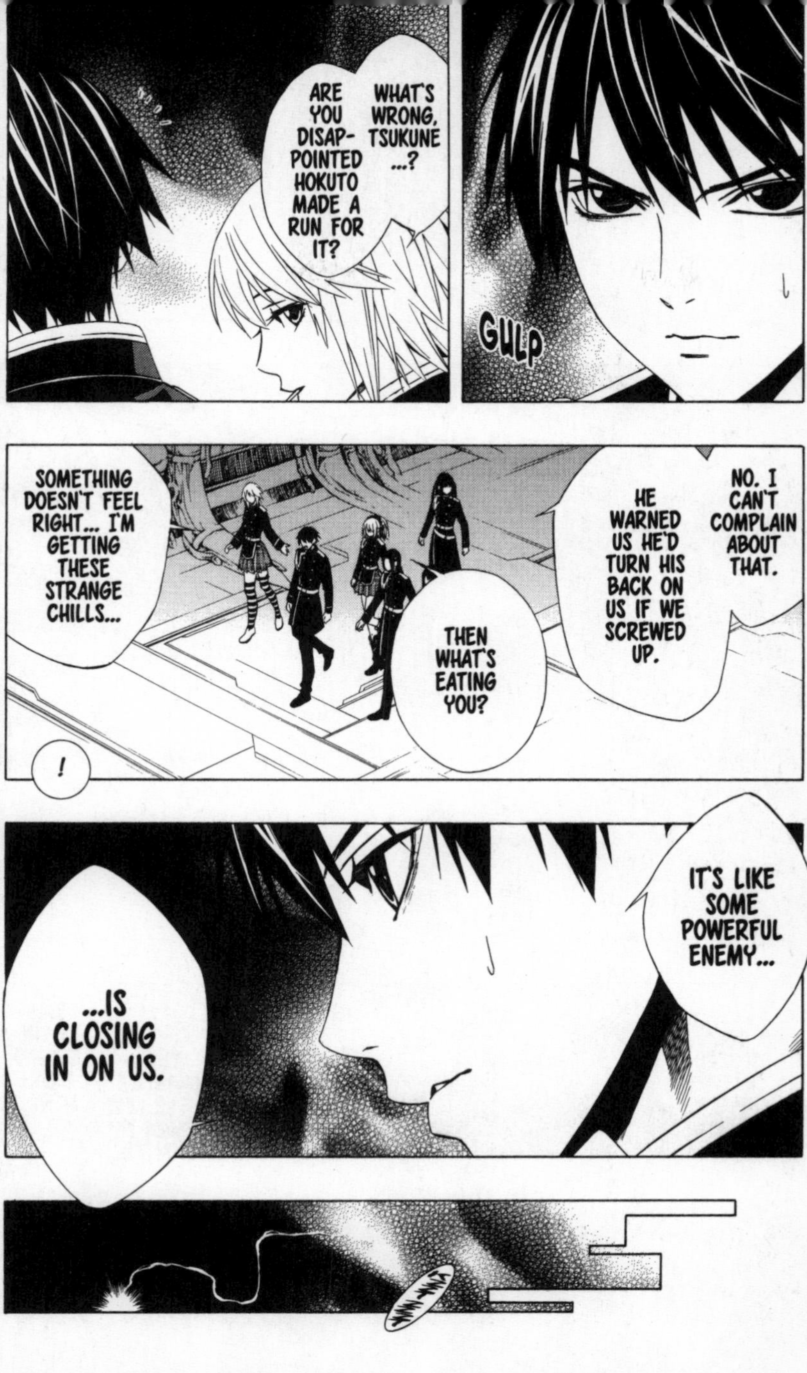
GULP
WHAT'S WRONG, TSUKUNE ...?
ARE YOU DISAPPOINTED HOKUTO MADE A RUN FOR IT?
NO. I CAN'T COMPLAIN ABOUT THAT.
HE WARNED US HE'D TURN HIS BACK ON US IF WE SCREWED UP.
THEN WHAT'S EATING YOU?
SOMETHING DOESN'T FEEL RIGHT... I'M GETTING THESE STRANGE CHILLS...
!
IT'S LIKE SOME POWERFUL ENEMY...
...IS CLOSING IN ON US.

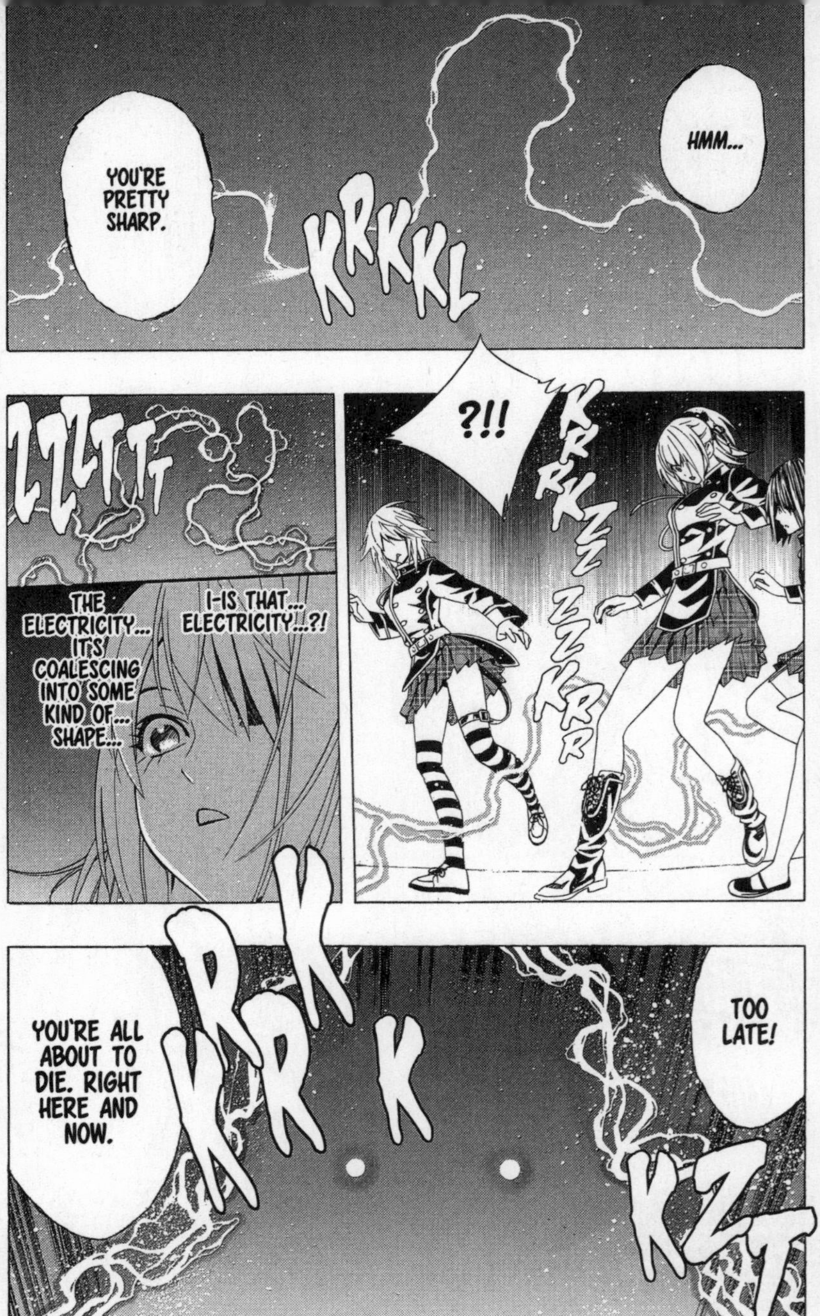
HMM...
KRKKL
YOU'RE PRETTY SHARP.
?!!
KRRKZZZZZKRRR
ZZZTTTT
I-IS THAT... ELECTRICITY...?!
THE ELECTRICITY... IT'S COALESCING INTO SOME KIND OF... SHAPE...
TOO LATE!
KZT
RK KRK
YOU'RE ALL ABOUT TO DIE. RIGHT HERE AND NOW.

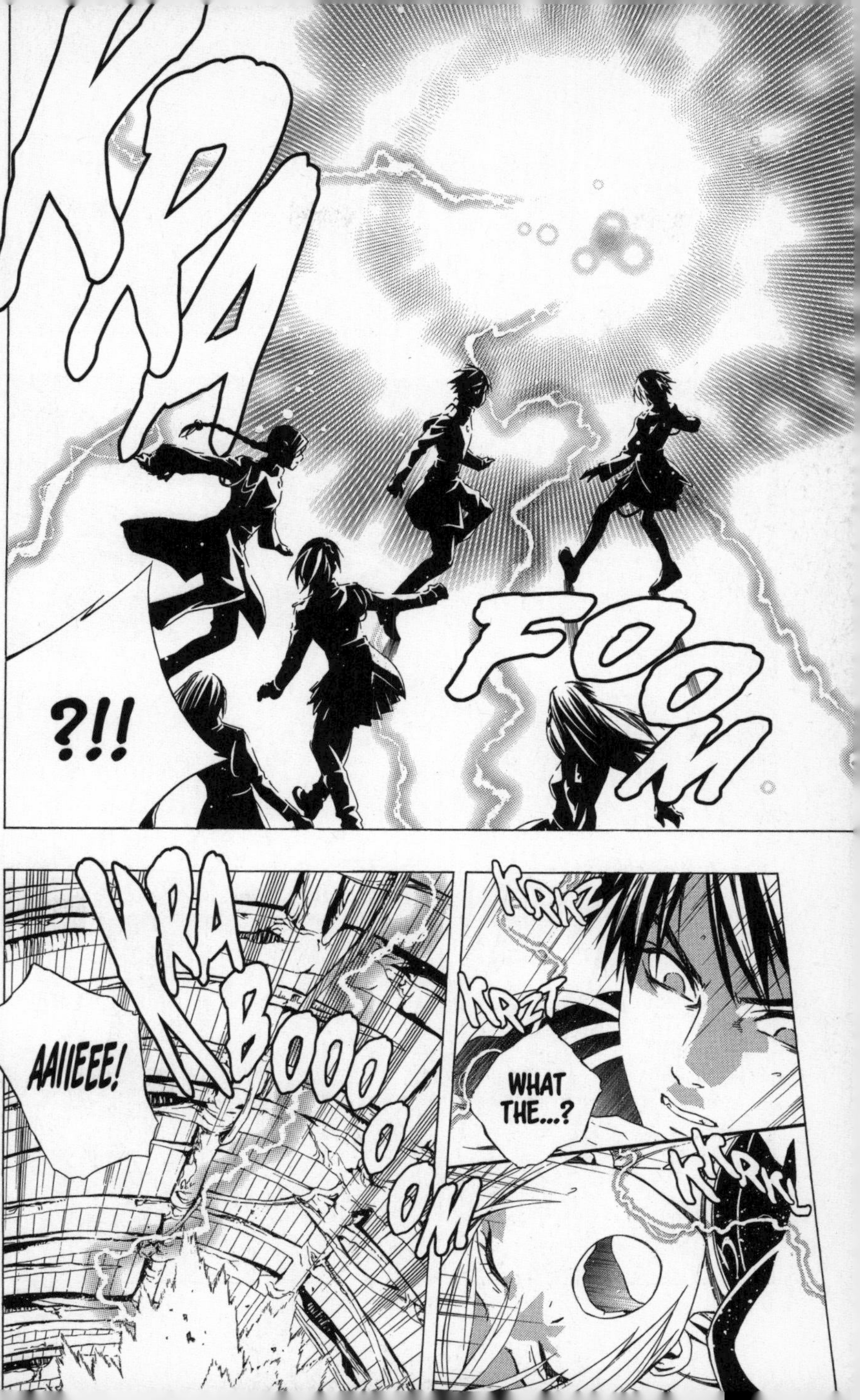
KRA
FOOM
?!!
KRKZ
KRZT
WHAT THE...?
KKRKL
VRABOOOOOM
AAIIEEE!

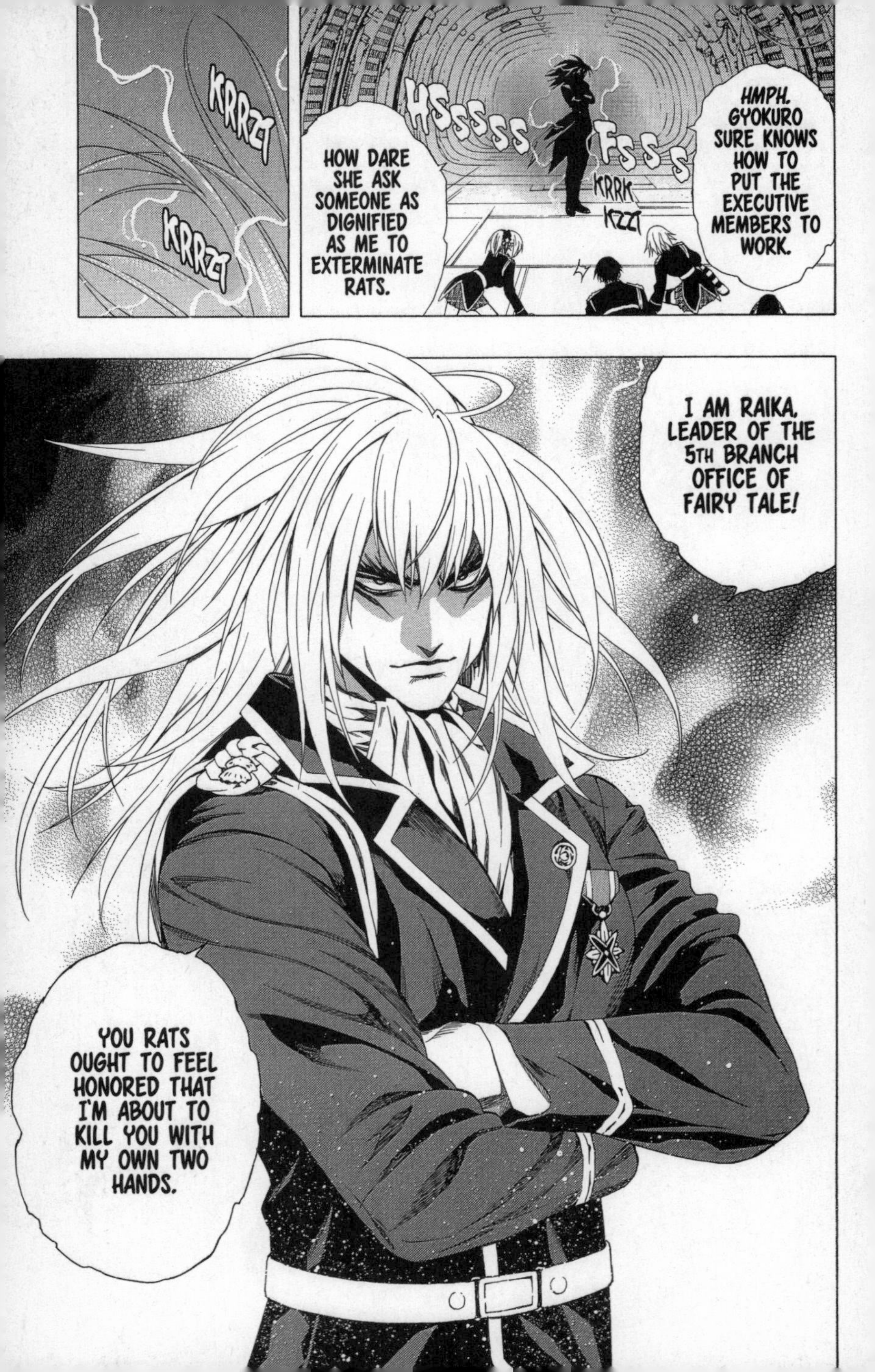
HMPH. GYOKURO SURE KNOWS HOW TO PUT THE EXECUTIVE MEMBERS TO WORK.
HSSSSS
FSSS
KRRK
KZZT
HOW DARE SHE ASK SOMEONE AS DIGNIFIED AS ME TO EXTERMINATE RATS.
KRRZT
KRRZT
I AM RAIKA, LEADER OF THE 5TH BRANCH OFFICE OF FAIRY TALE!
YOU RATS OUGHT TO FEEL HONORED THAT I'M ABOUT TO KILL YOU WITH MY OWN TWO HANDS.

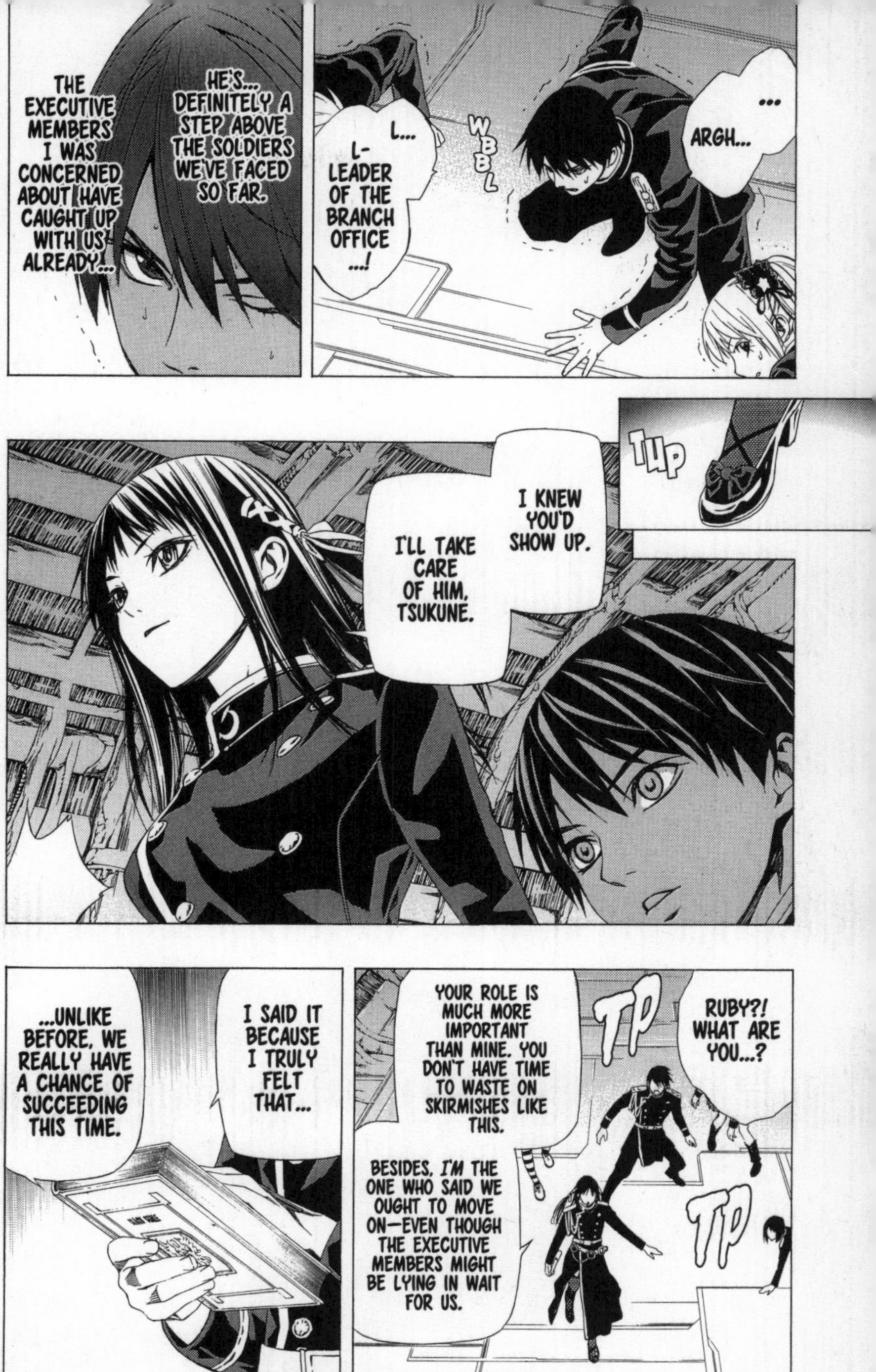
...
ARGH...
WBBL
L... L-LEADER OF THE BRANCH OFFICE ...!
HE'S... DEFINITELY A STEP ABOVE THE SOLDIERS WE'VE FACED SO FAR.
THE EXECUTIVE MEMBERS I WAS CONCERNED ABOUT HAVE CAUGHT UP WITH US ALREADY...!
TUP
I KNEW YOU'D SHOW UP.
I'LL TAKE CARE OF HIM, TSUKUNE.
RUBY?! WHAT ARE YOU...?
TP
YOUR ROLE IS MUCH MORE IMPORTANT THAN MINE. YOU DON'T HAVE TIME TO WASTE ON SKIRMISHES LIKE THIS.
TP
BESIDES, *I'M* THE ONE WHO SAID WE OUGHT TO MOVE ON—EVEN THOUGH THE EXECUTIVE MEMBERS MIGHT BE LYING IN WAIT FOR US.
I SAID IT BECAUSE I TRULY FELT THAT...
...UNLIKE BEFORE, WE REALLY HAVE A CHANCE OF SUCCEEDING THIS TIME.

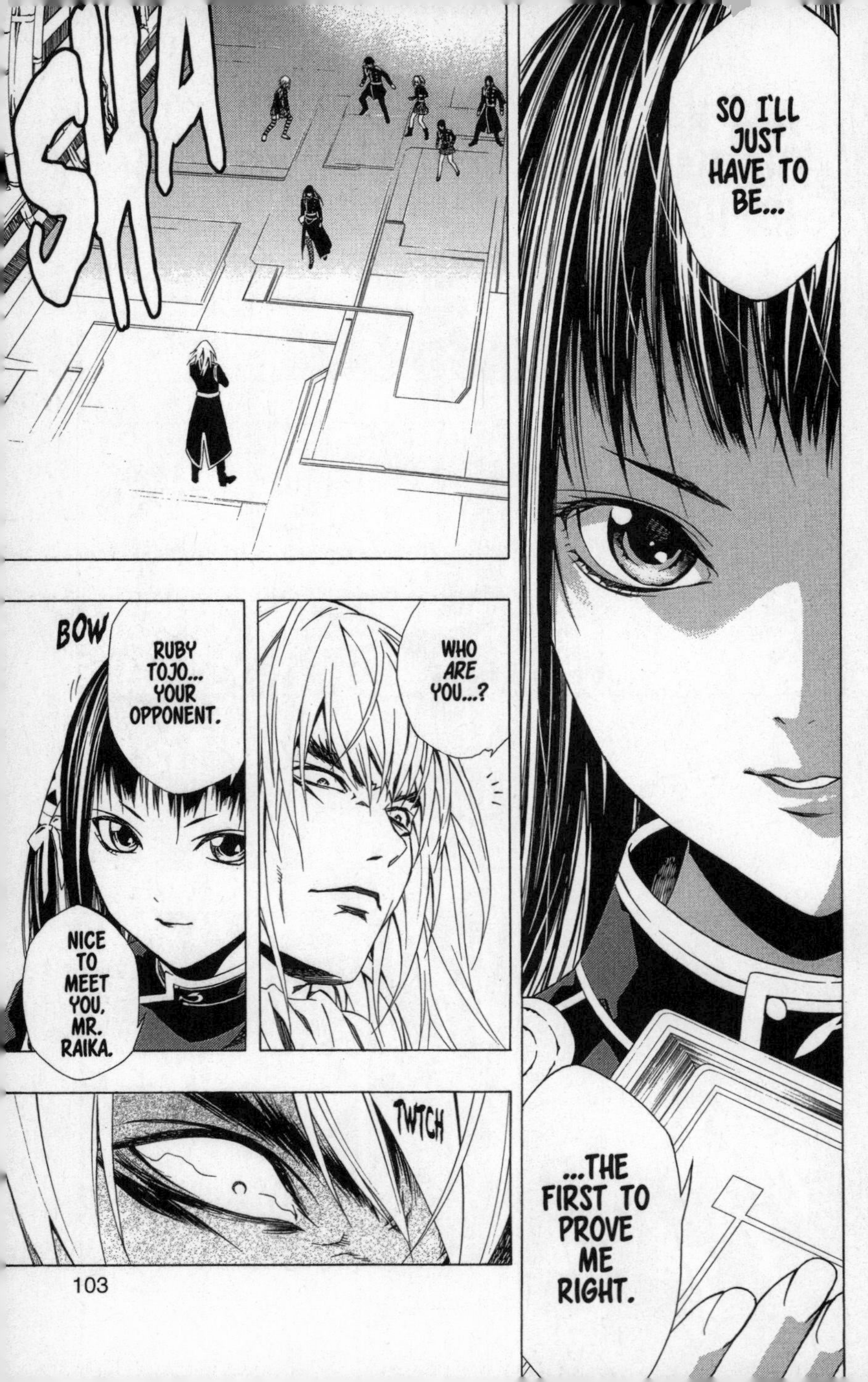
SO I'LL JUST HAVE TO BE...
...THE FIRST TO PROVE ME RIGHT.
SHA
WHO ARE YOU...?
BOW
RUBY TOJO... YOUR OPPONENT.
NICE TO MEET YOU, MR. RAIKA.
TWTCH

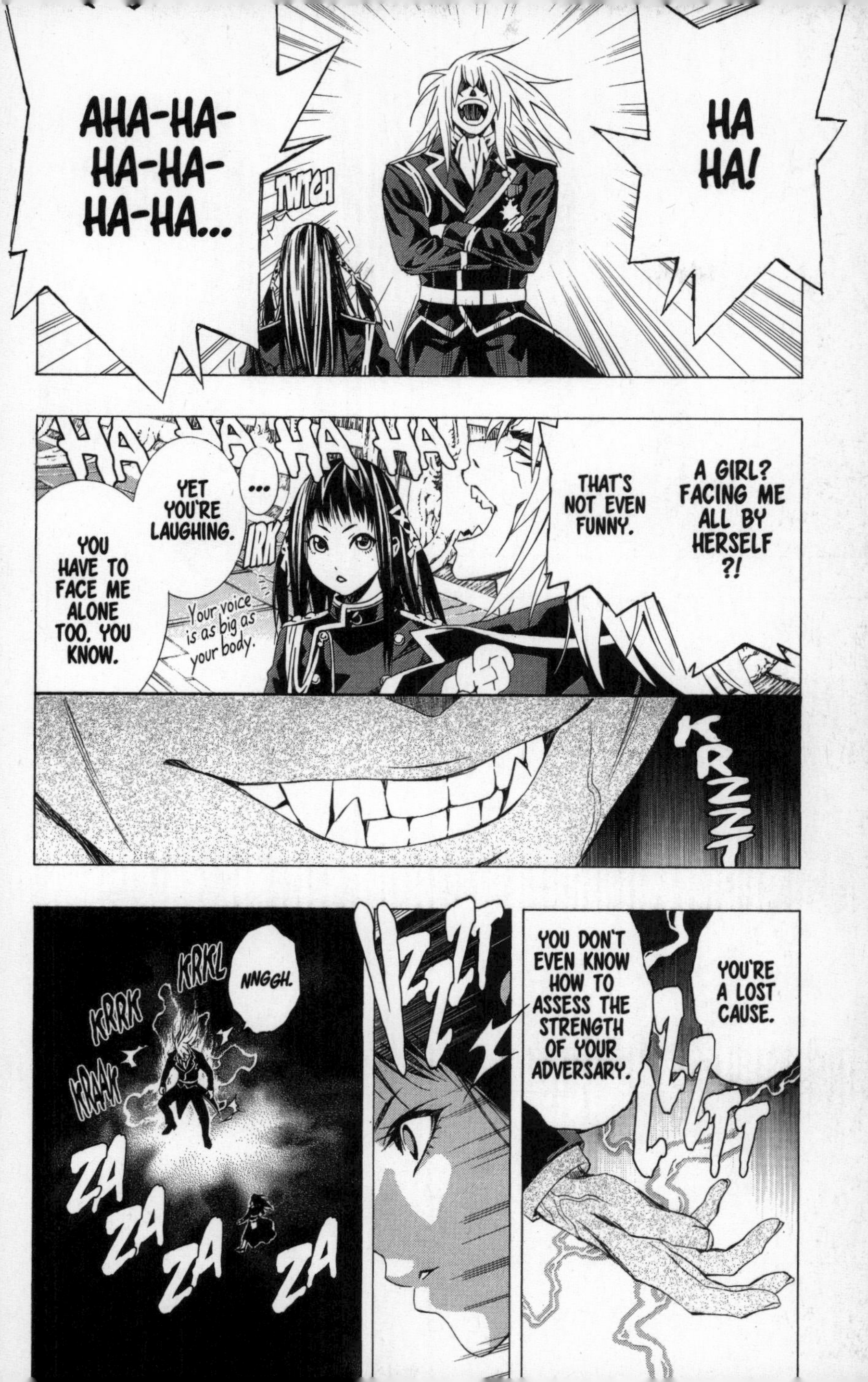
HA HA!
AHA-HA-HA-HA-HA-HA...
TWITCH
A GIRL? FACING ME ALL BY HERSELF?!
THAT'S NOT EVEN FUNNY.
...
IRK
YET YOU'RE LAUGHING.
YOU HAVE TO FACE ME ALONE TOO, YOU KNOW.
Your voice is as big as your body.
KRZZT
YOU'RE A LOST CAUSE.
YOU DON'T EVEN KNOW HOW TO ASSESS THE STRENGTH OF YOUR ADVERSARY.
ZZZT
VZZZT
NNGGH.
KRKL
KRRK
KRAAK
ZA ZA ZA ZA

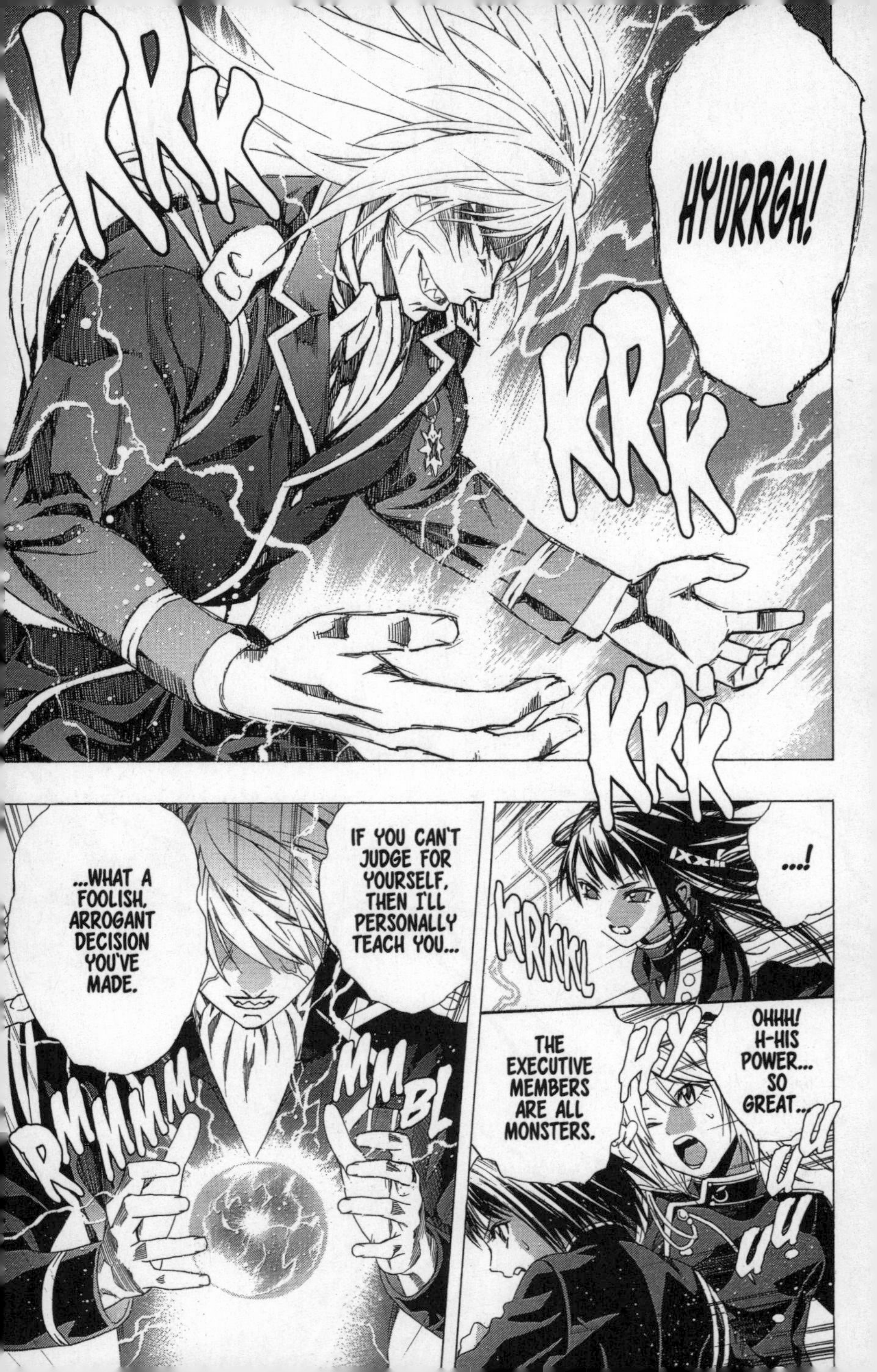
HYURRGH!
KRK
KRK
KRK
...!
KRKKL
OHHH! H-HIS POWER... SO GREAT...
HY
UUUUU!
THE EXECUTIVE MEMBERS ARE ALL MONSTERS.
...WHAT A FOOLISH, ARROGANT DECISION YOU'VE MADE.
IF YOU CAN'T JUDGE FOR YOURSELF, THEN I'LL PERSONALLY TEACH YOU...
MMBL
RMMMM

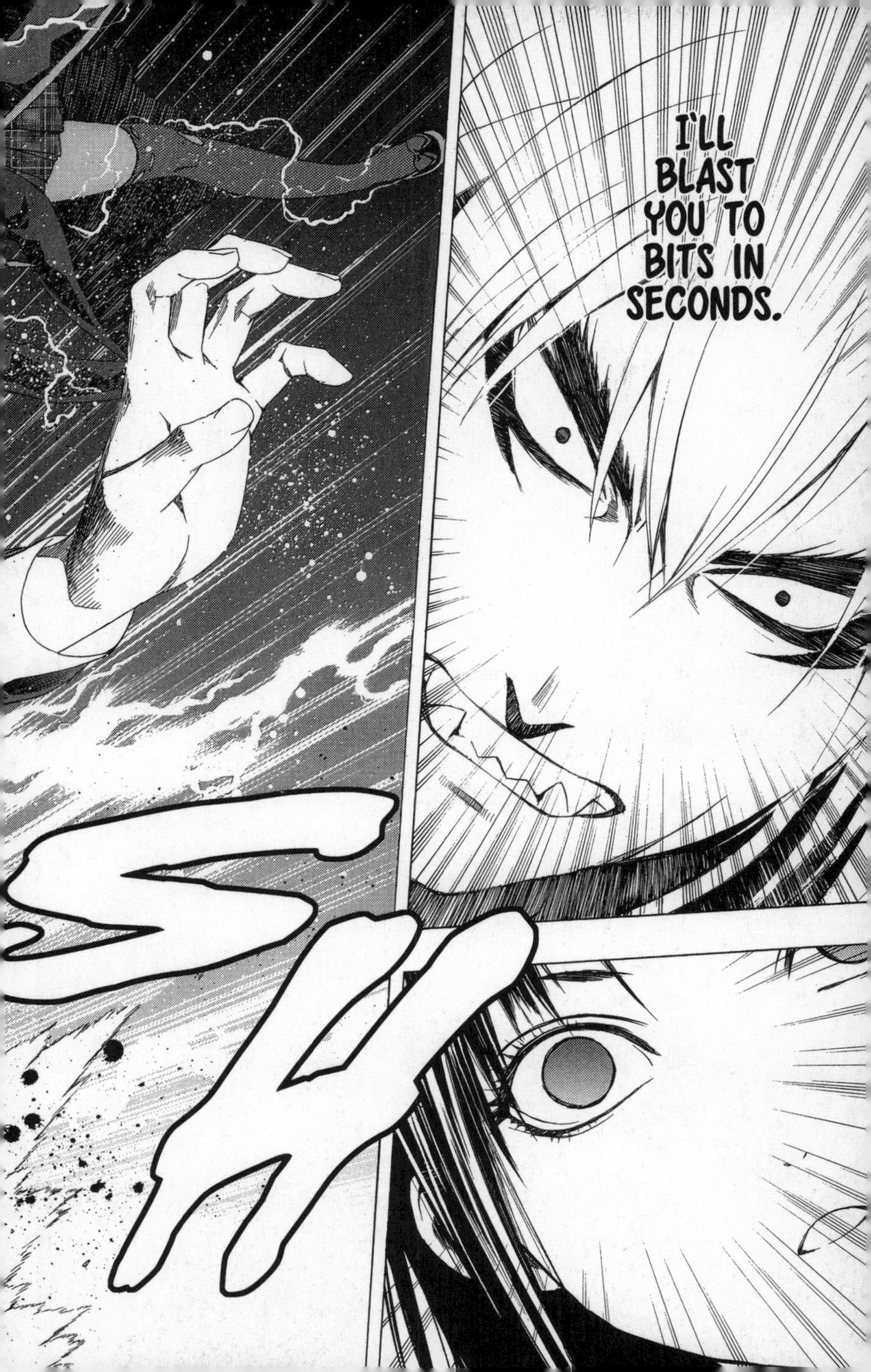
I'LL BLAST YOU TO BITS IN SECONDS.

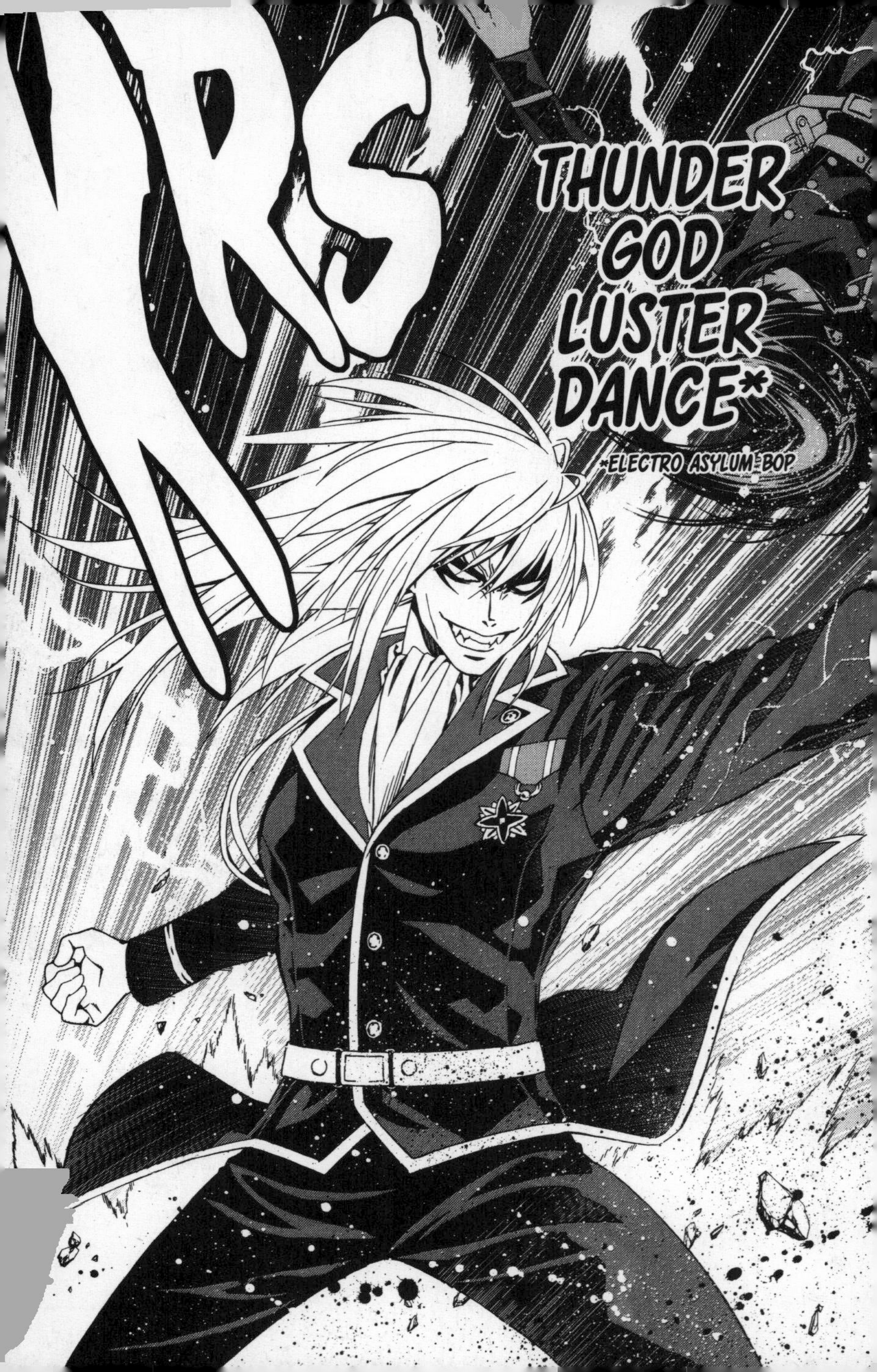
THUNDER GOD LUSTER DANCE*
*ELECTRO ASYLUM-BOP

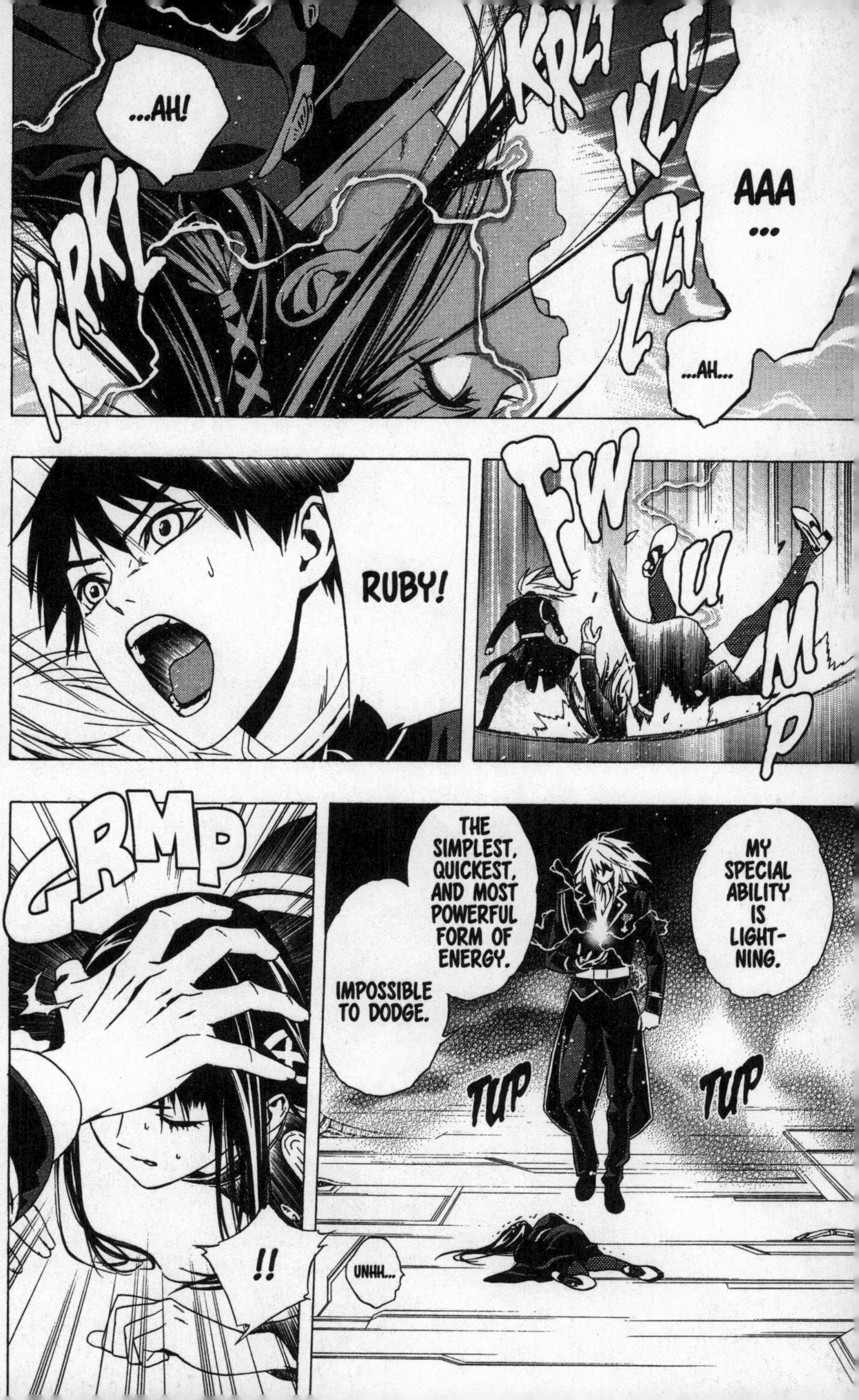
KRZT
KZT
AAA...
ZZT
...AH!
...AH...
KRKL
FWUMP
RUBY!
MY SPECIAL ABILITY IS LIGHT-NING.
THE SIMPLEST, QUICKEST, AND MOST POWERFUL FORM OF ENERGY.
IMPOSSIBLE TO DODGE.
TUP
TUP
UNHH...
GRMP
!!

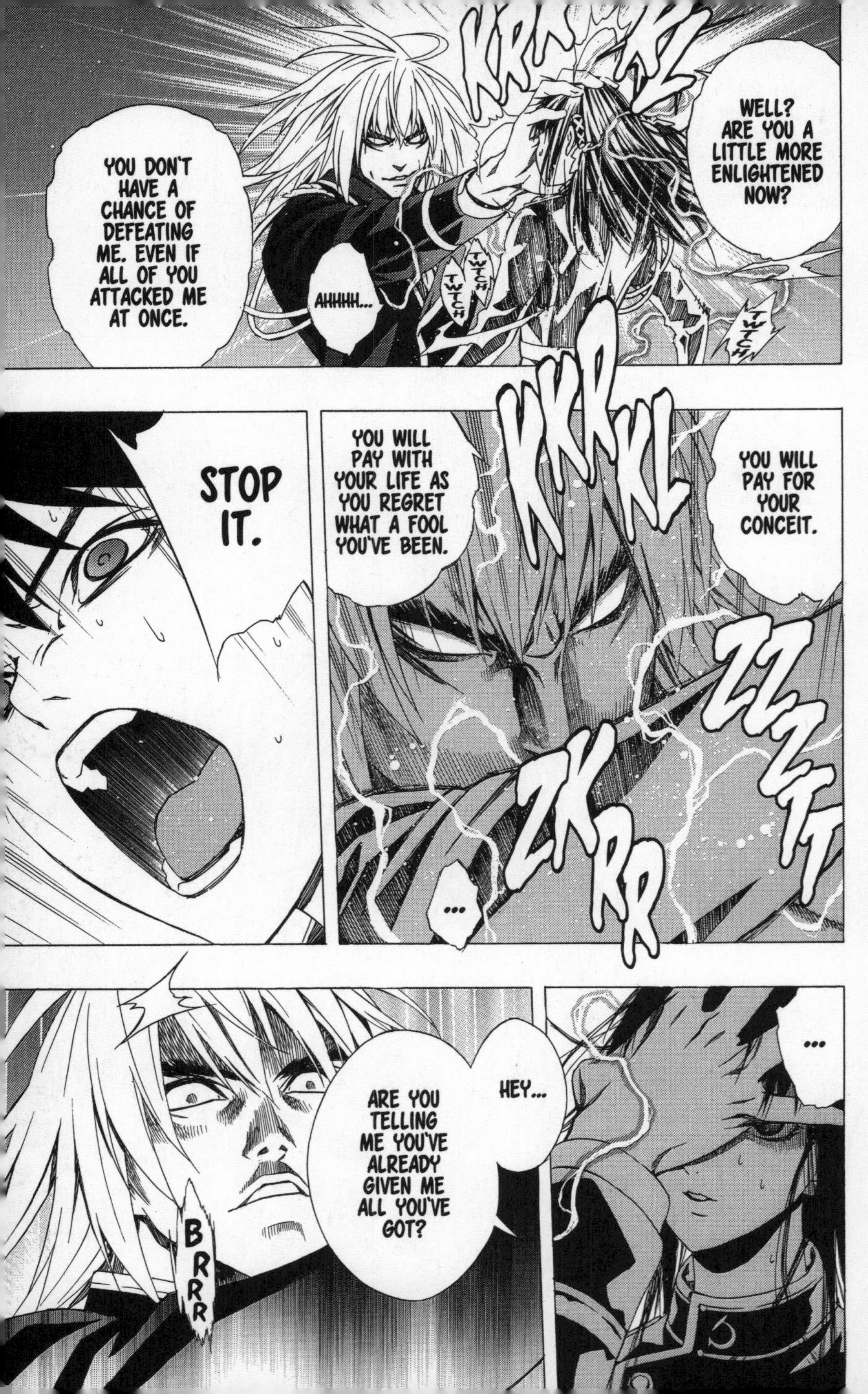
WELL? ARE YOU A LITTLE MORE ENLIGHTENED NOW?
TWITCH
TWITCH TWITCH
AHHHH...
YOU DON'T HAVE A CHANCE OF DEFEATING ME. EVEN IF ALL OF YOU ATTACKED ME AT ONCE.
KKRKL
YOU WILL PAY FOR YOUR CONCEIT.
YOU WILL PAY WITH YOUR LIFE AS YOU REGRET WHAT A FOOL YOU'VE BEEN.
ZZZTTT
ZKRR
...
STOP IT.
...
HEY...
ARE YOU TELLING ME YOU'VE ALREADY GIVEN ME ALL YOU'VE GOT?
BRRR

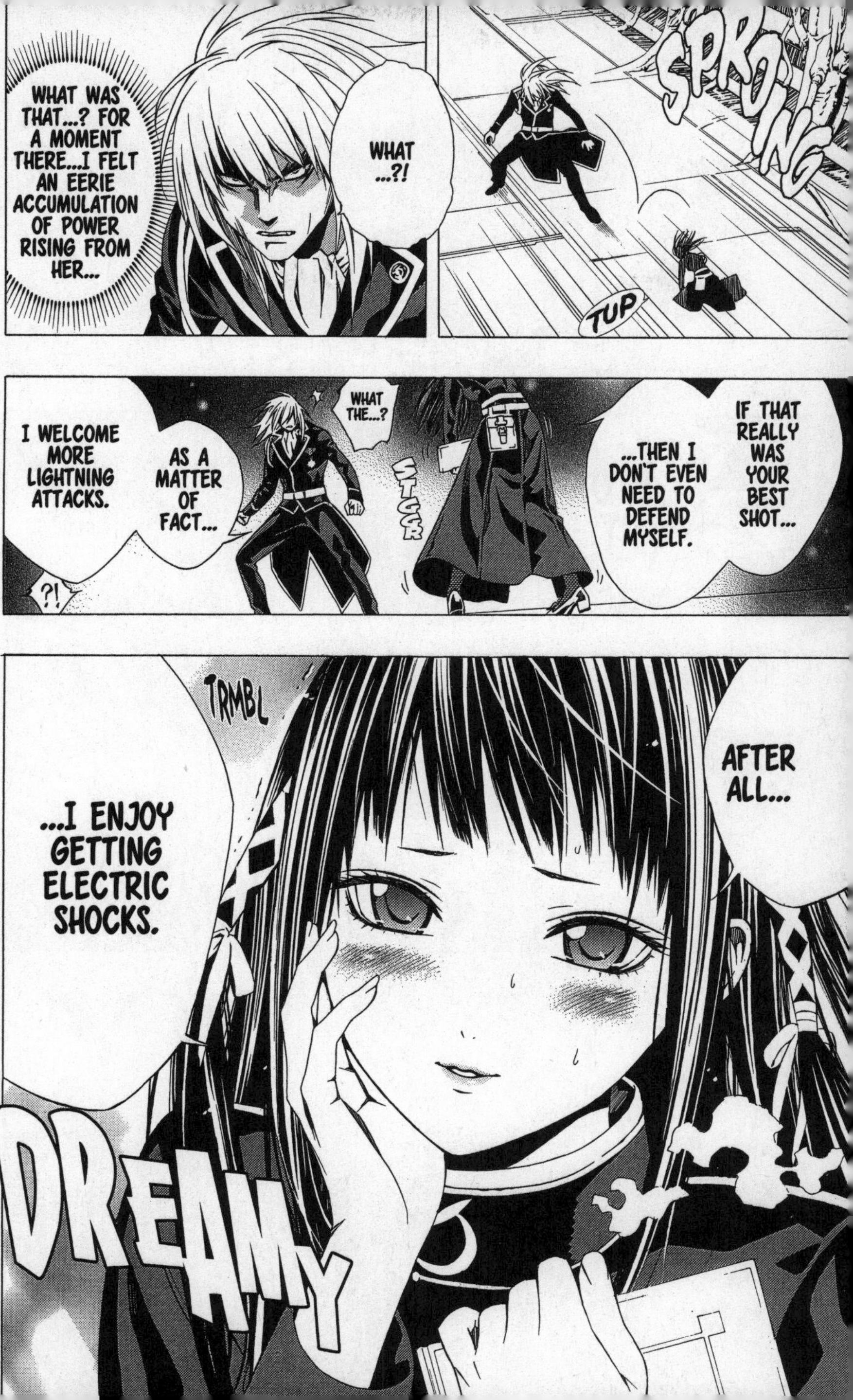
SPROING
TUP
WHAT ...?!
WHAT WAS THAT...? FOR A MOMENT THERE...I FELT AN EERIE ACCUMULATION OF POWER RISING FROM HER...
IF THAT REALLY WAS YOUR BEST SHOT...
...THEN I DON'T EVEN NEED TO DEFEND MYSELF.
STGGR
WHAT THE...?
AS A MATTER OF FACT...
I WELCOME MORE LIGHTNING ATTACKS.
?!
AFTER ALL...
TRMBL
...I ENJOY GETTING ELECTRIC SHOCKS.
DREAMY

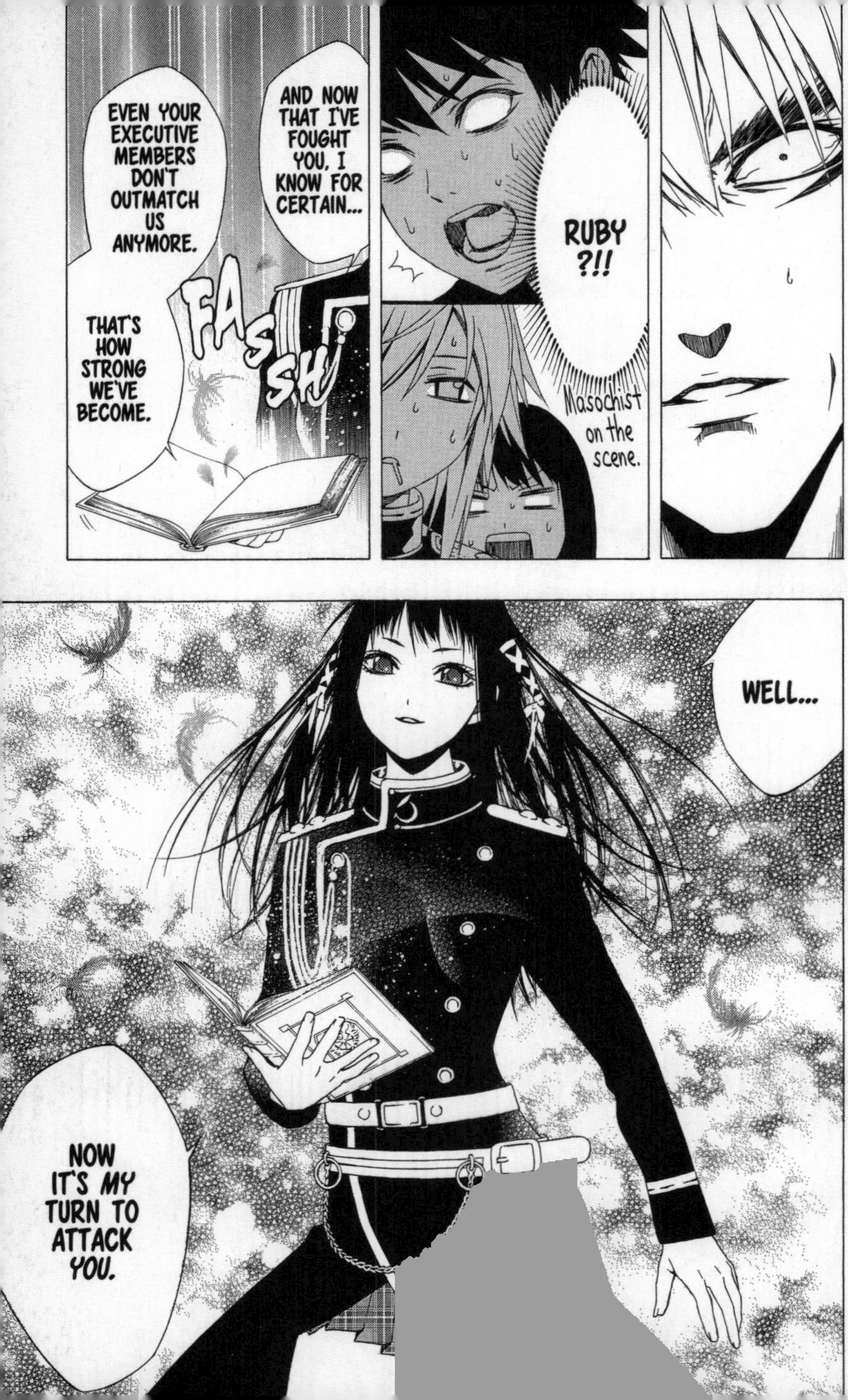
RUBY ?!!
Masochist on the scene.
AND NOW THAT I'VE FOUGHT YOU, I KNOW FOR CERTAIN...
EVEN YOUR EXECUTIVE MEMBERS DON'T OUTMATCH US ANYMORE.
FASSH
THAT'S HOW STRONG WE'VE BECOME.
WELL...
NOW IT'S MY TURN TO ATTACK YOU.

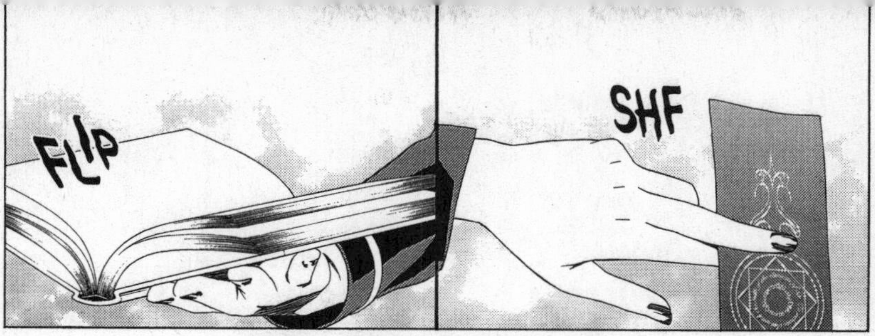
SHF
FLIP

45: Sorcerers

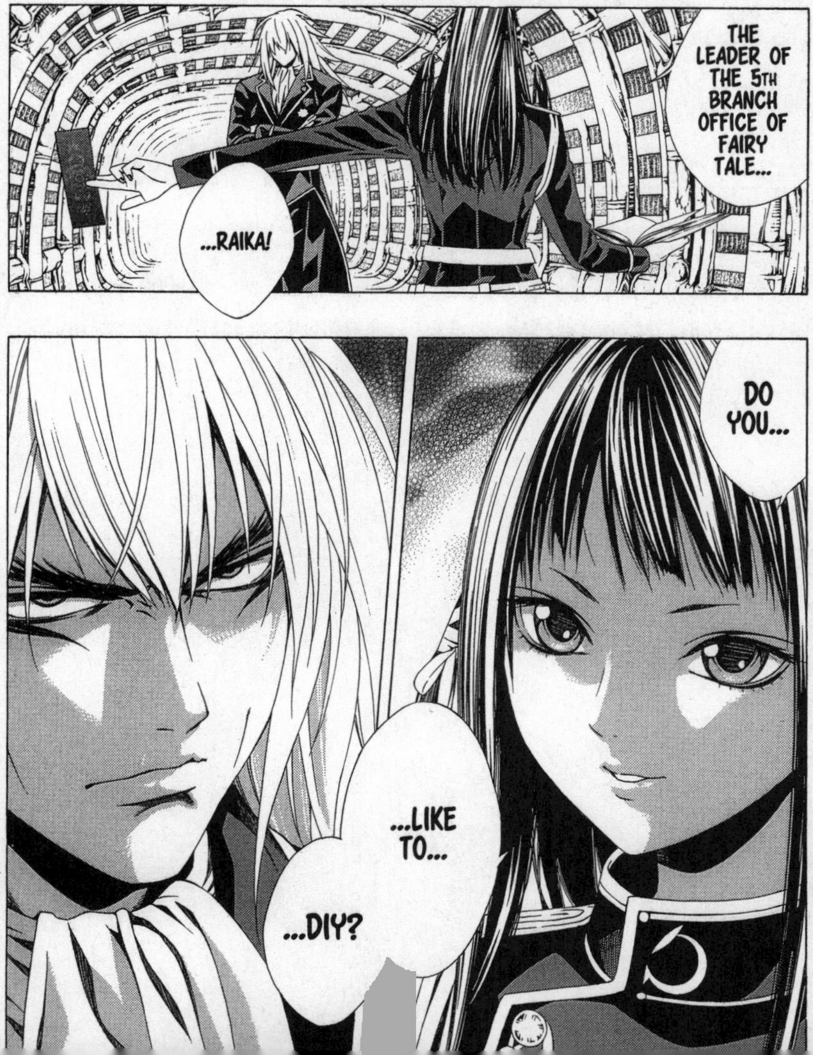
THE LEADER OF THE 5TH BRANCH OFFICE OF FAIRY TALE...
...RAIKA!
DO YOU...
...LIKE TO...
...DIY?

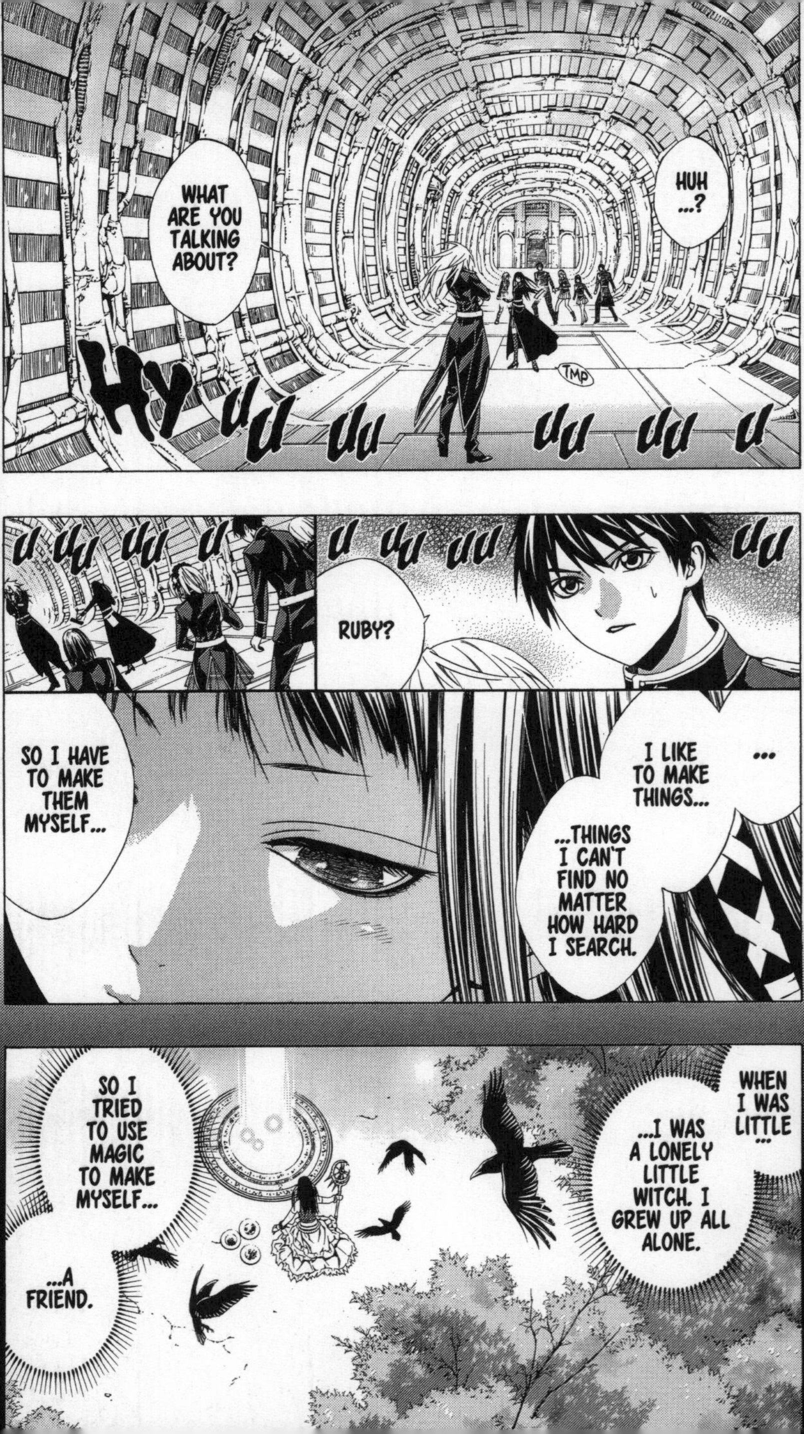
HUH ...?
WHAT ARE YOU TALKING ABOUT?
TMP
HYUUUUUUUUUUUU
UUUUUUU
RUBY?
UUUUUUU
...
I LIKE TO MAKE THINGS...
...THINGS I CAN'T FIND NO MATTER HOW HARD I SEARCH.
SO I HAVE TO MAKE THEM MYSELF...
WHEN I WAS LITTLE ...
...I WAS A LONELY LITTLE WITCH. I GREW UP ALL ALONE.
SO I TRIED TO USE MAGIC TO MAKE MYSELF...
...A FRIEND.

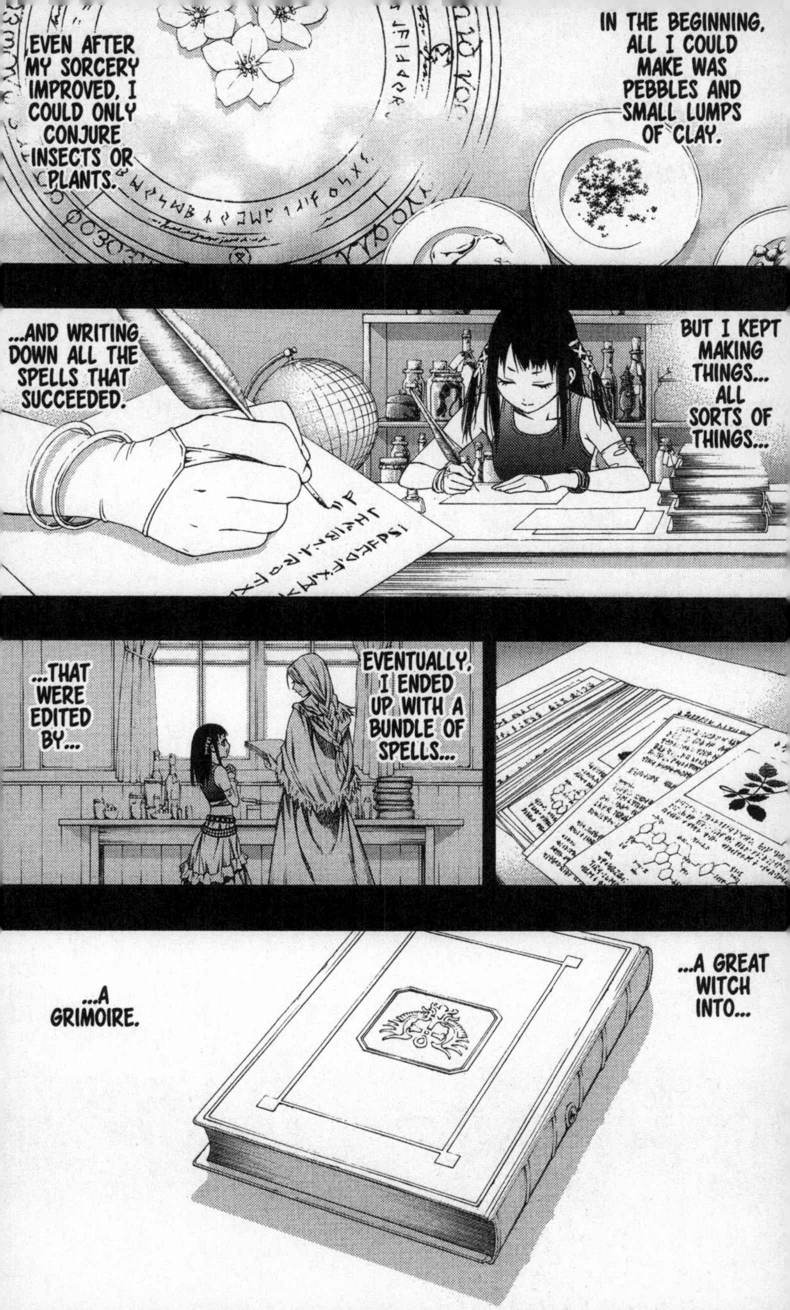
IN THE BEGINNING, ALL I COULD MAKE WAS PEBBLES AND SMALL LUMPS OF CLAY.
EVEN AFTER MY SORCERY IMPROVED, I COULD ONLY CONJURE INSECTS OR PLANTS.
BUT I KEPT MAKING THINGS... ALL SORTS OF THINGS...
...AND WRITING DOWN ALL THE SPELLS THAT SUCCEEDED.
EVENTUALLY, I ENDED UP WITH A BUNDLE OF SPELLS...
...THAT WERE EDITED BY...
...A GREAT WITCH INTO...
...A GRIMOIRE.

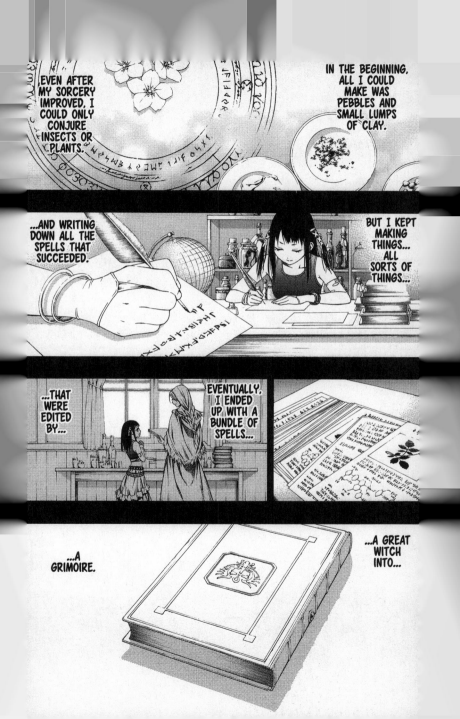

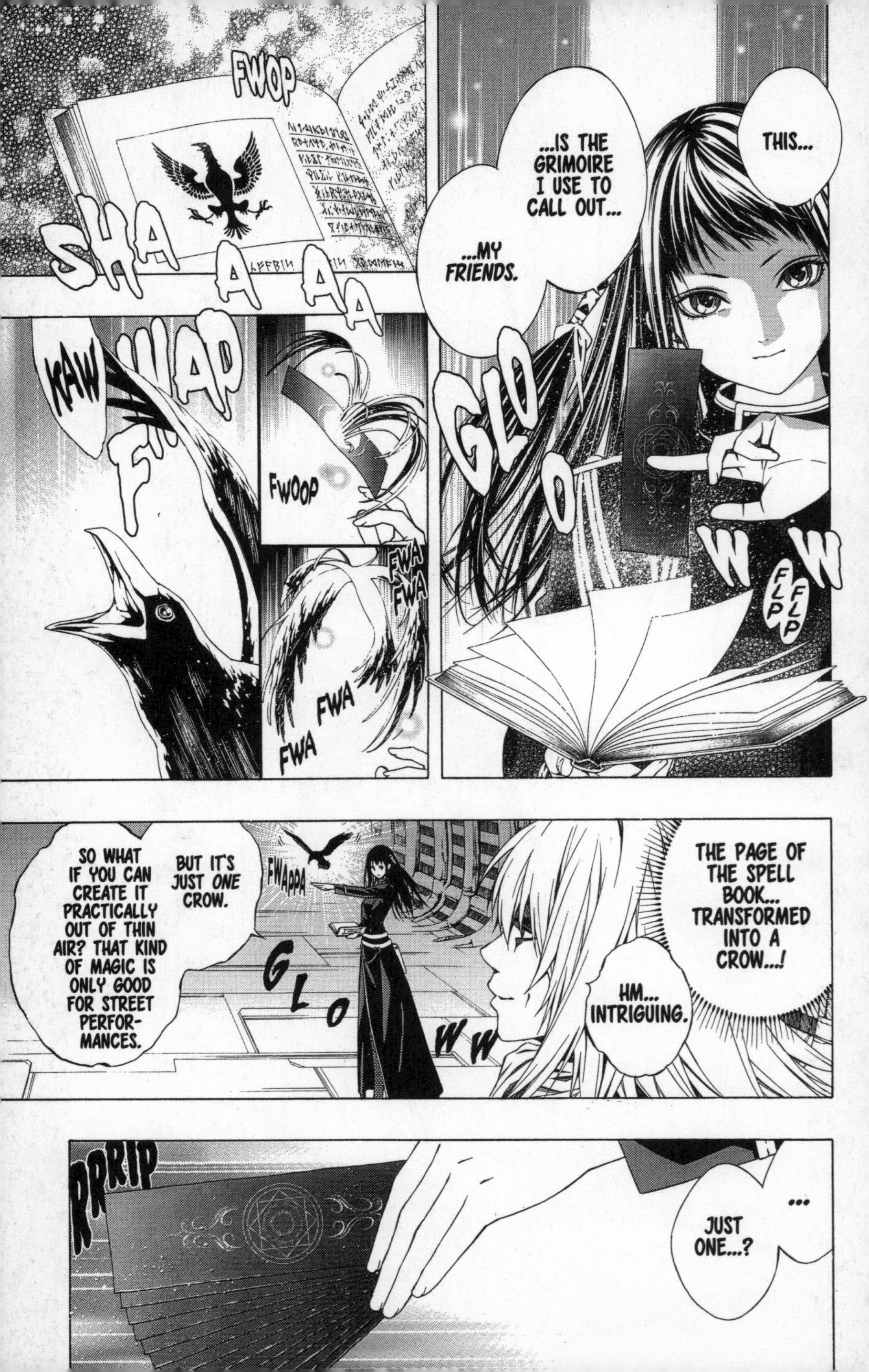
THIS...
...IS THE GRIMOIRE I USE TO CALL OUT...
...MY FRIENDS.
GLOOOW
FLP FLP
FWOP
SHAAAA
FWOOP
FWA FWA
FWA FWA
KAW
FWAP
THE PAGE OF THE SPELL BOOK... TRANSFORMED INTO A CROW...!
HM... INTRIGUING.
FWAPPA
GLOWW
BUT IT'S JUST *ONE* CROW.
SO WHAT IF YOU CAN CREATE IT PRACTICALLY OUT OF THIN AIR? THAT KIND OF MAGIC IS ONLY GOOD FOR STREET PERFORMANCES.
...
JUST ONE...?
RRRIP

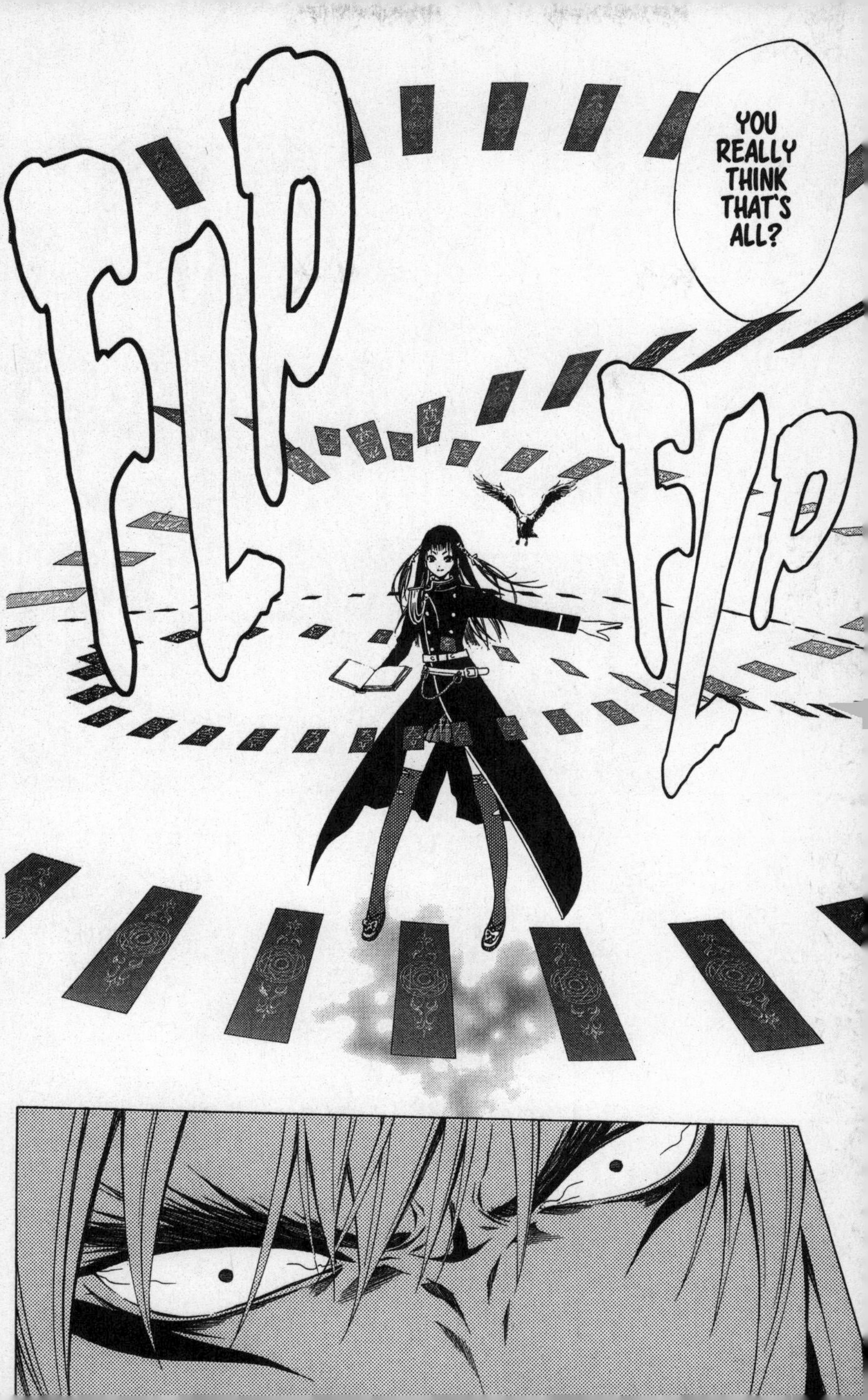
YOU REALLY THINK THAT'S ALL?
FLIP
FLIP

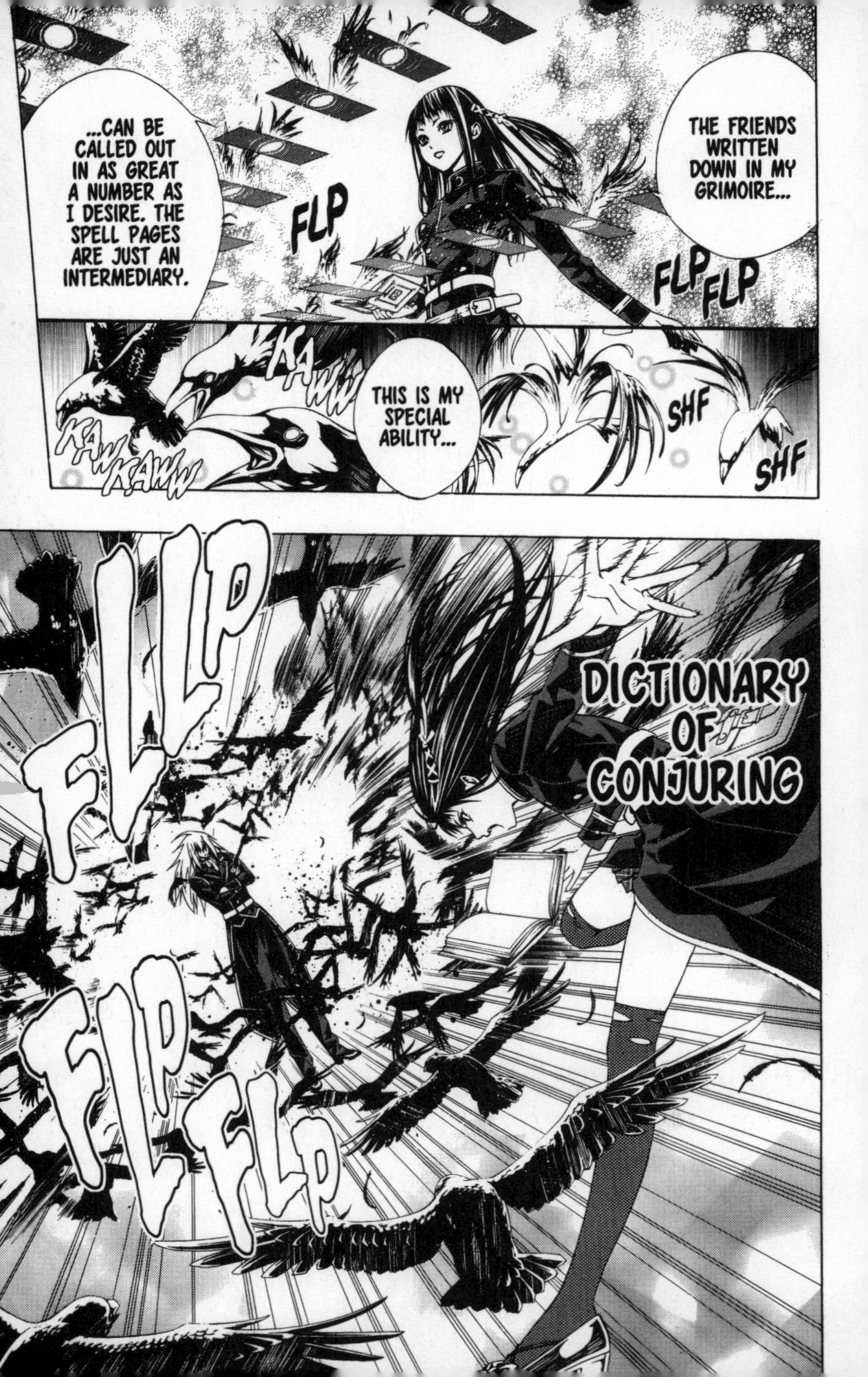
THE FRIENDS WRITTEN DOWN IN MY GRIMOIRE...
...CAN BE CALLED OUT IN AS GREAT A NUMBER AS I DESIRE. THE SPELL PAGES ARE JUST AN INTERMEDIARY.
FLP FLP
FLP
SHF
SHF
THIS IS MY SPECIAL ABILITY...
KAWW
KAW KAWW
DICTIONARY OF CONJURING
FLP
FLP
FLP

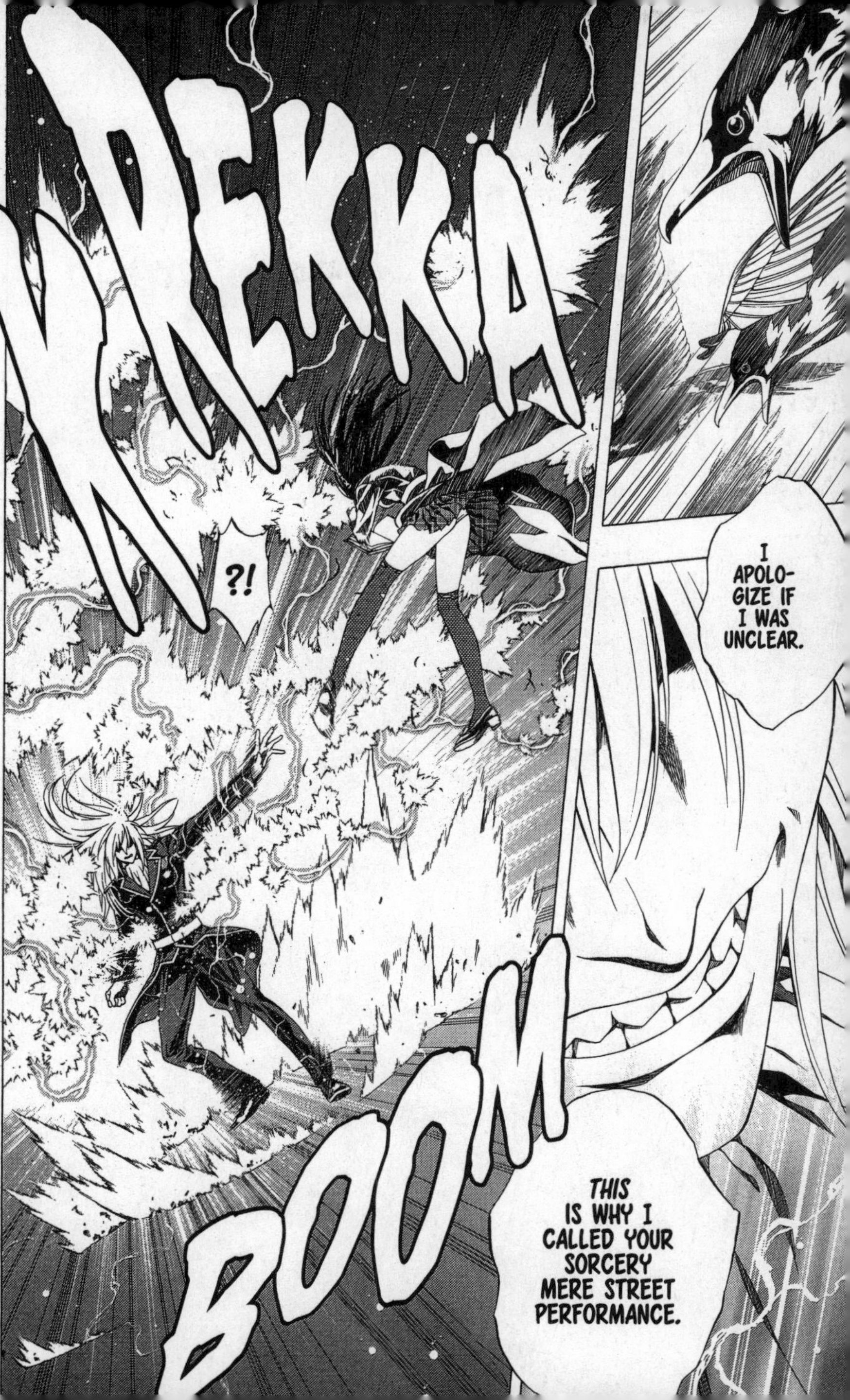
I APOLOGIZE IF I WAS UNCLEAR.
THIS IS WHY I CALLED YOUR SORCERY MERE STREET PERFORMANCE.
KREKKA
?!
BOOM

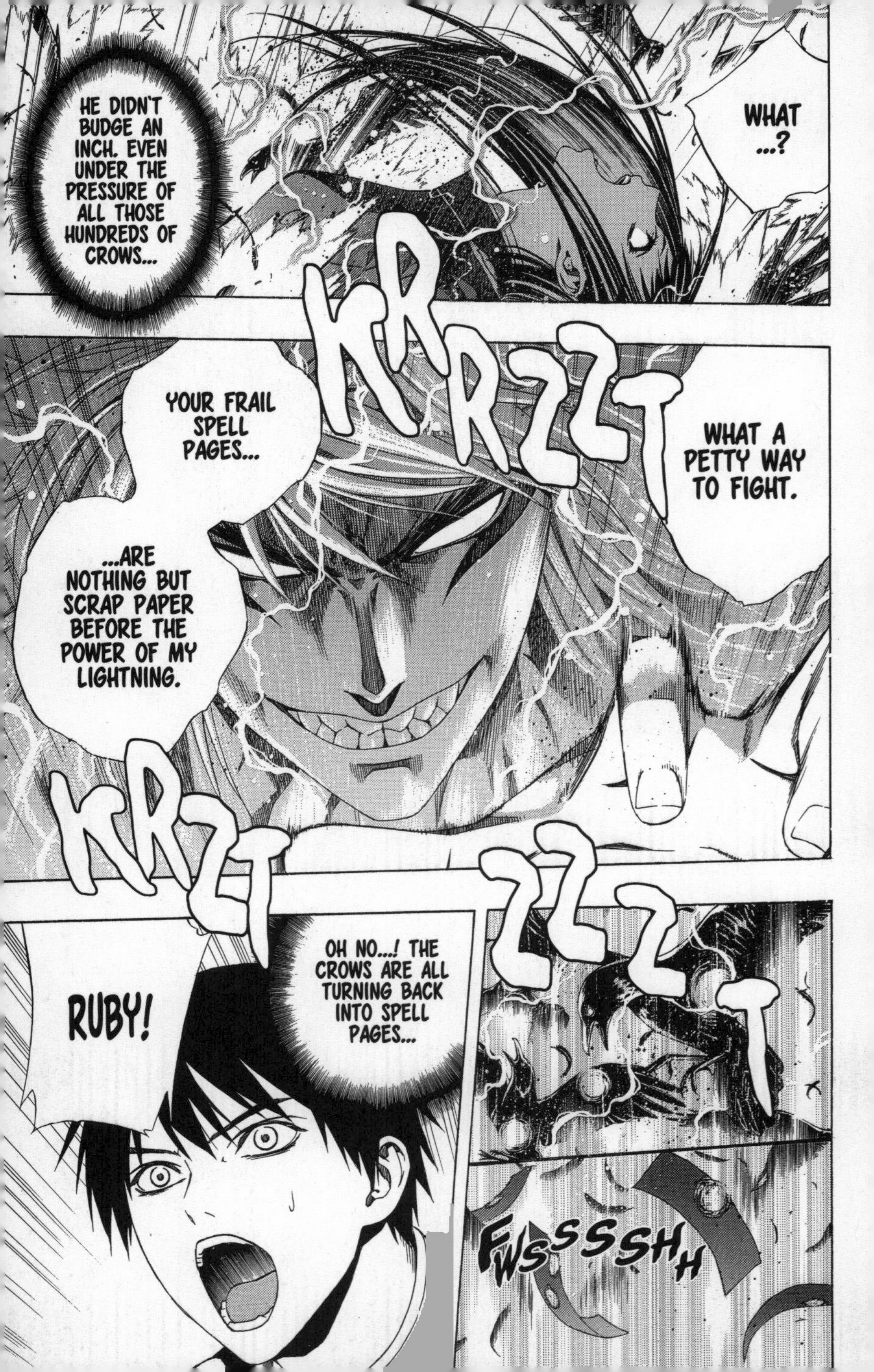
WHAT ...?
HE DIDN'T BUDGE AN INCH. EVEN UNDER THE PRESSURE OF ALL THOSE HUNDREDS OF CROWS...
KRRZZT
WHAT A PETTY WAY TO FIGHT.
YOUR FRAIL SPELL PAGES...
...ARE NOTHING BUT SCRAP PAPER BEFORE THE POWER OF MY LIGHTNING.
KRZT
ZZZT
FWSSSSHH
OH NO...! THE CROWS ARE ALL TURNING BACK INTO SPELL PAGES...
RUBY!

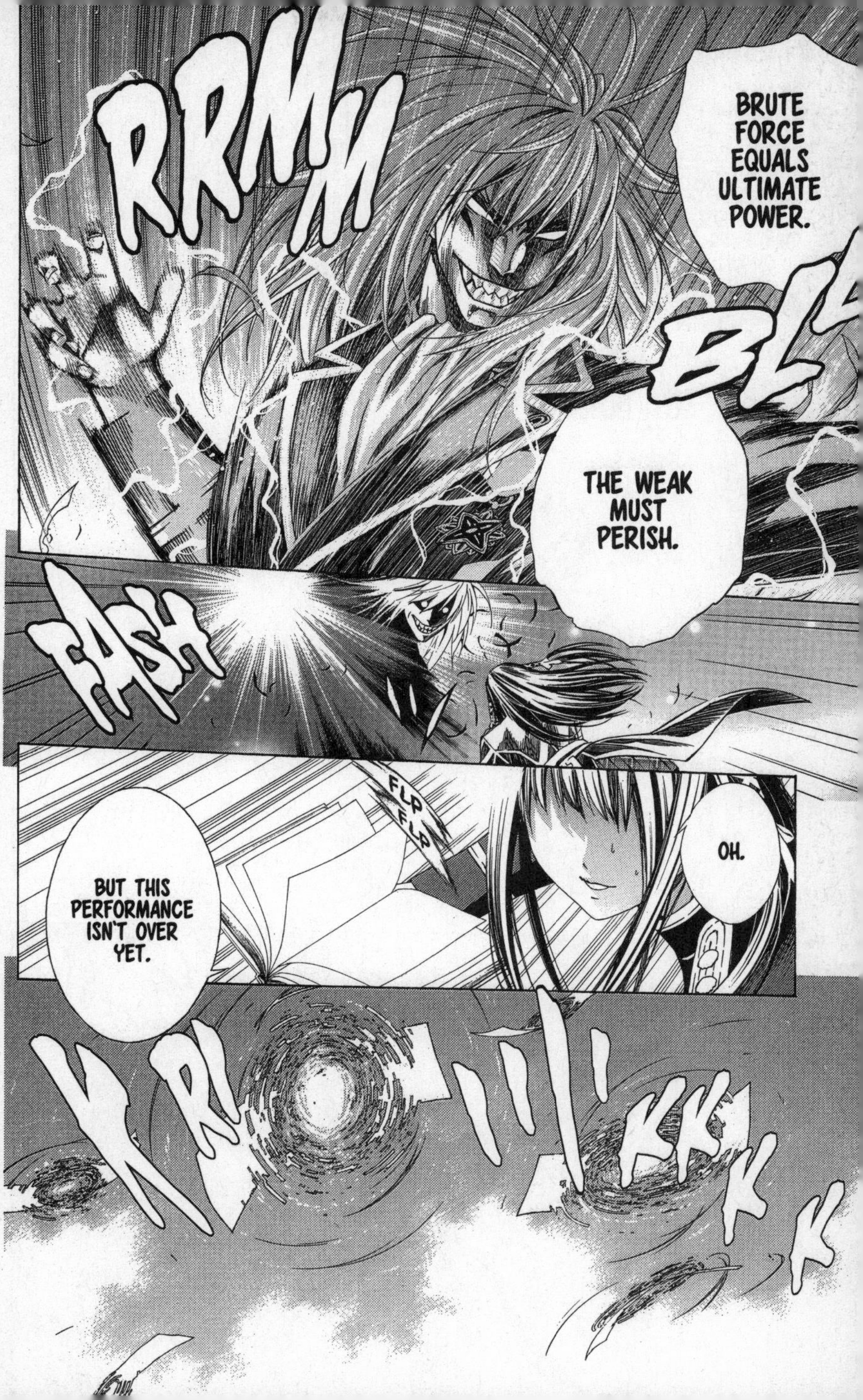
RRMM
BRUTE FORCE EQUALS ULTIMATE POWER.
BL
THE WEAK MUST PERISH.
OH.
FLP FLP
BUT THIS PERFORMANCE ISN'T OVER YET.

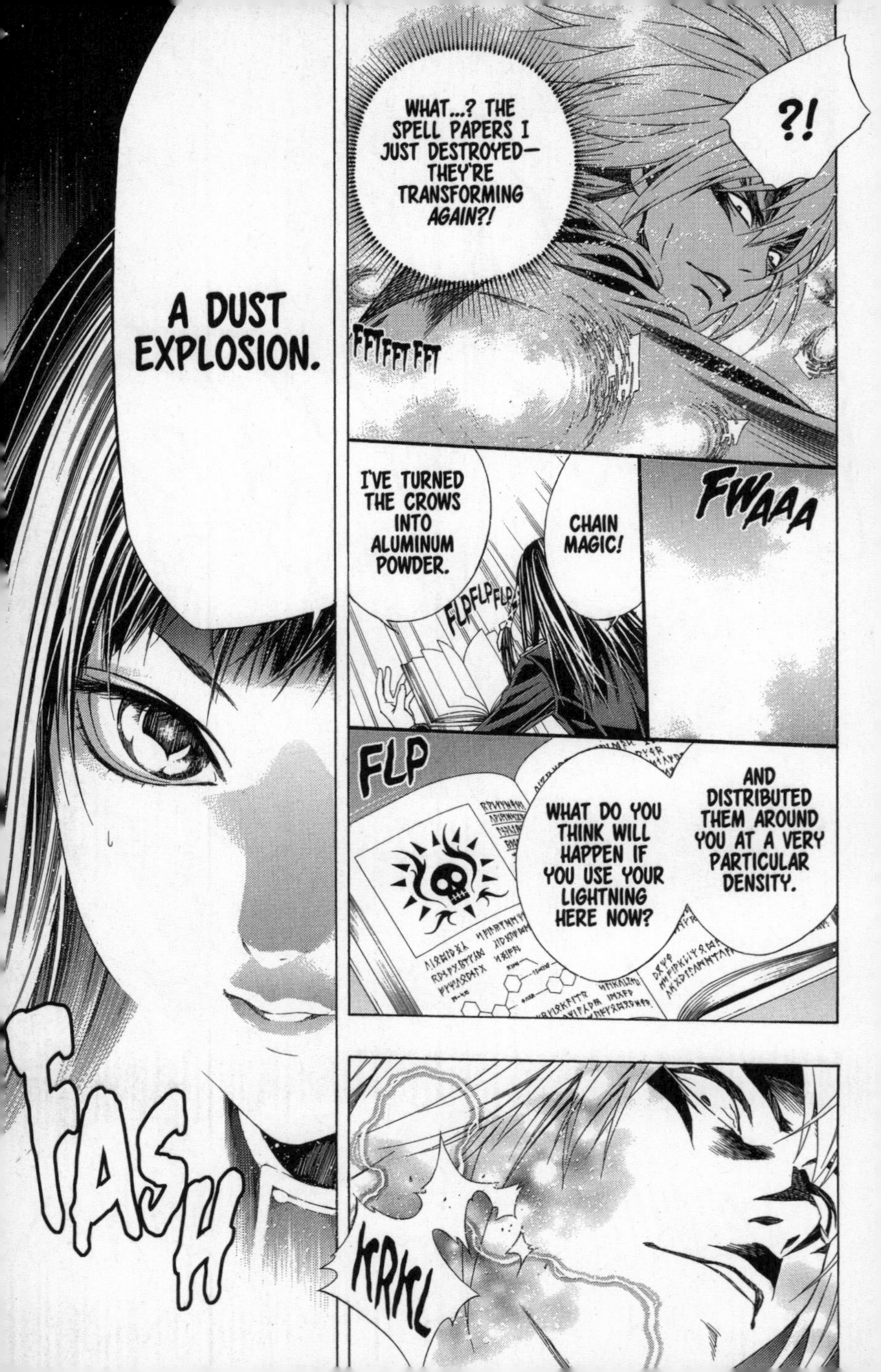
?!
WHAT...? THE SPELL PAPERS I JUST DESTROYED—THEY'RE TRANSFORMING AGAIN?!
FFT FFT FFT
FWAAAA
CHAIN MAGIC!
I'VE TURNED THE CROWS INTO ALUMINUM POWDER.
FLPFLPFLP
AND DISTRIBUTED THEM AROUND YOU AT A VERY PARTICULAR DENSITY.
WHAT DO YOU THINK WILL HAPPEN IF YOU USE YOUR LIGHTNING HERE NOW?
FLP
KRKL
A DUST EXPLOSION.
TASH

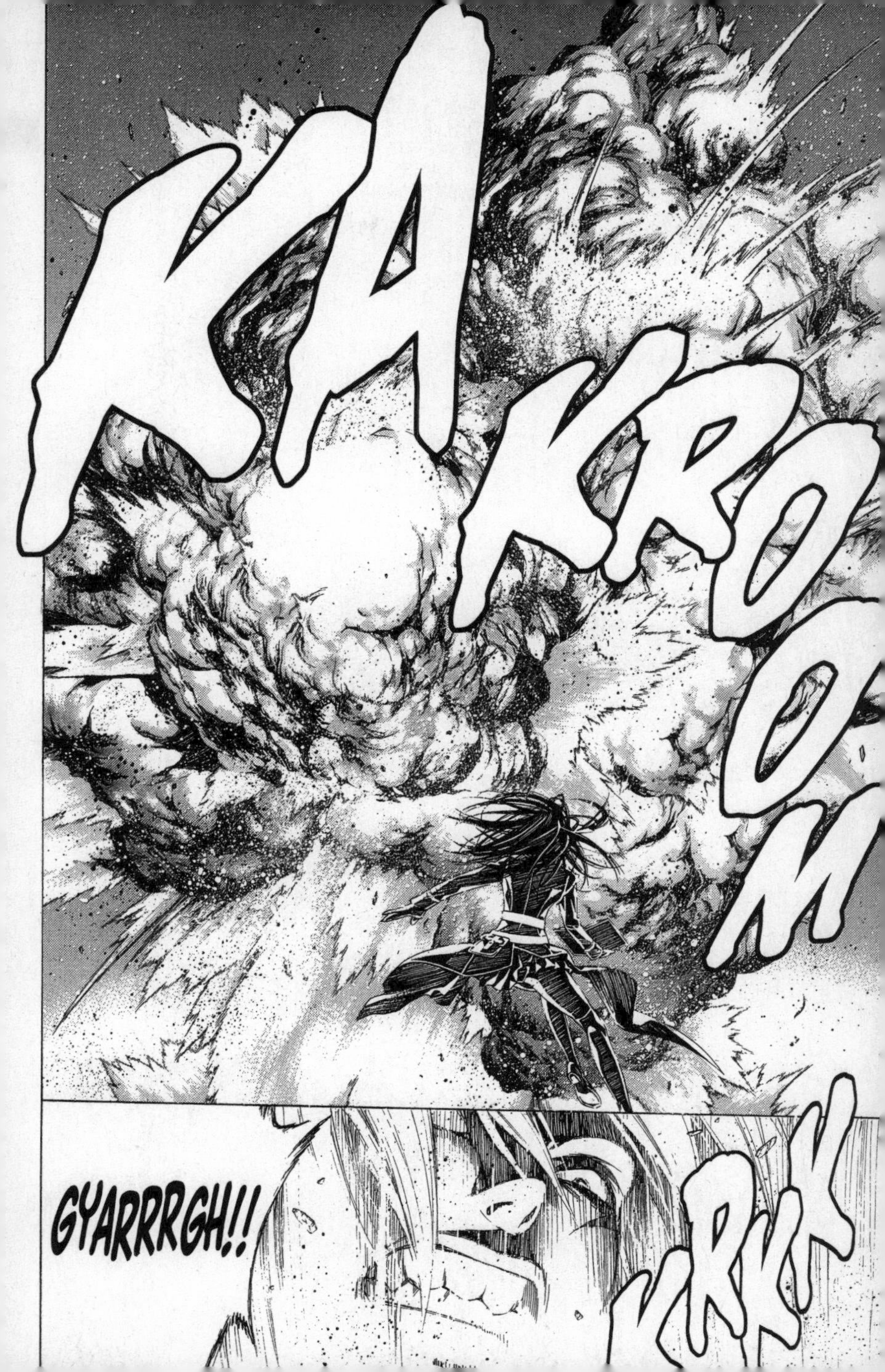
KA KROOM
URK
GYARRRGH!!

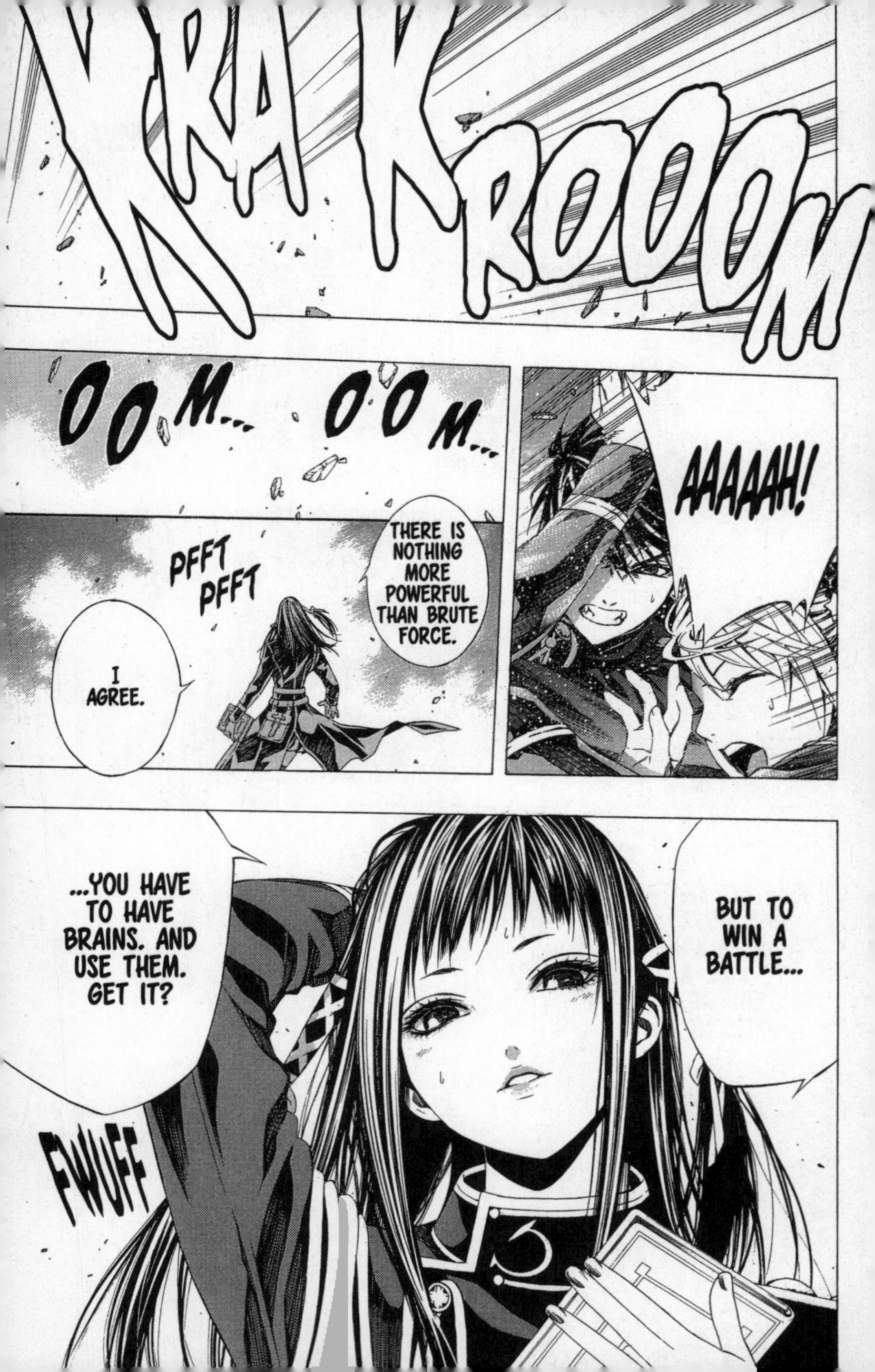
KRA KROOOM
AAAAAH!
OOM... OOM...
THERE IS NOTHING MORE POWERFUL THAN BRUTE FORCE.
PFFT PFFT
I AGREE.
BUT TO WIN A BATTLE...
...YOU HAVE TO HAVE BRAINS. AND USE THEM. GET IT?
FWUFF

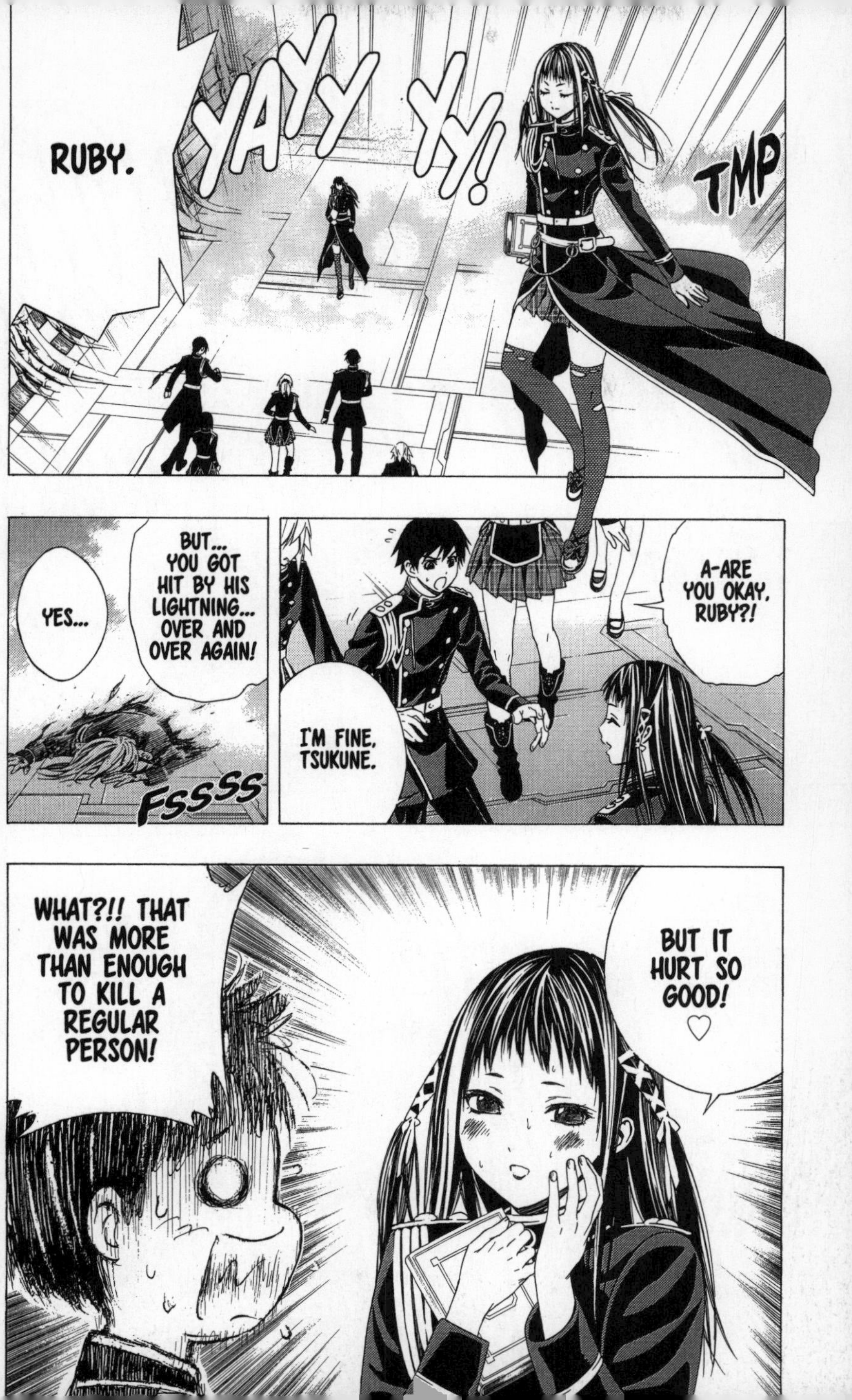
TMP
YAYY YY!
RUBY.
A-ARE YOU OKAY, RUBY?!
I'M FINE, TSUKUNE.
BUT... YOU GOT HIT BY HIS LIGHTNING... OVER AND OVER AGAIN!
YES...
FSSSS
BUT IT HURT SO GOOD! ♡
WHAT?!! THAT WAS MORE THAN ENOUGH TO KILL A REGULAR PERSON!

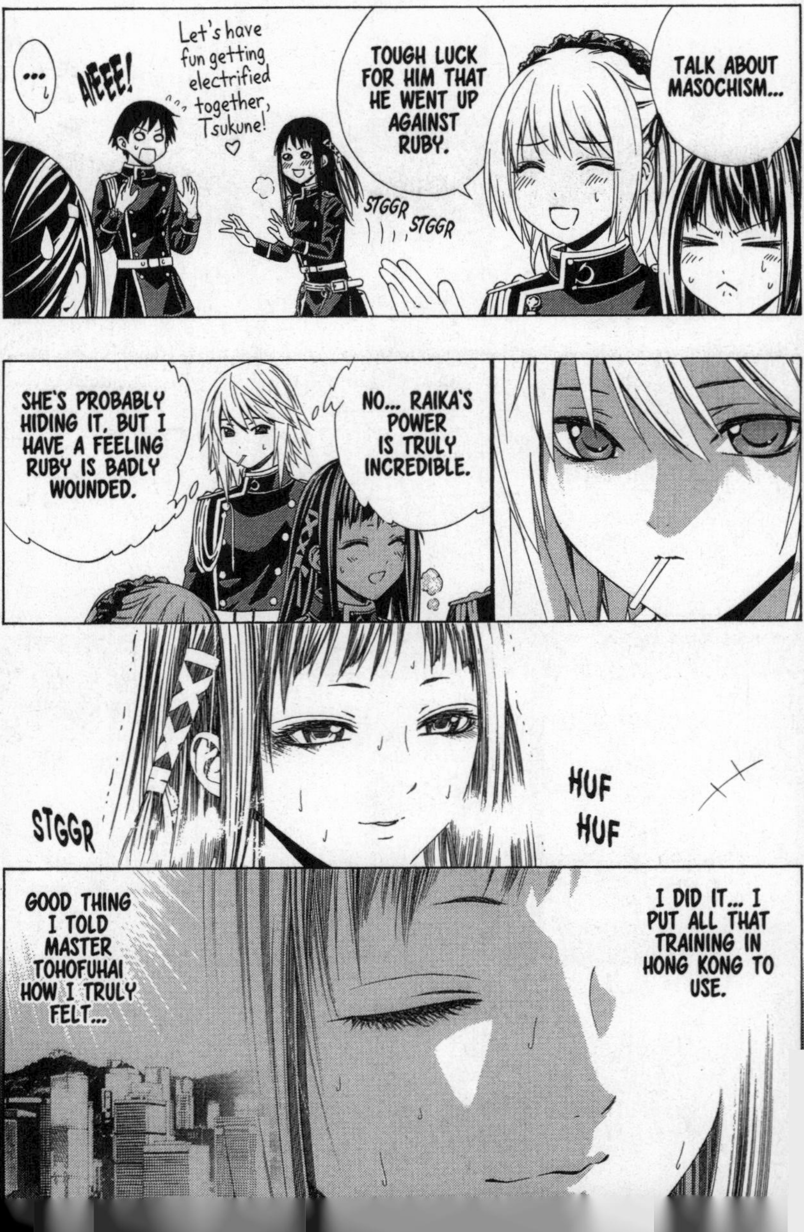
TALK ABOUT MASOCHISM...
TOUGH LUCK FOR HIM THAT HE WENT UP AGAINST RUBY.
STGGR
STGGR
Let's have fun getting electrified together, Tsukune! ♡
AIEEE!
...
NO... RAIKA'S POWER IS TRULY INCREDIBLE.
SHE'S PROBABLY HIDING IT, BUT I HAVE A FEELING RUBY IS BADLY WOUNDED.
HUF
HUF
STGGR
I DID IT... I PUT ALL THAT TRAINING IN HONG KONG TO USE.
GOOD THING I TOLD MASTER TOHOFUHAI HOW I TRULY FELT...

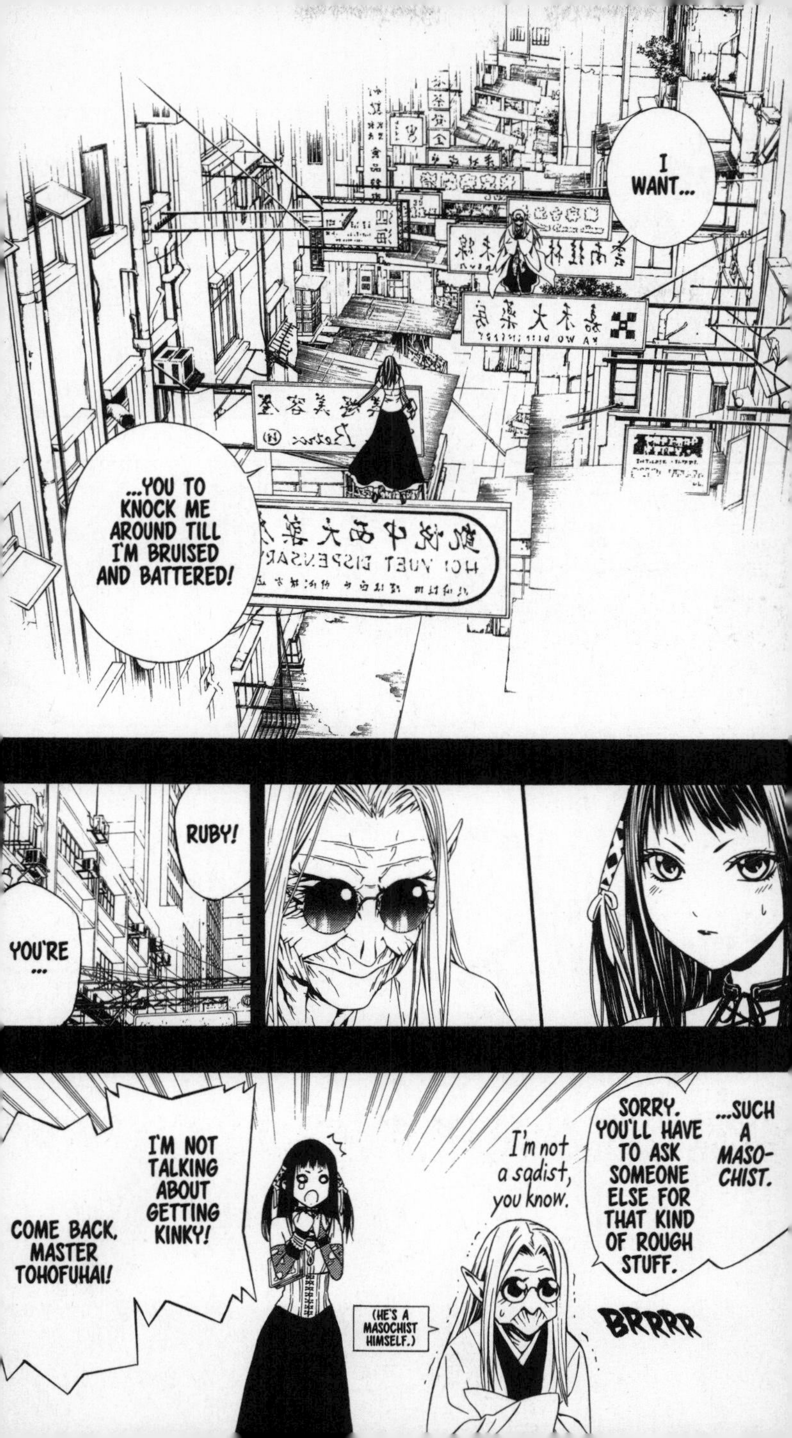
I WANT...
...YOU TO KNOCK ME AROUND TILL I'M BRUISED AND BATTERED!
RUBY!
YOU'RE ...
...SUCH A MASOCHIST.
SORRY. YOU'LL HAVE TO ASK SOMEONE ELSE FOR THAT KIND OF ROUGH STUFF.
I'm not a sadist, you know.
BRRRR
(HE'S A MASOCHIST HIMSELF.)
I'M NOT TALKING ABOUT GETTING KINKY!
COME BACK, MASTER TOHOFUHAI!

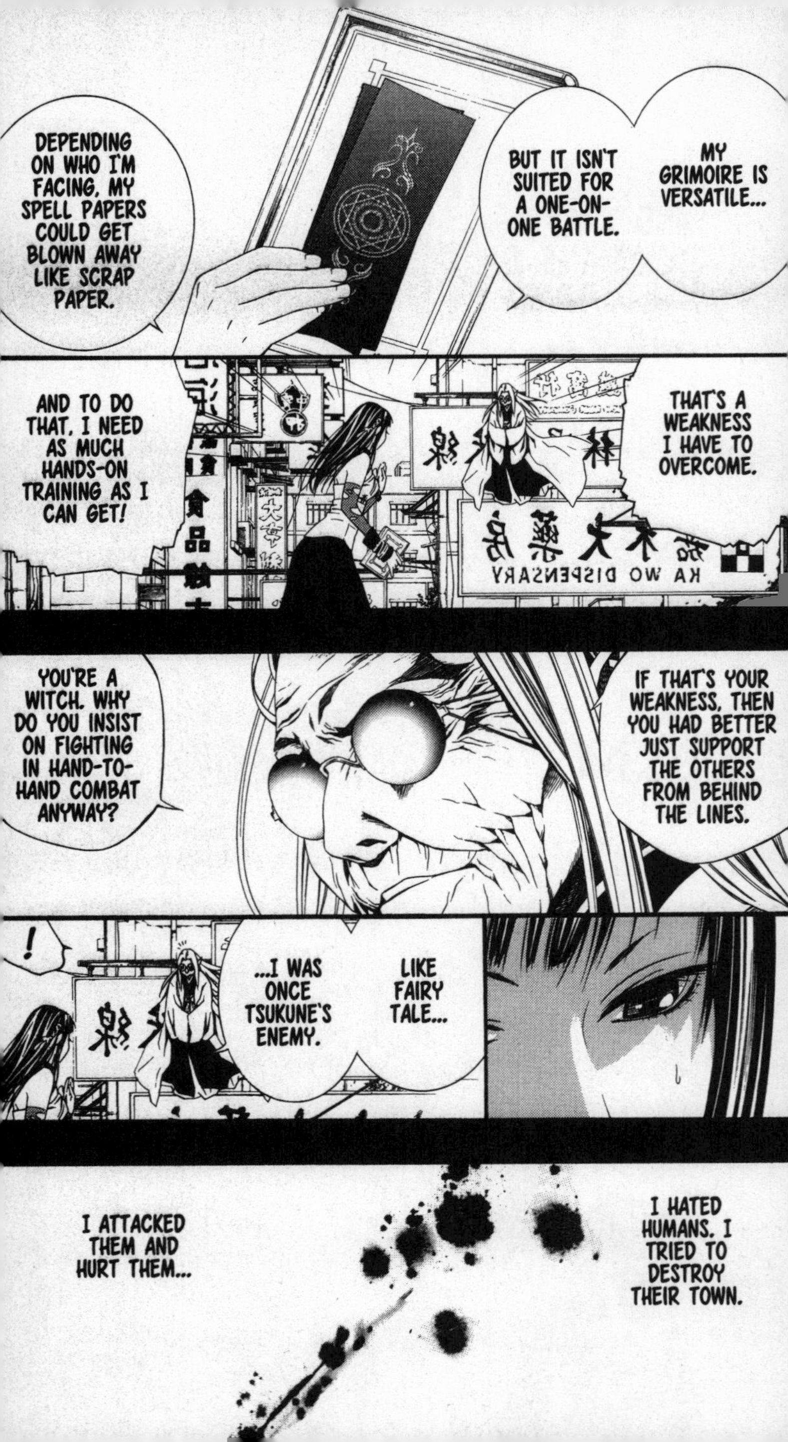
MY GRIMOIRE IS VERSATILE...
BUT IT ISN'T SUITED FOR A ONE-ON-ONE BATTLE.
DEPENDING ON WHO I'M FACING, MY SPELL PAPERS COULD GET BLOWN AWAY LIKE SCRAP PAPER.
THAT'S A WEAKNESS I HAVE TO OVERCOME.
AND TO DO THAT, I NEED AS MUCH HANDS-ON TRAINING AS I CAN GET!
IF THAT'S YOUR WEAKNESS, THEN YOU HAD BETTER JUST SUPPORT THE OTHERS FROM BEHIND THE LINES.
YOU'RE A WITCH. WHY DO YOU INSIST ON FIGHTING IN HAND-TO-HAND COMBAT ANYWAY?
LIKE FAIRY TALE...
...I WAS ONCE TSUKUNE'S ENEMY.
!
I HATED HUMANS. I TRIED TO DESTROY THEIR TOWN.
I ATTACKED THEM AND HURT THEM...

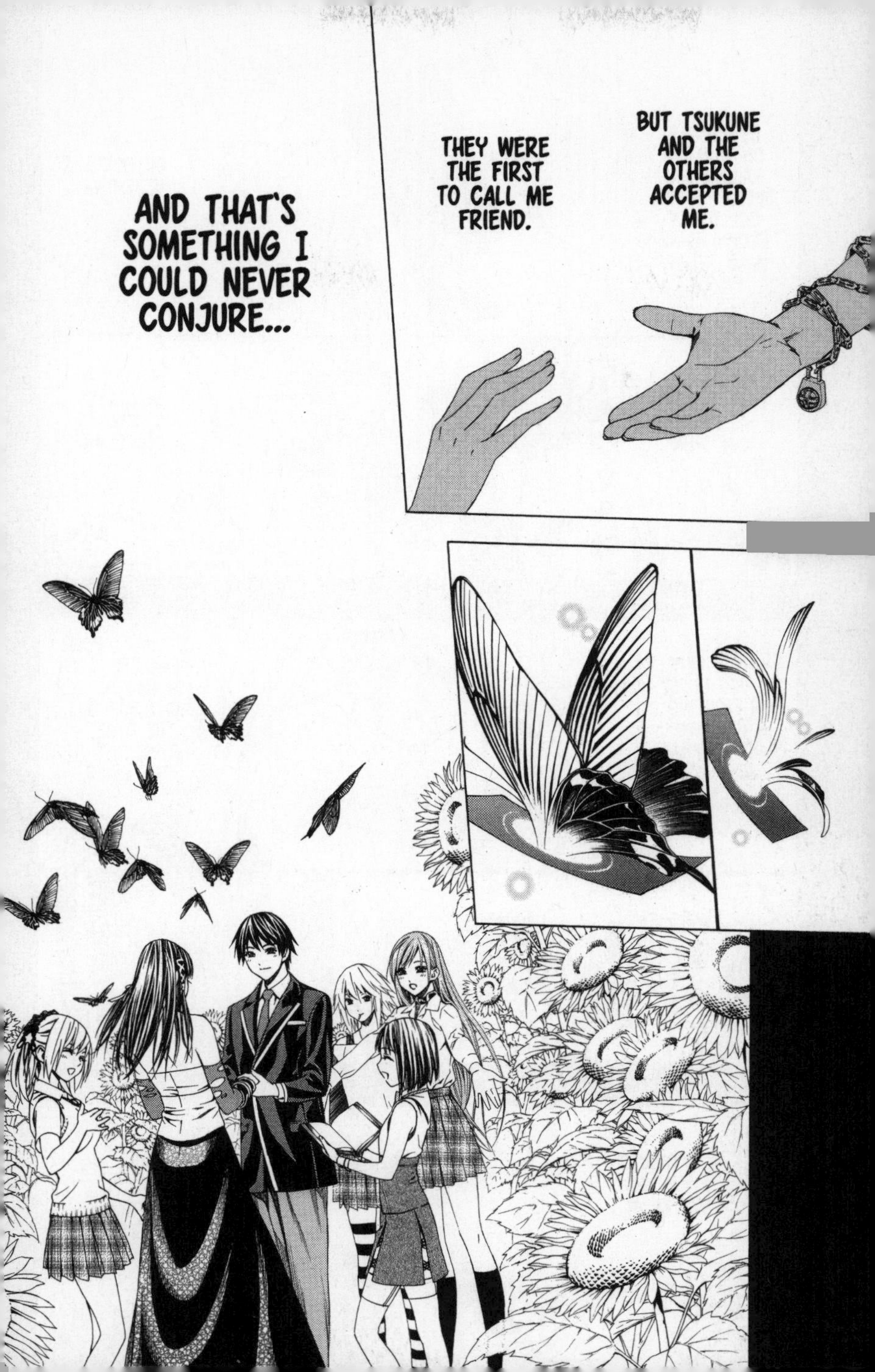
BUT TSUKUNE AND THE OTHERS ACCEPTED ME.
THEY WERE THE FIRST TO CALL ME FRIEND.
AND THAT'S SOMETHING I COULD NEVER CONJURE...

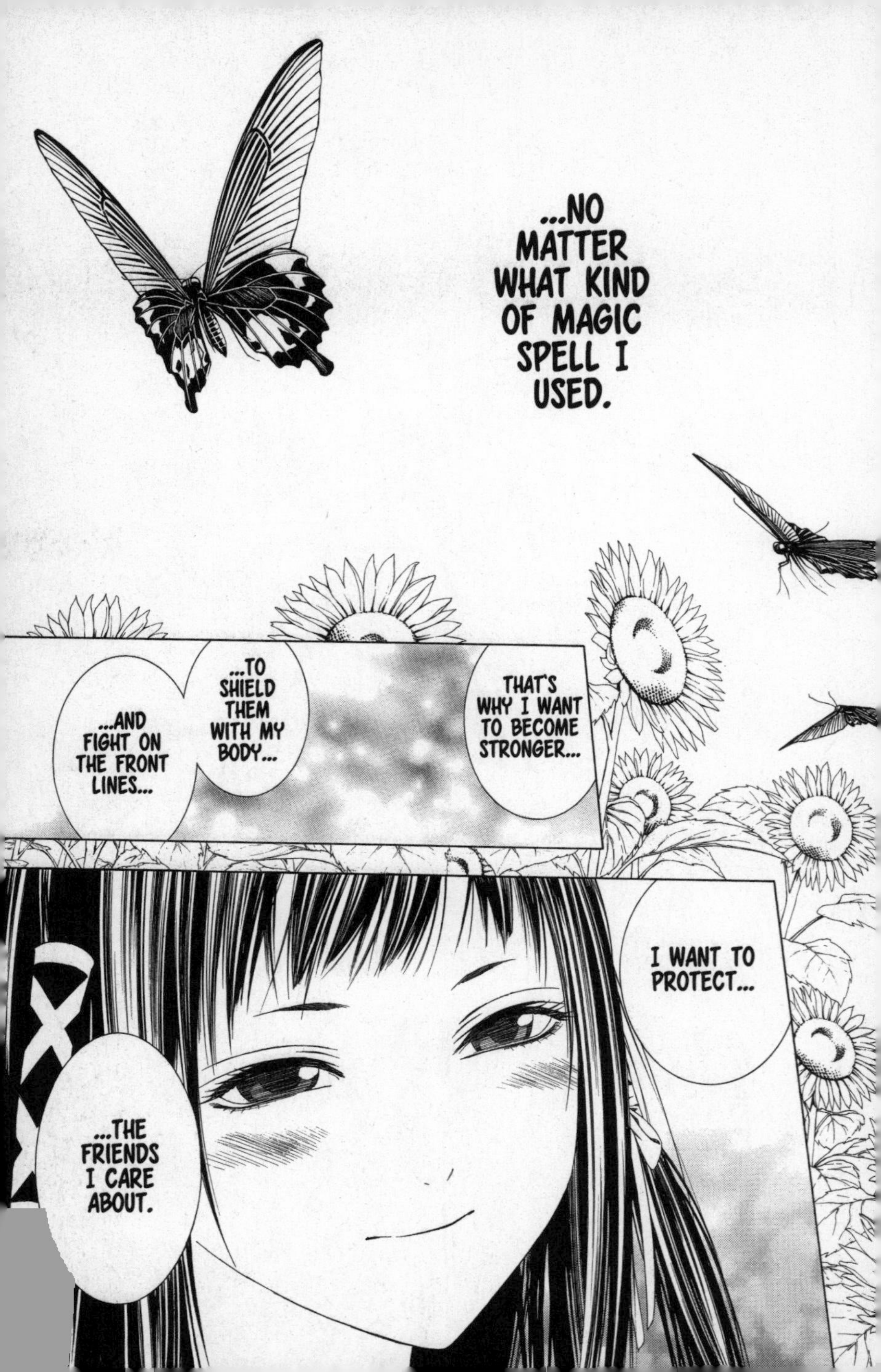
...NO MATTER WHAT KIND OF MAGIC SPELL I USED.
THAT'S WHY I WANT TO BECOME STRONGER...
...TO SHIELD THEM WITH MY BODY...
...AND FIGHT ON THE FRONT LINES...
I WANT TO PROTECT...
...THE FRIENDS I CARE ABOUT.

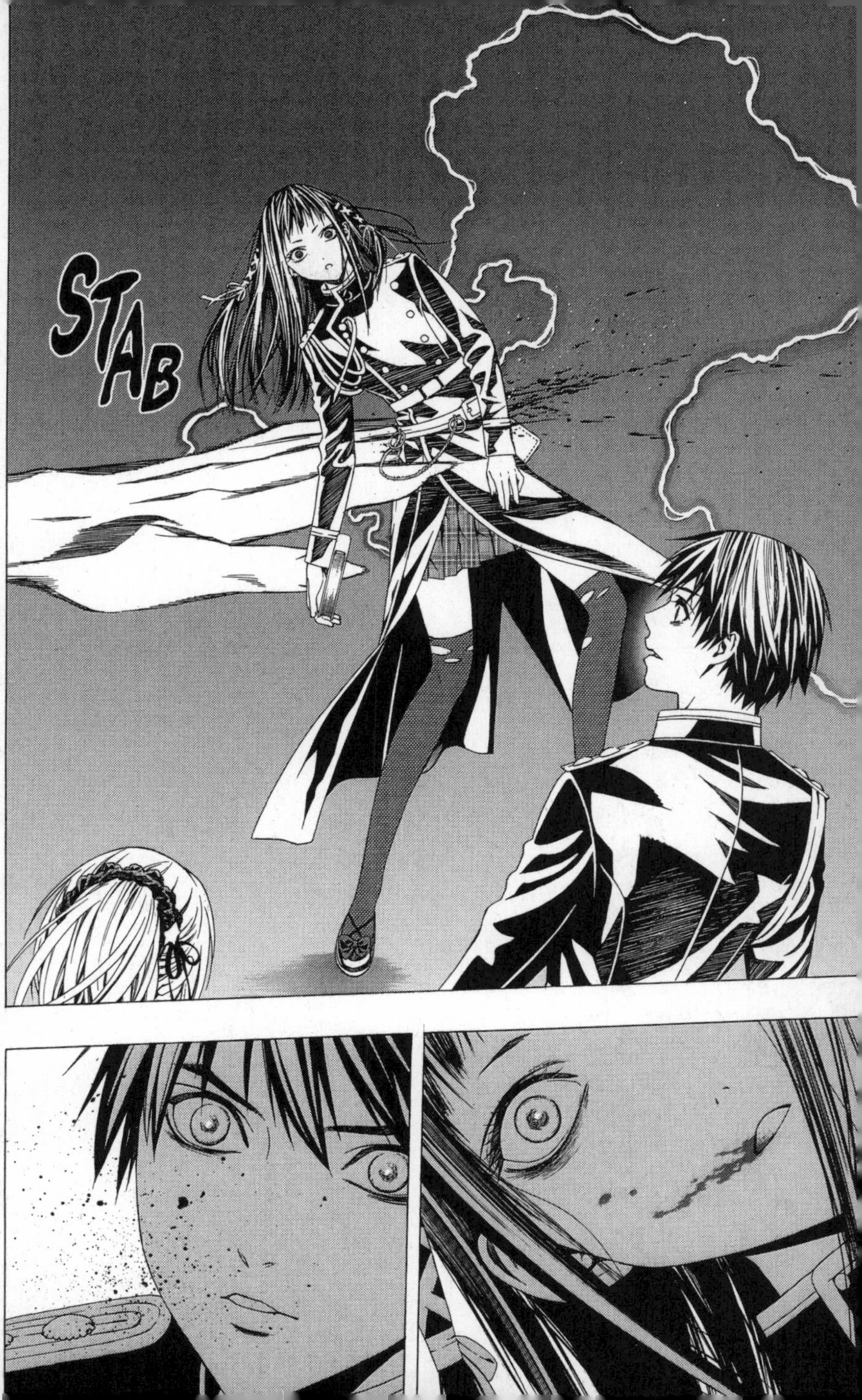
STAB

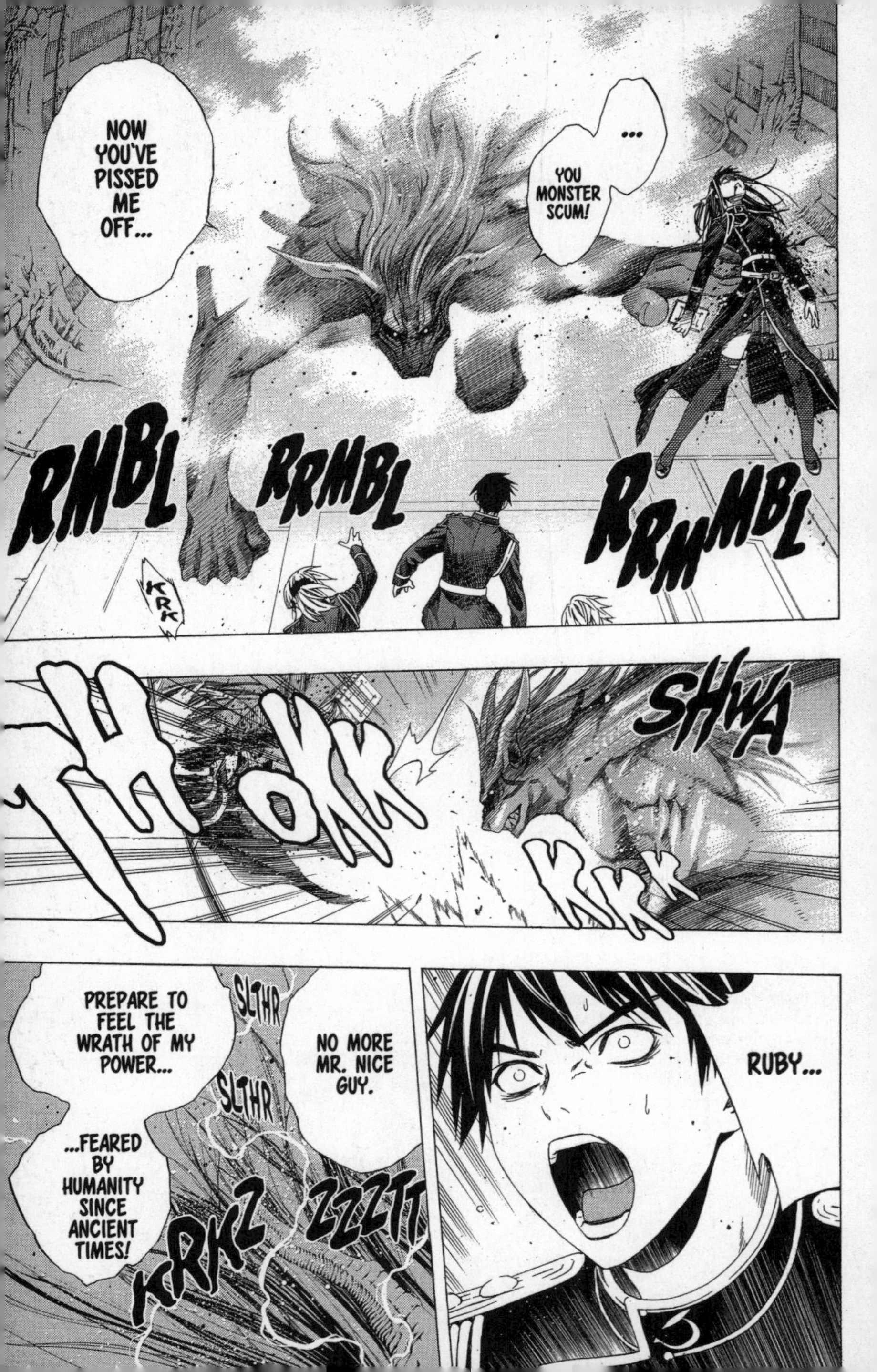
...
YOU MONSTER SCUM!
NOW YOU'VE PISSED ME OFF...
RRMMBL
RRMBL
RMBL
KRK
SHWA
KRK
THOKK
RUBY...
NO MORE MR. NICE GUY.
SLTHR
PREPARE TO FEEL THE WRATH OF MY POWER...
SLTHR
...FEARED BY HUMANITY SINCE ANCIENT TIMES!
ZZZTT
KRKZ

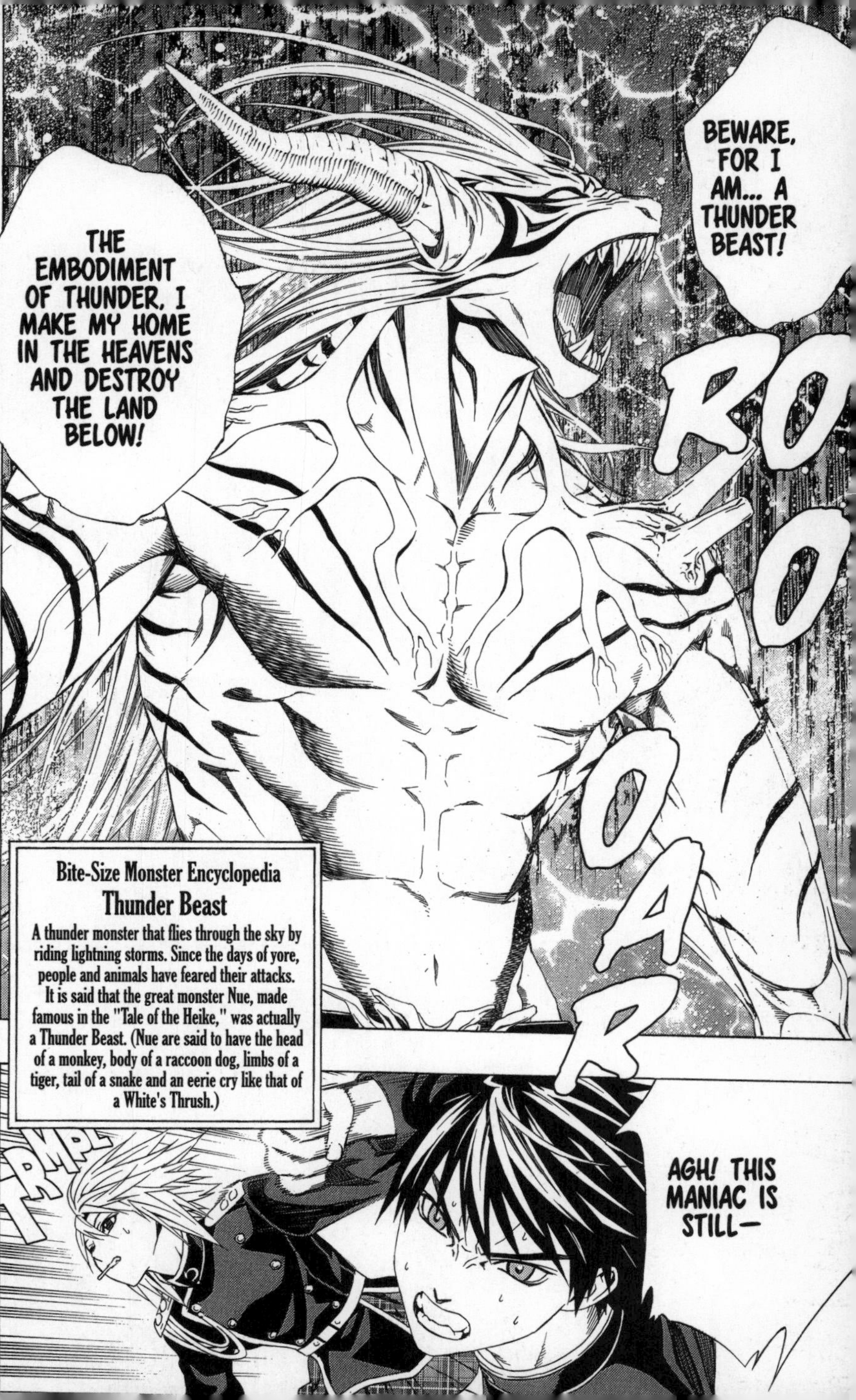
BEWARE, FOR I AM... A THUNDER BEAST!
THE EMBODIMENT OF THUNDER, I MAKE MY HOME IN THE HEAVENS AND DESTROY THE LAND BELOW!
ROOOOAR
Bite-Size Monster Encyclopedia
Thunder Beast
A thunder monster that flies through the sky by riding lightning storms. Since the days of yore, people and animals have feared their attacks. It is said that the great monster Nue, made famous in the "Tale of the Heike," was actually a Thunder Beast. (Nue are said to have the head of a monkey, body of a raccoon dog, limbs of a tiger, tail of a snake and an eerie cry like that of a White's Thrush.)
AGH! THIS MANIAC IS STILL—

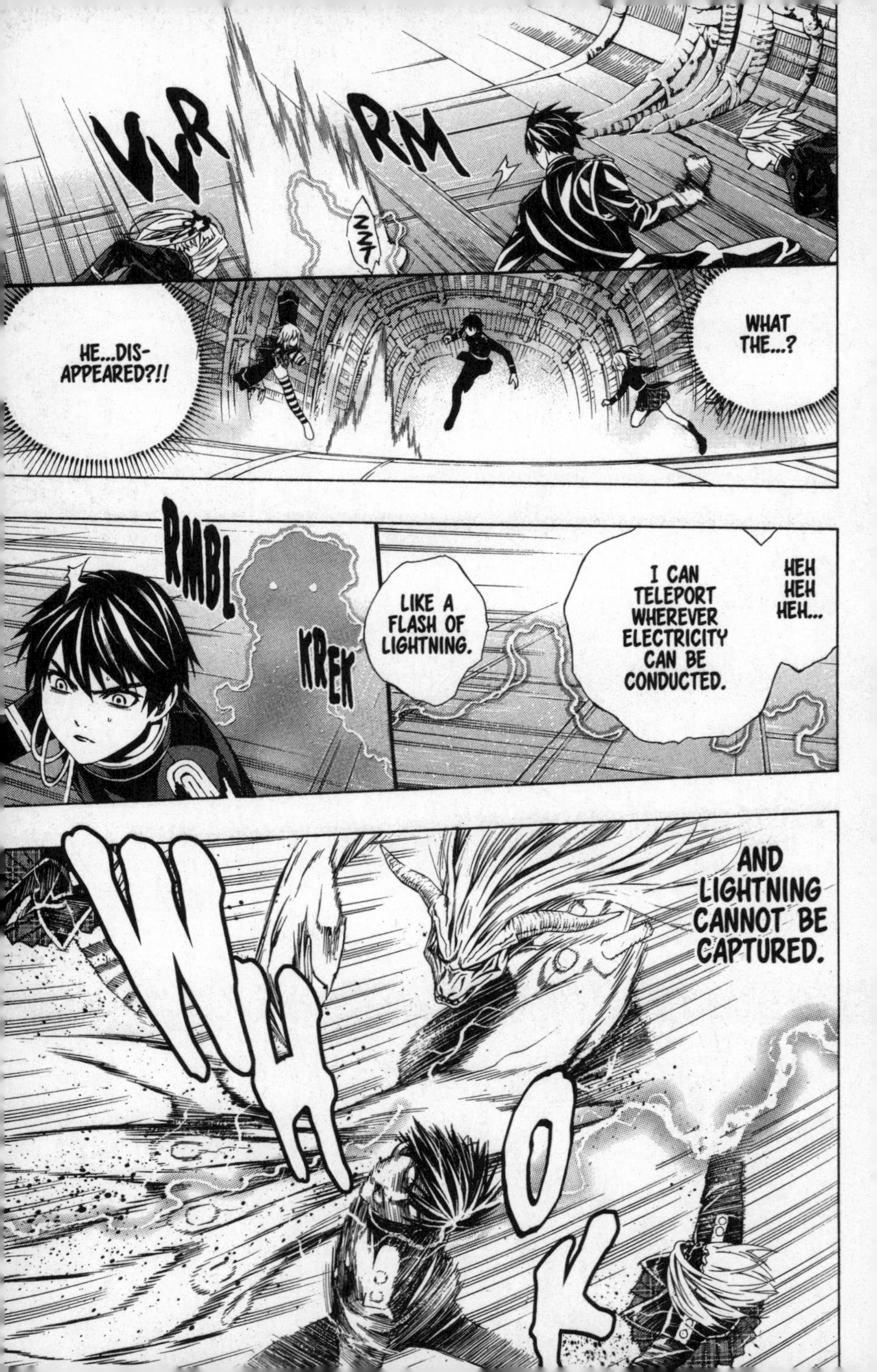
VVRRM
ZZZT
WHAT THE...?
HE...DIS-APPEARED?!!
HEH HEH HEH...
I CAN TELEPORT WHEREVER ELECTRICITY CAN BE CONDUCTED.
LIKE A FLASH OF LIGHTNING.
RMBL
KREK
AND LIGHTNING CANNOT BE CAPTURED.

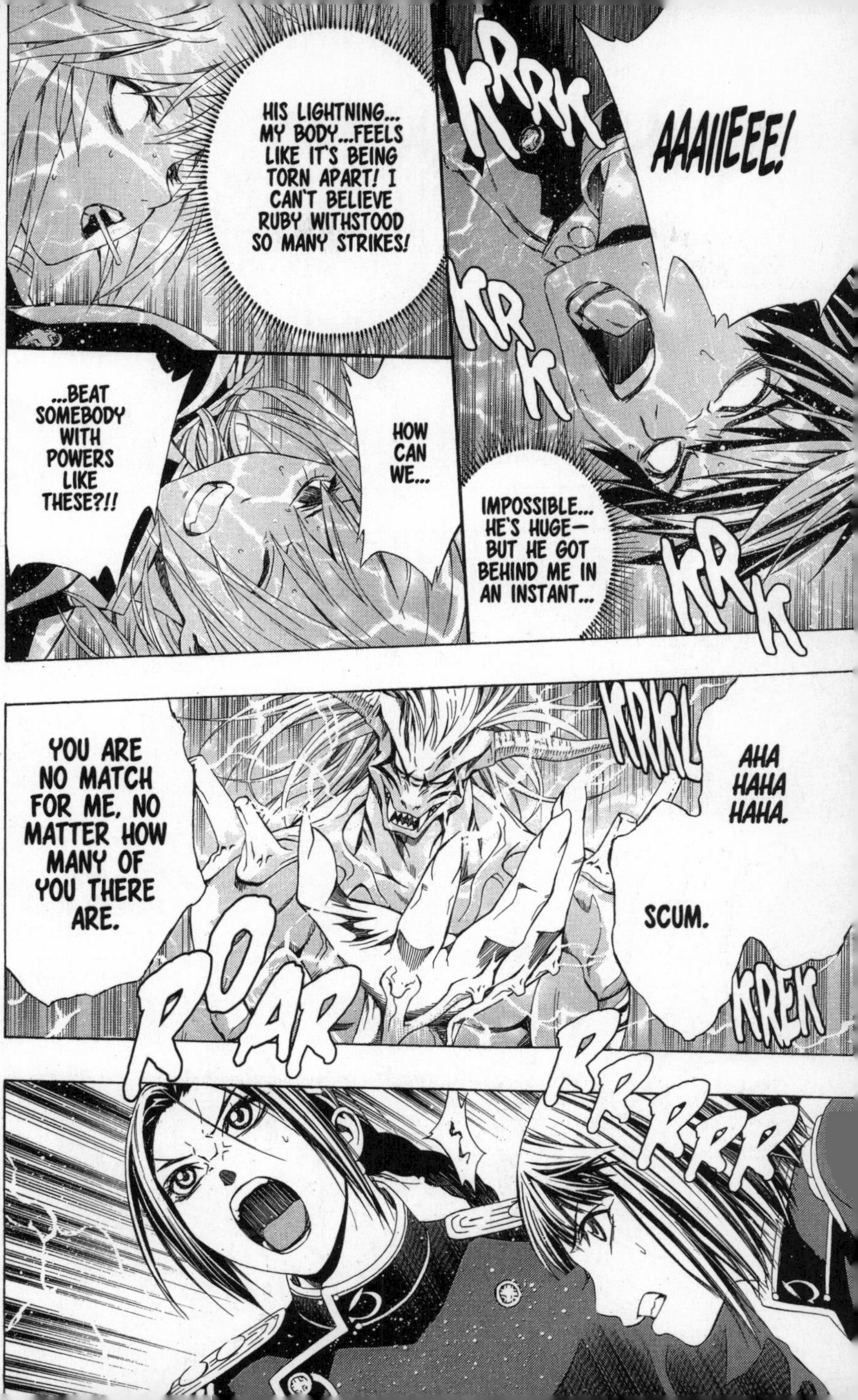
KRRK
AAAIIEEE!
KRK
IMPOSSIBLE... HE'S HUGE—BUT HE GOT BEHIND ME IN AN INSTANT...
KRK
HIS LIGHTNING... MY BODY...FEELS LIKE IT'S BEING TORN APART! I CAN'T BELIEVE RUBY WITHSTOOD SO MANY STRIKES!
HOW CAN WE...
...BEAT SOMEBODY WITH POWERS LIKE THESE?!!
KRRKL
AHA HAHA HAHA.
SCUM.
KREK
YOU ARE NO MATCH FOR ME, NO MATTER HOW MANY OF YOU THERE ARE.
ROAR
RRRRRR

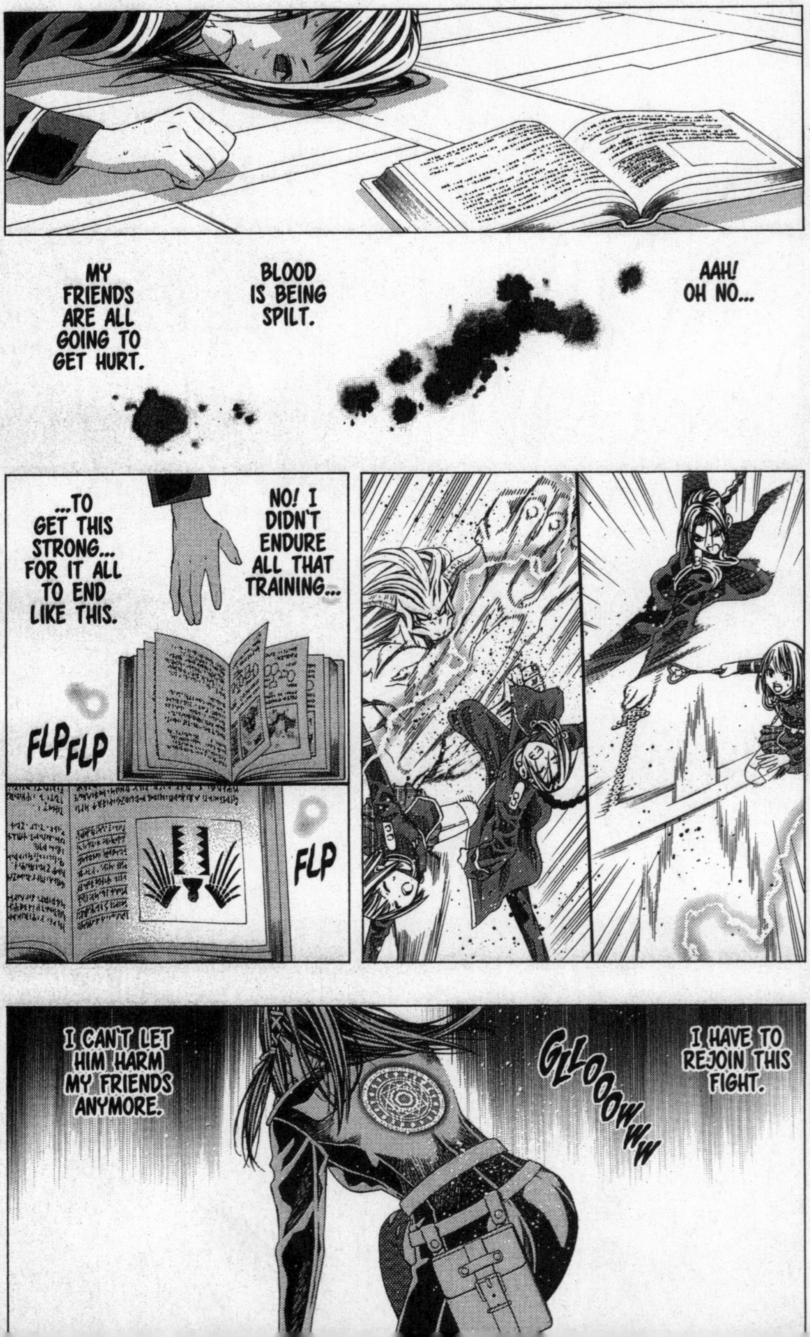
AAH! OH NO...
BLOOD IS BEING SPILT.
MY FRIENDS ARE ALL GOING TO GET HURT.
NO! I DIDN'T ENDURE ALL THAT TRAINING...
...TO GET THIS STRONG... FOR IT ALL TO END LIKE THIS.
FLP FLP
FLP
I HAVE TO REJOIN THIS FIGHT.
GLOOOWWW
I CAN'T LET HIM HARM MY FRIENDS ANYMORE.

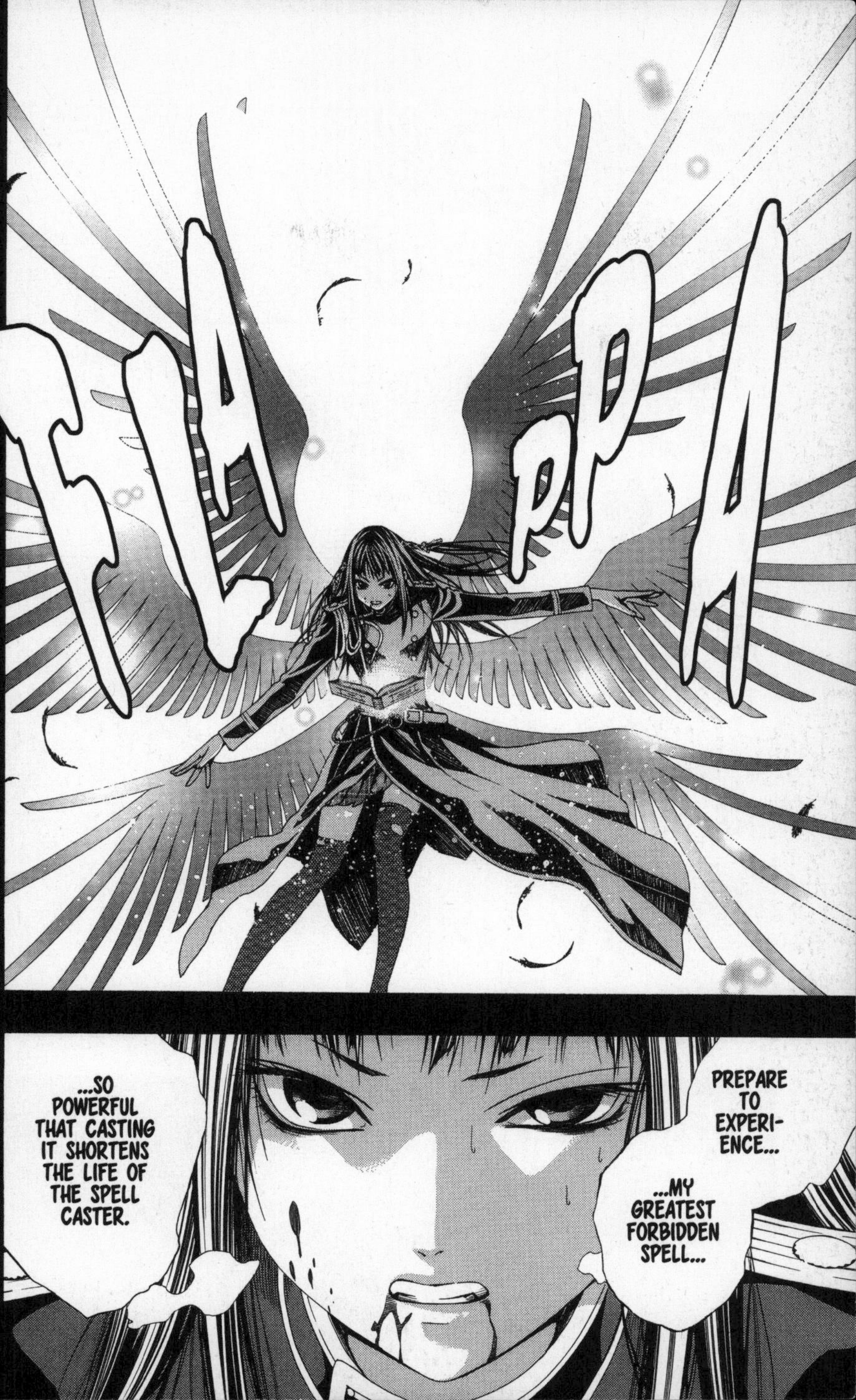
FLAPPA
PREPARE TO EXPERI-ENCE...
...MY GREATEST FORBIDDEN SPELL...
...SO POWERFUL THAT CASTING IT SHORTENS THE LIFE OF THE SPELL CASTER.

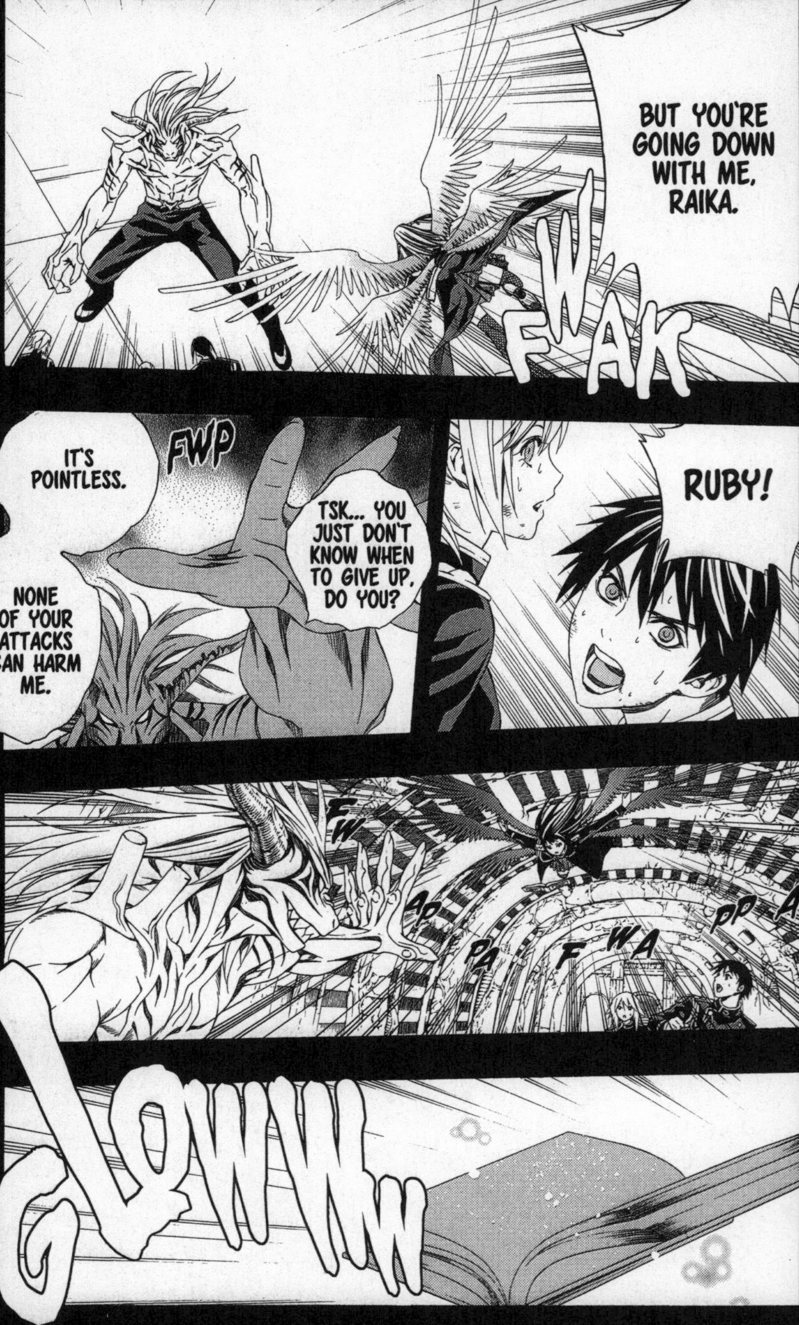
BUT YOU'RE GOING DOWN WITH ME, RAIKA.
FWAK
RUBY!
FWP
TSK... YOU JUST DON'T KNOW WHEN TO GIVE UP, DO YOU?
IT'S POINTLESS.
NONE OF YOUR ATTACKS CAN HARM ME.
FW
AP
PA
FWA
PP
A
GLOWWW

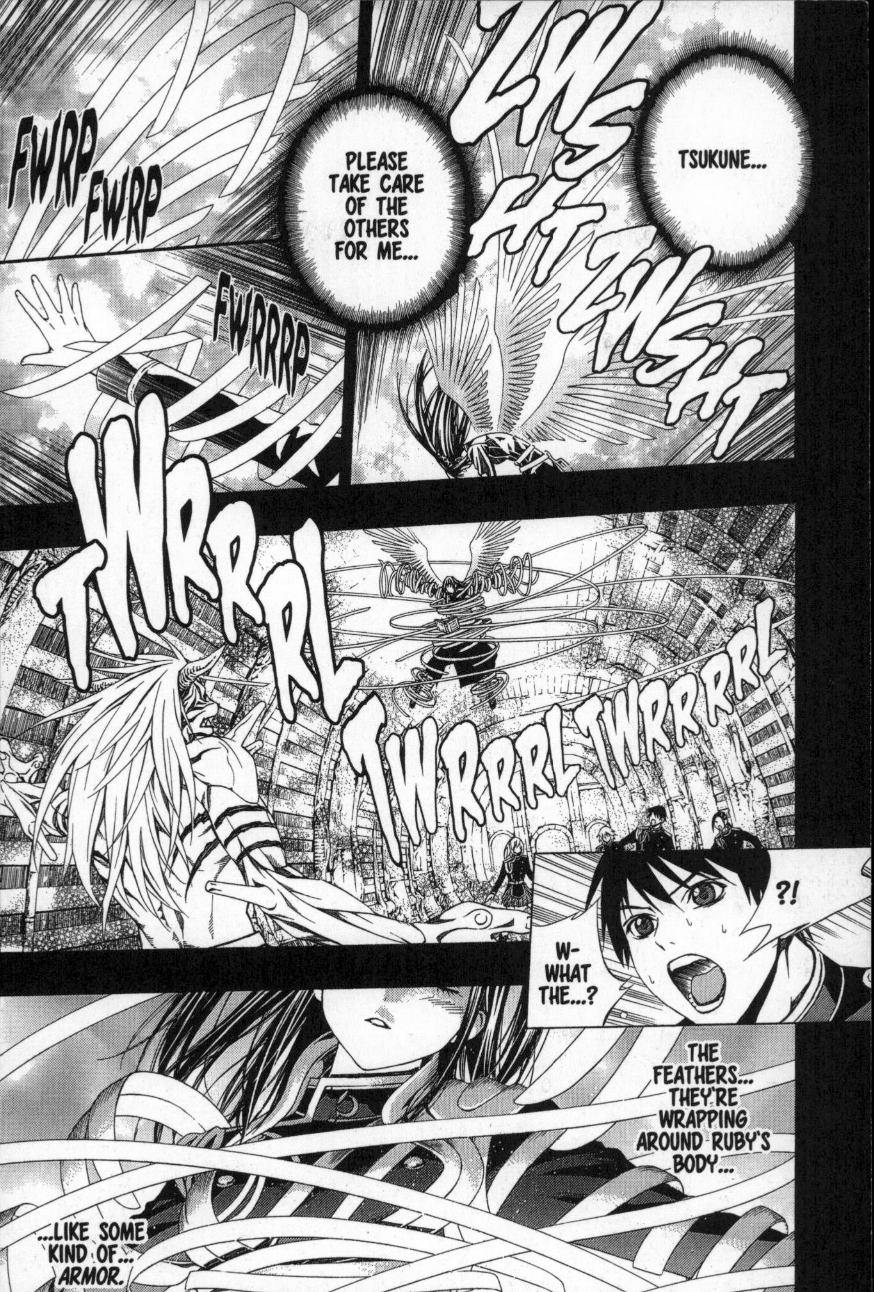
TSUKUNE...
PLEASE TAKE CARE OF THE OTHERS FOR ME...
FWRP FWRP
FWRRRP
TWRRRL
TWRRRL TWRRRRL
?!
W-WHAT THE...?
THE FEATHERS... THEY'RE WRAPPING AROUND RUBY'S BODY...
...LIKE SOME KIND OF... ARMOR.

46: If My Love Reaches Him

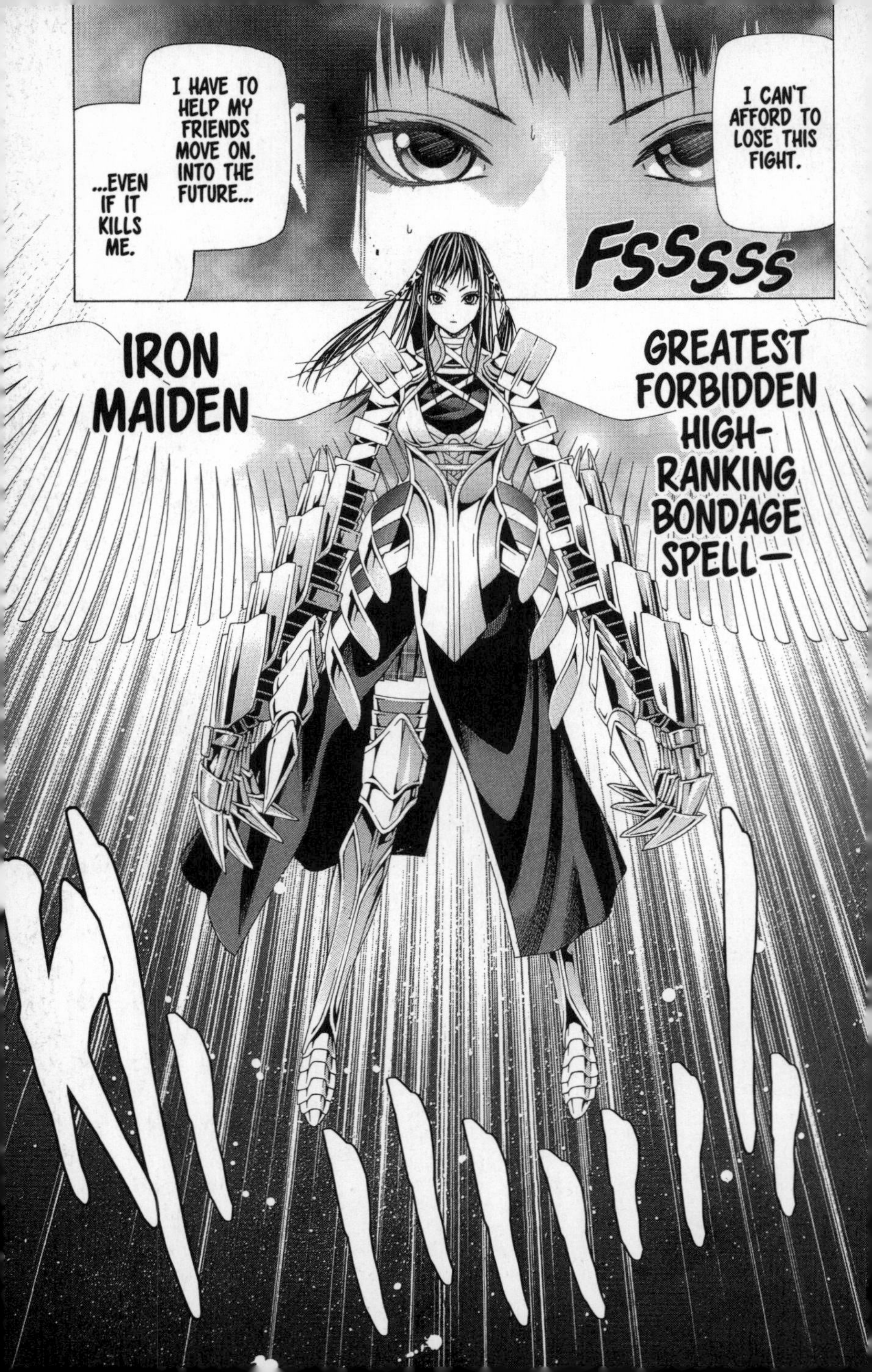
I CAN'T AFFORD TO LOSE THIS FIGHT.
I HAVE TO HELP MY FRIENDS MOVE ON. INTO THE FUTURE...
...EVEN IF IT KILLS ME.
FSSSSS
GREATEST FORBIDDEN HIGH-RANKING BONDAGE SPELL—
IRON MAIDEN

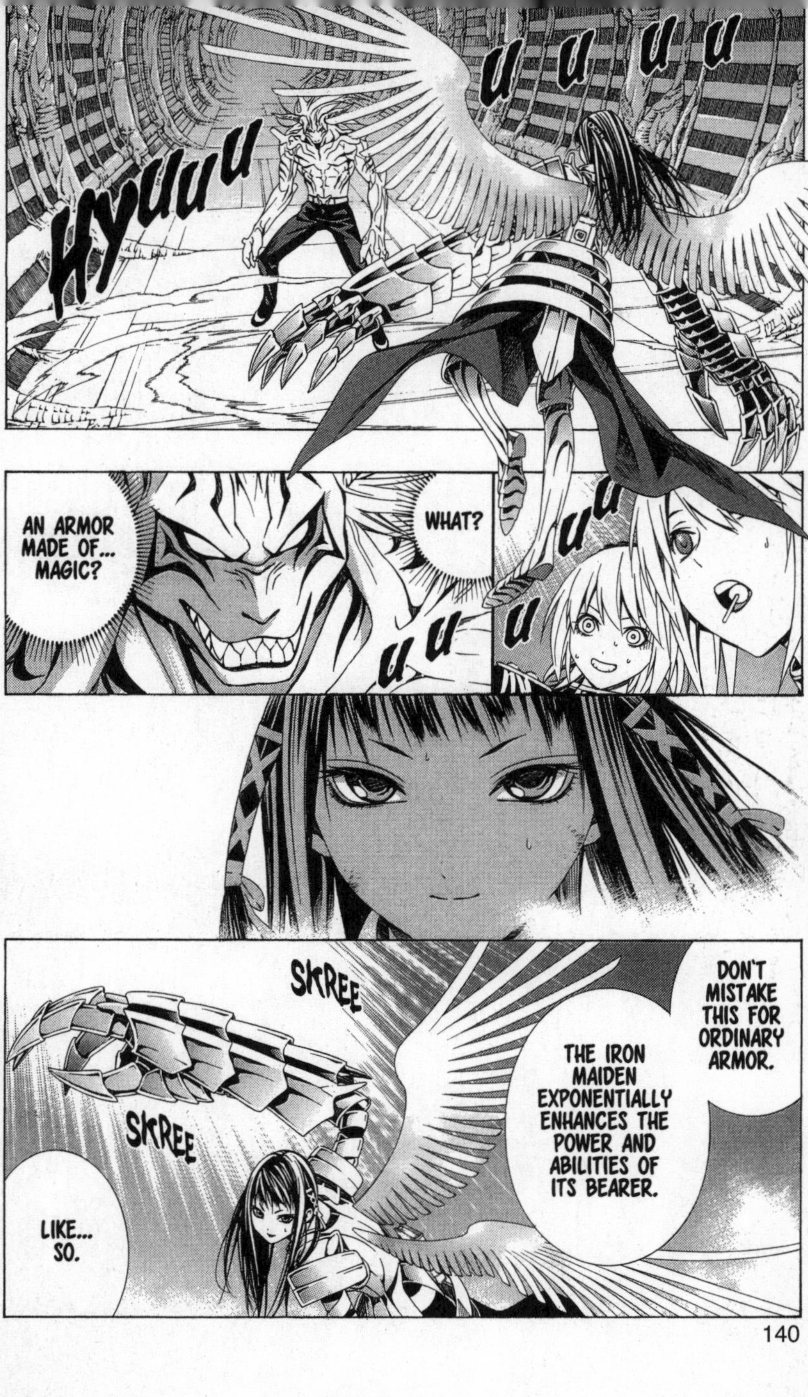
UUUUU
HYUUU
UUUU
WHAT?
AN ARMOR MADE OF... MAGIC?
UU
DON'T MISTAKE THIS FOR ORDINARY ARMOR.
THE IRON MAIDEN EXPONENTIALLY ENHANCES THE POWER AND ABILITIES OF ITS BEARER.
SKREE
SKREE
LIKE... SO.

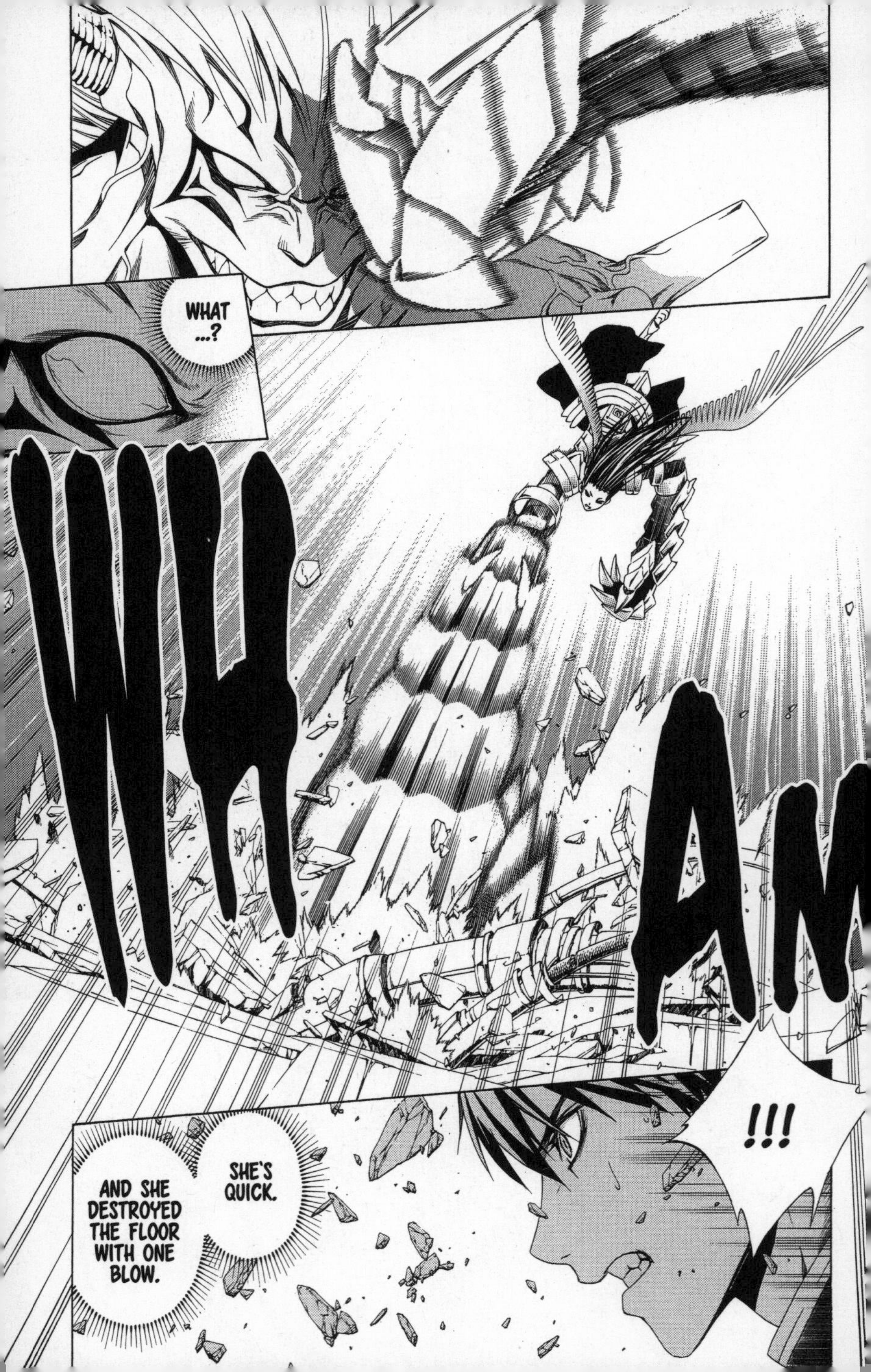
WHAT ...?
WHAM
!!!
SHE'S QUICK.
AND SHE DESTROYED THE FLOOR WITH ONE BLOW.

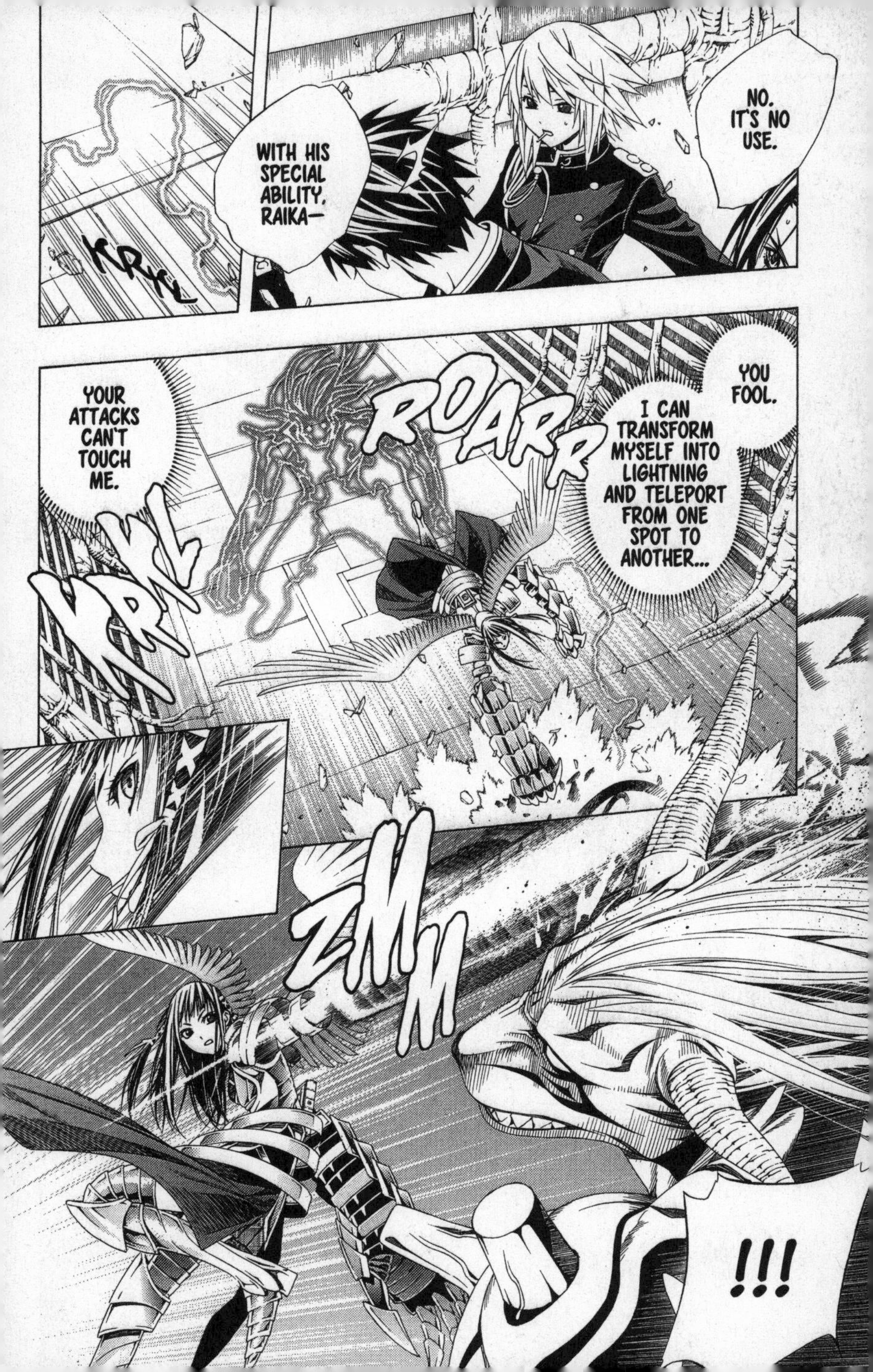
NO. IT'S NO USE.
WITH HIS SPECIAL ABILITY, RAIKA—
KRKL
YOU FOOL.
I CAN TRANSFORM MYSELF INTO LIGHTNING AND TELEPORT FROM ONE SPOT TO ANOTHER...
ROARR
YOUR ATTACKS CAN'T TOUCH ME.
VRKL
ZMMM
!!!

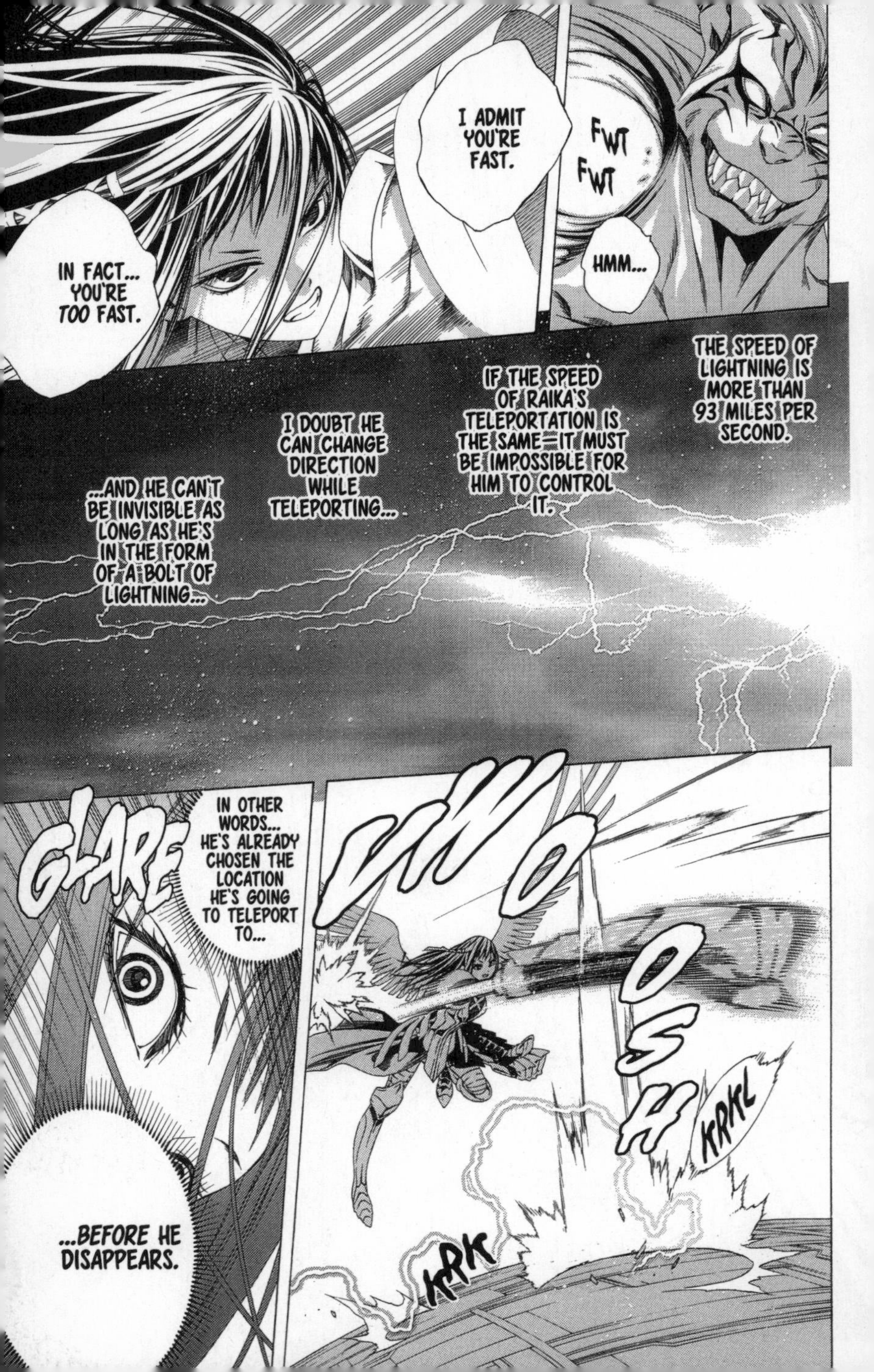
I ADMIT YOU'RE FAST.
FWT FWT
HMM...
IN FACT... YOU'RE TOO FAST.
THE SPEED OF LIGHTNING IS MORE THAN 93 MILES PER SECOND.
IF THE SPEED OF RAIKA'S TELEPORTATION IS THE SAME—IT MUST BE IMPOSSIBLE FOR HIM TO CONTROL IT.
I DOUBT HE CAN CHANGE DIRECTION WHILE TELEPORTING...
...AND HE CAN'T BE INVISIBLE AS LONG AS HE'S IN THE FORM OF A BOLT OF LIGHTNING...
WHOOSH
KRKL
KRK
GLARE
IN OTHER WORDS... HE'S ALREADY CHOSEN THE LOCATION HE'S GOING TO TELEPORT TO...
...BEFORE HE DISAPPEARS.

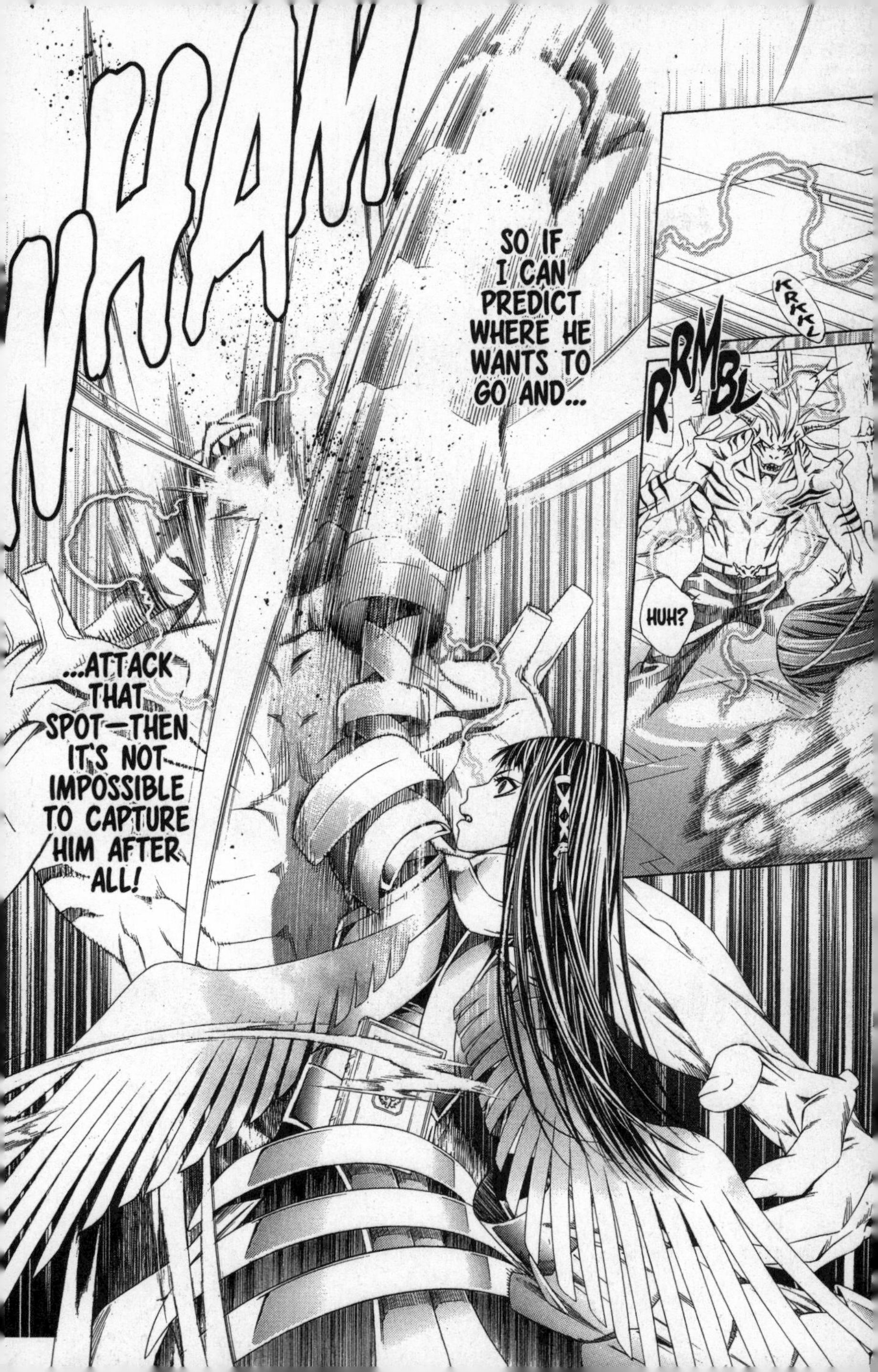
KRKKL
RRMBL
HUH?
WHAM
SO IF I CAN PREDICT WHERE HE WANTS TO GO AND...
...ATTACK THAT SPOT—THEN IT'S NOT IMPOSSIBLE TO CAPTURE HIM AFTER ALL!

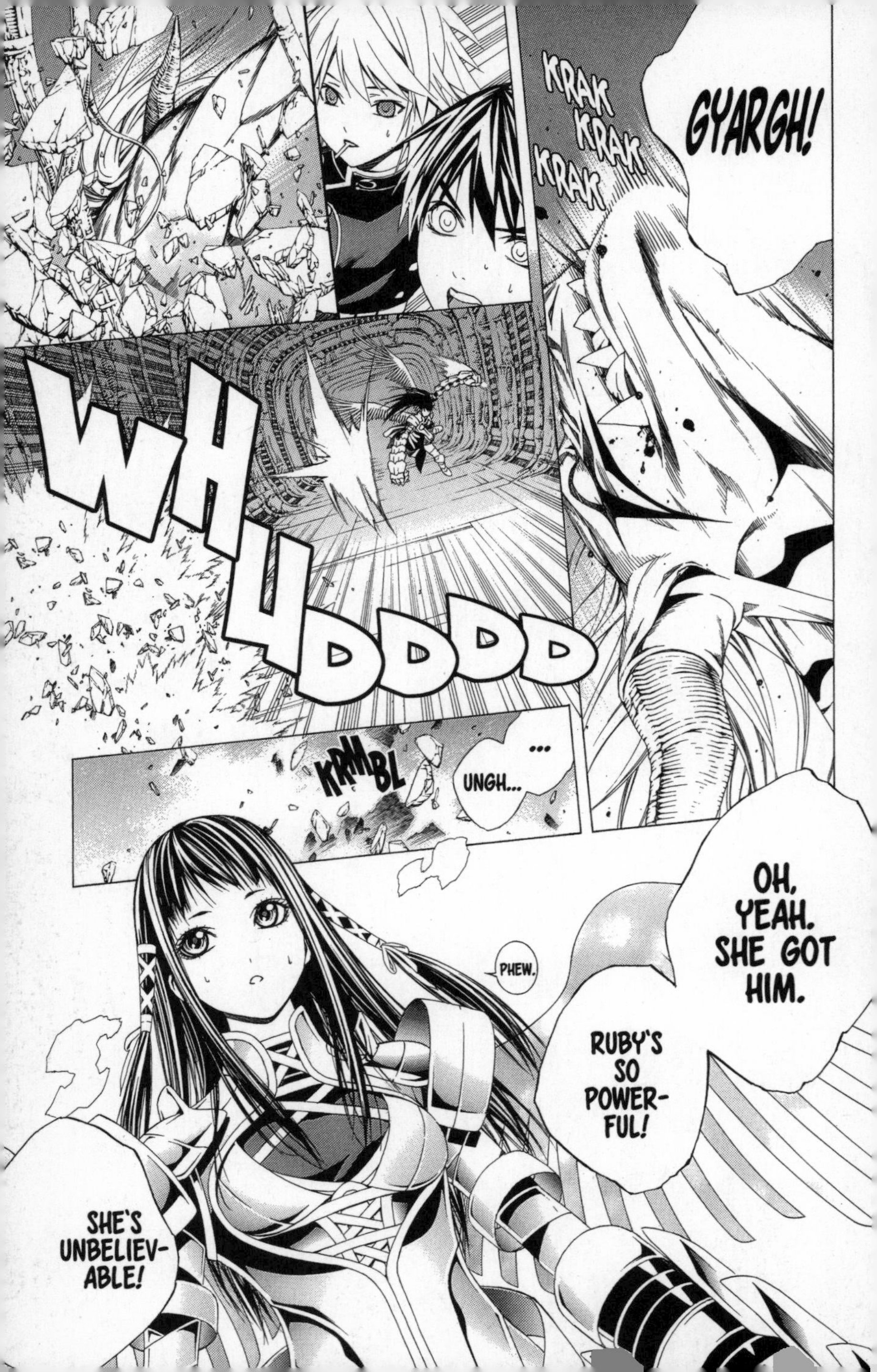
GYARGH!
KRAK KRAK KRAK
WHUDDDDD
...
UNGH...
KRMBL
OH, YEAH. SHE GOT HIM.
PHEW.
RUBY'S SO POWER-FUL!
SHE'S UNBELIEV-ABLE!

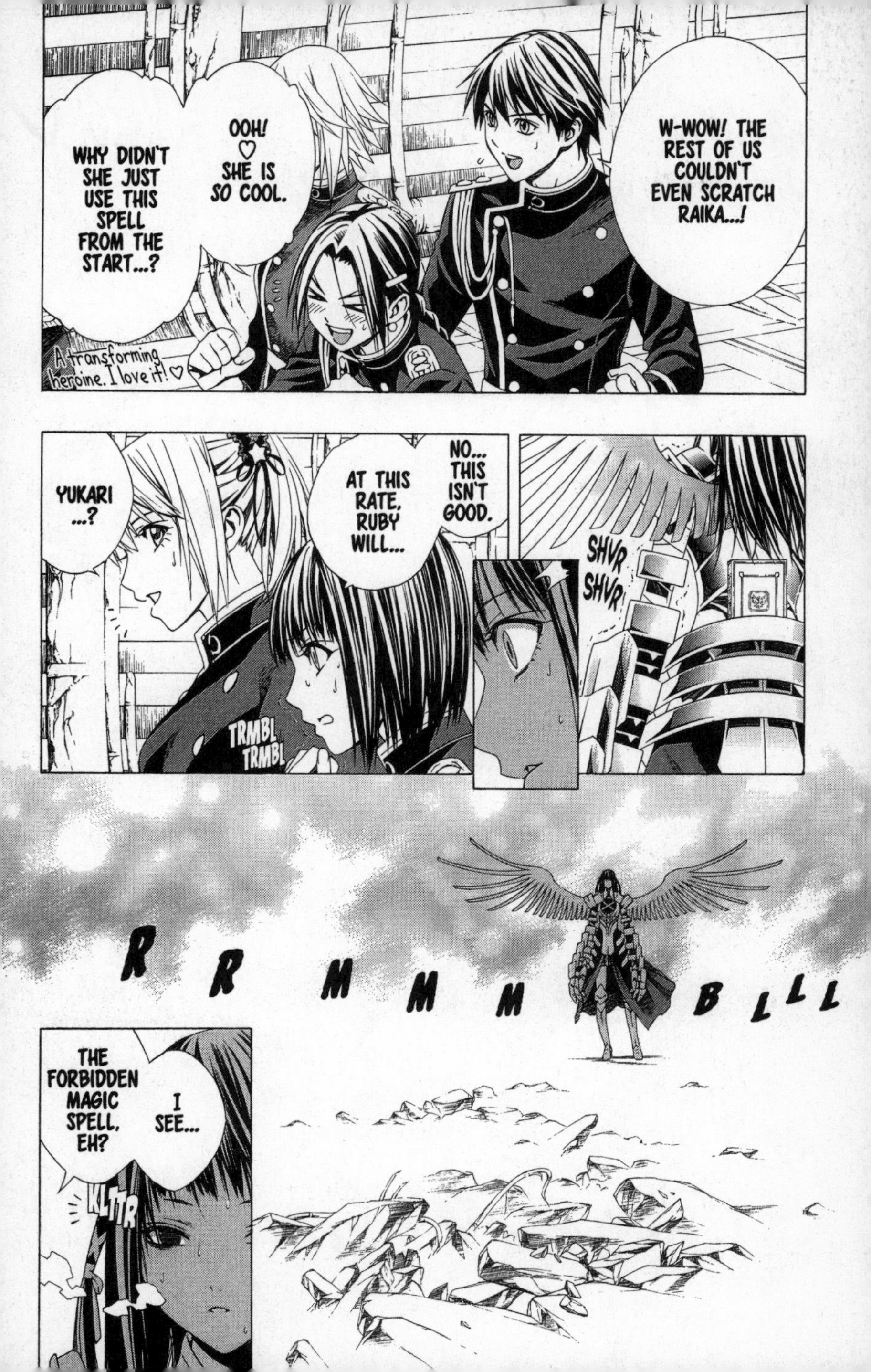
W-WOW! THE REST OF US COULDN'T EVEN SCRATCH RAIKA...!
OOH! ♡ SHE IS SO COOL.
WHY DIDN'T SHE JUST USE THIS SPELL FROM THE START...?
A transforming heroine. I love it! ♡
SHVR SHVR
NO... THIS ISN'T GOOD.
AT THIS RATE, RUBY WILL...
YUKARI ...?
TRMBL TRMBL
RRMMMBLLL
I SEE...
THE FORBIDDEN MAGIC SPELL, EH?
KLTTR

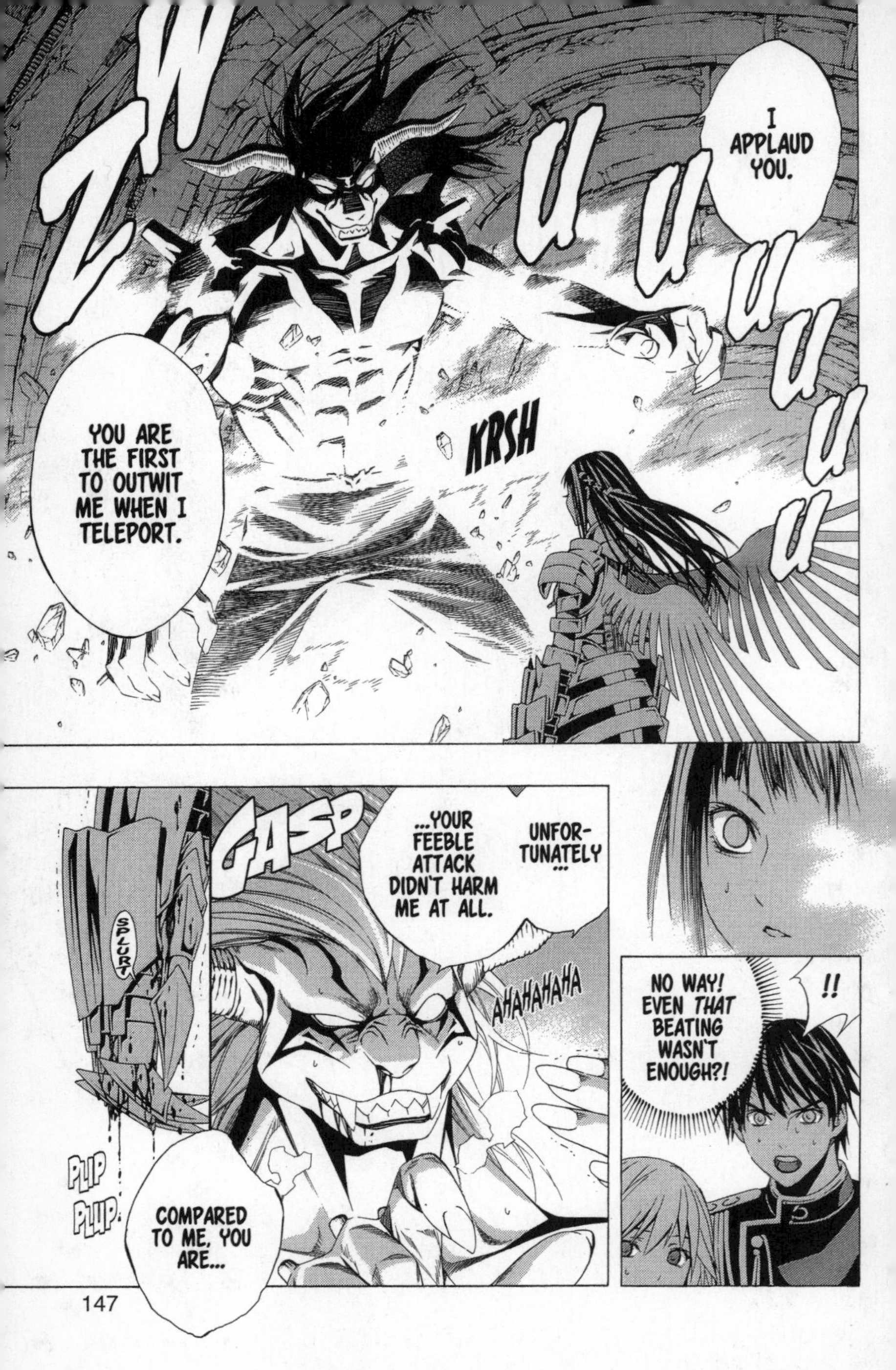
ZWUUUUUUUUU
I APPLAUD YOU.
KRSH
YOU ARE THE FIRST TO OUTWIT ME WHEN I TELEPORT.
!!
NO WAY! EVEN *THAT* BEATING WASN'T ENOUGH?!
UNFOR-TUNATELY...
...YOUR FEEBLE ATTACK DIDN'T HARM ME AT ALL.
GASP
AHAHAHAHA
COMPARED TO ME, YOU ARE...
SPLURT
PLIP
PLIP

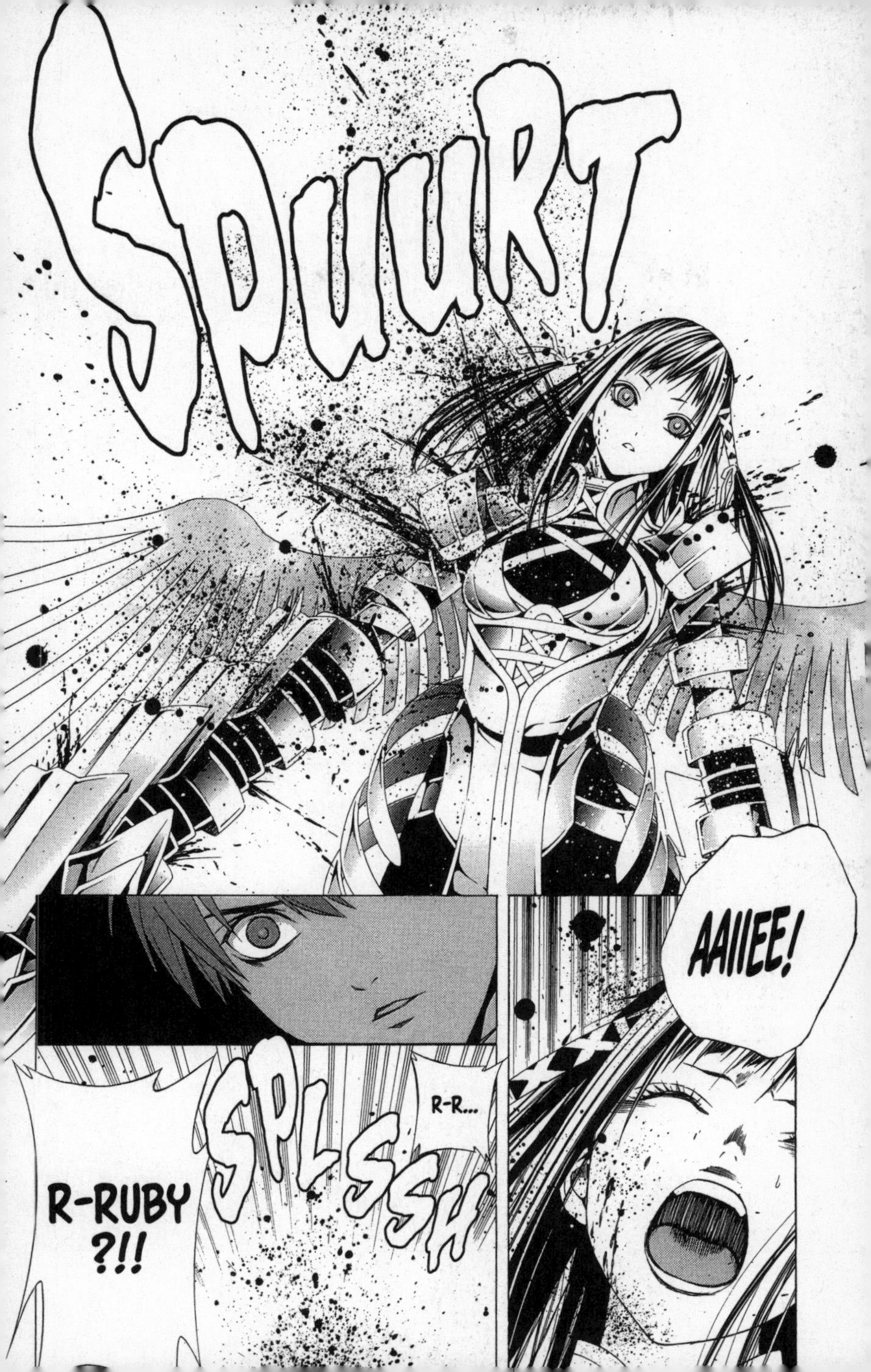
SPUURT
AAIIEE!
R-R...
SPLSSH
R-RUBY ?!!

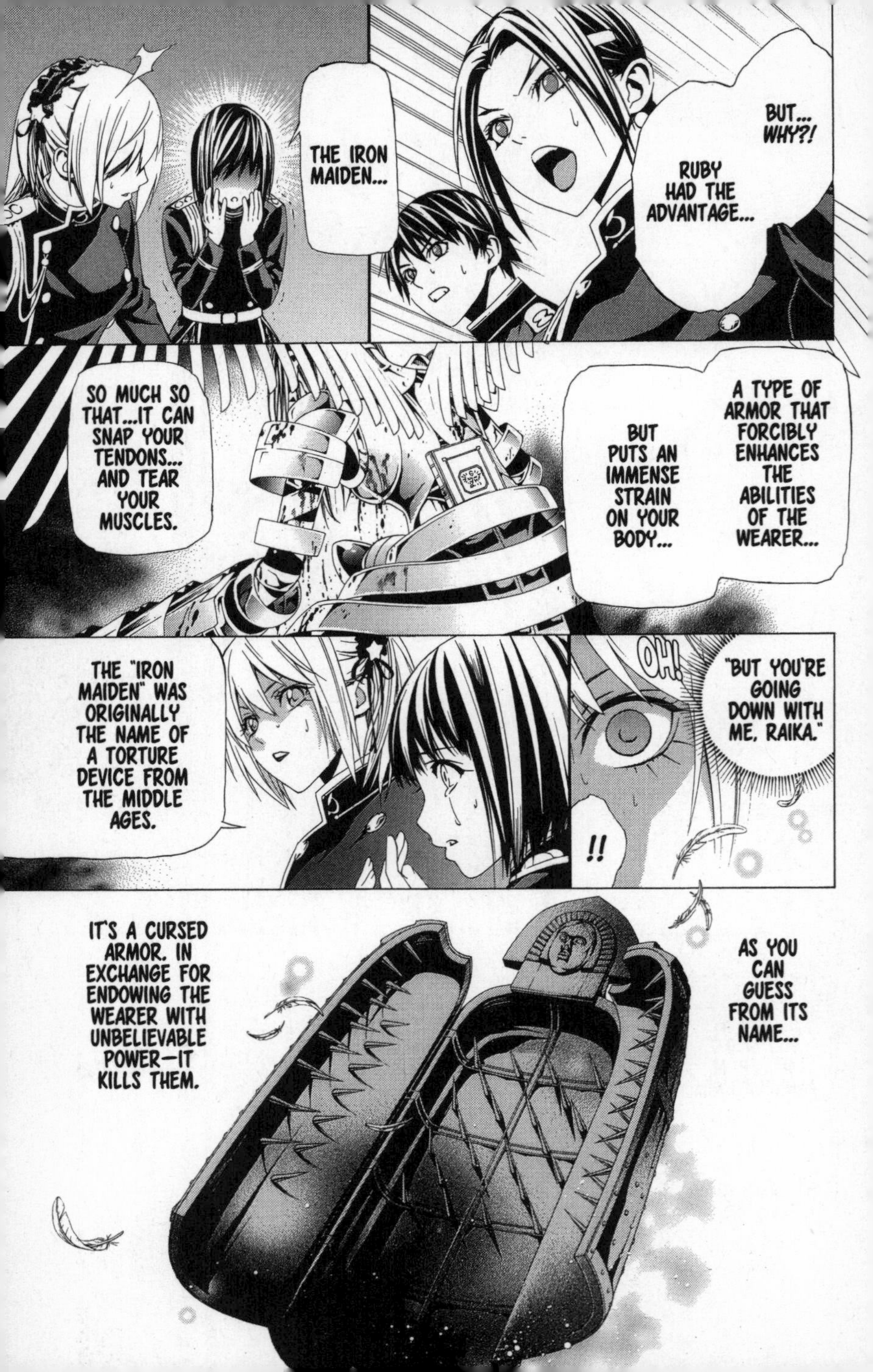
BUT... WHY?!
RUBY HAD THE ADVANTAGE...
THE IRON MAIDEN...
A TYPE OF ARMOR THAT FORCIBLY ENHANCES THE ABILITIES OF THE WEARER...
BUT PUTS AN IMMENSE STRAIN ON YOUR BODY...
SO MUCH SO THAT...IT CAN SNAP YOUR TENDONS... AND TEAR YOUR MUSCLES.
OH!
"BUT YOU'RE GOING DOWN WITH ME, RAIKA."
!!
THE "IRON MAIDEN" WAS ORIGINALLY THE NAME OF A TORTURE DEVICE FROM THE MIDDLE AGES.
AS YOU CAN GUESS FROM ITS NAME...
IT'S A CURSED ARMOR. IN EXCHANGE FOR ENDOWING THE WEARER WITH UNBELIEVABLE POWER—IT KILLS THEM.

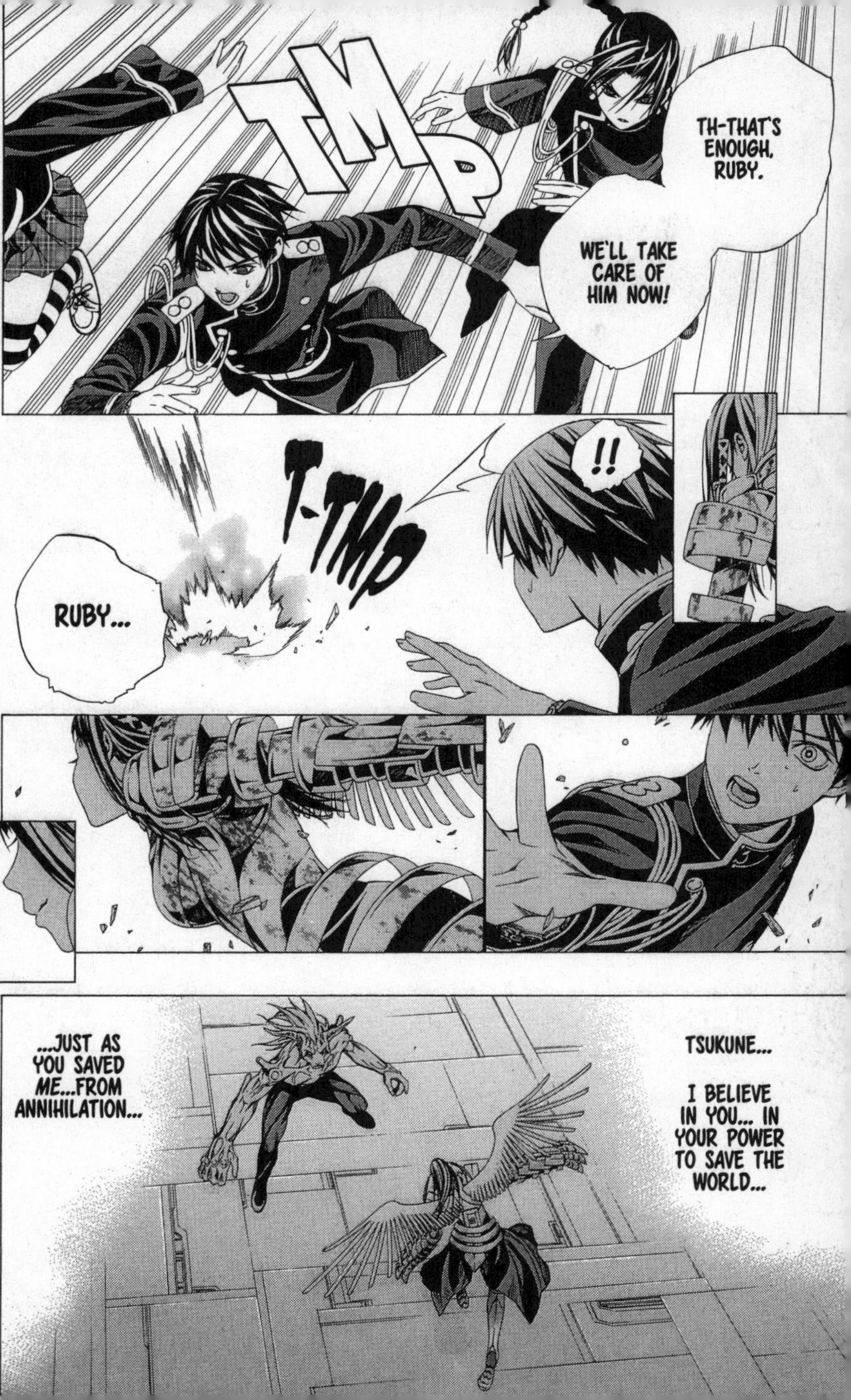
TH-THAT'S ENOUGH, RUBY.
WE'LL TAKE CARE OF HIM NOW!
TMP
!!
T-TMP
RUBY...
TSUKUNE...
I BELIEVE IN YOU... IN YOUR POWER TO SAVE THE WORLD...
...JUST AS YOU SAVED *ME*...FROM ANNIHILATION...

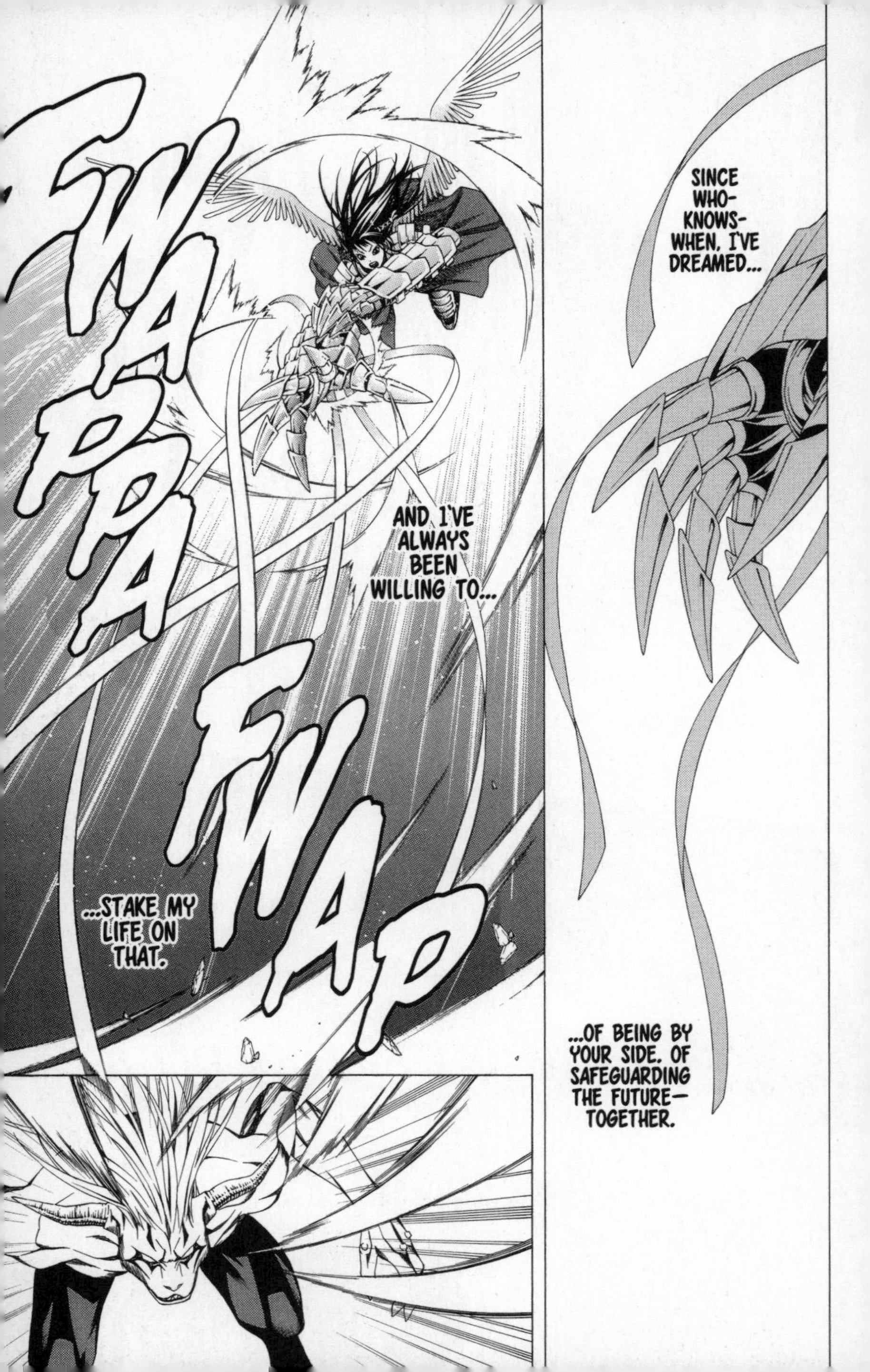
SINCE WHO-KNOWS-WHEN, I'VE DREAMED...
...OF BEING BY YOUR SIDE. OF SAFEGUARDING THE FUTURE—TOGETHER.
FWAPPA
AND I'VE ALWAYS BEEN WILLING TO...
FWAP
...STAKE MY LIFE ON THAT.

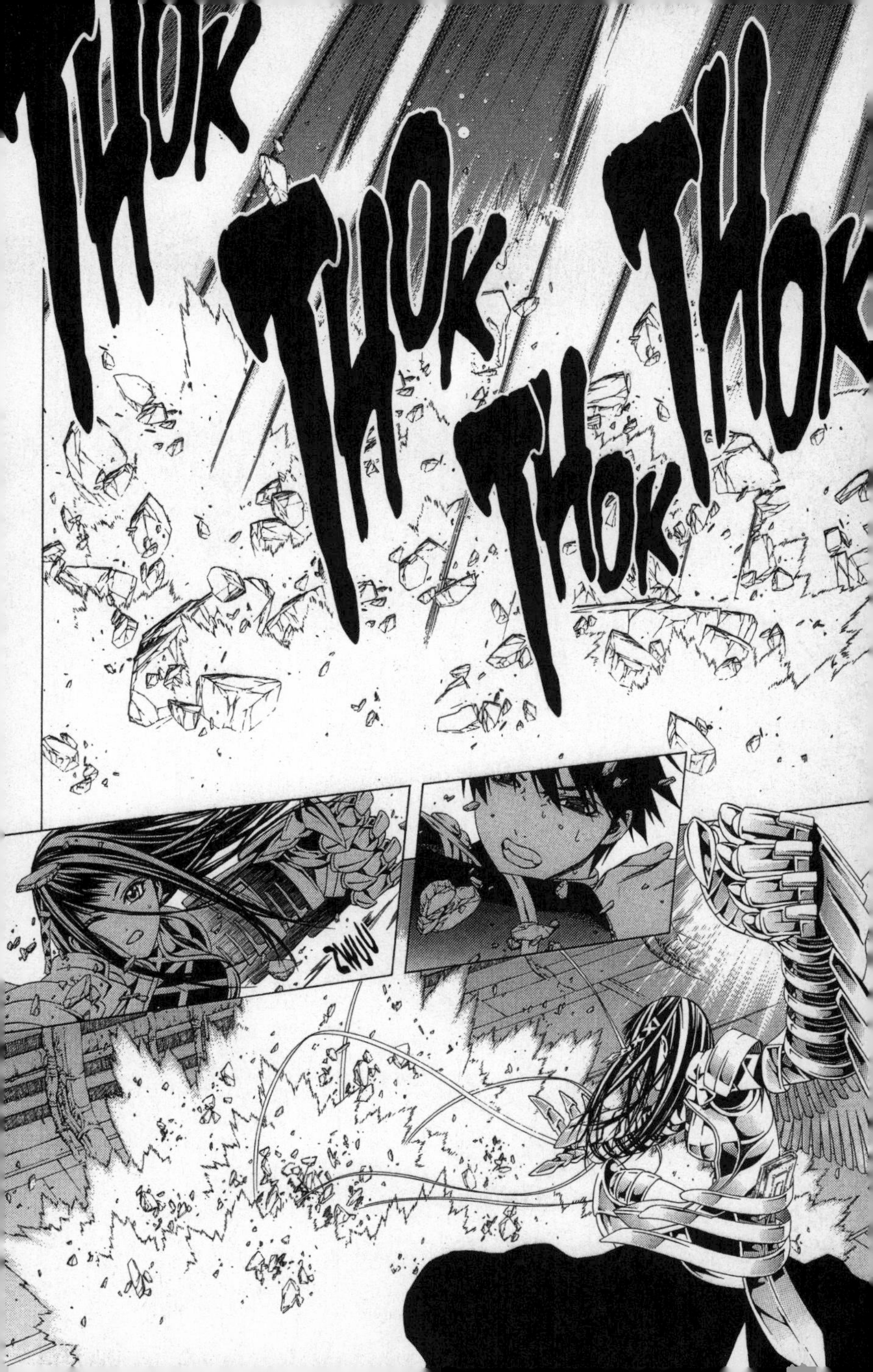
THOK
THOK
THOK
THOK
ZWUU

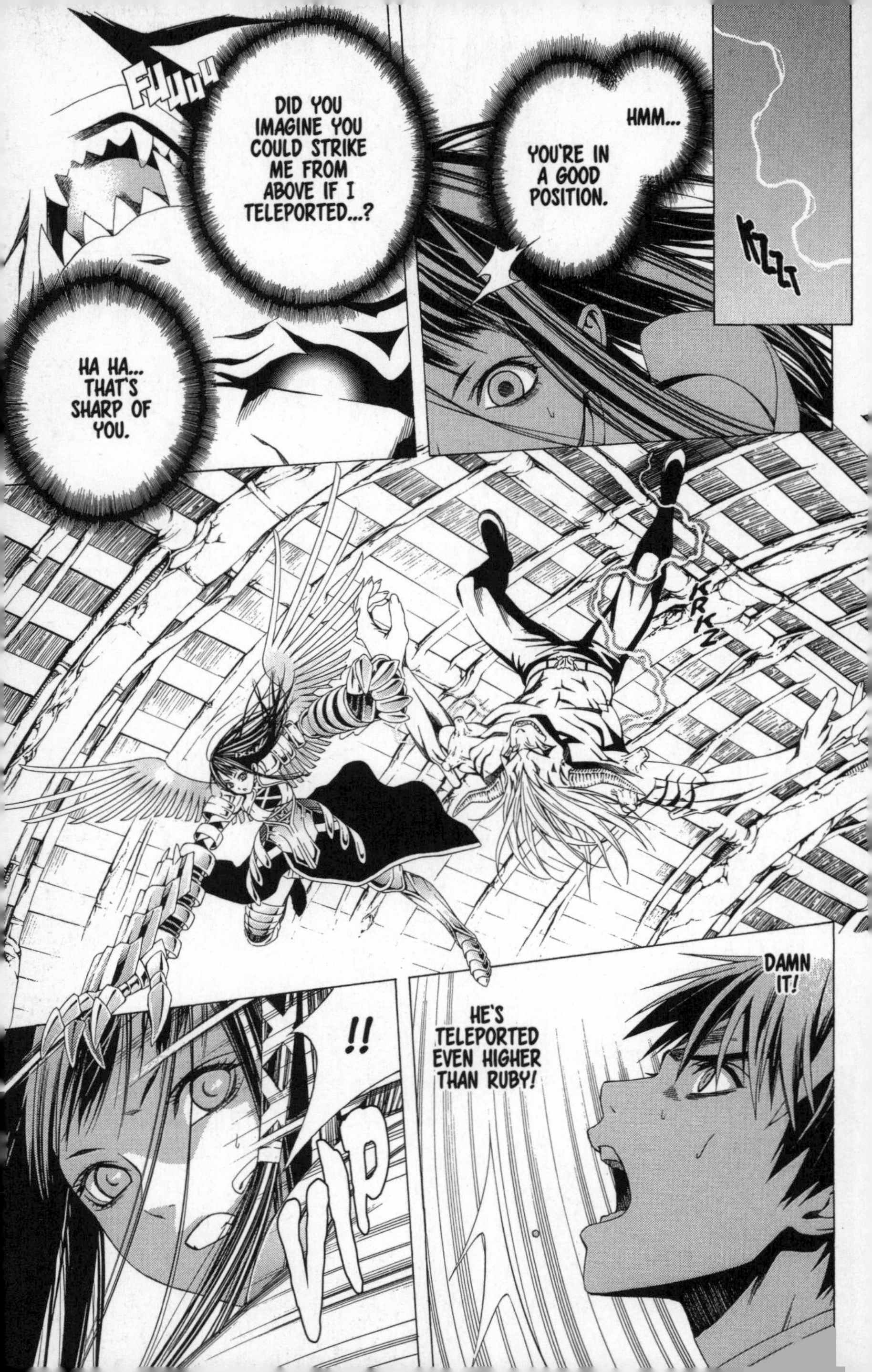
KZZZT
HMM...
YOU'RE IN A GOOD POSITION.
FUUUU
DID YOU IMAGINE YOU COULD STRIKE ME FROM ABOVE IF I TELEPORTED...?
HA HA... THAT'S SHARP OF YOU.
KRKZ
DAMN IT!
HE'S TELEPORTED EVEN HIGHER THAN RUBY!
!!
VIP

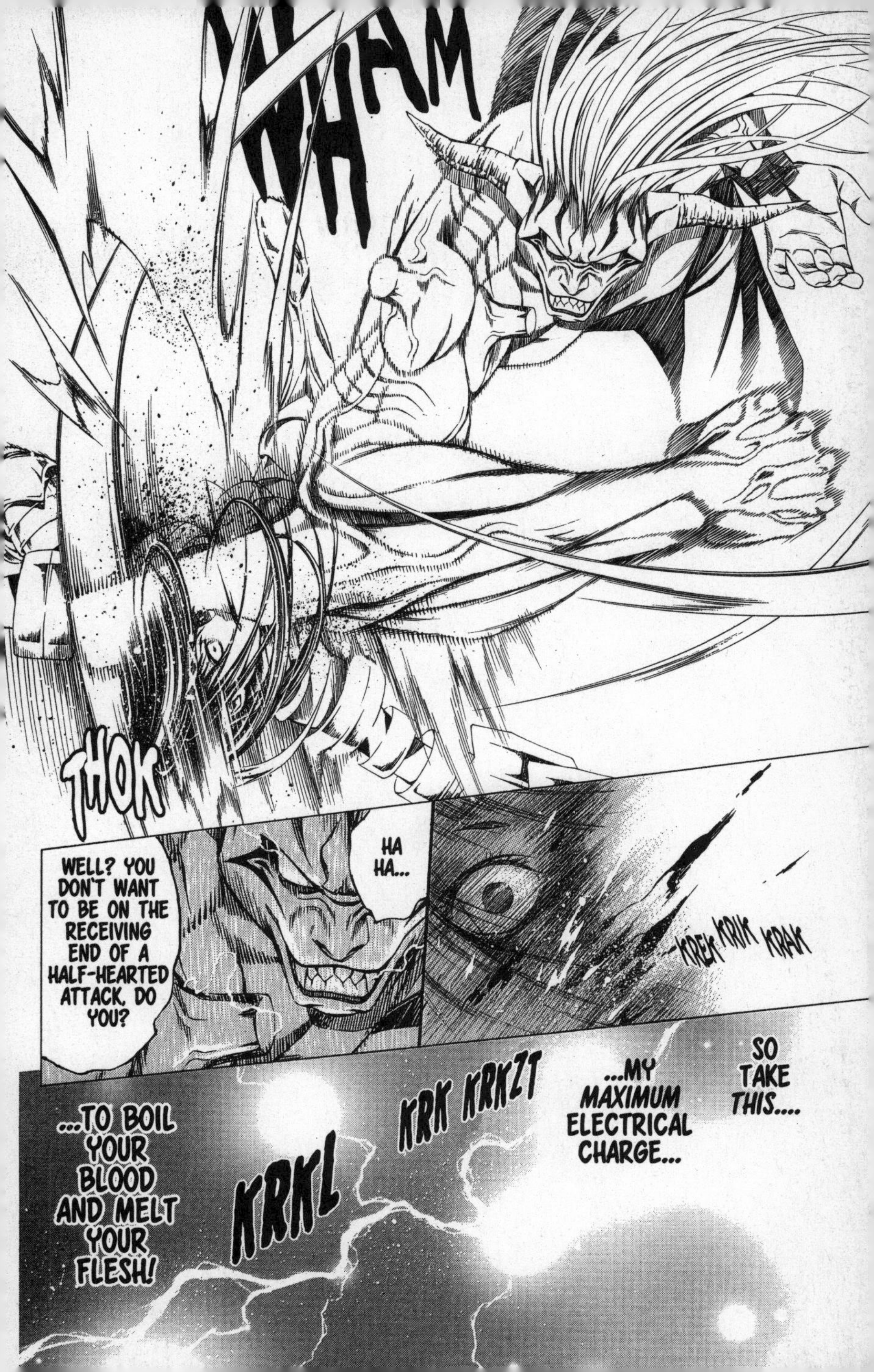
WHAM
THOK
KREK KRIK KRAK
HA HA...
WELL? YOU DON'T WANT TO BE ON THE RECEIVING END OF A HALF-HEARTED ATTACK, DO YOU?
SO TAKE THIS....
...MY MAXIMUM ELECTRICAL CHARGE...
KRK KRKZT
KRKL
...TO BOIL YOUR BLOOD AND MELT YOUR FLESH!

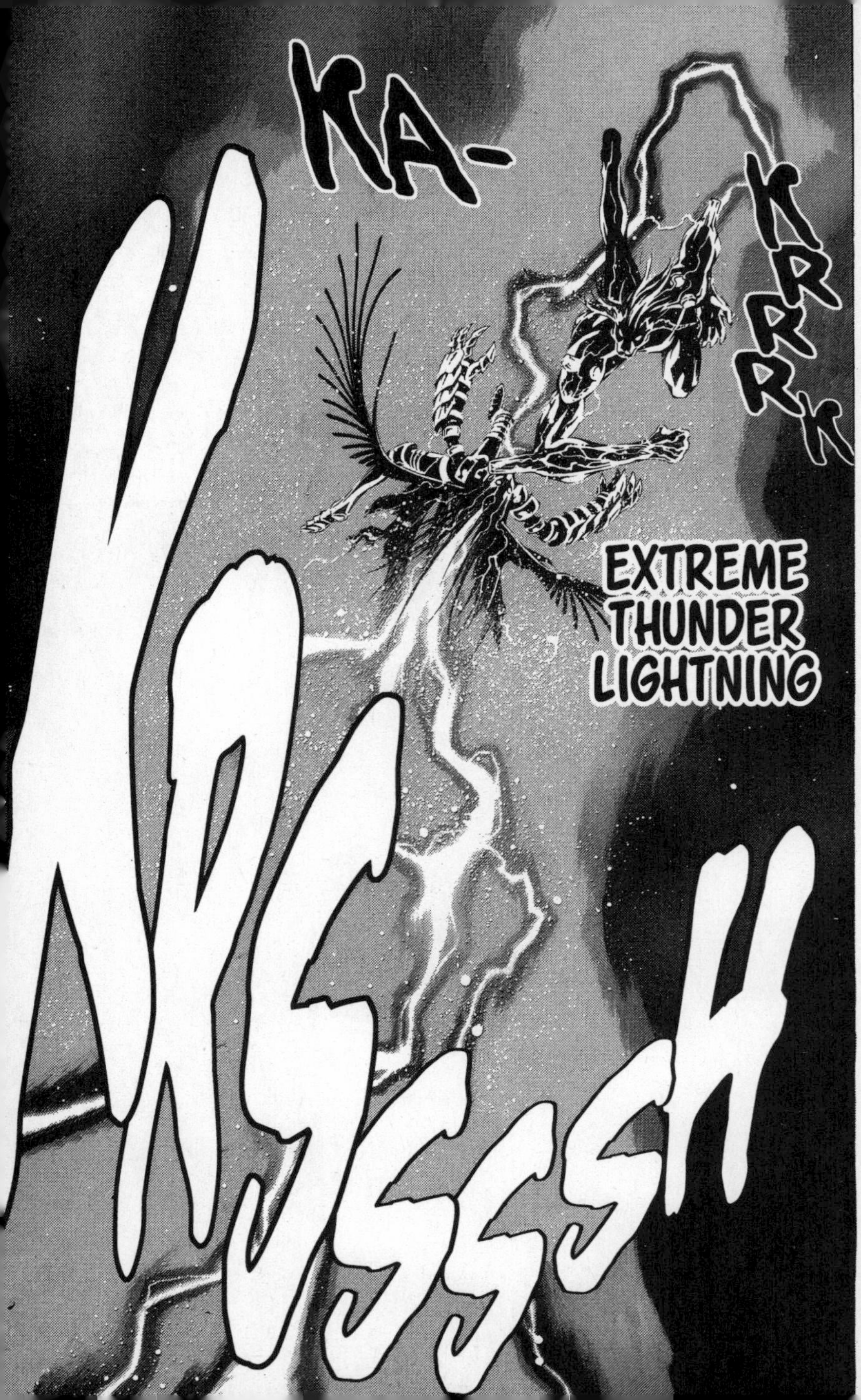
KA-KRRRK
EXTREME THUNDER LIGHTNING

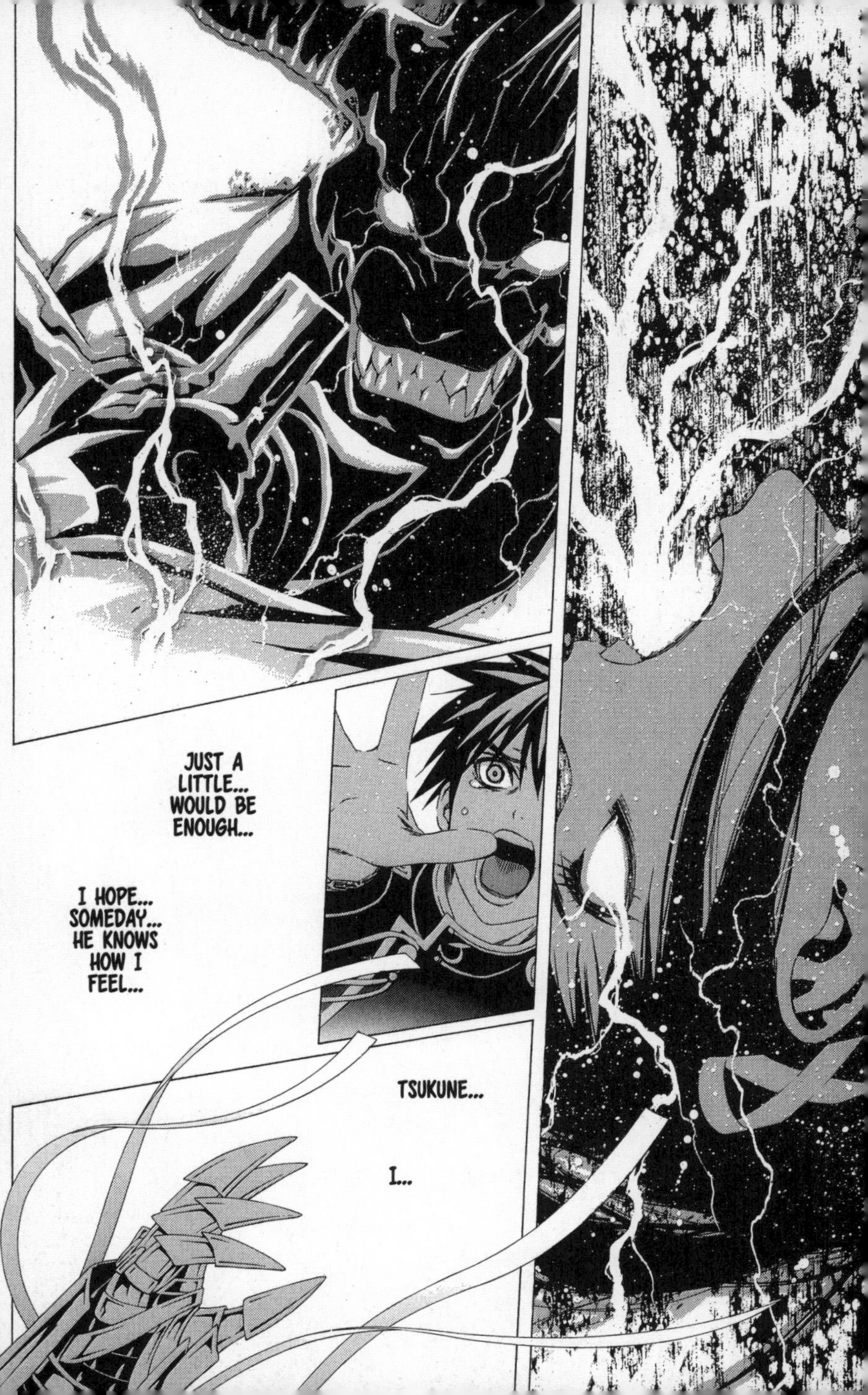
JUST A LITTLE... WOULD BE ENOUGH...
I HOPE... SOMEDAY... HE KNOWS HOW I FEEL...
TSUKUNE...
I...

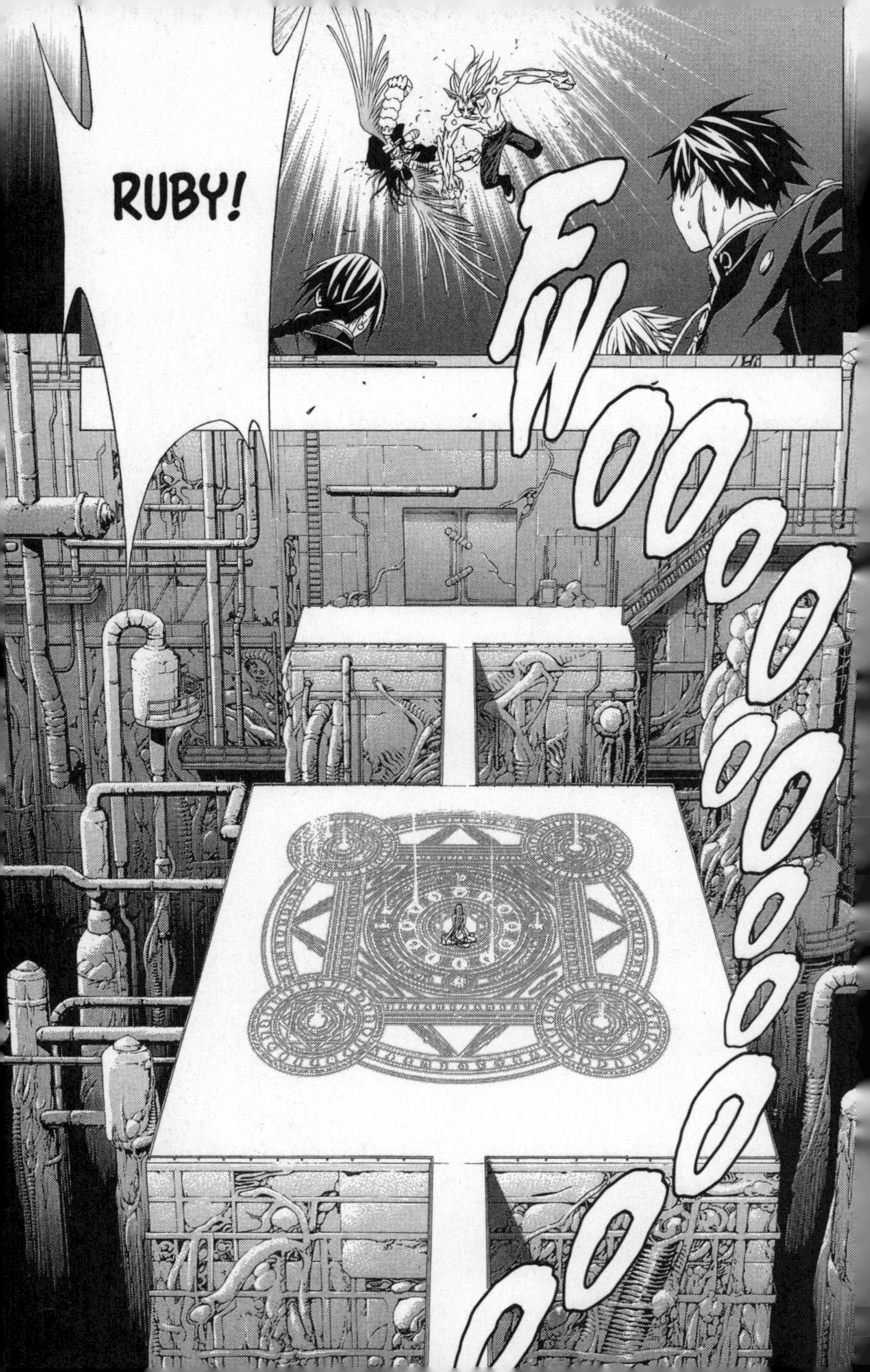
RUBY!
FWOOOOOOOOOOOOOO

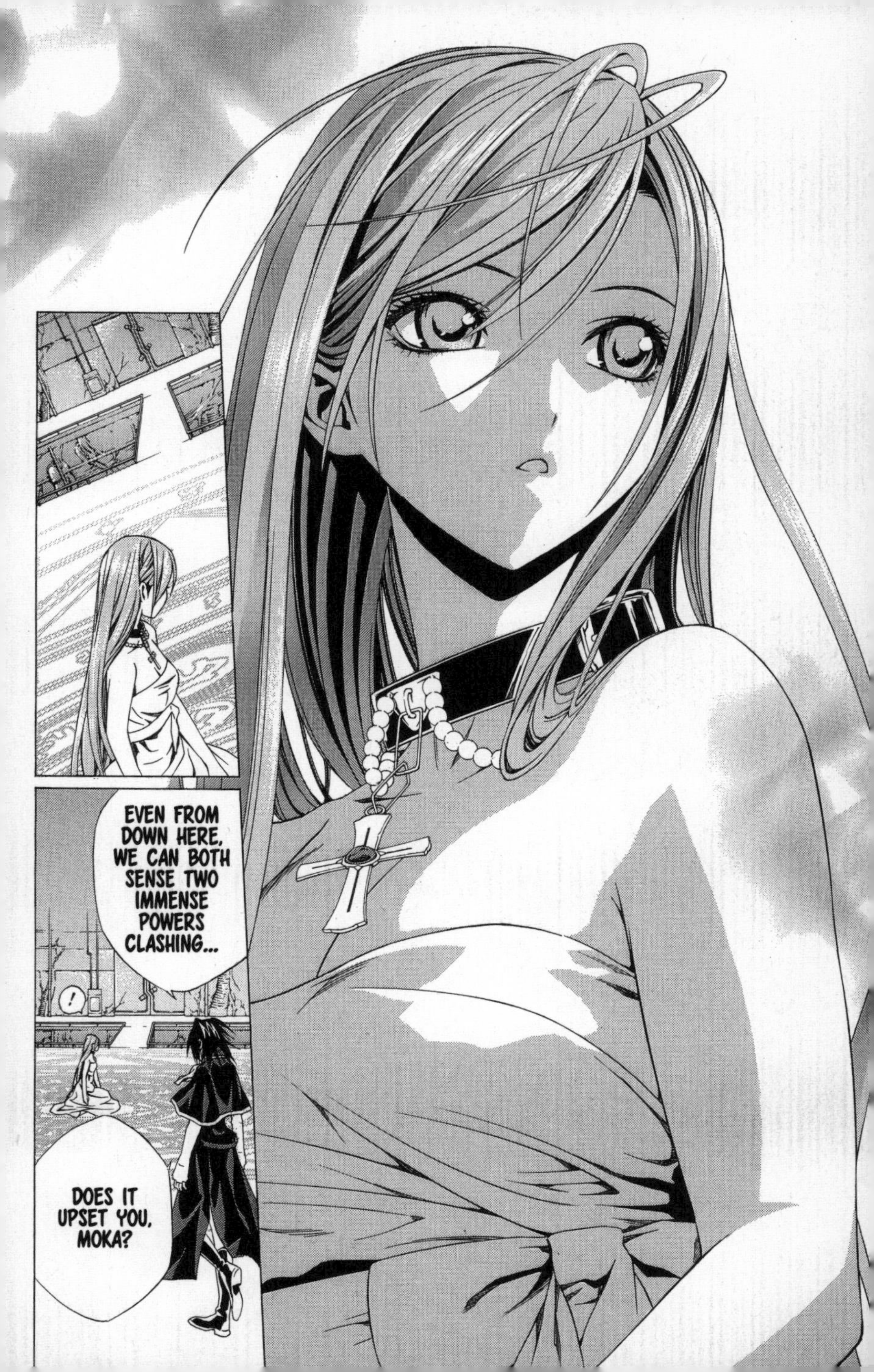
EVEN FROM DOWN HERE, WE CAN BOTH SENSE TWO IMMENSE POWERS CLASHING...
!
DOES IT UPSET YOU, MOKA?

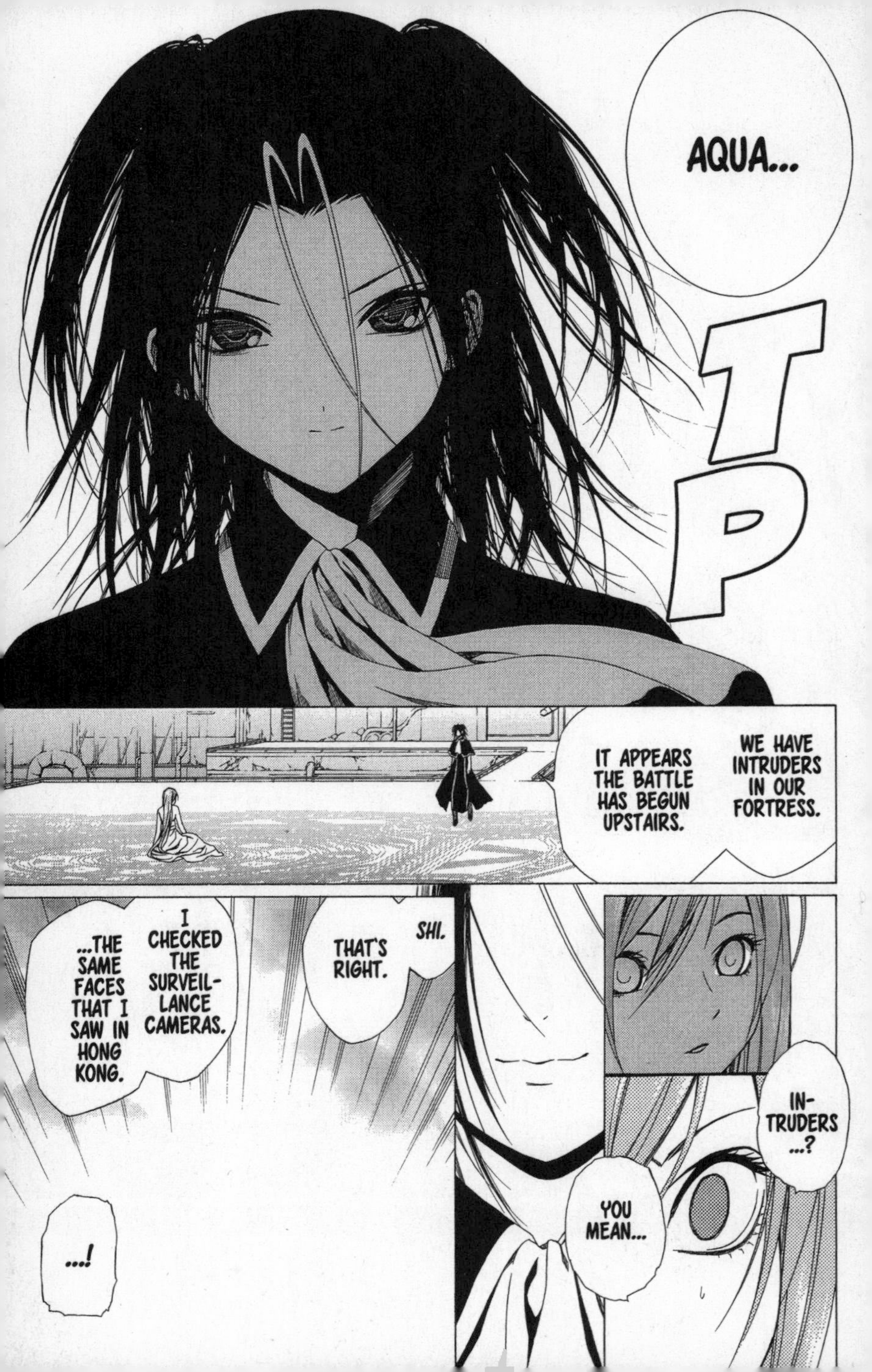

AQUA...
TP
WE HAVE INTRUDERS IN OUR FORTRESS.
IT APPEARS THE BATTLE HAS BEGUN UPSTAIRS.
IN-TRUDERS ...?
YOU MEAN...
SHI.
THAT'S RIGHT.
I CHECKED THE SURVEIL-LANCE CAMERAS.
...THE SAME FACES THAT I SAW IN HONG KONG.
...!

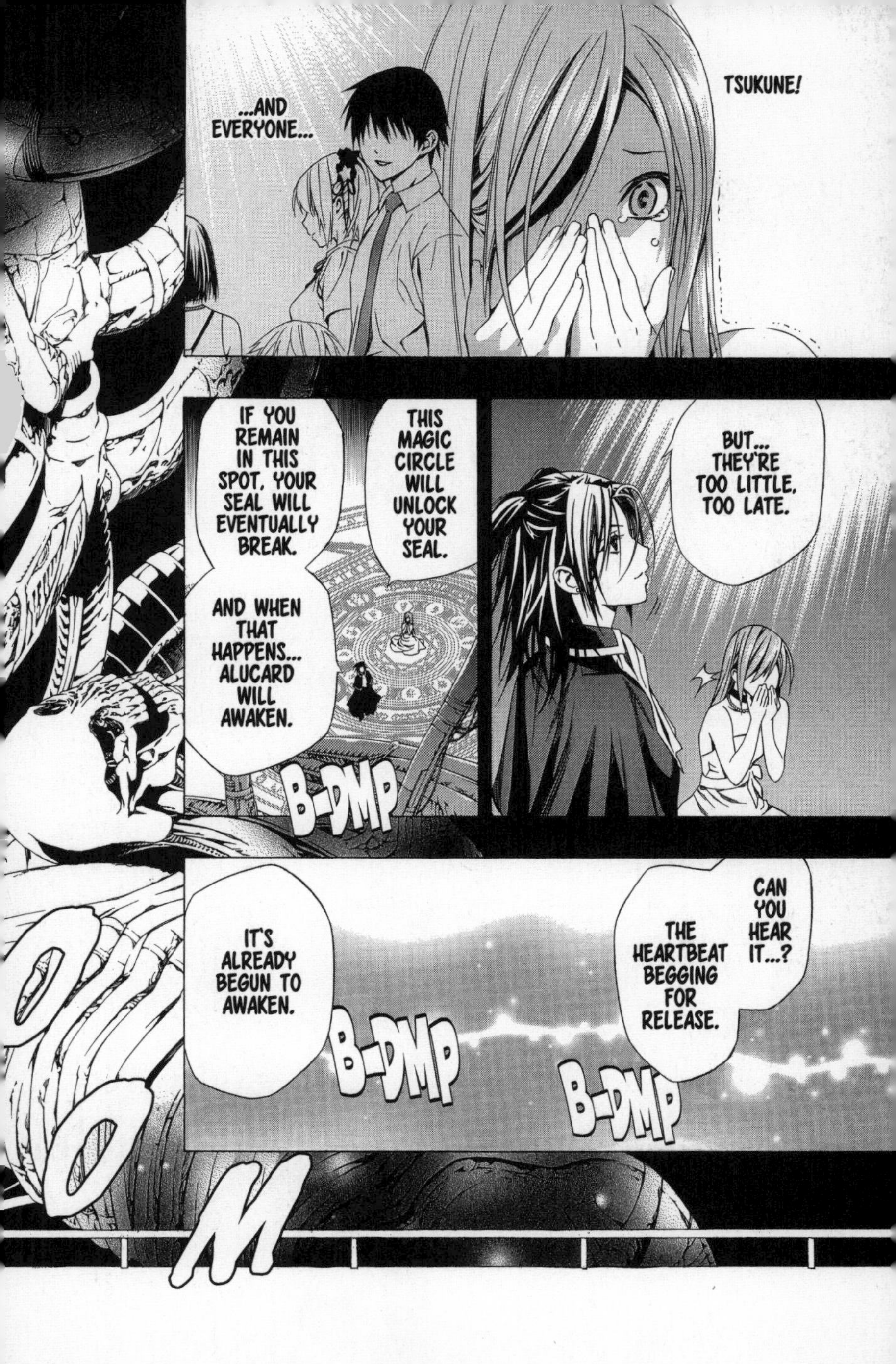
TSUKUNE!
...AND EVERYONE...
BUT... THEY'RE TOO LITTLE, TOO LATE.
THIS MAGIC CIRCLE WILL UNLOCK YOUR SEAL.
IF YOU REMAIN IN THIS SPOT, YOUR SEAL WILL EVENTUALLY BREAK.
AND WHEN THAT HAPPENS... ALUCARD WILL AWAKEN.
B-DMP
CAN YOU HEAR IT...?
THE HEARTBEAT BEGGING FOR RELEASE.
B-DMP
IT'S ALREADY BEGUN TO AWAKEN.
B-DMP
OOOM

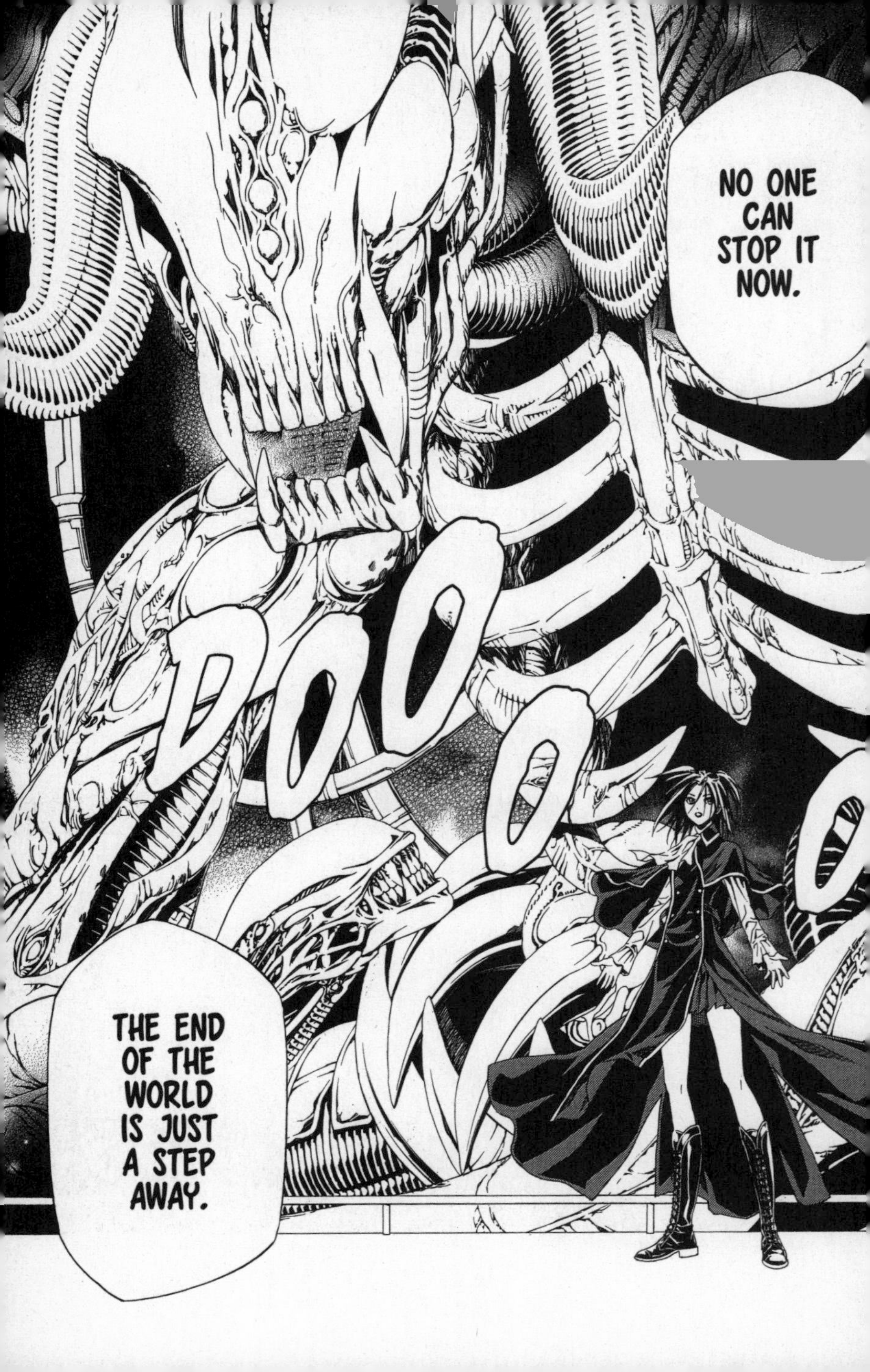
NO ONE CAN STOP IT NOW.
DOOOOO
THE END OF THE WORLD IS JUST A STEP AWAY.

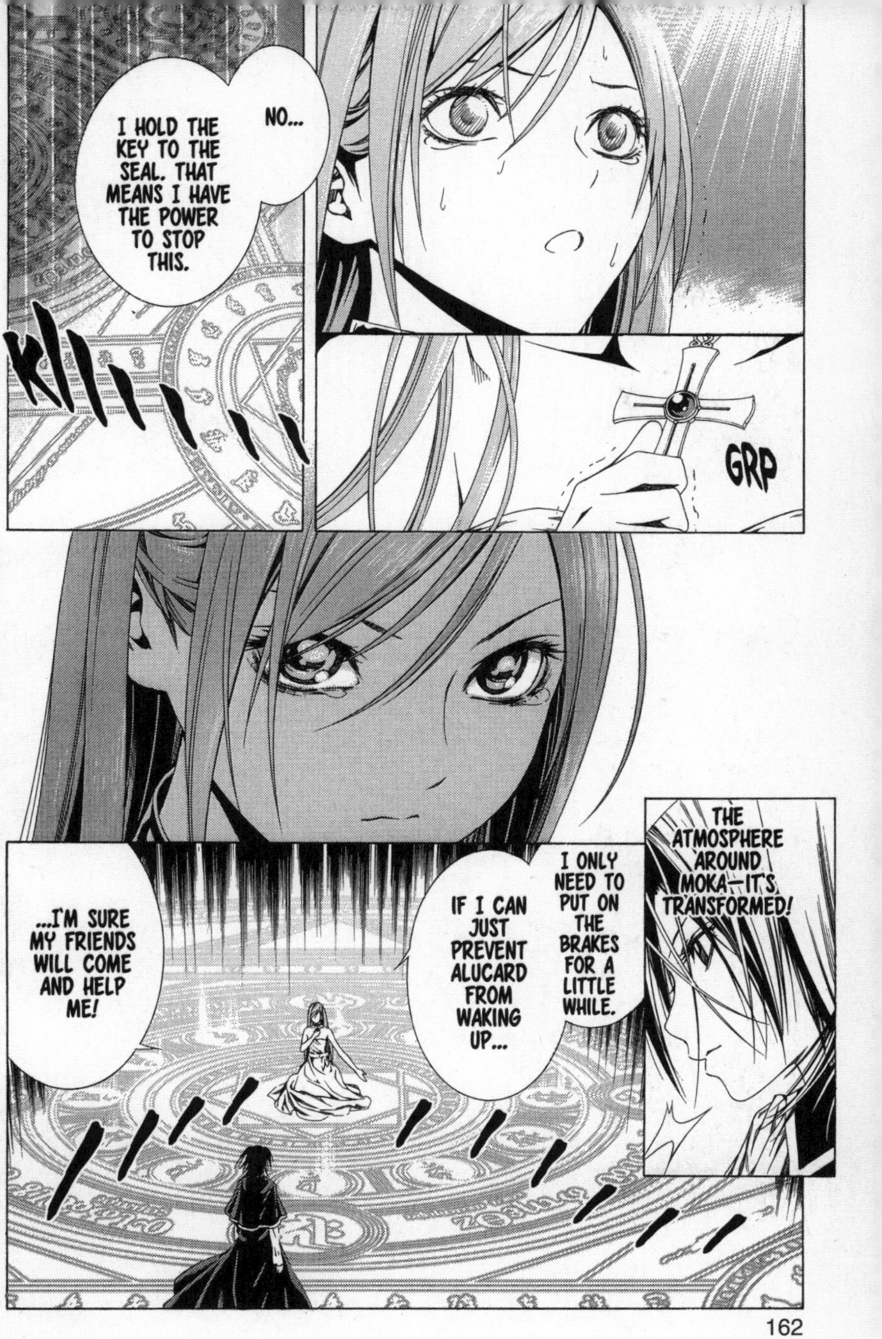
NO...
I HOLD THE KEY TO THE SEAL. THAT MEANS I HAVE THE POWER TO STOP THIS.
KRIIIIIII
GRP
THE ATMOSPHERE AROUND MOKA—IT'S TRANSFORMED!
I ONLY NEED TO PUT ON THE BRAKES FOR A LITTLE WHILE.
IF I CAN JUST PREVENT ALUCARD FROM WAKING UP...
...I'M SURE MY FRIENDS WILL COME AND HELP ME!

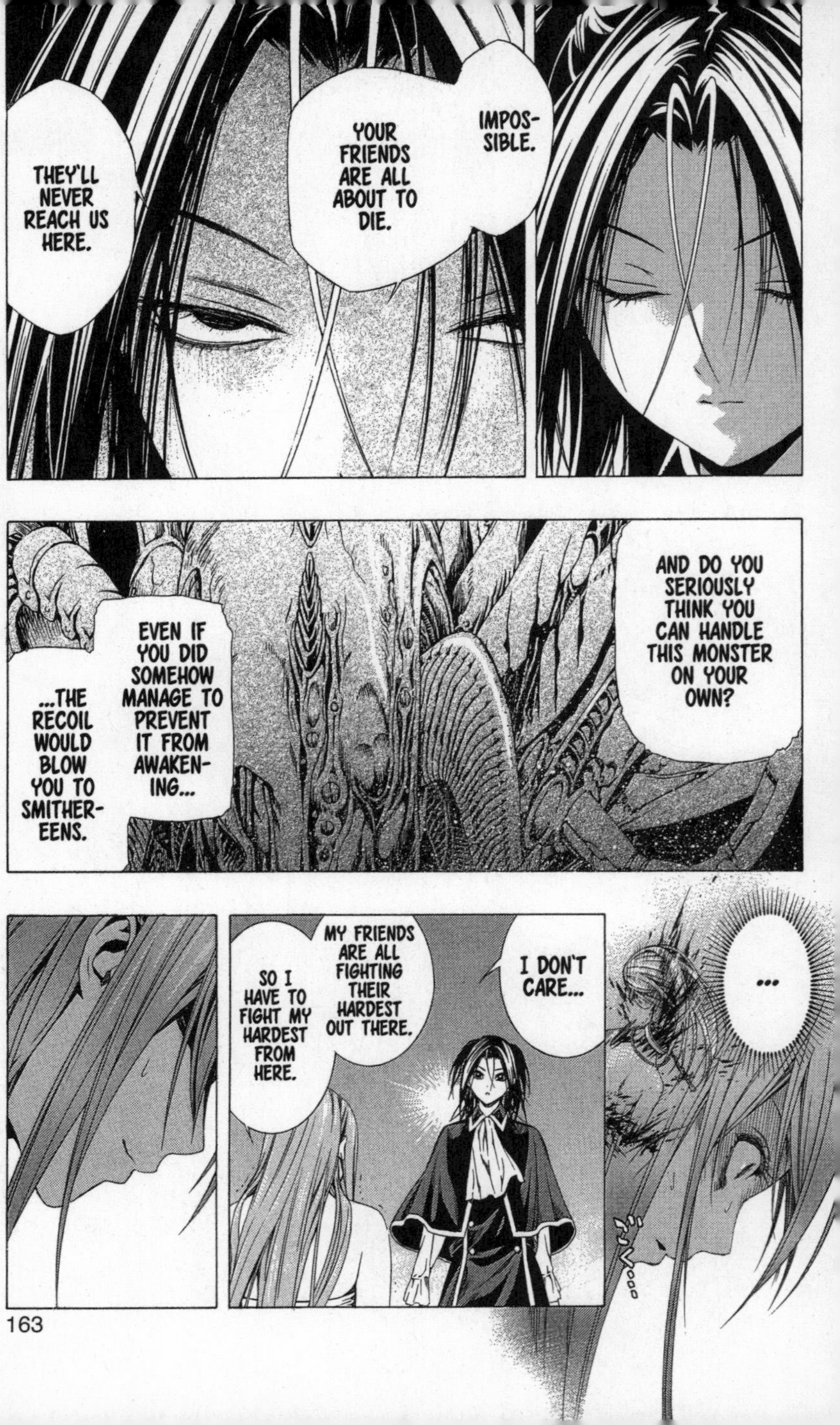
IMPOS-SIBLE.
YOUR FRIENDS ARE ALL ABOUT TO DIE.
THEY'LL NEVER REACH US HERE.
AND DO YOU SERIOUSLY THINK YOU CAN HANDLE THIS MONSTER ON YOUR OWN?
EVEN IF YOU DID SOMEHOW MANAGE TO PREVENT IT FROM AWAKEN-ING...
...THE RECOIL WOULD BLOW YOU TO SMITHER-EENS.
...
I DON'T CARE...
MY FRIENDS ARE ALL FIGHTING THEIR HARDEST OUT THERE.
SO I HAVE TO FIGHT MY HARDEST FROM HERE.

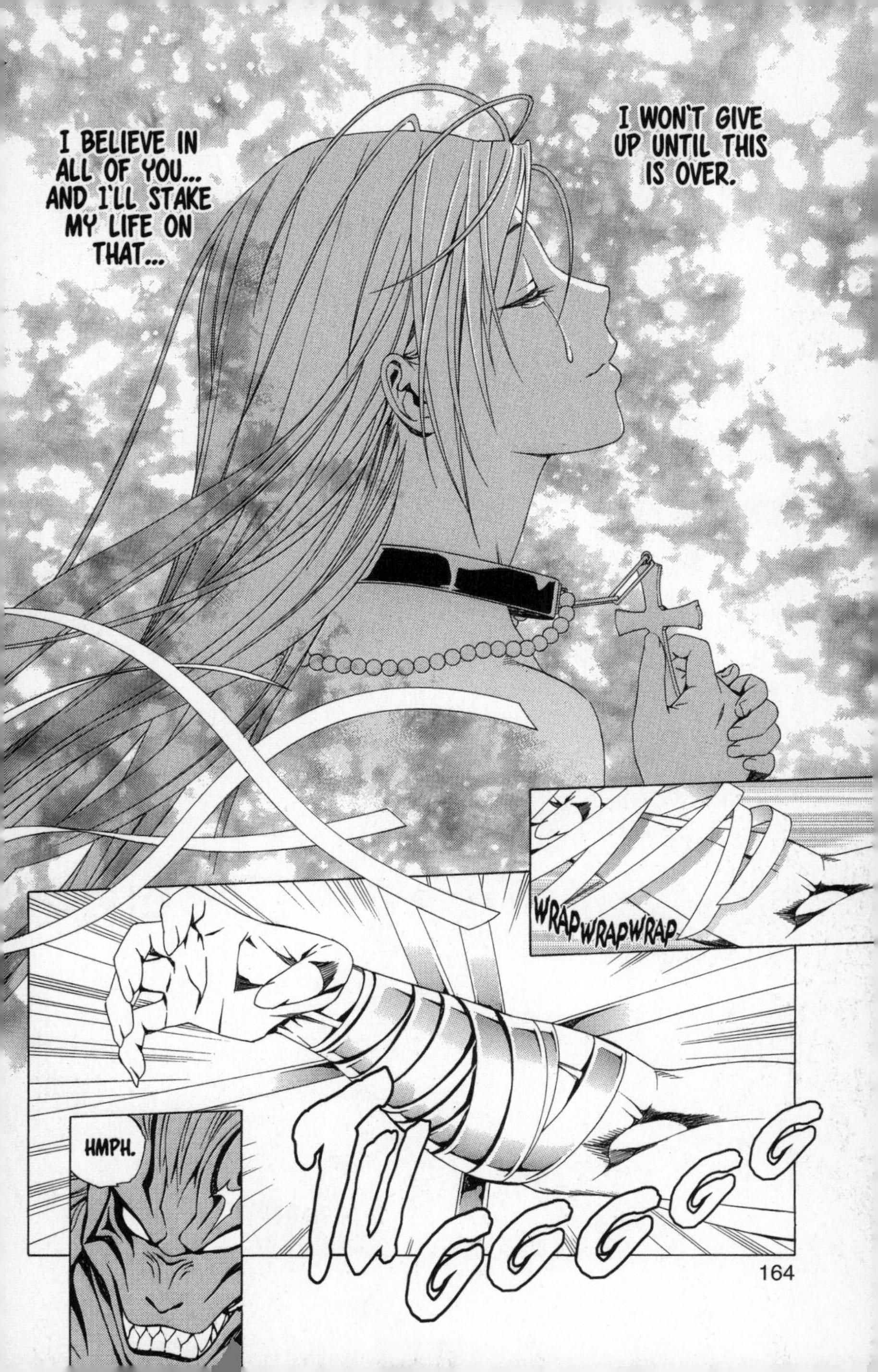
I WON'T GIVE UP UNTIL THIS IS OVER.
I BELIEVE IN ALL OF YOU... AND I'LL STAKE MY LIFE ON THAT...
WRAPWRAPWRAP
TUGGGGGG
HMPH.

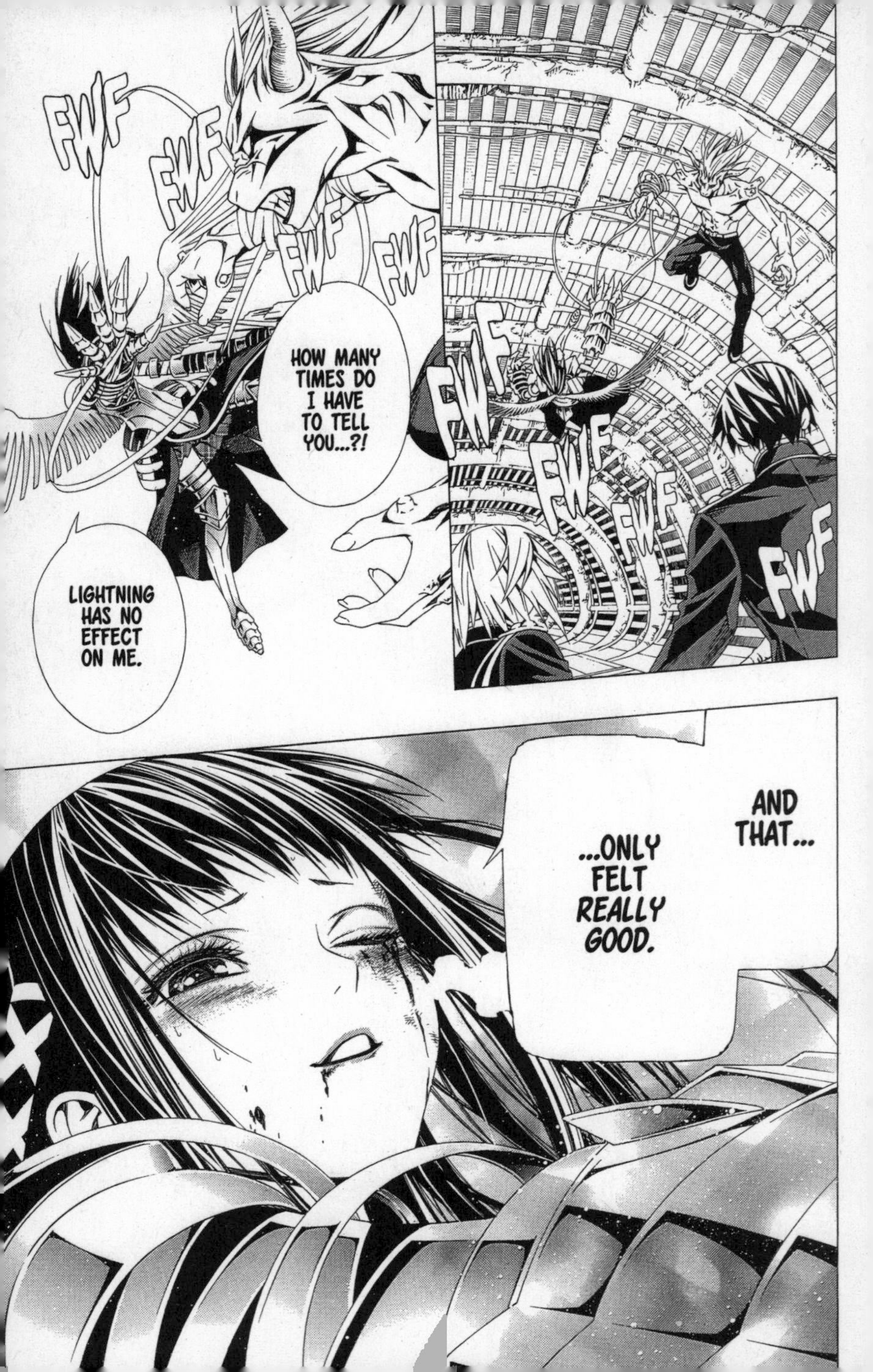
FWF
FWF
FWF
FWF
FWF
FWF
FWF
FWF
HOW MANY TIMES DO I HAVE TO TELL YOU...?!
LIGHTNING HAS NO EFFECT ON ME.
AND THAT...
...ONLY FELT REALLY GOOD.

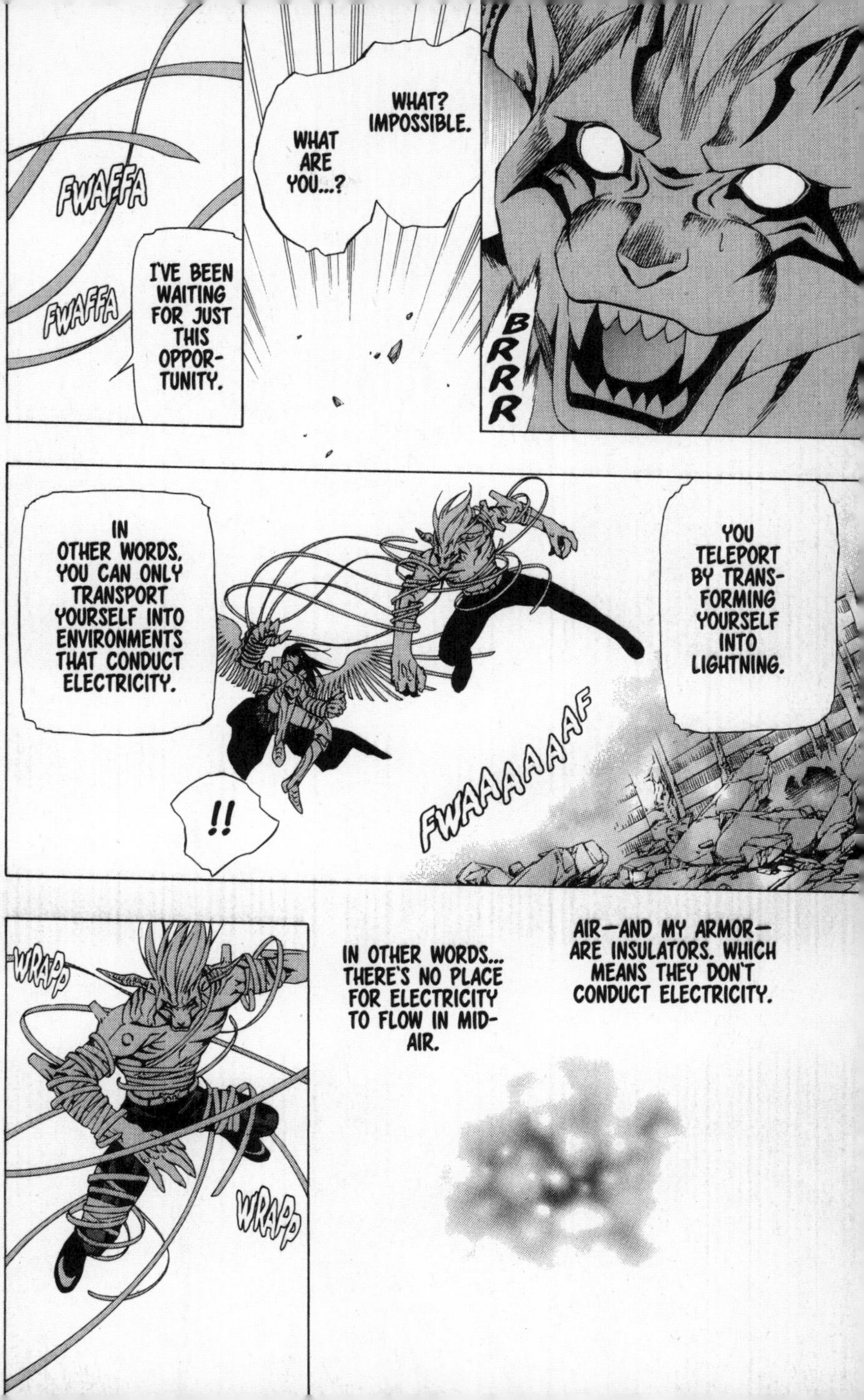
BRRR
WHAT? IMPOSSIBLE.
WHAT ARE YOU...?
FWAFFA
I'VE BEEN WAITING FOR JUST THIS OPPORTUNITY.
FWAFFA
YOU TELEPORT BY TRANSFORMING YOURSELF INTO LIGHTNING.
IN OTHER WORDS, YOU CAN ONLY TRANSPORT YOURSELF INTO ENVIRONMENTS THAT CONDUCT ELECTRICITY.
FWAAAAAAF
!!
AIR—AND MY ARMOR—ARE INSULATORS. WHICH MEANS THEY DON'T CONDUCT ELECTRICITY.
IN OTHER WORDS... THERE'S NO PLACE FOR ELECTRICITY TO FLOW IN MID-AIR.
WRAPP
WRAPP

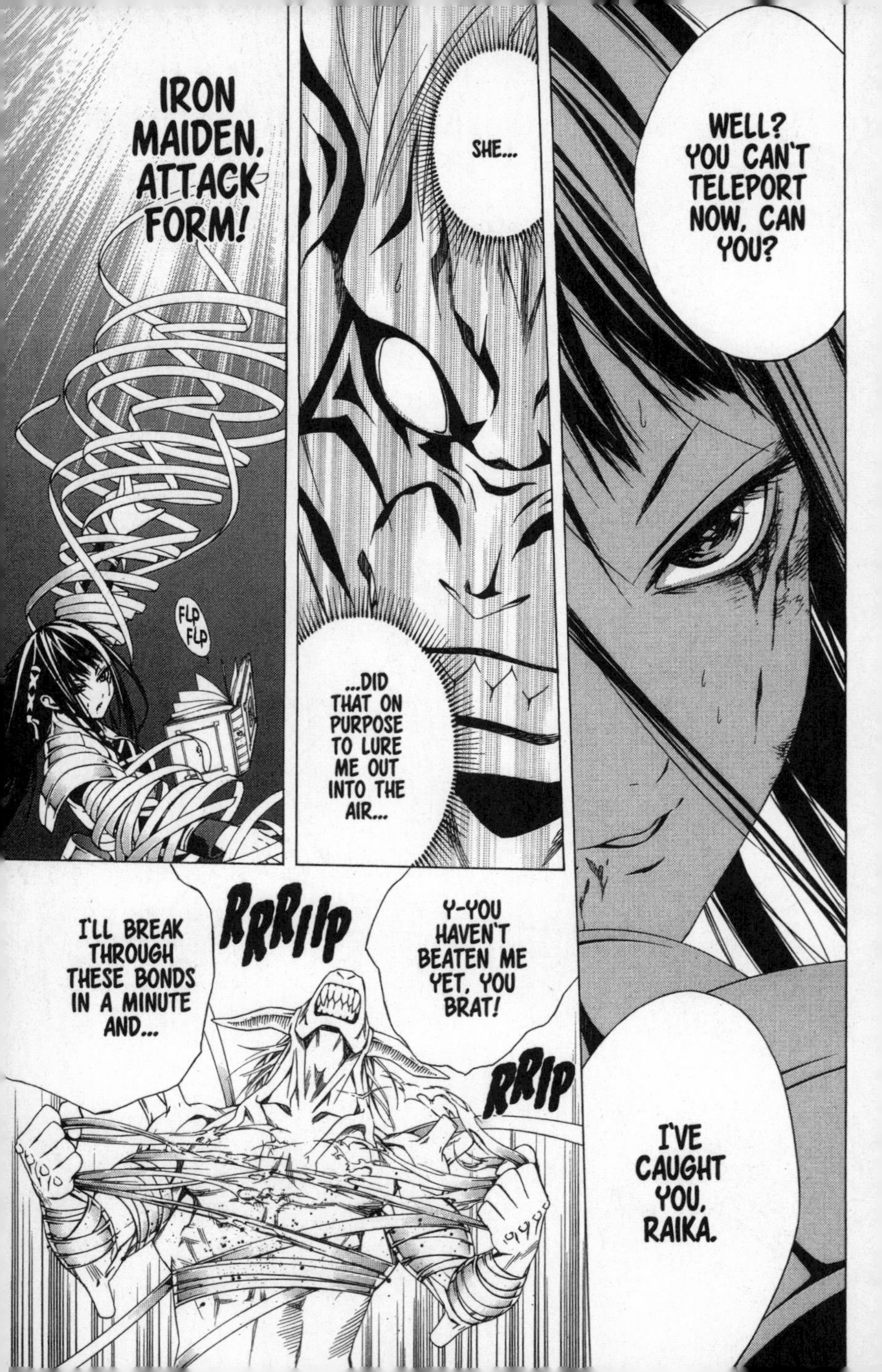
WELL? YOU CAN'T TELEPORT NOW, CAN YOU?
I'VE CAUGHT YOU, RAIKA.
SHE...
...DID THAT ON PURPOSE TO LURE ME OUT INTO THE AIR...
IRON MAIDEN, ATTACK FORM!
FLP FLP
Y-YOU HAVEN'T BEATEN ME YET, YOU BRAT!
RRRIIP
I'LL BREAK THROUGH THESE BONDS IN A MINUTE AND...
RRIP

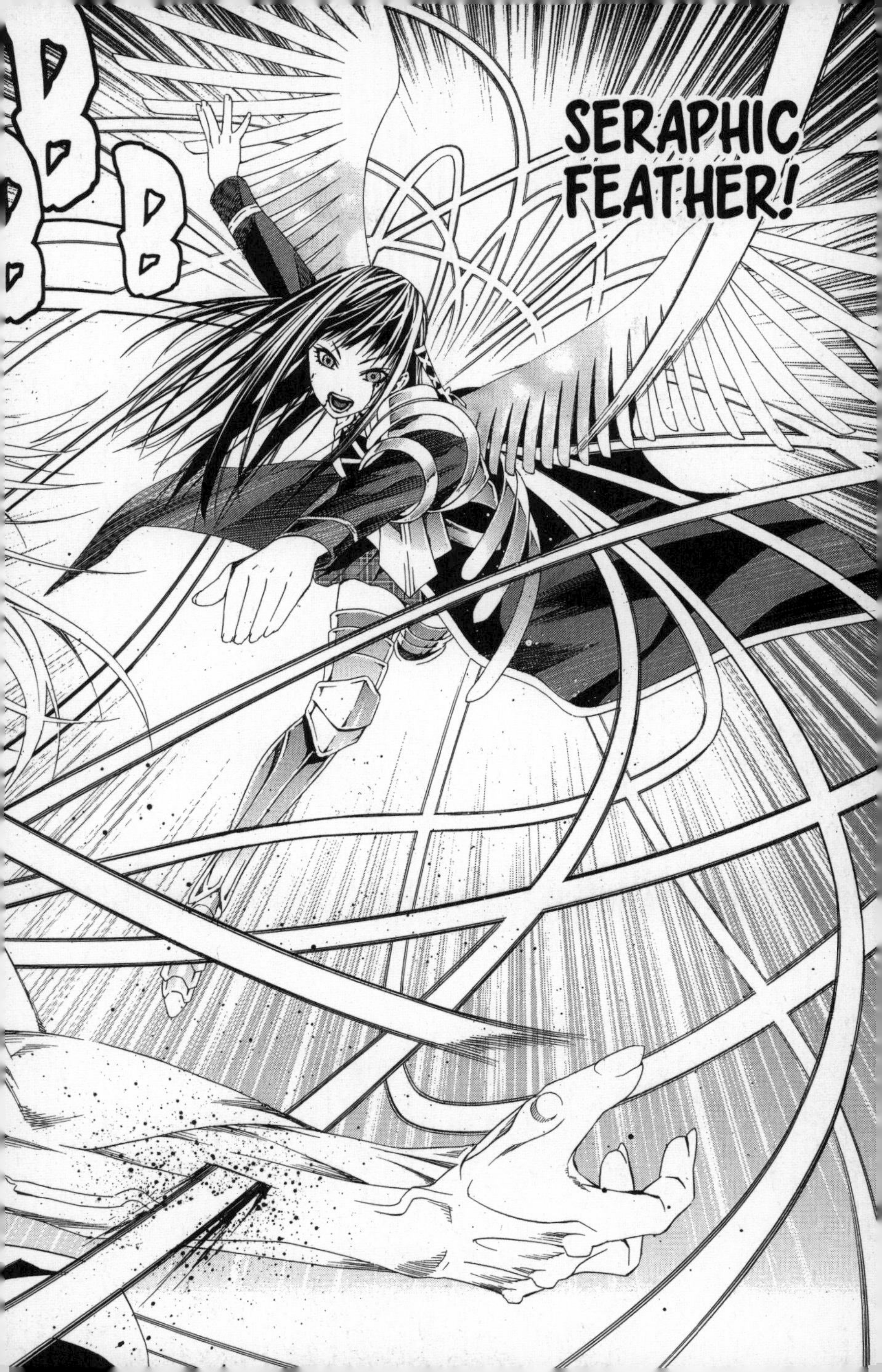
SERAPHIC FEATHER!
BBB

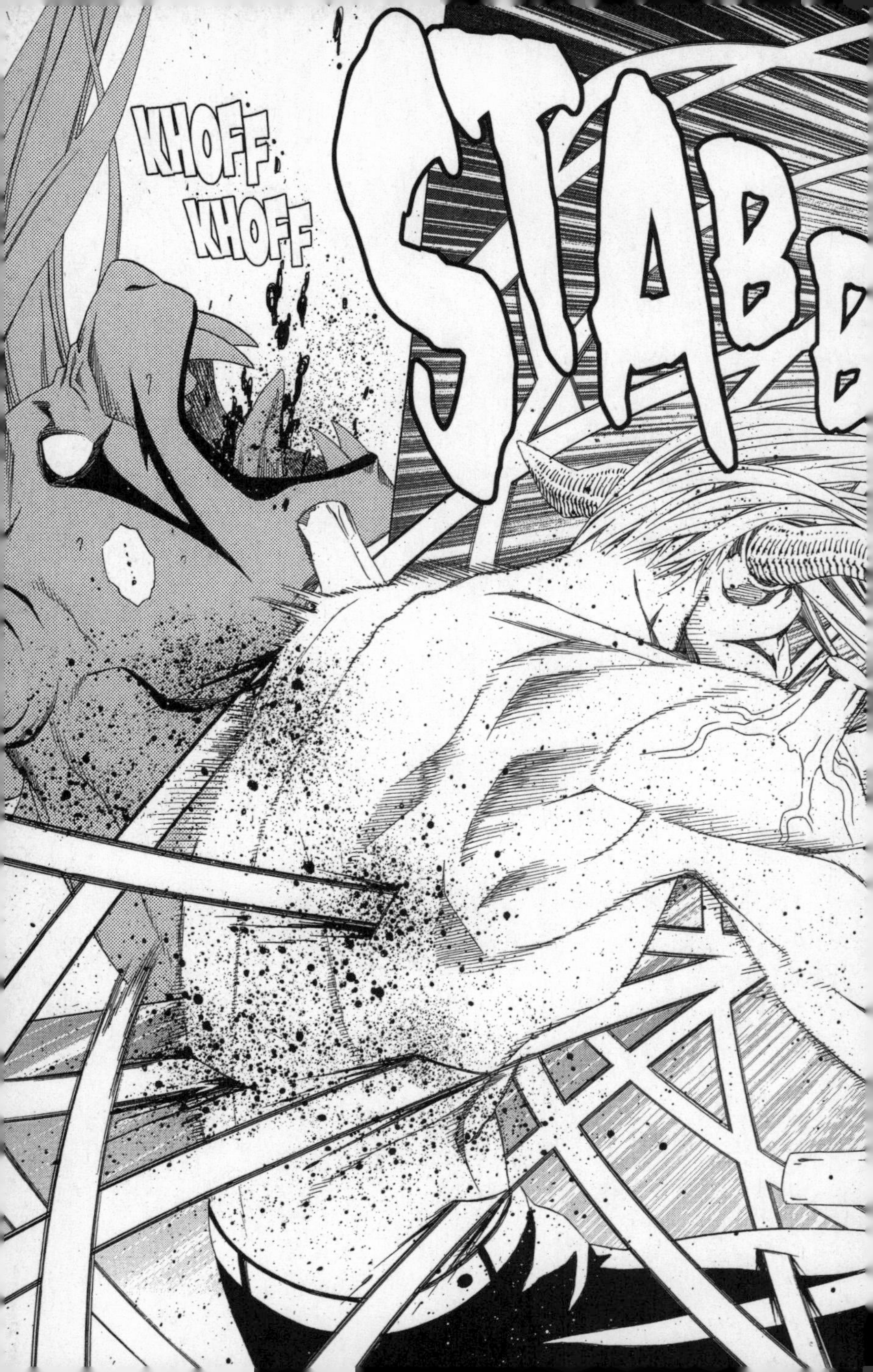
STAB
KHOFF
KHOFF
...

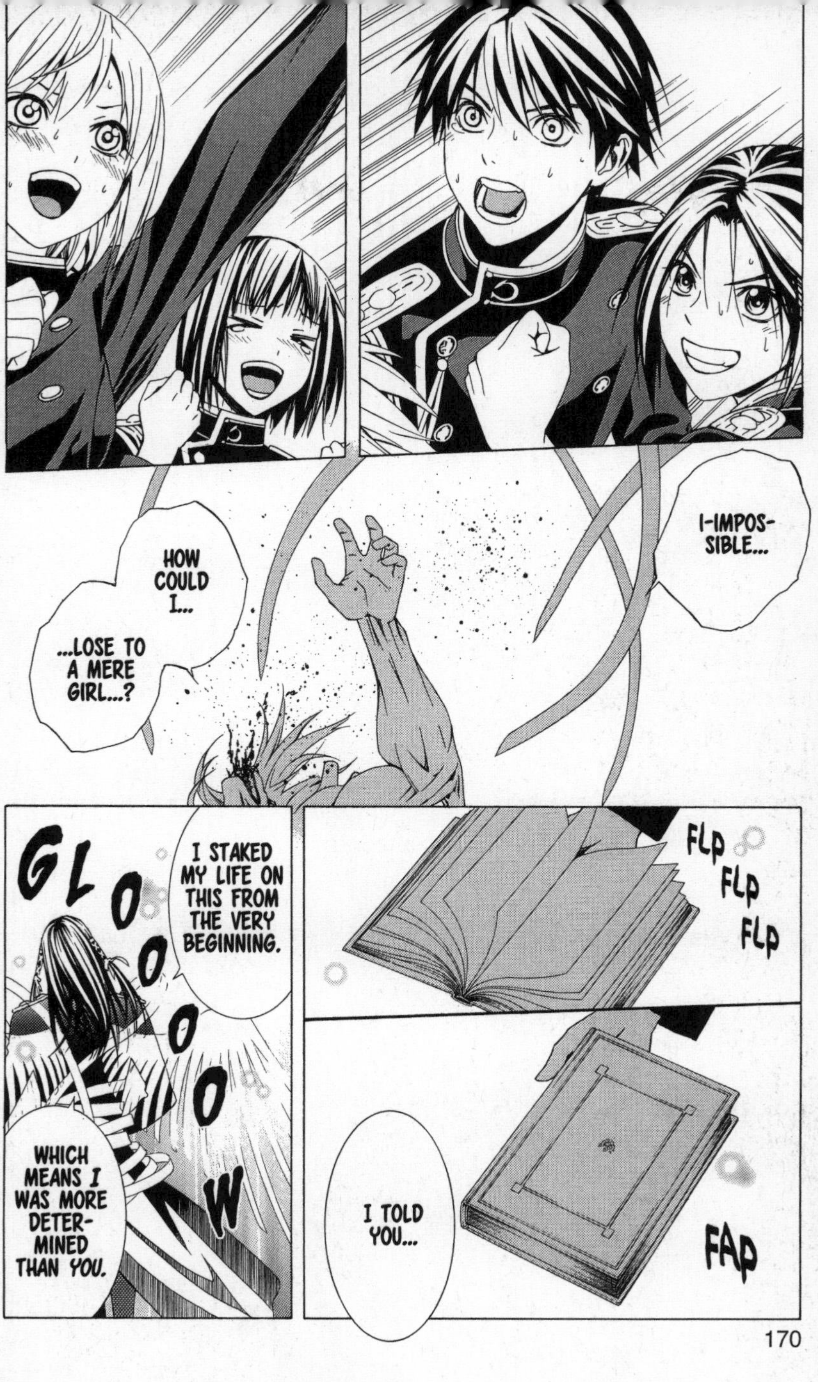
I-IMPOS-SIBLE...
HOW COULD I...
...LOSE TO A MERE GIRL...?
FLP FLP FLP
I TOLD YOU...
FAP
GLOOOOOOW
I STAKED MY LIFE ON THIS FROM THE VERY BEGINNING.
WHICH MEANS *I* WAS MORE DETER-MINED THAN *YOU*.

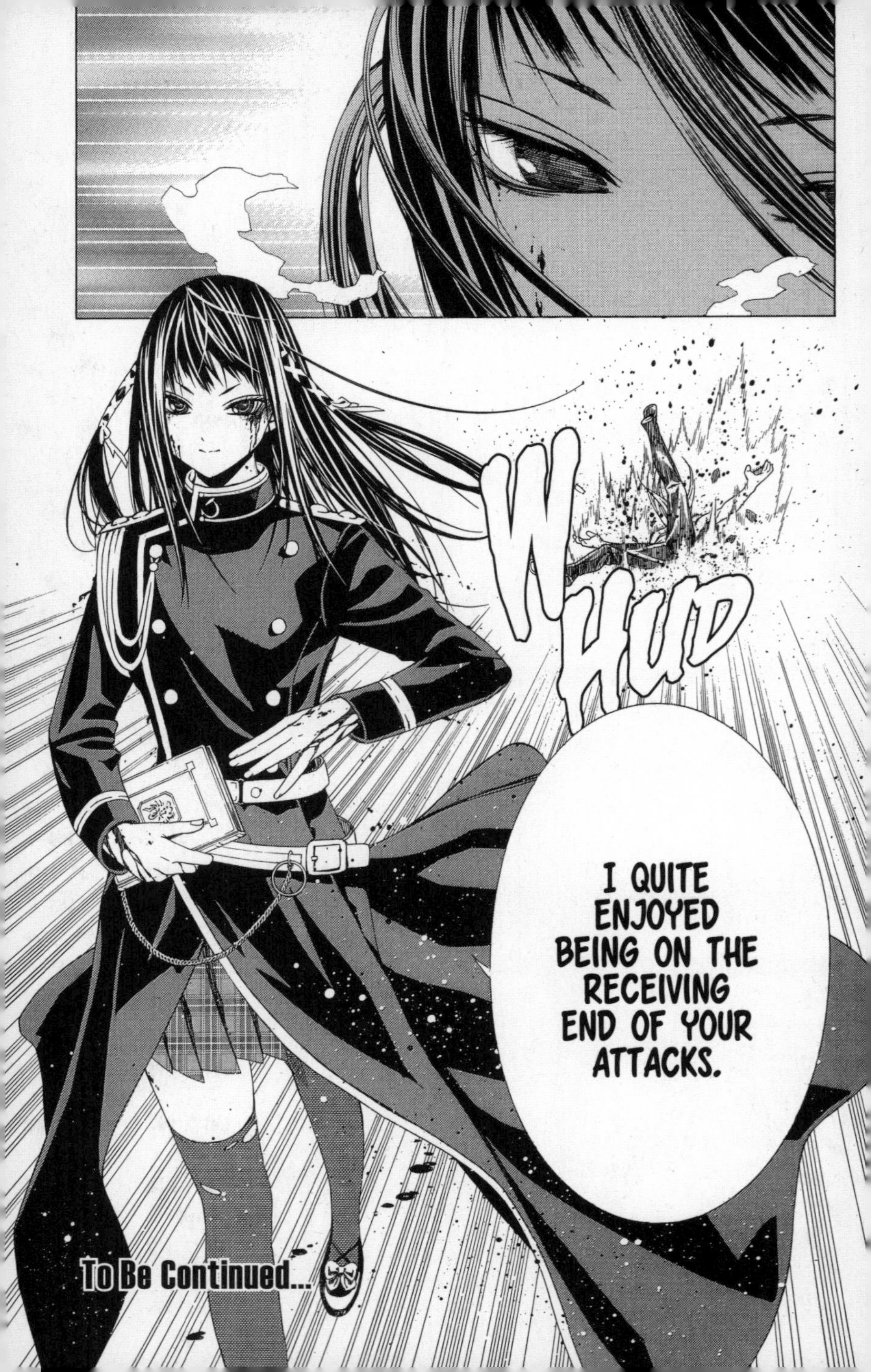
WHUD
I QUITE ENJOYED BEING ON THE RECEIVING END OF YOUR ATTACKS.
To Be Continued...

ROSARIO + VAMPIRE Season II

Extra Bite-Size Notes

The Secret to Lessening The Effect of The Electric Shocks.

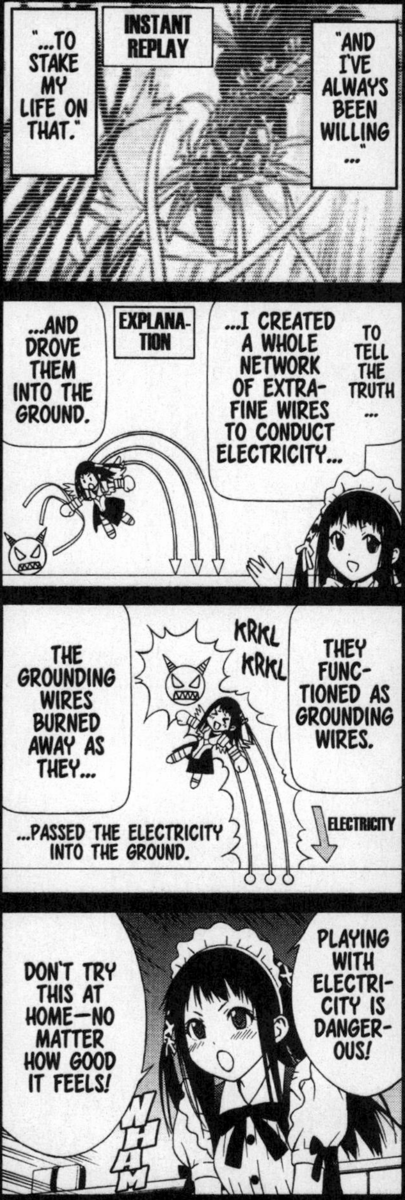
INSTANT REPLAY
"AND I'VE ALWAYS BEEN WILLING"...
"...TO STAKE MY LIFE ON THAT."
TO TELL THE TRUTH...
...I CREATED A WHOLE NETWORK OF EXTRA-FINE WIRES TO CONDUCT ELECTRICITY...
EXPLANATION
...AND DROVE THEM INTO THE GROUND.
KRKL KRKL
THEY FUNCTIONED AS GROUNDING WIRES.
THE GROUNDING WIRES BURNED AWAY AS THEY...
ELECTRICITY
...PASSED THE ELECTRICITY INTO THE GROUND.
PLAYING WITH ELECTRICITY IS DANGEROUS!
DON'T TRY THIS AT HOME—NO MATTER HOW GOOD IT FEELS!
WHAM

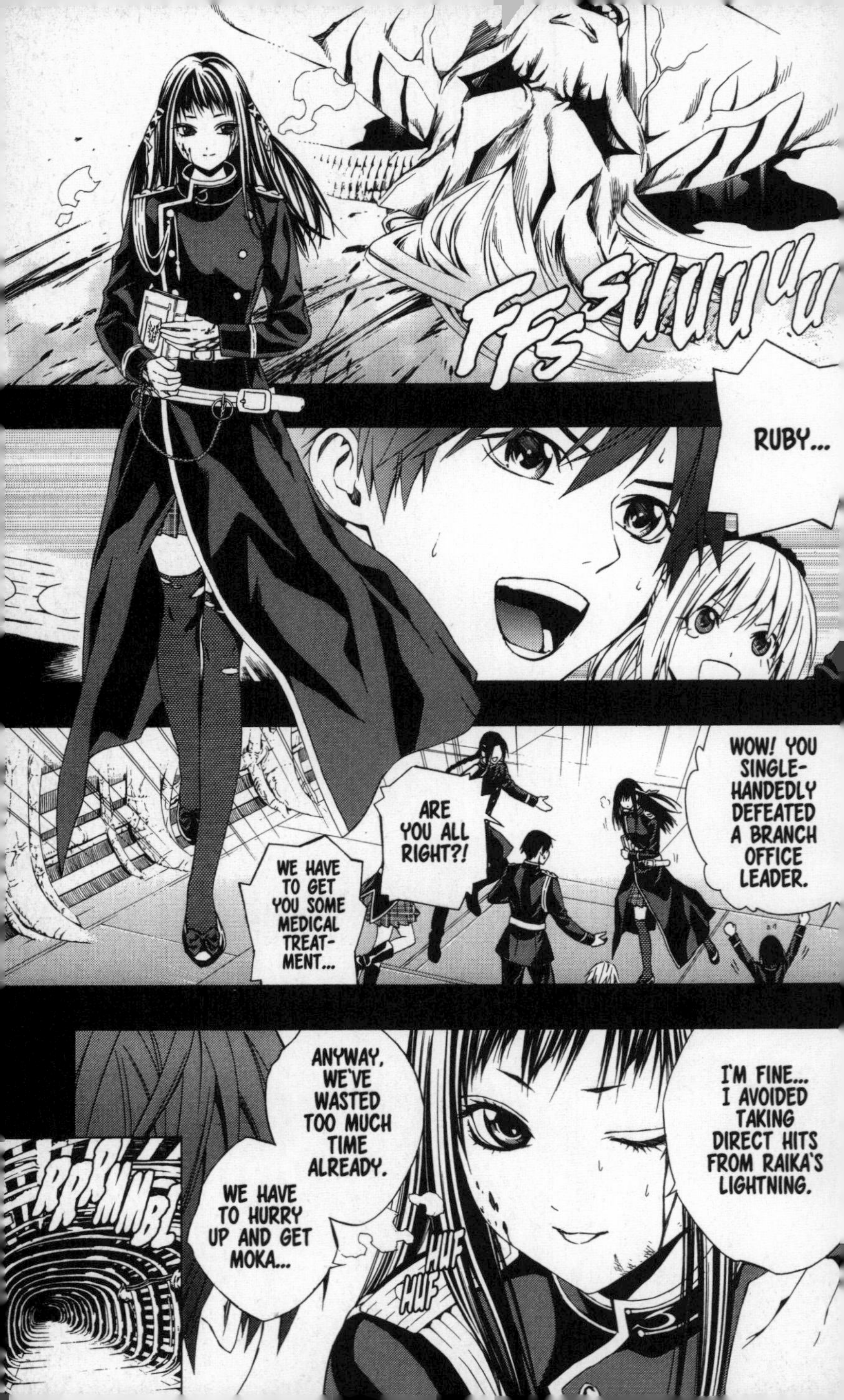
FFSSUUUUU
RUBY...
WOW! YOU SINGLE-HANDEDLY DEFEATED A BRANCH OFFICE LEADER.
ARE YOU ALL RIGHT?!
WE HAVE TO GET YOU SOME MEDICAL TREAT-MENT...
I'M FINE... I AVOIDED TAKING DIRECT HITS FROM RAIKA'S LIGHTNING.
HUF HUF
ANYWAY, WE'VE WASTED TOO MUCH TIME ALREADY.
WE HAVE TO HURRY UP AND GET MOKA...
RRRMMBL

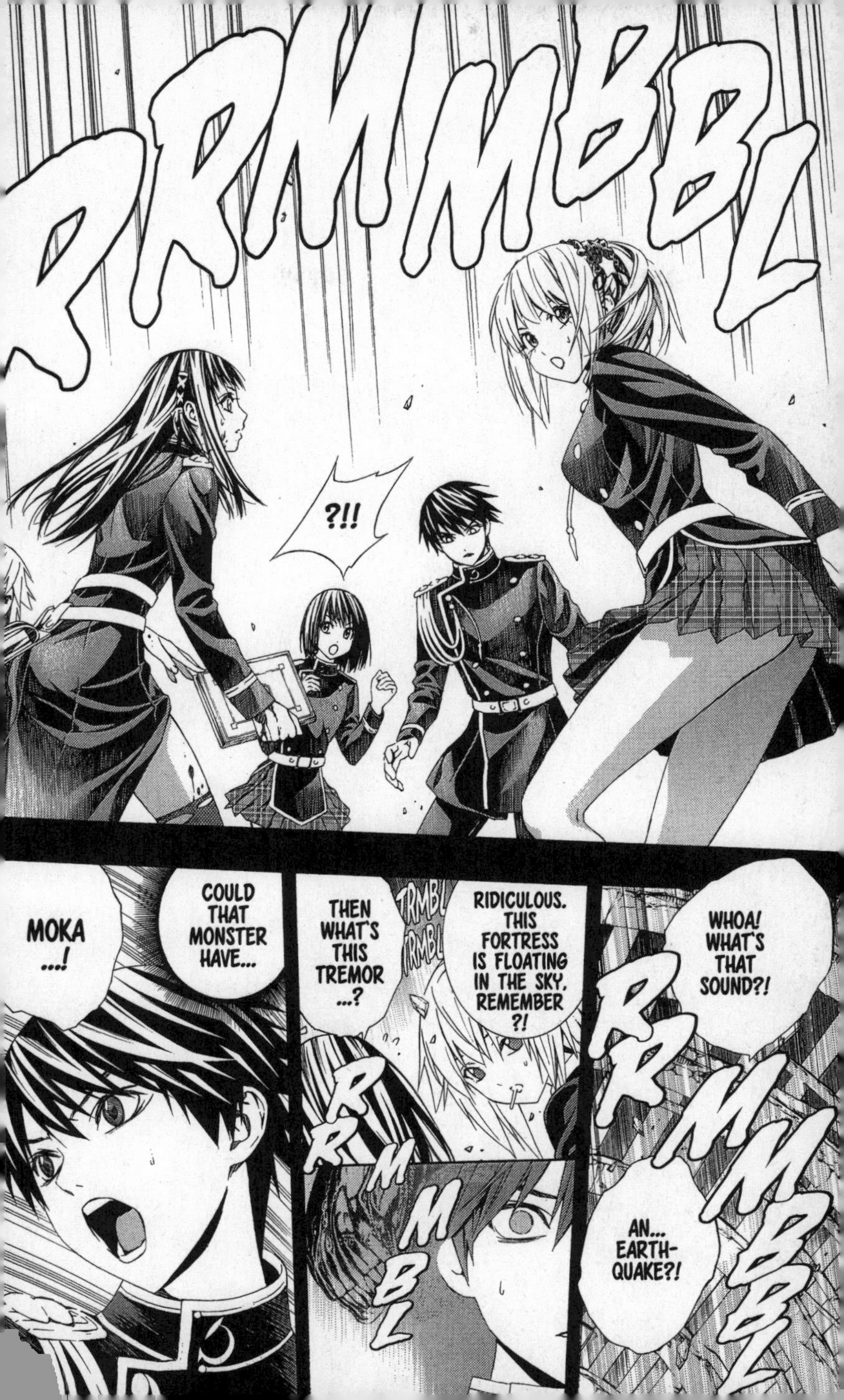
RRMMBBL
?!!
WHOA! WHAT'S THAT SOUND?!
RRMMBBB
AN... EARTHQUAKE?!
RIDICULOUS. THIS FORTRESS IS FLOATING IN THE SKY, REMEMBER ?!
TRMBL TRMBL
THEN WHAT'S THIS TREMOR ...?
RRMMBL
COULD THAT MONSTER HAVE...
MOKA ...!

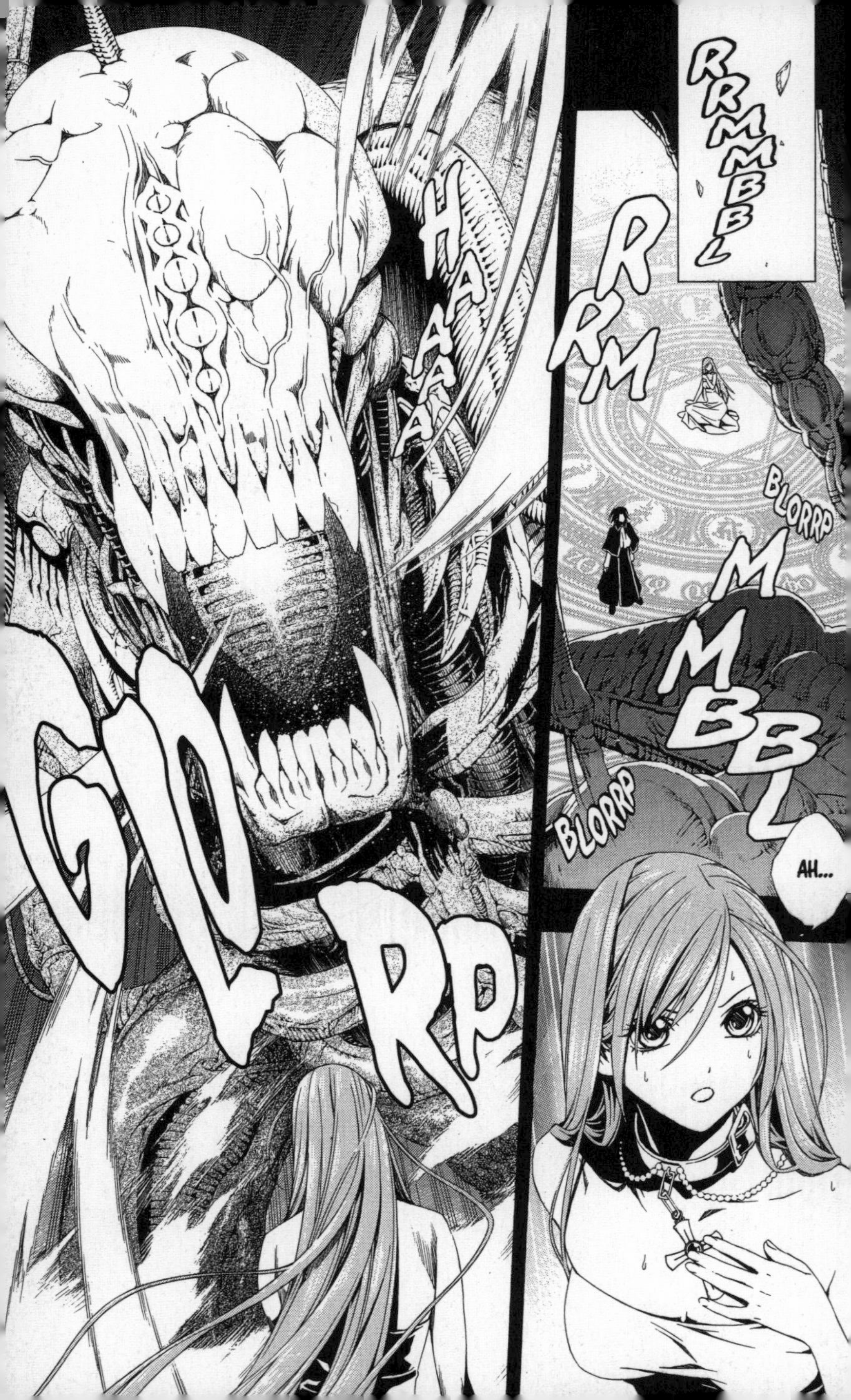
RRMMBBL
RRM
BLORRP
MMBBL
BLORRP
AH...
HAAAAA
GORP

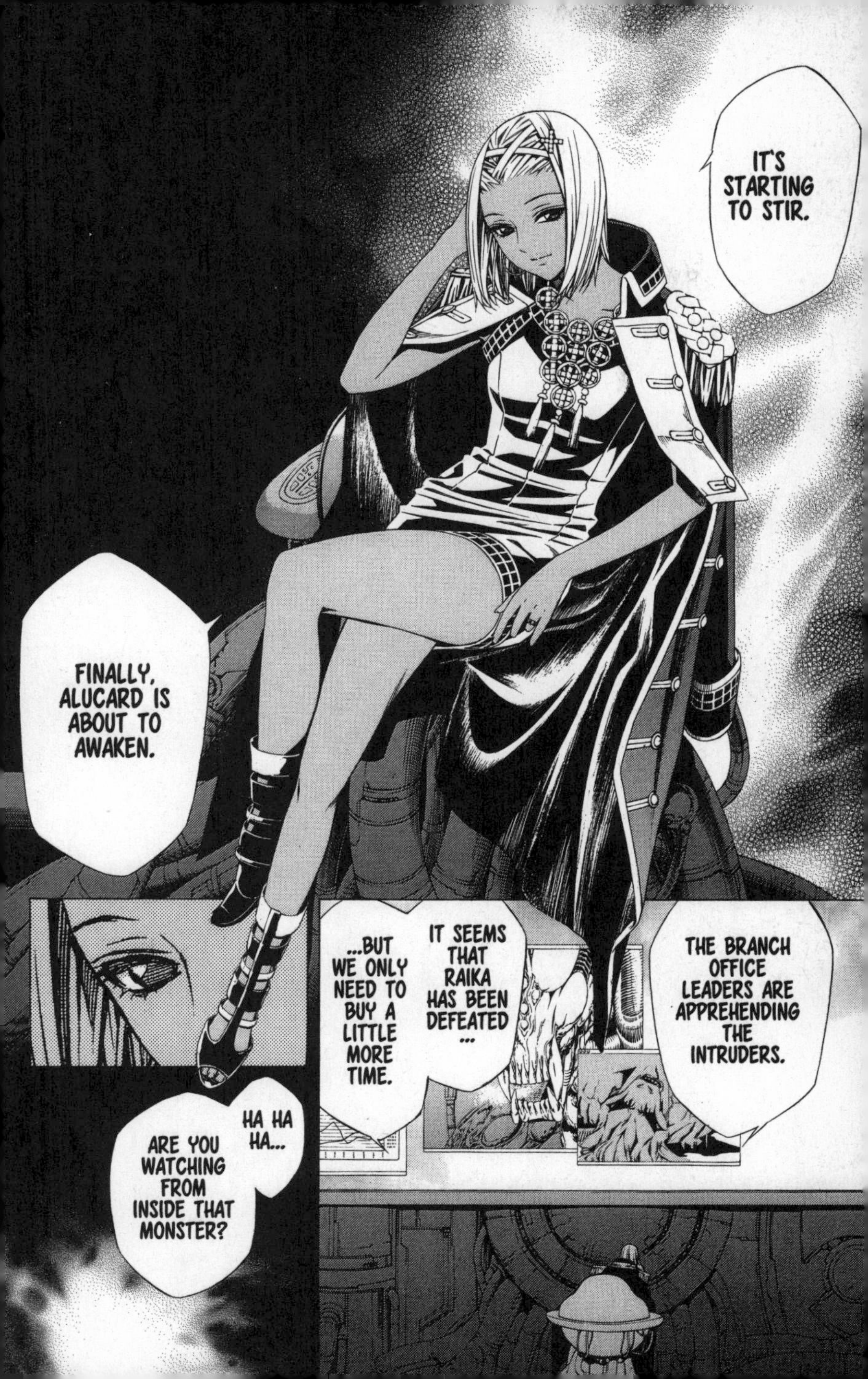
IT'S STARTING TO STIR.
FINALLY, ALUCARD IS ABOUT TO AWAKEN.
THE BRANCH OFFICE LEADERS ARE APPREHENDING THE INTRUDERS.
IT SEEMS THAT RAIKA HAS BEEN DEFEATED...
...BUT WE ONLY NEED TO BUY A LITTLE MORE TIME.
HA HA HA...
ARE YOU WATCHING FROM INSIDE THAT MONSTER?

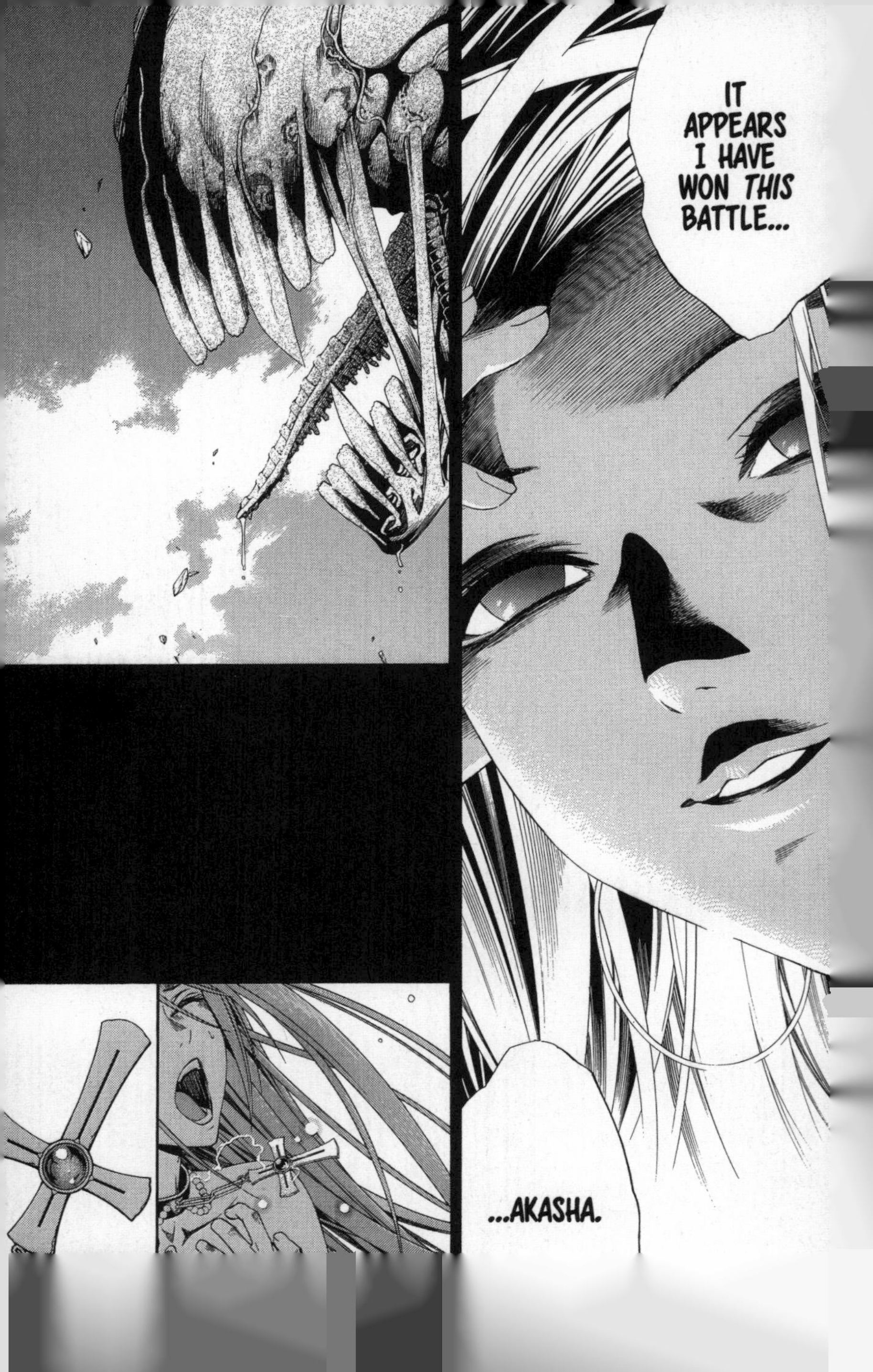
IT APPEARS I HAVE WON *THIS* BATTLE...
...AKASHA.

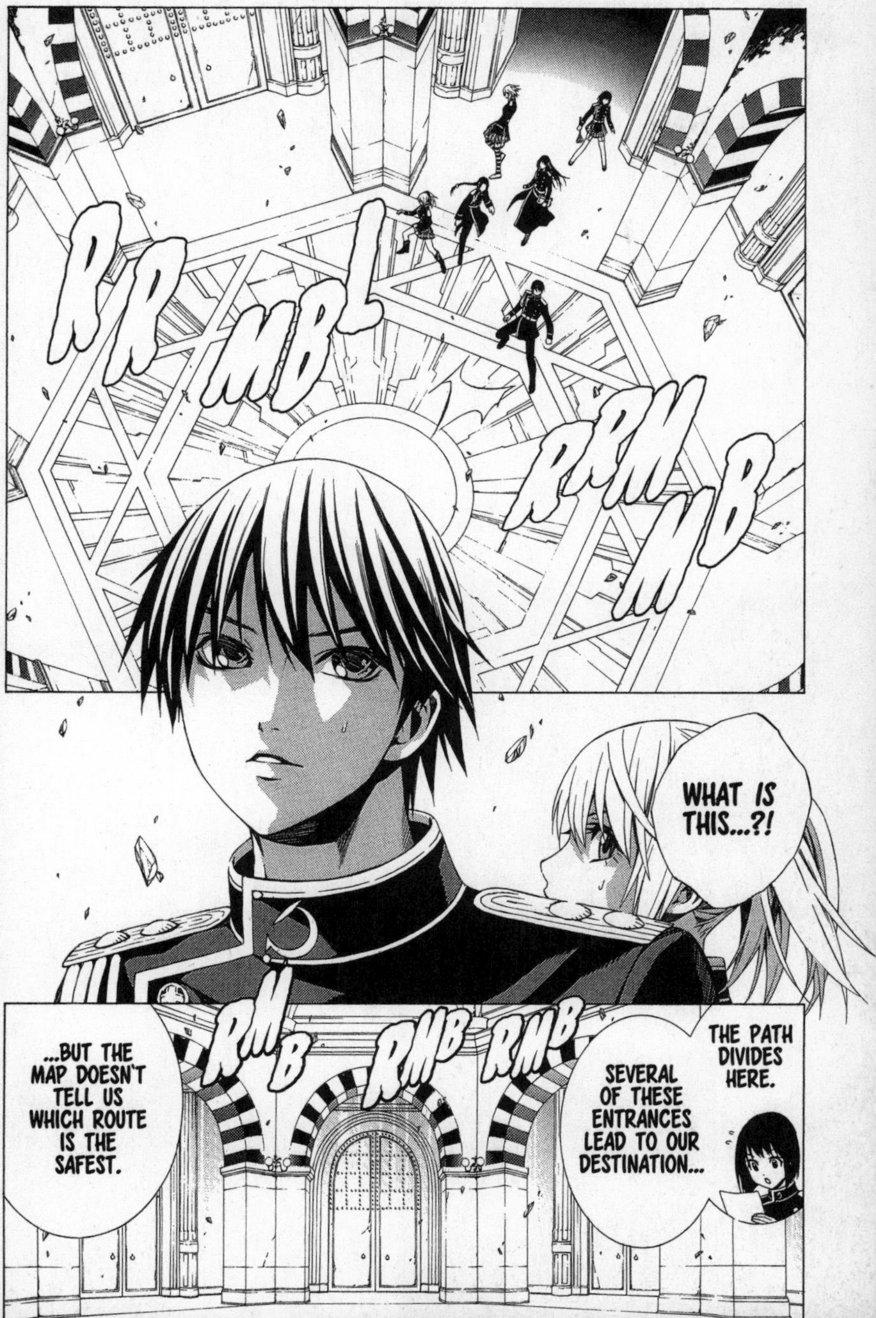
RRMMB
RRMBL
WHAT IS THIS...?!
THE PATH DIVIDES HERE.
SEVERAL OF THESE ENTRANCES LEAD TO OUR DESTINATION...
RMB RMB RMB
...BUT THE MAP DOESN'T TELL US WHICH ROUTE IS THE SAFEST.

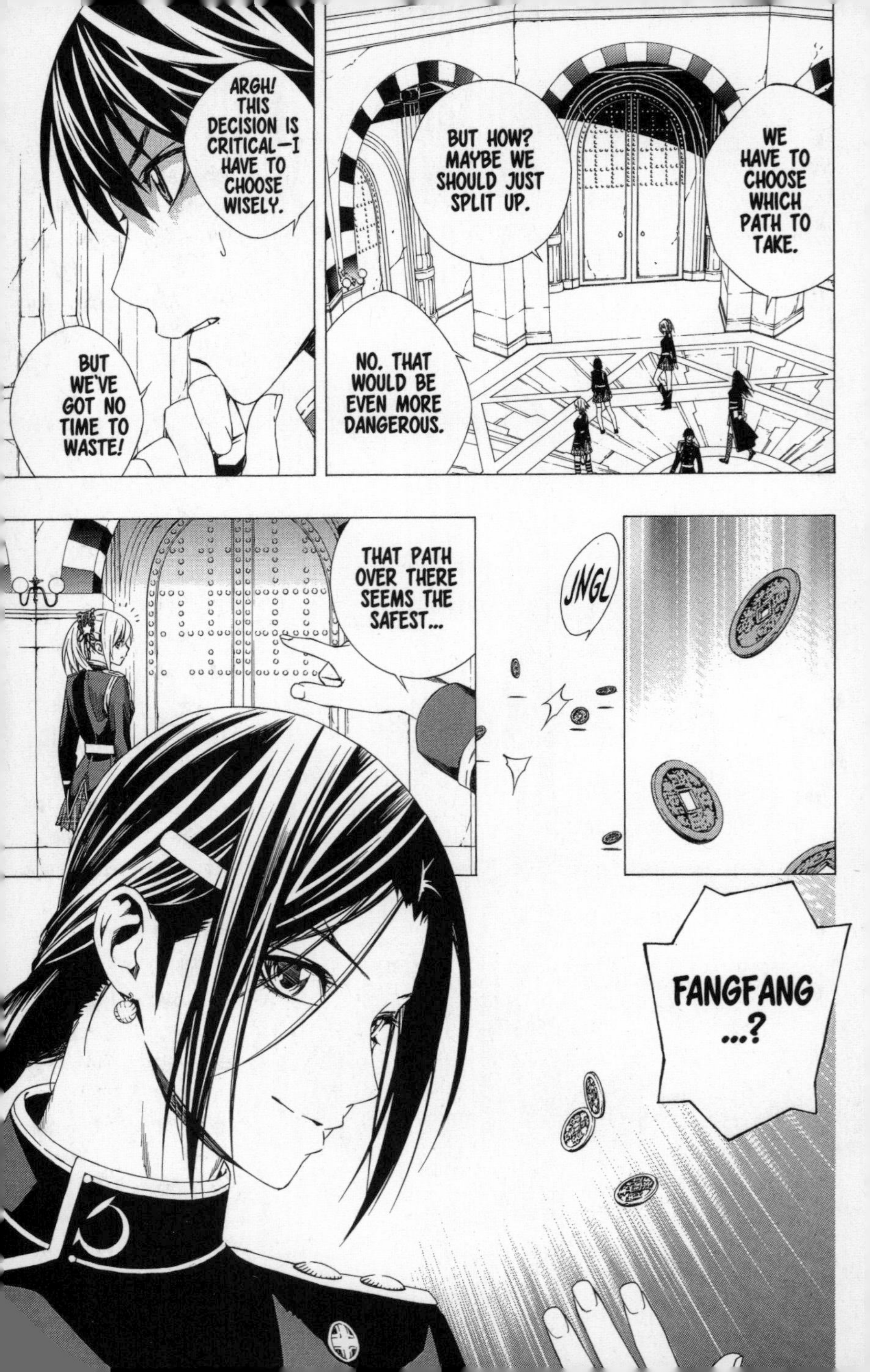
WE HAVE TO CHOOSE WHICH PATH TO TAKE.
BUT HOW? MAYBE WE SHOULD JUST SPLIT UP.
NO. THAT WOULD BE EVEN MORE DANGEROUS.
ARGH! THIS DECISION IS CRITICAL—I HAVE TO CHOOSE WISELY.
BUT WE'VE GOT NO TIME TO WASTE!
JNGL
THAT PATH OVER THERE SEEMS THE SAFEST...
FANGFANG ...?

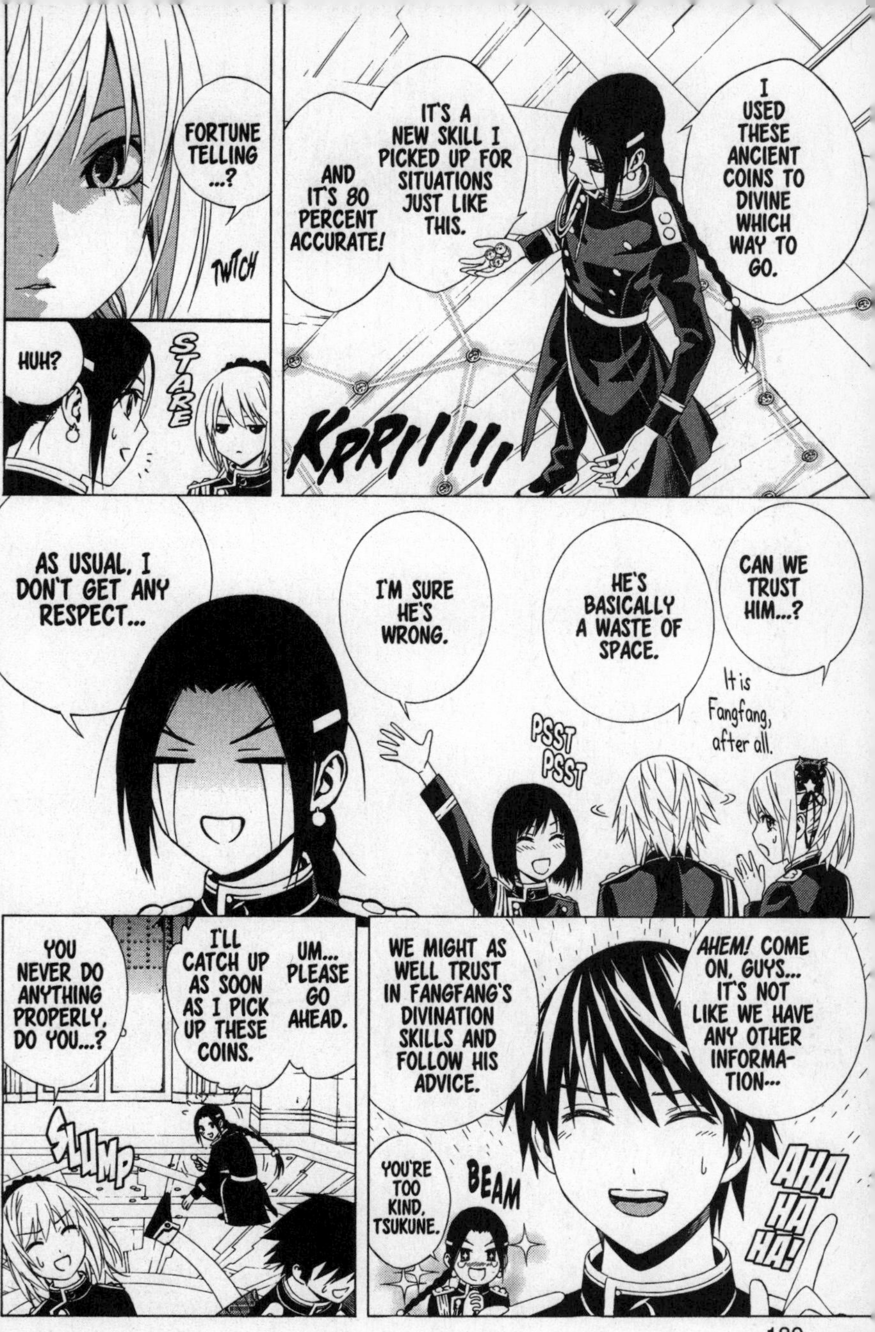
I USED THESE ANCIENT COINS TO DIVINE WHICH WAY TO GO.
IT'S A NEW SKILL I PICKED UP FOR SITUATIONS JUST LIKE THIS.
AND IT'S 80 PERCENT ACCURATE!
KRRIIIII
FORTUNE TELLING ...?
TWITCH
HUH?
STARE
CAN WE TRUST HIM...?
HE'S BASICALLY A WASTE OF SPACE.
I'M SURE HE'S WRONG.
It is Fangfang, after all.
PSST PSST
AS USUAL, I DON'T GET ANY RESPECT...
AHEM! COME ON, GUYS... IT'S NOT LIKE WE HAVE ANY OTHER INFORMA-TION...
WE MIGHT AS WELL TRUST IN FANGFANG'S DIVINATION SKILLS AND FOLLOW HIS ADVICE.
AHAHAHA!
BEAM
YOU'RE TOO KIND, TSUKUNE.
UM... PLEASE GO AHEAD.
I'LL CATCH UP AS SOON AS I PICK UP THESE COINS.
YOU NEVER DO ANYTHING PROPERLY, DO YOU...?
SLUMP

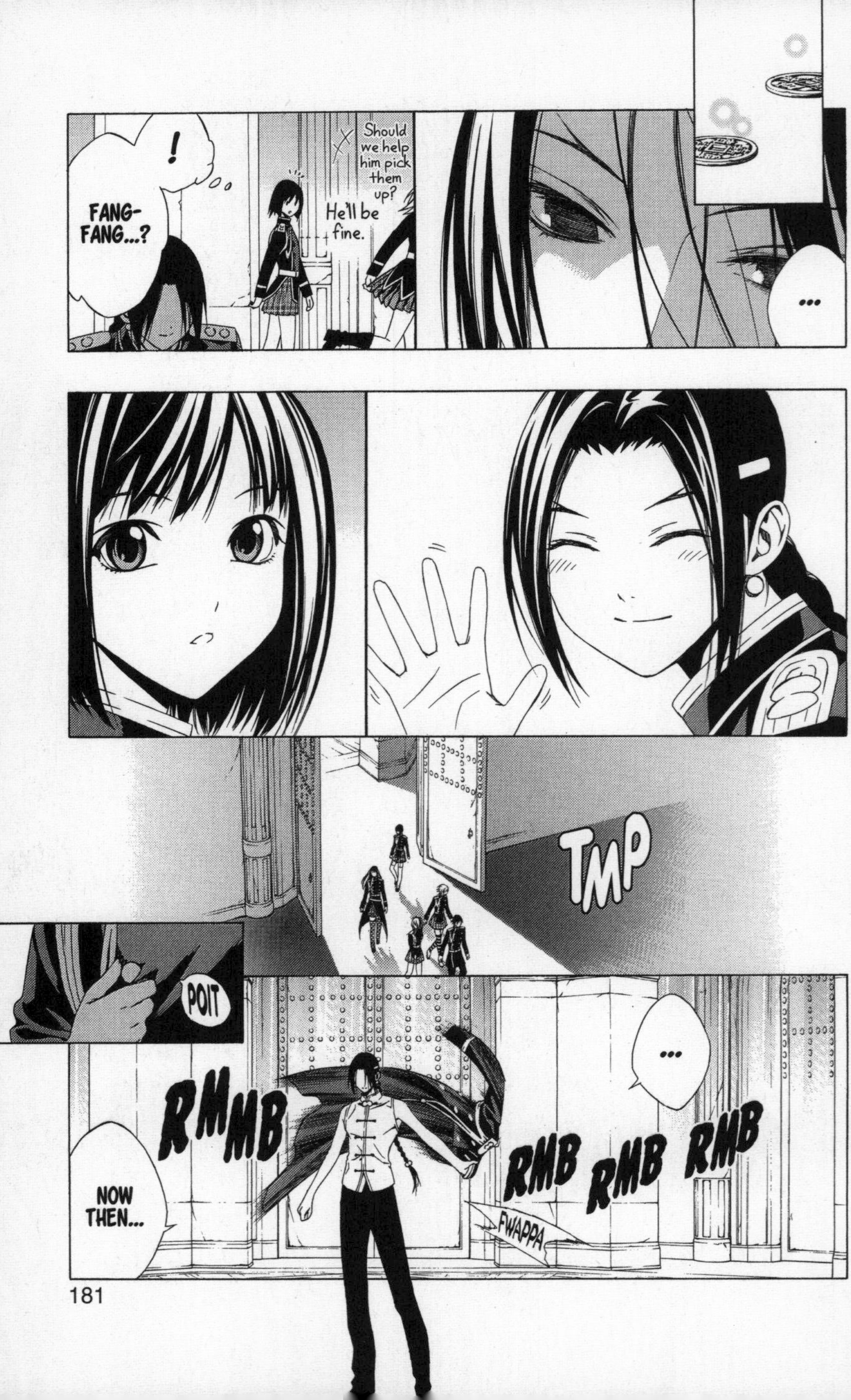
...
Should we help him pick them up?
He'll be fine.
!
FANG-FANG...?
TMP
POIT
...
RMB RMB RMB
FWAPPA
RMMB
NOW THEN...

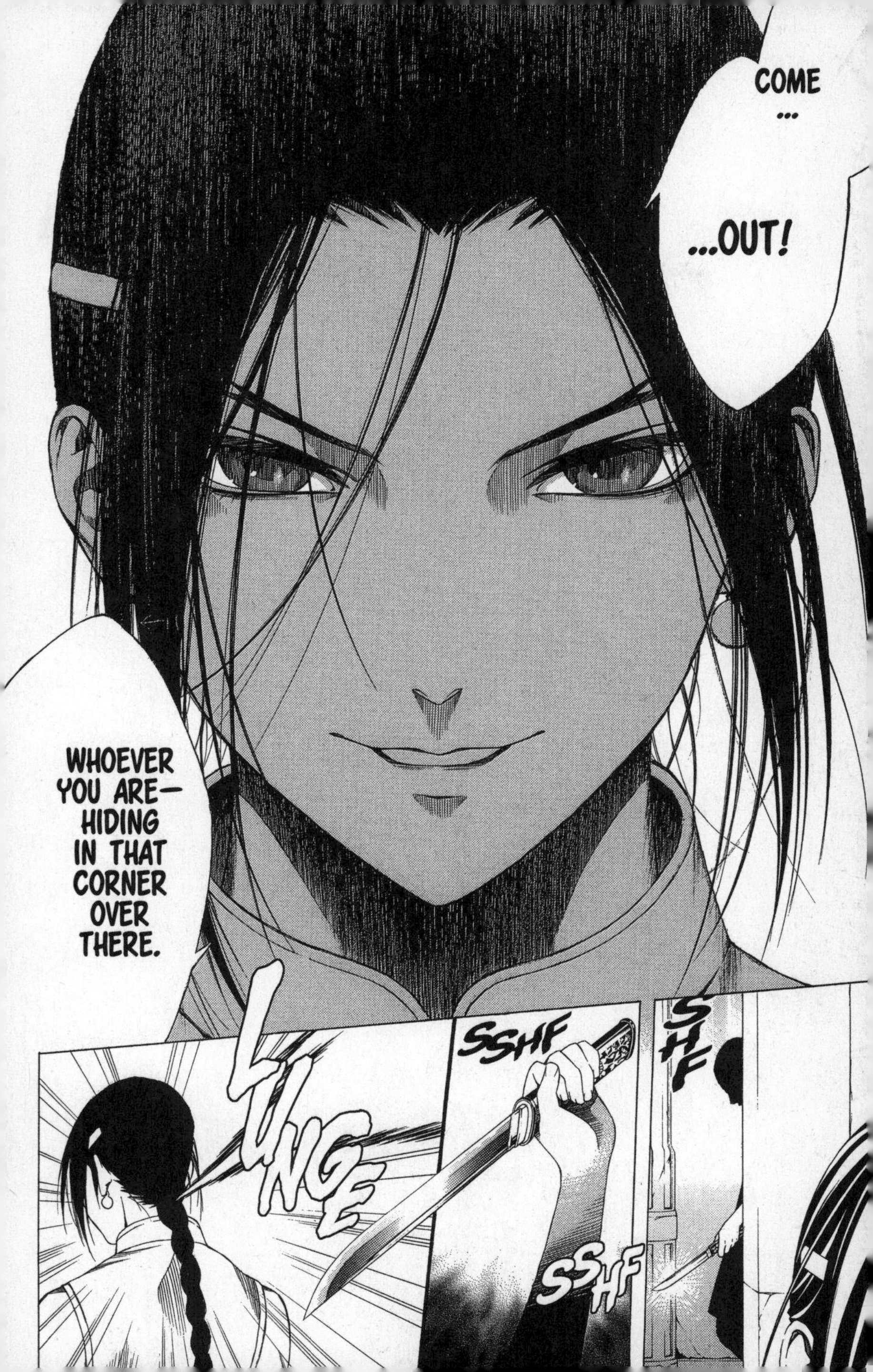
COME ...
...OUT!
WHOEVER YOU ARE— HIDING IN THAT CORNER OVER THERE.
SHF
SSHF
SSHF
LUNGE

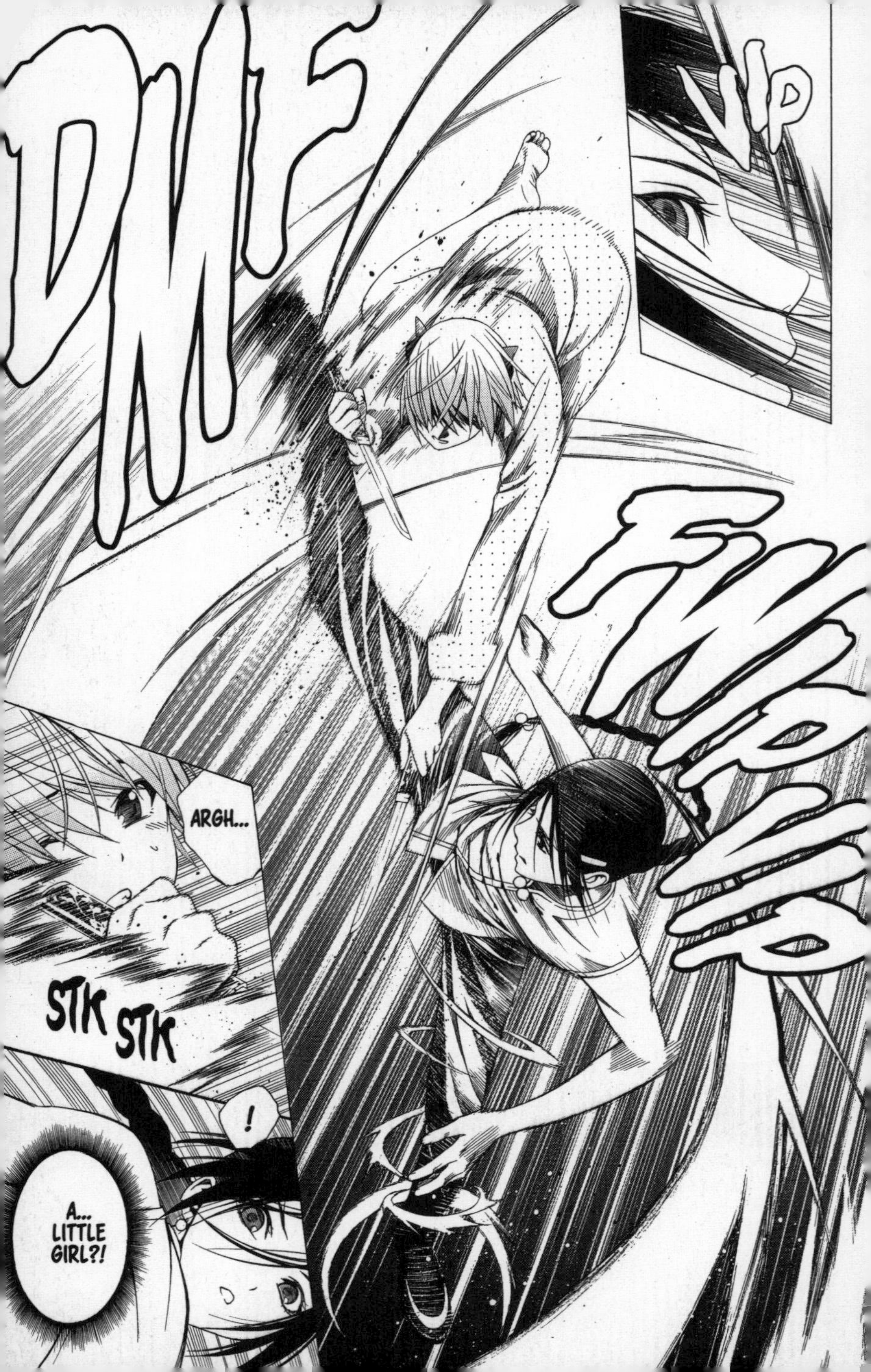
VIP
DMF
FWIP
ARGH...
STK STK
!
A... LITTLE GIRL?!

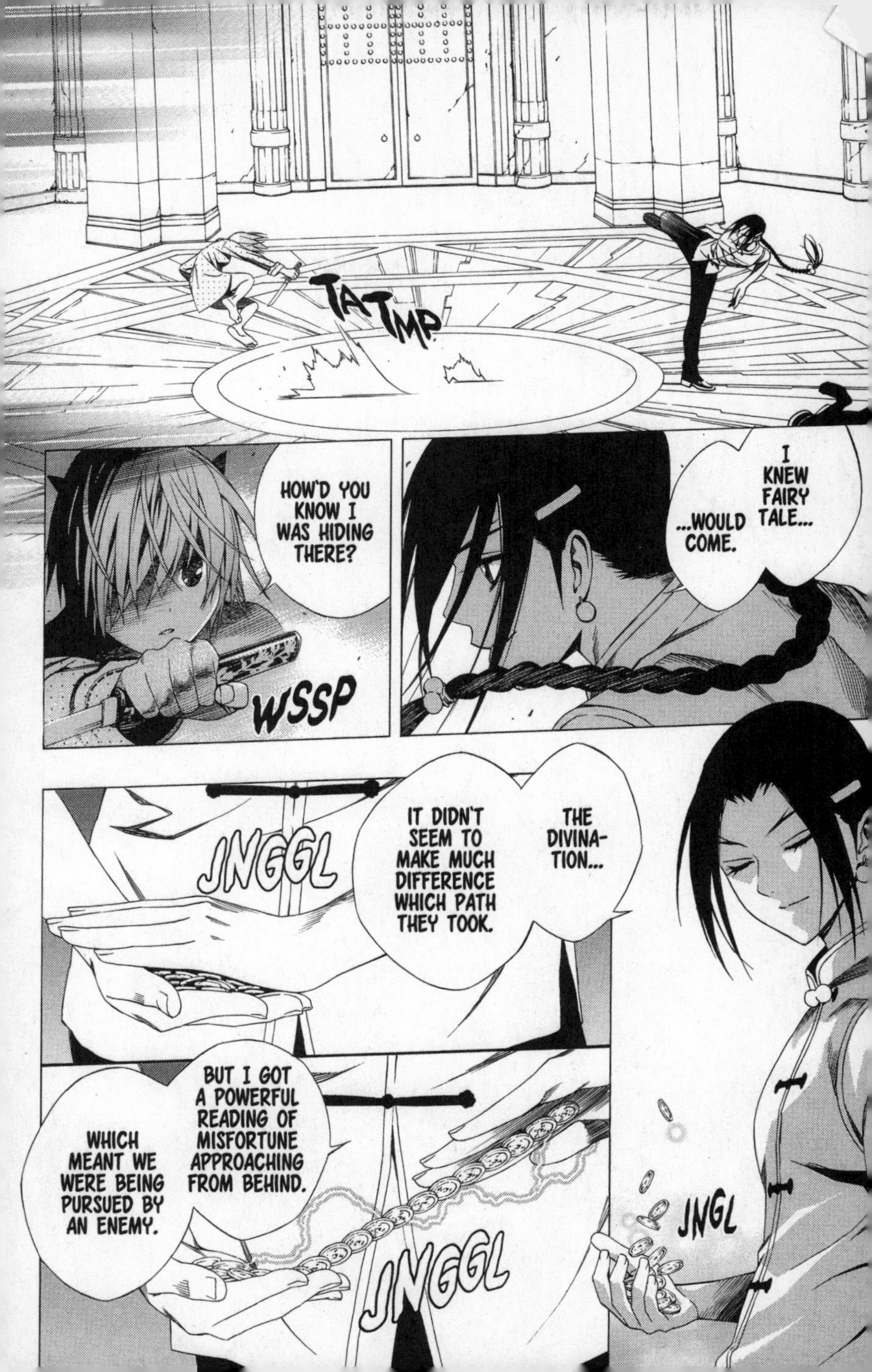
TATMP
I KNEW FAIRY TALE...
...WOULD COME.
HOW'D YOU KNOW I WAS HIDING THERE?
WSSP
JNGL
THE DIVINATION...
IT DIDN'T SEEM TO MAKE MUCH DIFFERENCE WHICH PATH THEY TOOK.
JNGGL
BUT I GOT A POWERFUL READING OF MISFORTUNE APPROACHING FROM BEHIND.
WHICH MEANT WE WERE BEING PURSUED BY AN ENEMY.
JNGGL

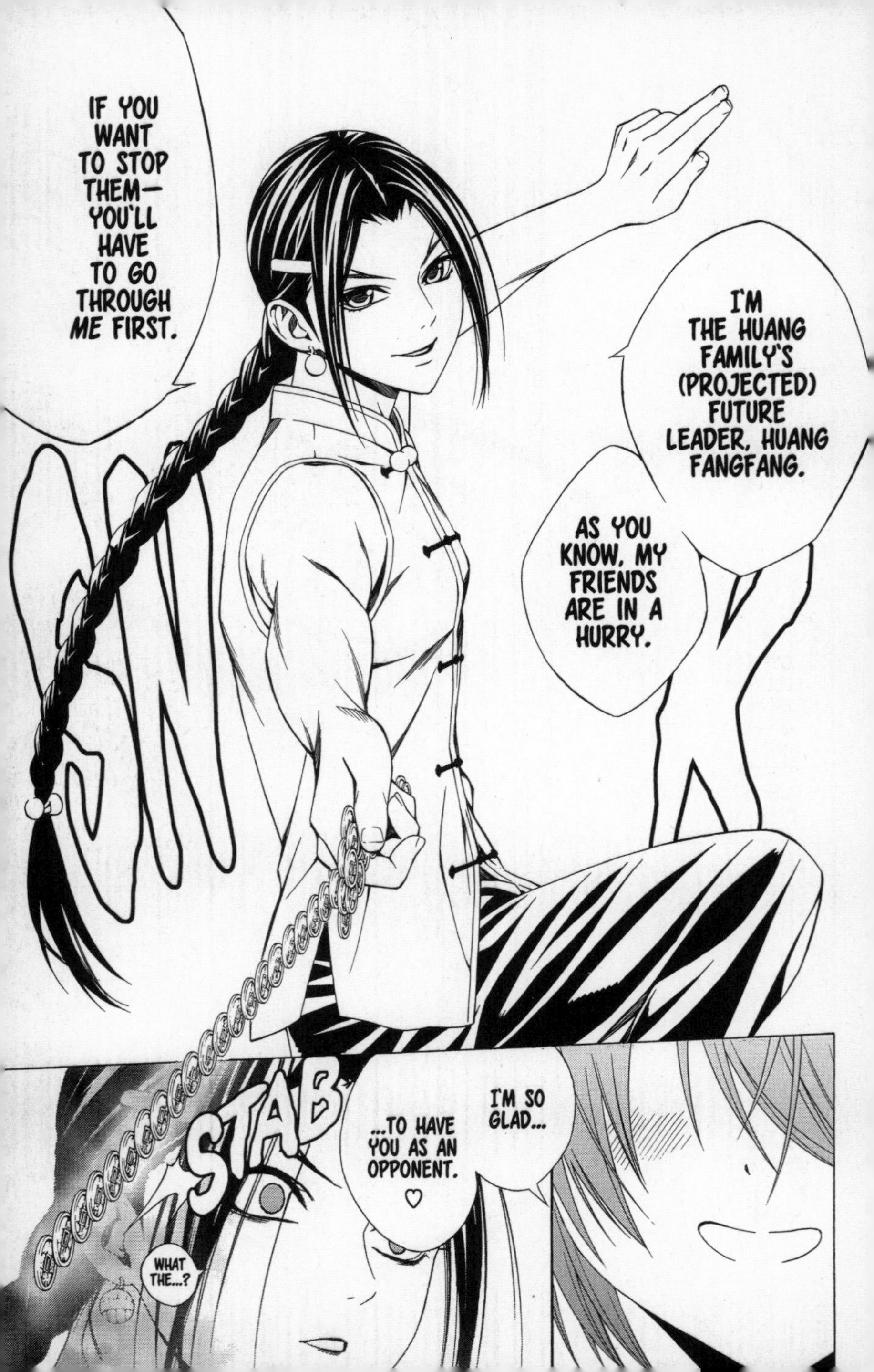
I'M THE HUANG FAMILY'S (PROJECTED) FUTURE LEADER, HUANG FANGFANG.
AS YOU KNOW, MY FRIENDS ARE IN A HURRY.
IF YOU WANT TO STOP THEM— YOU'LL HAVE TO GO THROUGH ME FIRST.
I'M SO GLAD...
...TO HAVE YOU AS AN OPPONENT. ♡
STAB
WHAT THE...?

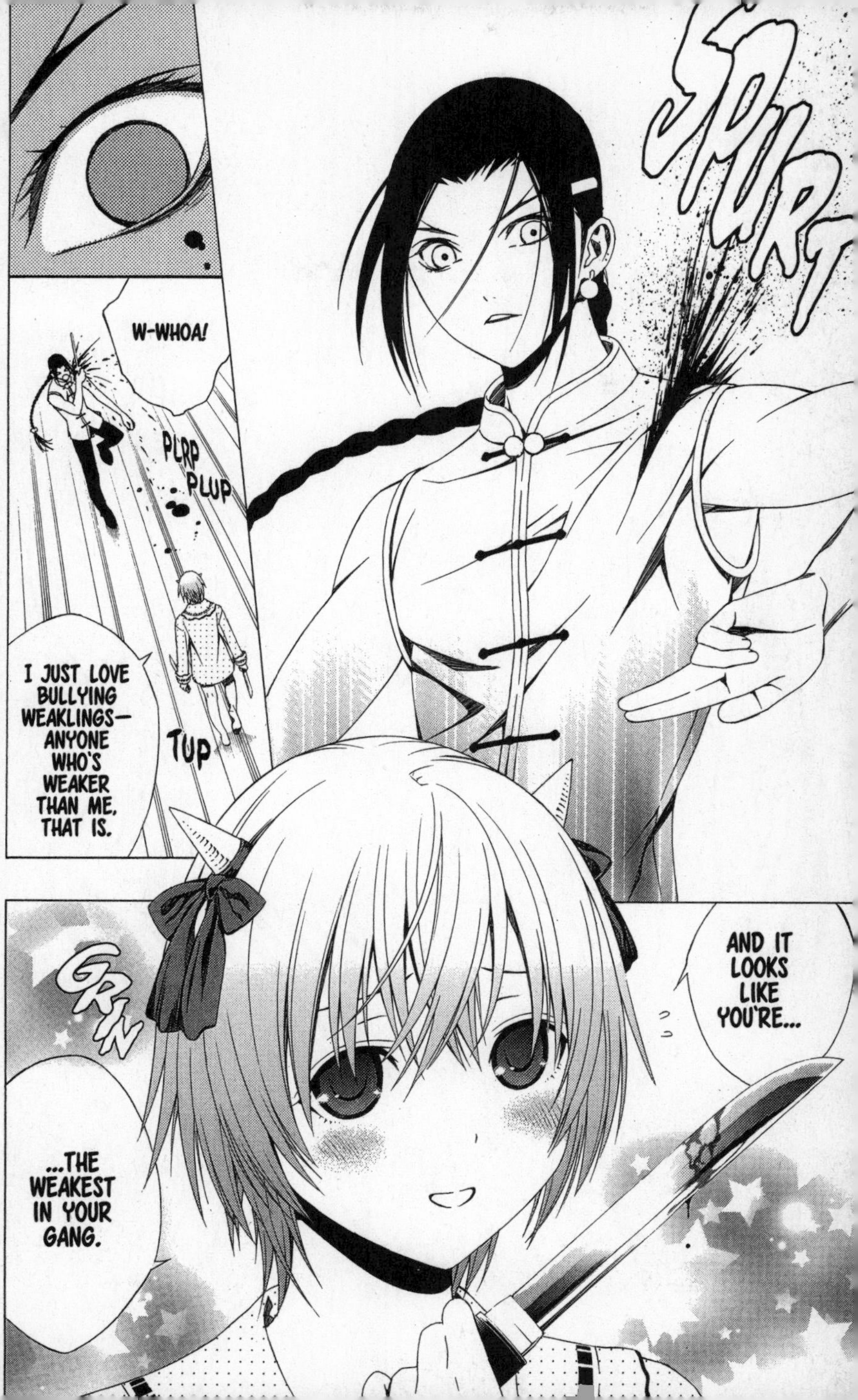
SPURT
W-WHOA!
PLRP PLUP
TUP
I JUST LOVE BULLYING WEAKLINGS— ANYONE WHO'S WEAKER THAN ME, THAT IS.
AND IT LOOKS LIKE YOU'RE...
GRIN
...THE WEAKEST IN YOUR GANG.

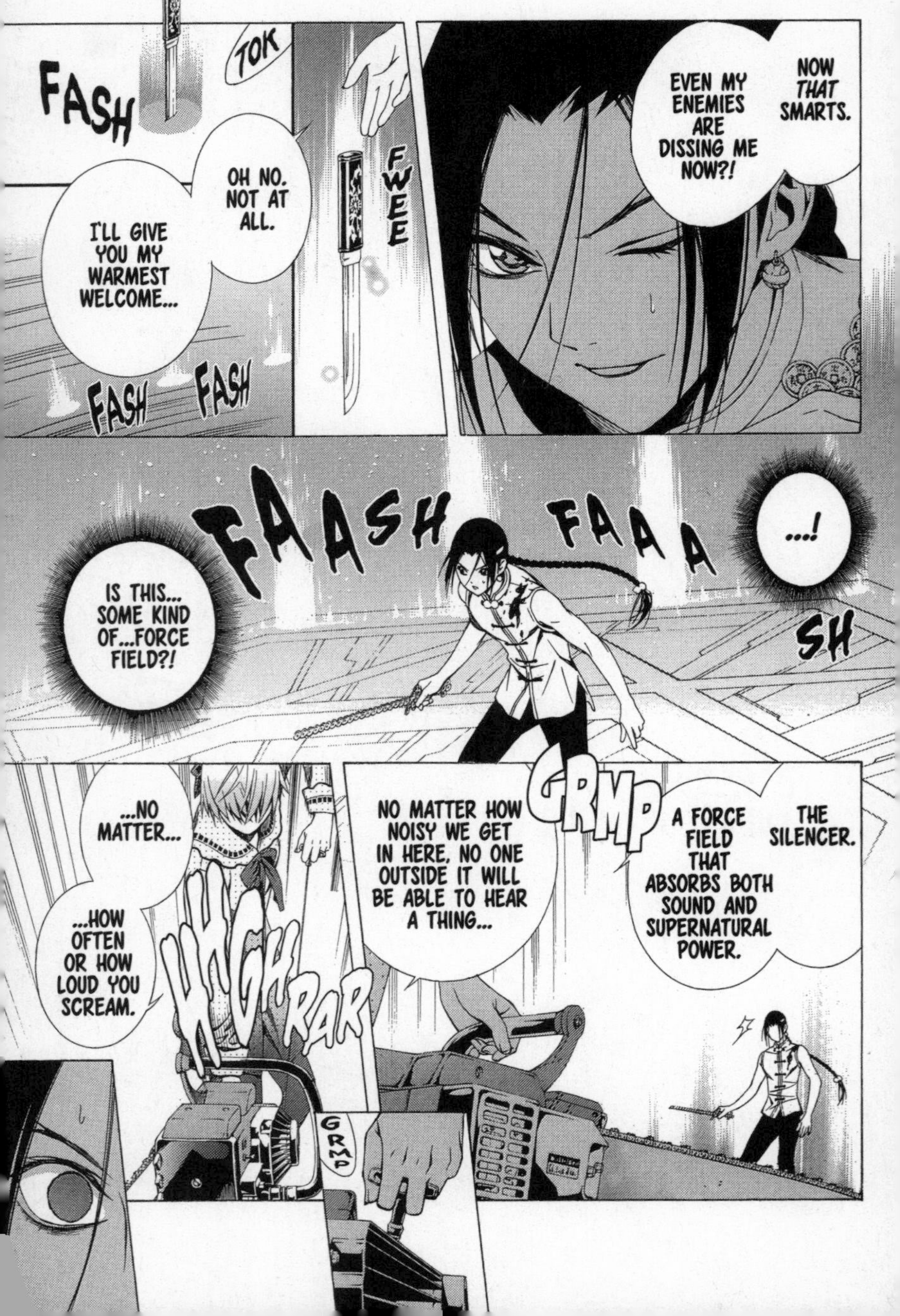
NOW THAT SMARTS.
EVEN MY ENEMIES ARE DISSING ME NOW?!
FWEE
OH NO. NOT AT ALL.
TOK
FASH
I'LL GIVE YOU MY WARMEST WELCOME...
FASH FASH
...!
FAAA
SH
FAASH
IS THIS... SOME KIND OF...FORCE FIELD?!
THE SILENCER.
A FORCE FIELD THAT ABSORBS BOTH SOUND AND SUPERNATURAL POWER.
GRMP
NO MATTER HOW NOISY WE GET IN HERE, NO ONE OUTSIDE IT WILL BE ABLE TO HEAR A THING...
...NO MATTER...
...HOW OFTEN OR HOW LOUD YOU SCREAM.
RAR
GRMP

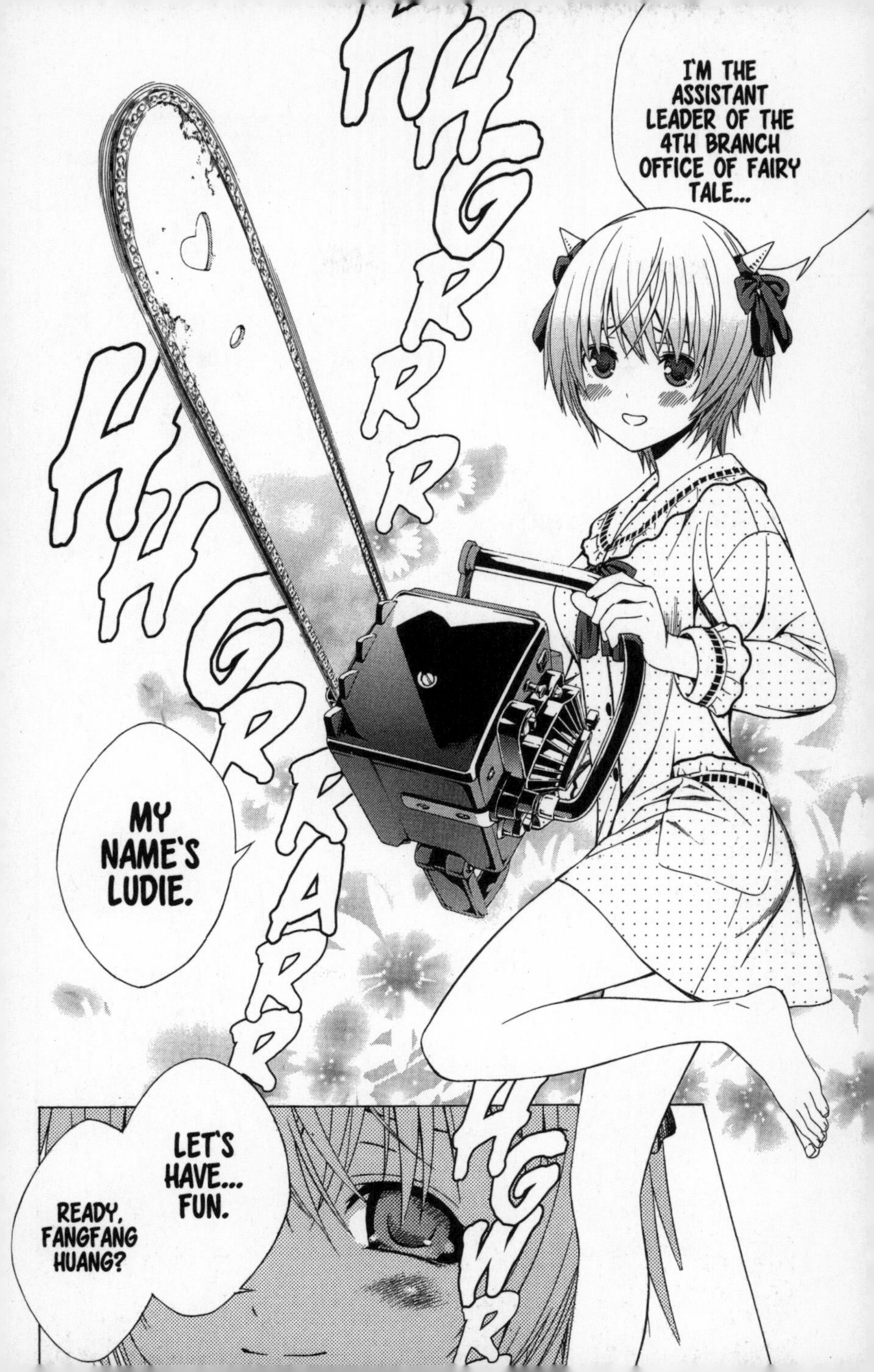
I'M THE ASSISTANT LEADER OF THE 4TH BRANCH OFFICE OF FAIRY TALE...
MY NAME'S LUDIE.
LET'S HAVE... FUN.
READY, FANGFANG HUANG?

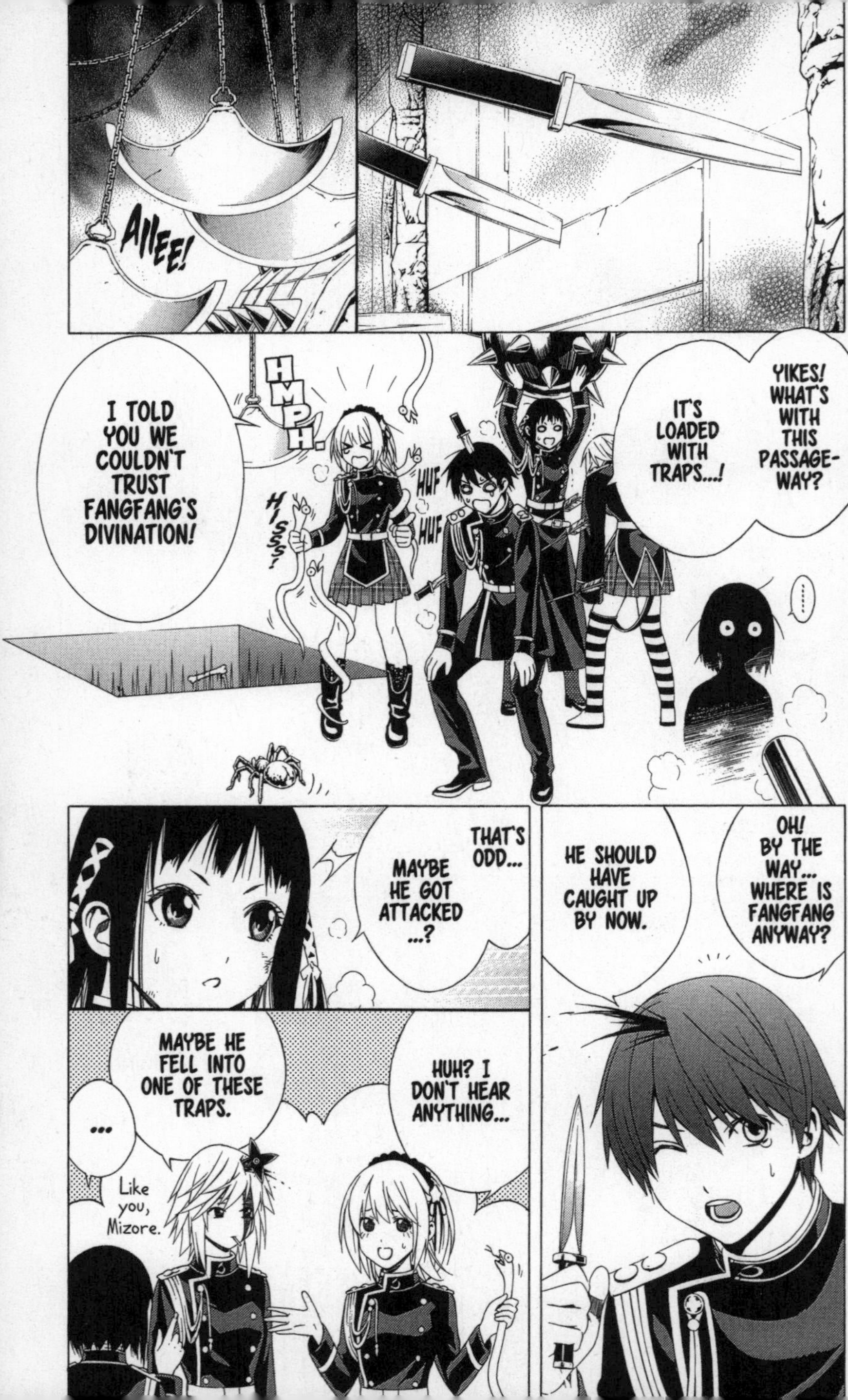
AIIEE!
YIKES! WHAT'S WITH THIS PASSAGE-WAY?
IT'S LOADED WITH TRAPS...!
HUF HUF
HISS!
HMPH.
I TOLD YOU WE COULDN'T TRUST FANGFANG'S DIVINATION!
OH! BY THE WAY... WHERE IS FANGFANG ANYWAY?
HE SHOULD HAVE CAUGHT UP BY NOW.
THAT'S ODD...
MAYBE HE GOT ATTACKED ...?
HUH? I DON'T HEAR ANYTHING...
MAYBE HE FELL INTO ONE OF THESE TRAPS.
...
Like you, Mizore.

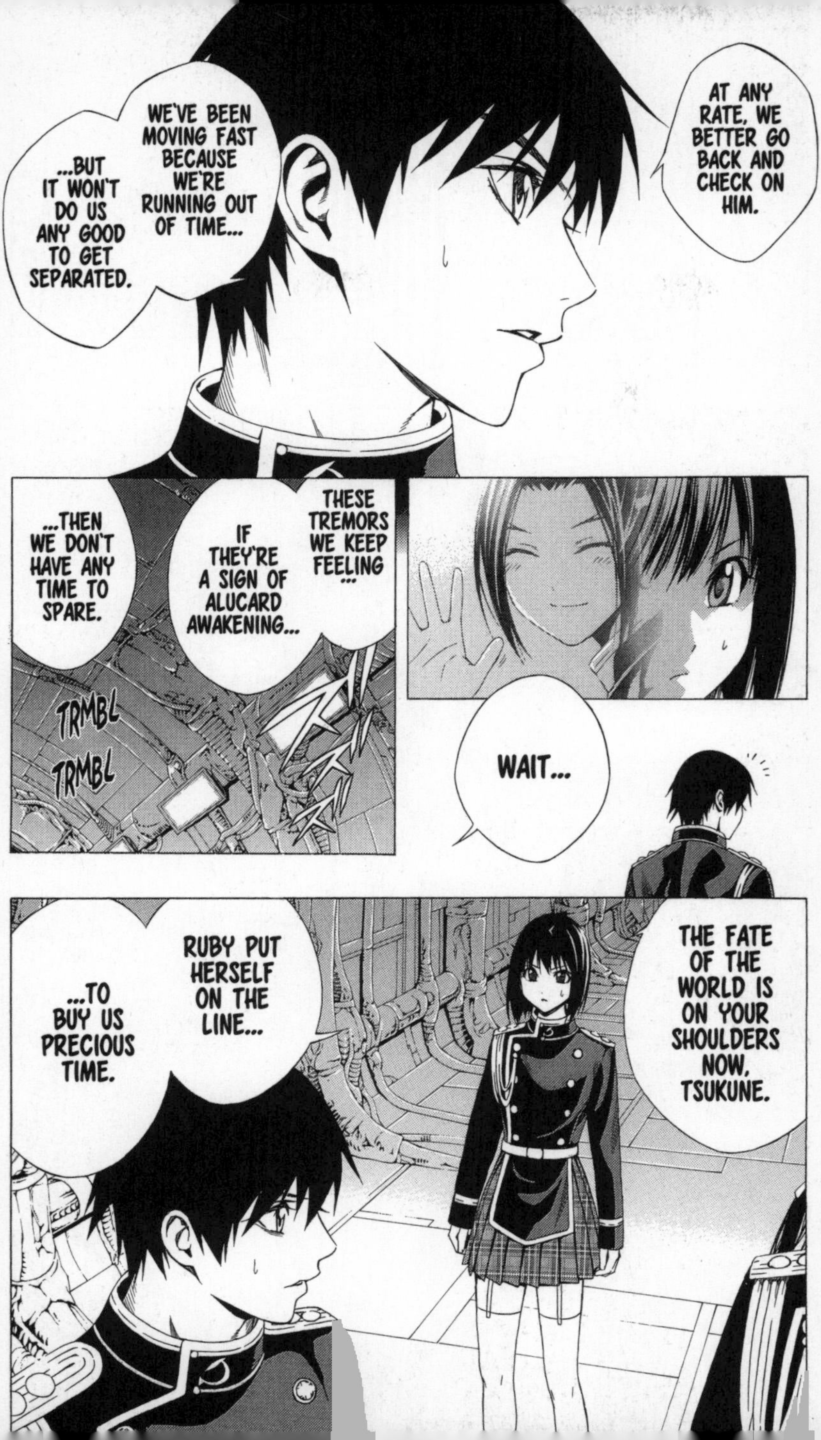
AT ANY RATE, WE BETTER GO BACK AND CHECK ON HIM.
WE'VE BEEN MOVING FAST BECAUSE WE'RE RUNNING OUT OF TIME...
...BUT IT WON'T DO US ANY GOOD TO GET SEPARATED.
THESE TREMORS WE KEEP FEELING...
IF THEY'RE A SIGN OF ALUCARD AWAKENING...
...THEN WE DON'T HAVE ANY TIME TO SPARE.
TRMBL
TRMBL
WAIT...
THE FATE OF THE WORLD IS ON YOUR SHOULDERS NOW, TSUKUNE.
RUBY PUT HERSELF ON THE LINE...
...TO BUY US PRECIOUS TIME.

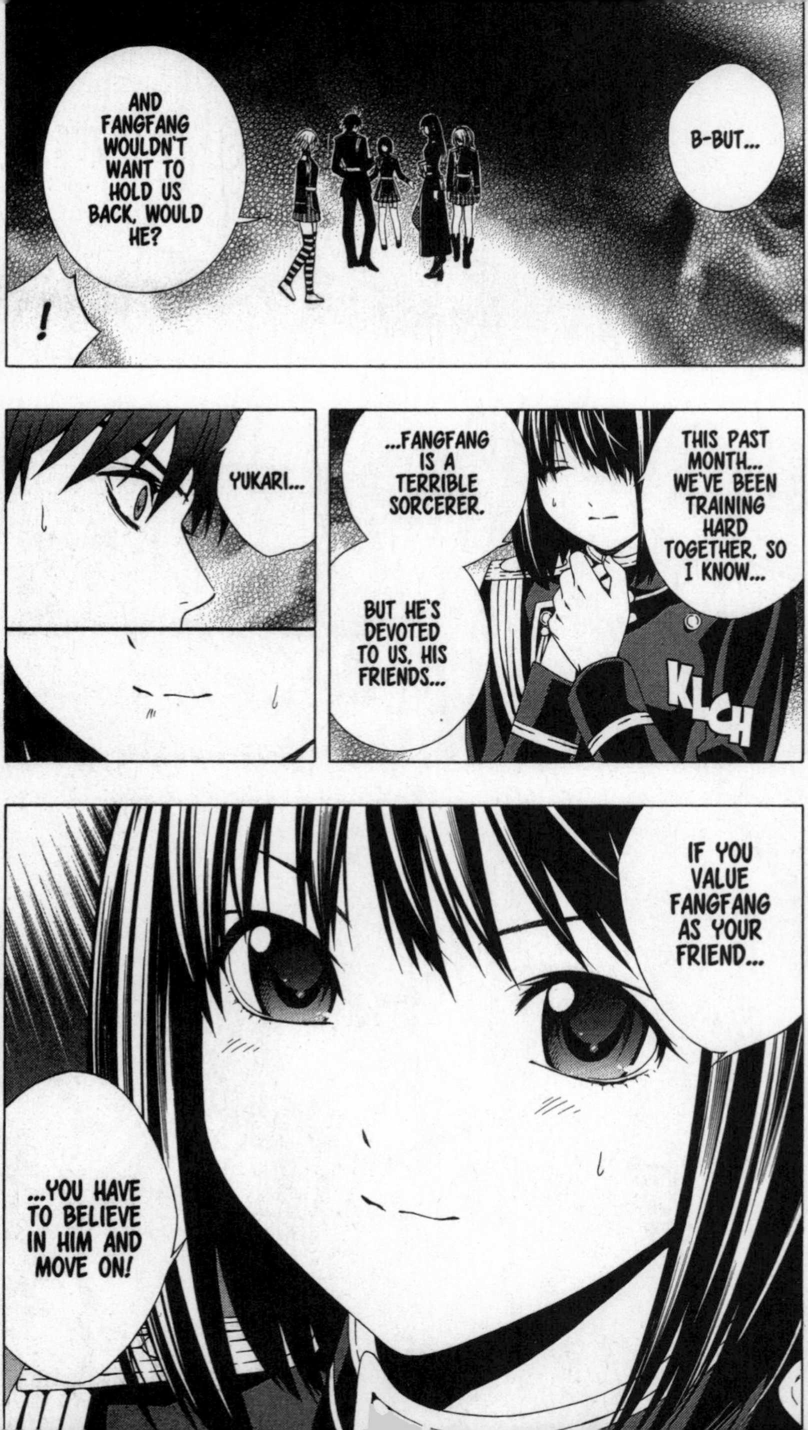
B-BUT...
AND FANGFANG WOULDN'T WANT TO HOLD US BACK, WOULD HE?
!
THIS PAST MONTH... WE'VE BEEN TRAINING HARD TOGETHER, SO I KNOW...
...FANGFANG IS A TERRIBLE SORCERER.
BUT HE'S DEVOTED TO US, HIS FRIENDS...
KLCH
YUKARI...
IF YOU VALUE FANGFANG AS YOUR FRIEND...
...YOU HAVE TO BELIEVE IN HIM AND MOVE ON!

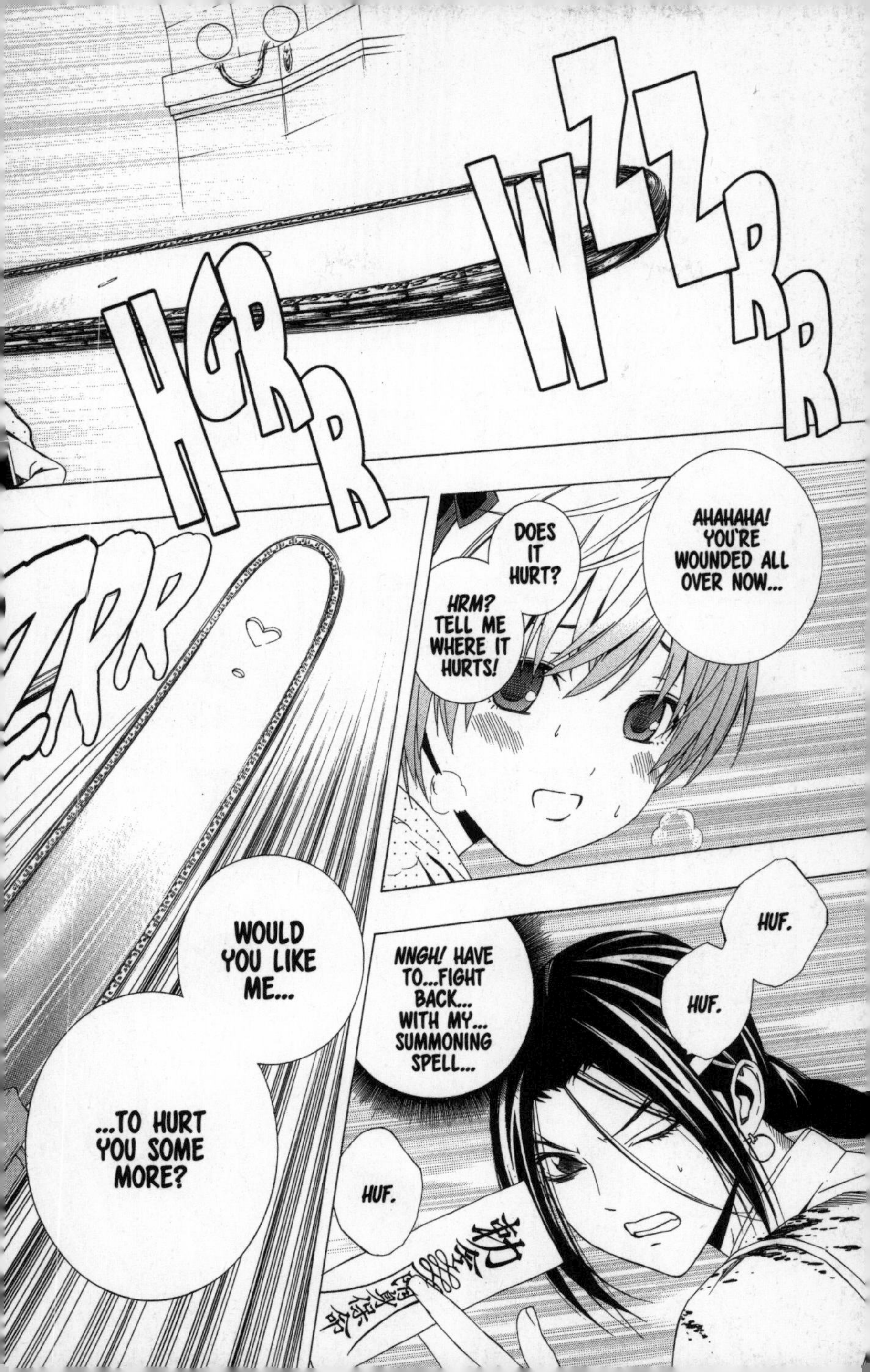
WZZRRR
HGRR
AHAHAHA! YOU'RE WOUNDED ALL OVER NOW...
DOES IT HURT?
HRM? TELL ME WHERE IT HURTS!
ZRR
HUF.
HUF.
NNGH! HAVE TO...FIGHT BACK... WITH MY... SUMMONING SPELL...
HUF.
WOULD YOU LIKE ME...
...TO HURT YOU SOME MORE?

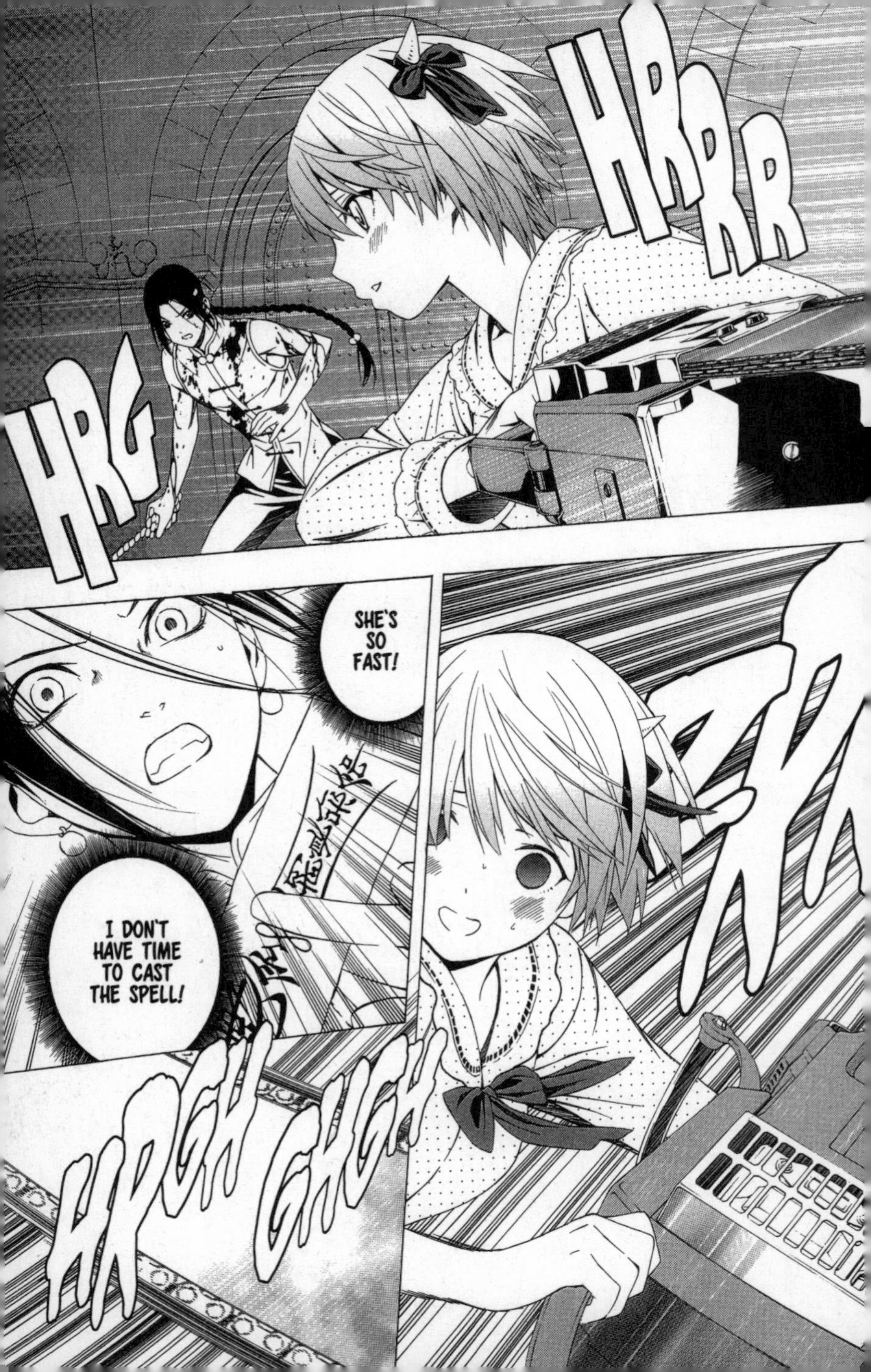
HRRRR
HRG
SHE'S SO FAST!
I DON'T HAVE TIME TO CAST THE SPELL!

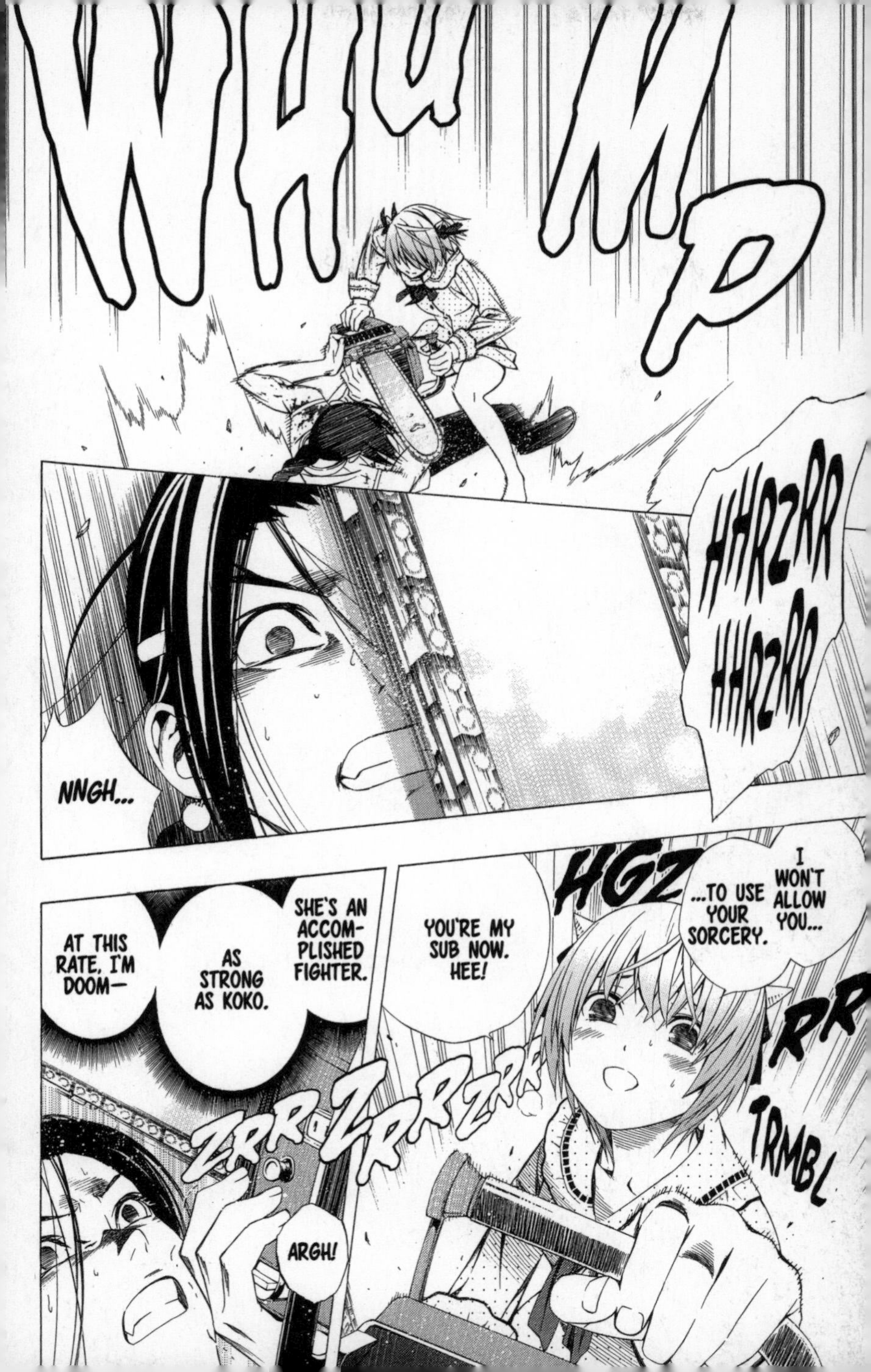
WHUMP
HHRZRR
HHRZRR
NNGH...
I WON'T ALLOW YOU...
...TO USE YOUR SORCERY.
HGZ
YOU'RE MY SUB NOW. HEE!
RR
TRMBL
ZRR ZRR ZRRZRR
SHE'S AN ACCOM-PLISHED FIGHTER.
AS STRONG AS KOKO.
AT THIS RATE, I'M DOOM—
ARGH!

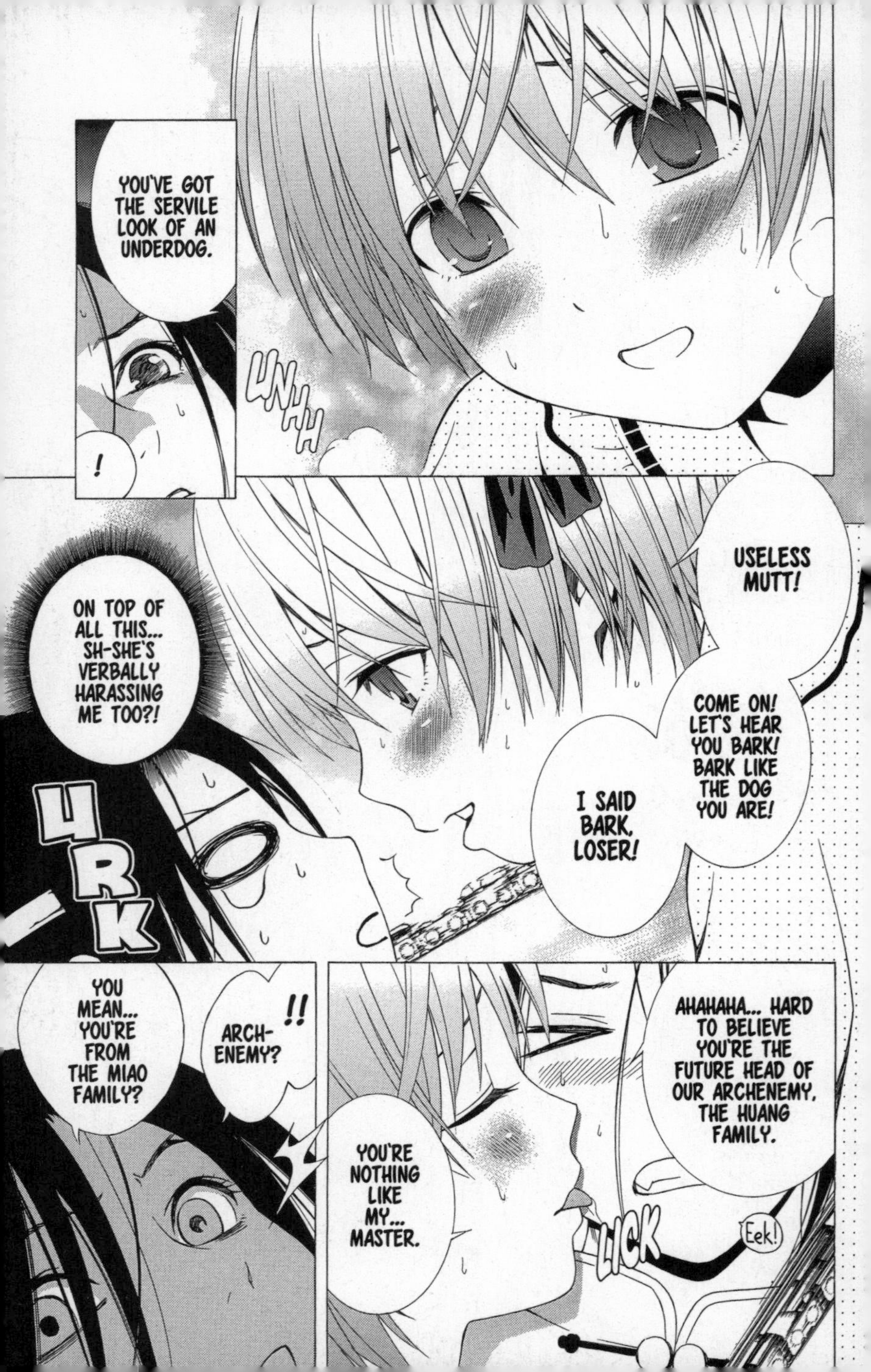
UNHH
YOU'VE GOT THE SERVILE LOOK OF AN UNDERDOG.
!
USELESS MUTT!
COME ON! LET'S HEAR YOU BARK! BARK LIKE THE DOG YOU ARE!
I SAID BARK, LOSER!
ON TOP OF ALL THIS... SH-SHE'S VERBALLY HARASSING ME TOO?!
URK
AHAHAHA... HARD TO BELIEVE YOU'RE THE FUTURE HEAD OF OUR ARCHENEMY, THE HUANG FAMILY.
Eek!
LICK
YOU'RE NOTHING LIKE MY... MASTER.
!!
ARCH-ENEMY?
YOU MEAN... YOU'RE FROM THE MIAO FAMILY?

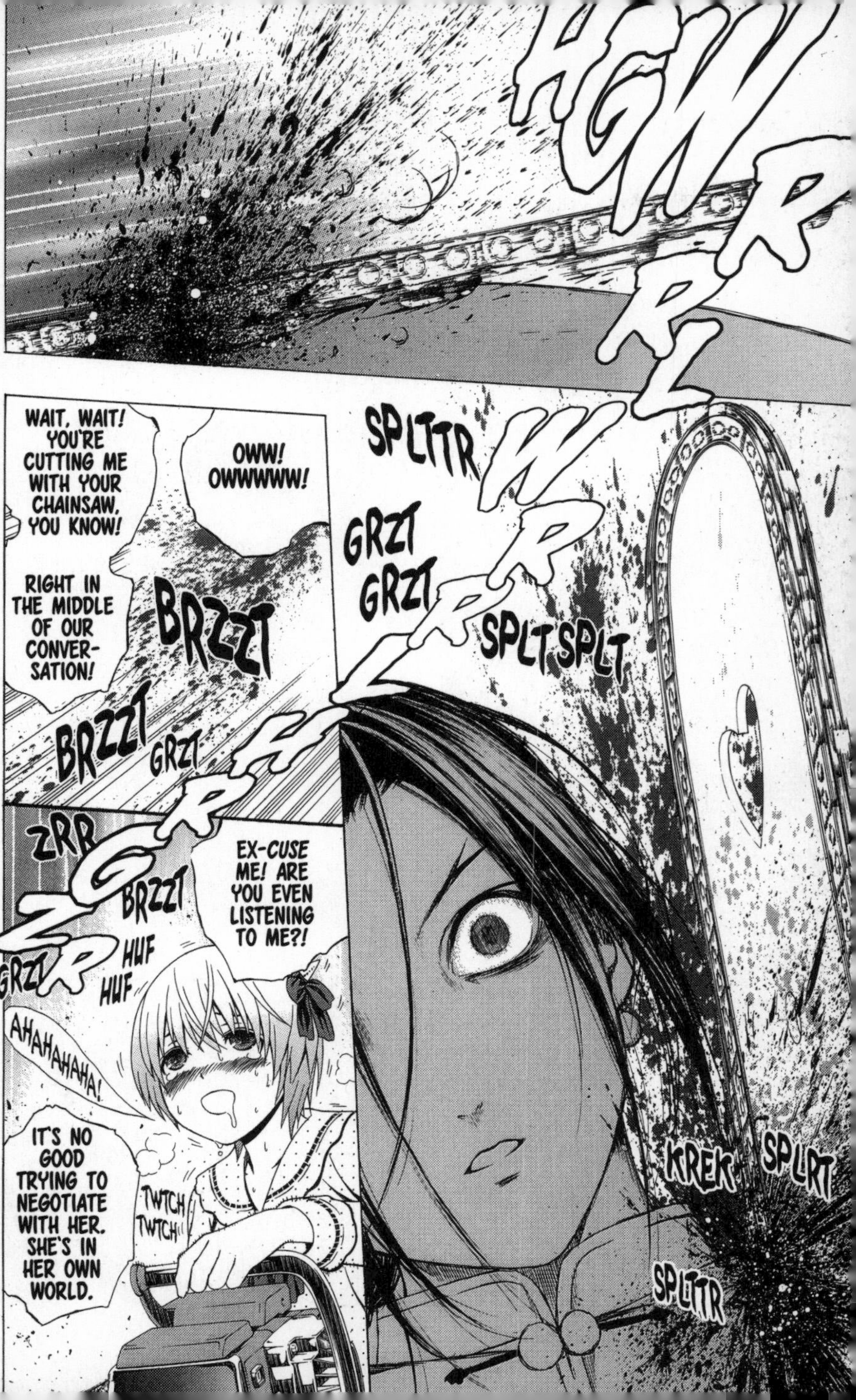
HGWRRL
SPLTTR
WRRLH
GRZT GRZT
SPLT SPLT
KREK
SPLRT
SPLTTR
OWW! OWWWWW!
WAIT, WAIT! YOU'RE CUTTING ME WITH YOUR CHAINSAW, YOU KNOW!
RIGHT IN THE MIDDLE OF OUR CONVER-SATION!
BRZZZT
BRZZZT
GRZT
RGZR
ZRR
EX-CUSE ME! ARE YOU EVEN LISTENING TO ME?!
BRZZZT
GRZT
HUF HUF
AHAHAHAHA!
IT'S NO GOOD TRYING TO NEGOTIATE WITH HER. SHE'S IN HER OWN WORLD.
TWTCH TWTCH

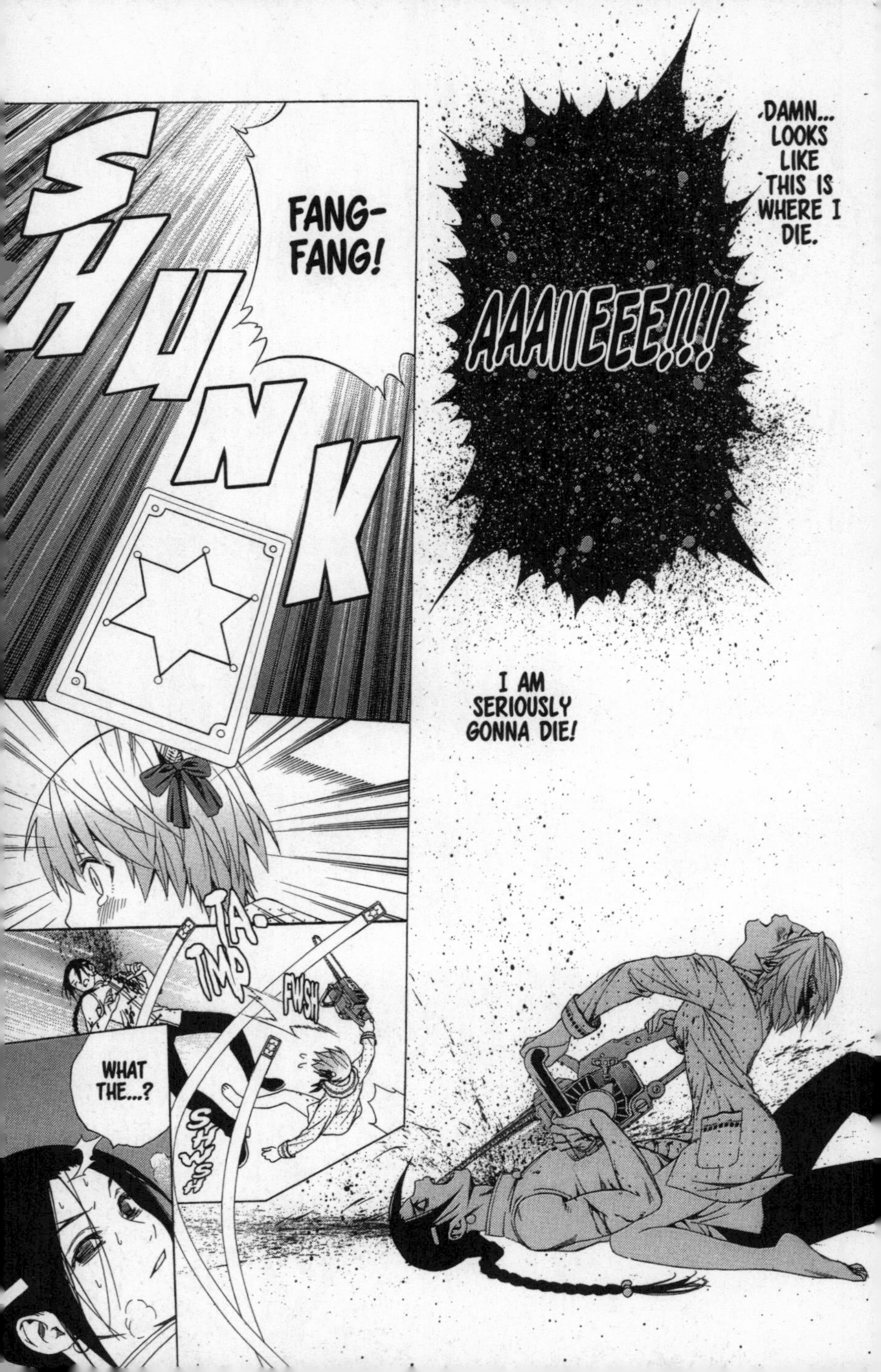

DAMN... LOOKS LIKE THIS IS WHERE I DIE.
AAAIIEEE!!!
I AM SERIOUSLY GONNA DIE!
SHUNK
FANG-FANG!
TA-TMP
FWSH
WHAT THE...?
SHWSH

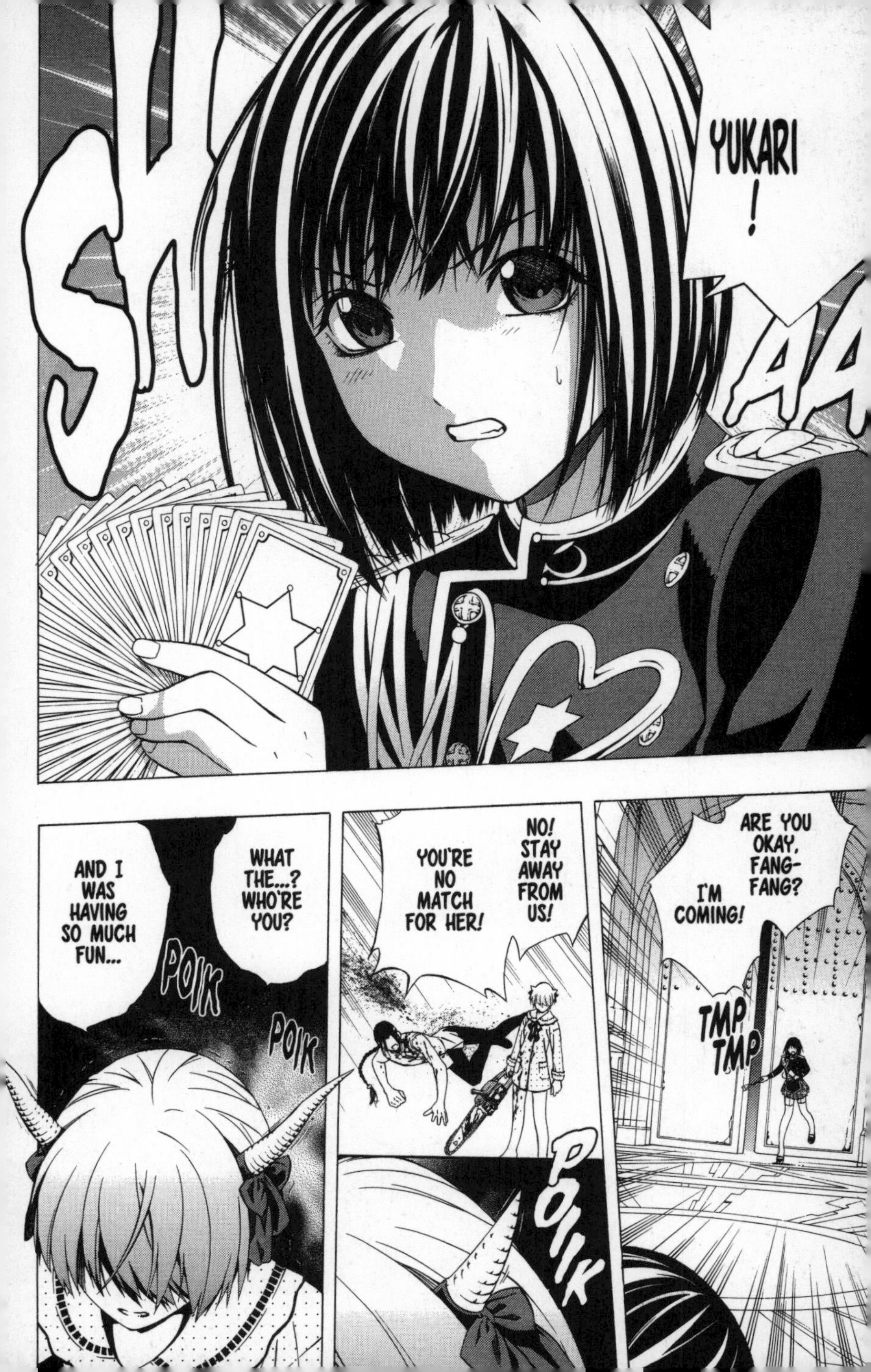
YUKARI!
ARE YOU OKAY, FANG-FANG?
I'M COMING!
TMP TMP
NO! STAY AWAY FROM US!
YOU'RE NO MATCH FOR HER!
POIIK
WHAT THE...? WHO'RE YOU?
AND I WAS HAVING SO MUCH FUN...
POIK
POIK

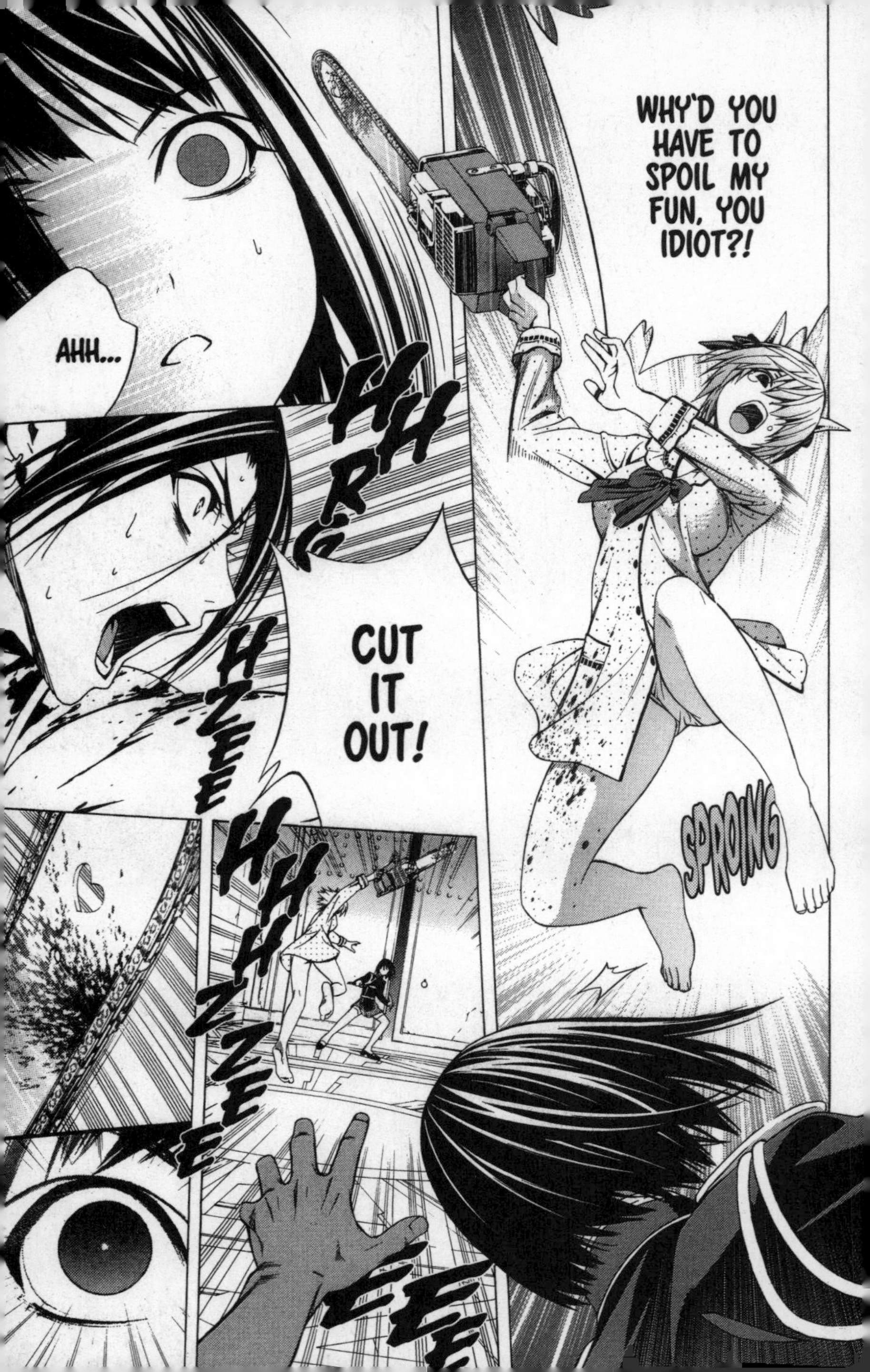
WHY'D YOU HAVE TO SPOIL MY FUN, YOU IDIOT?!
SPROING
AHH...
HHRRG
CUT IT OUT!
HZEEE
HHHHZZZEEE

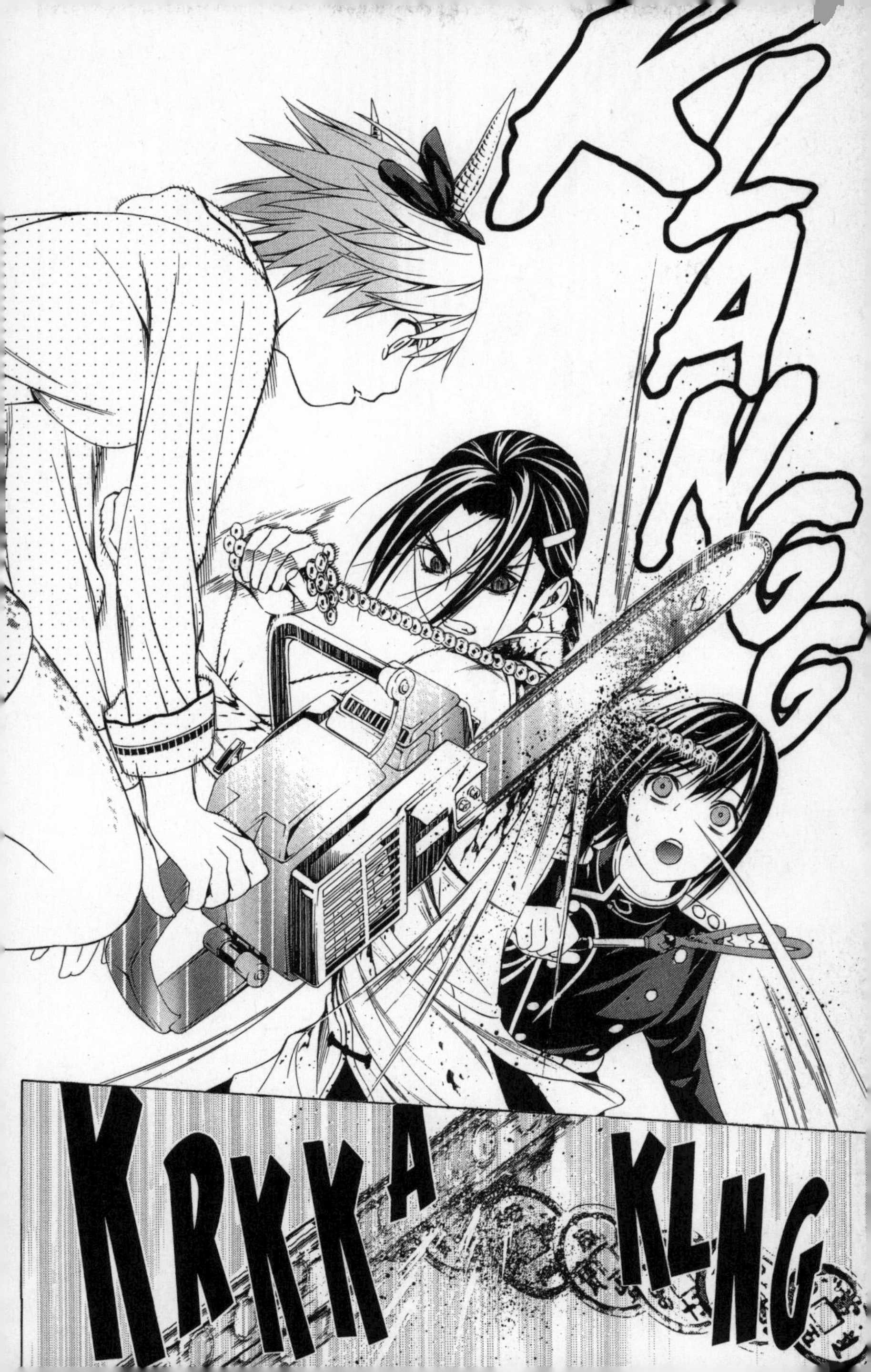
KLANGG
KRKKA KLNG

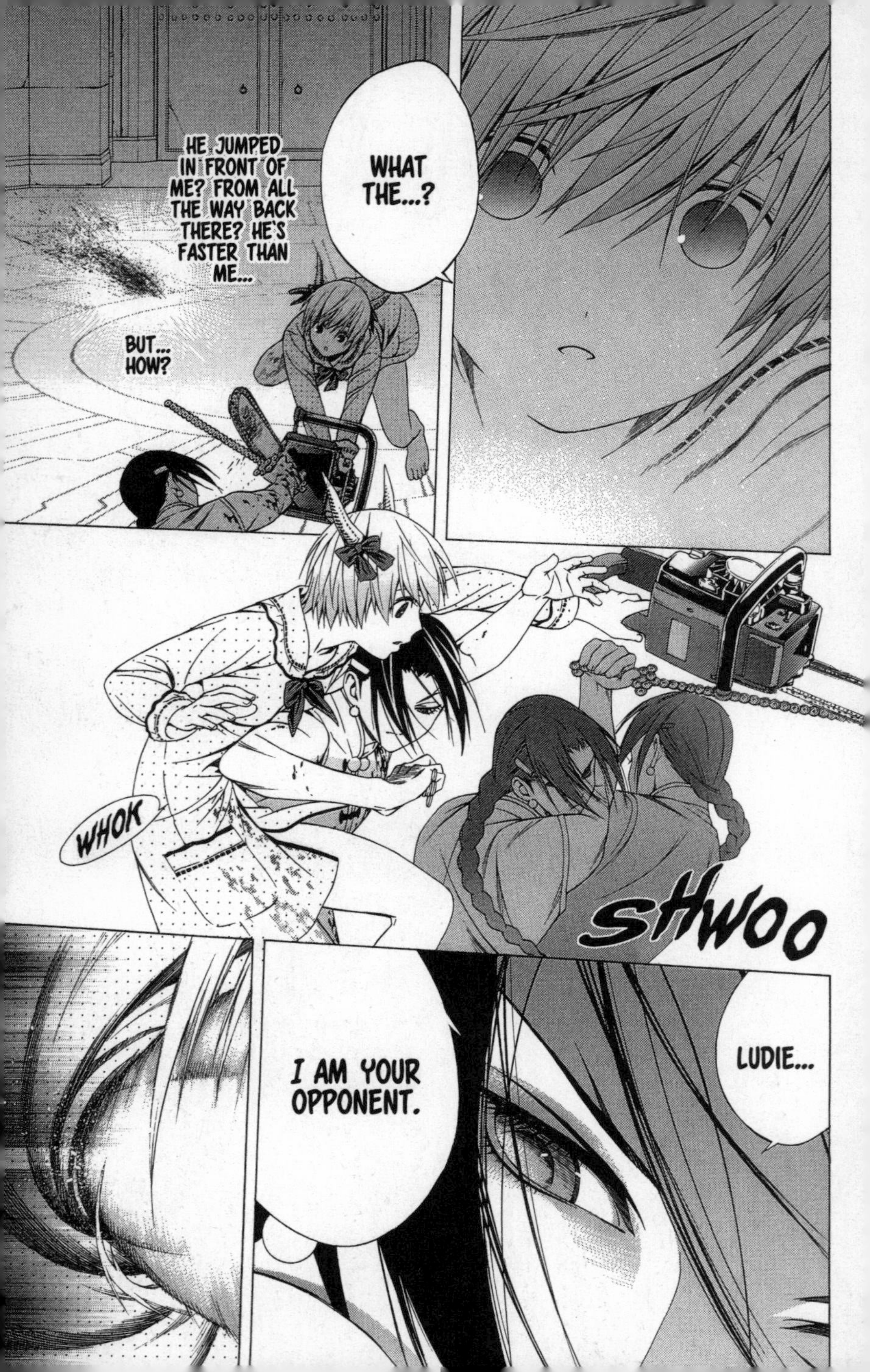
WHAT THE...?
HE JUMPED IN FRONT OF ME? FROM ALL THE WAY BACK THERE? HE'S FASTER THAN ME...
BUT... HOW?
SHWOO
WHOK
LUDIE...
I AM YOUR OPPONENT.

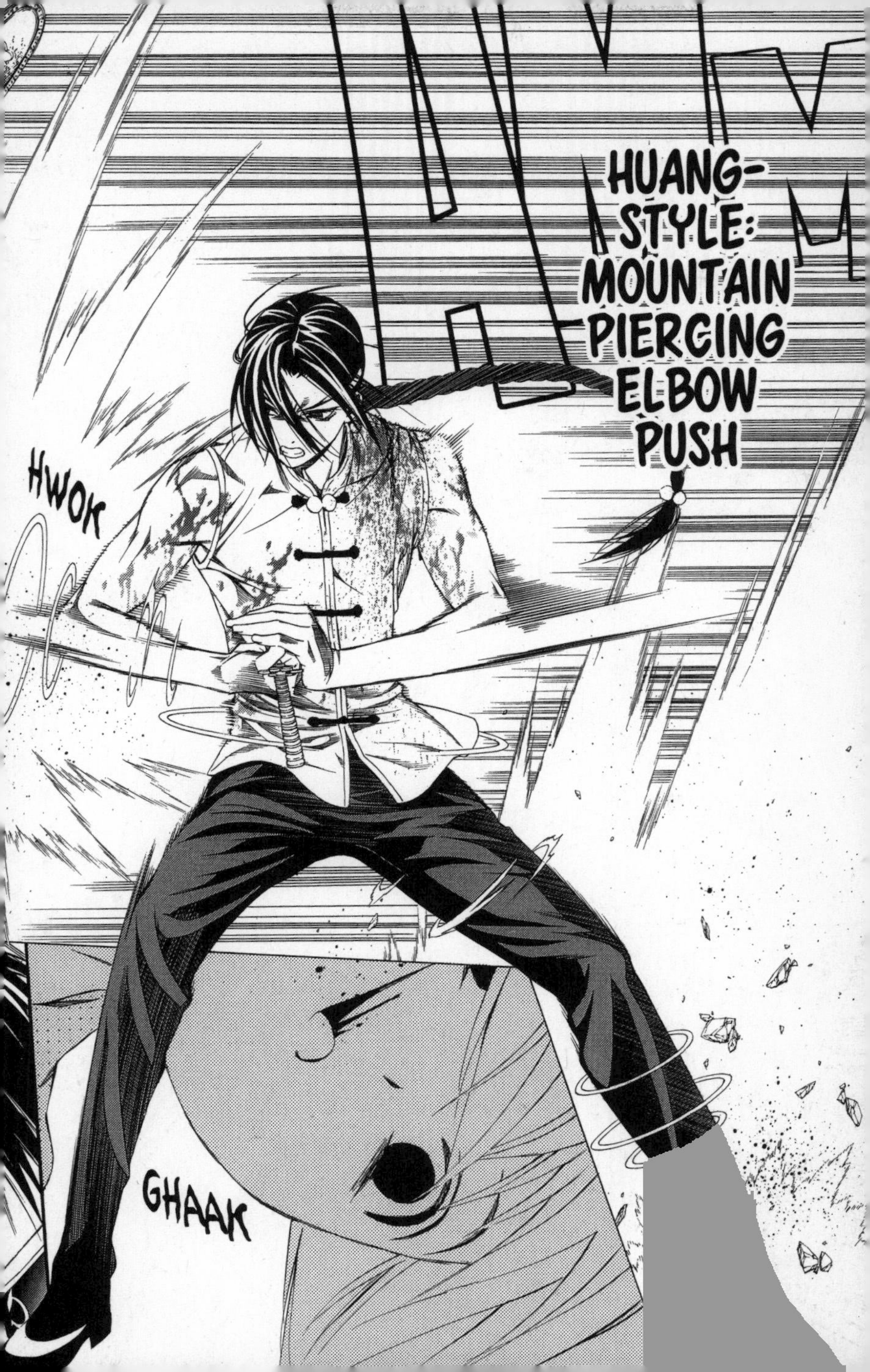
HUANG-STYLE: MOUNTAIN PIERCING ELBOW PUSH
HWOK
GHAAK

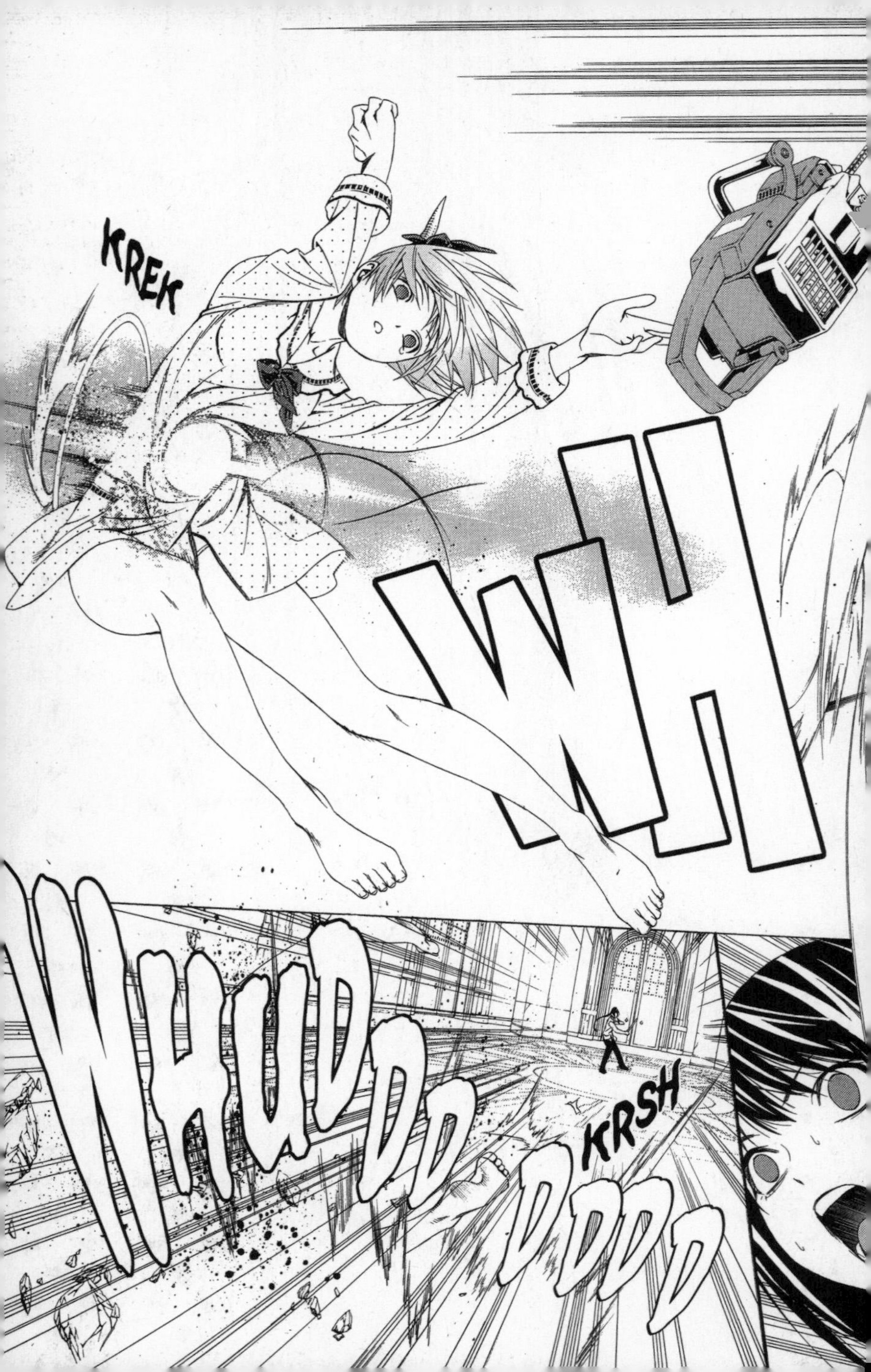
KREK
WH
WHUDDDDDDD
KRSH

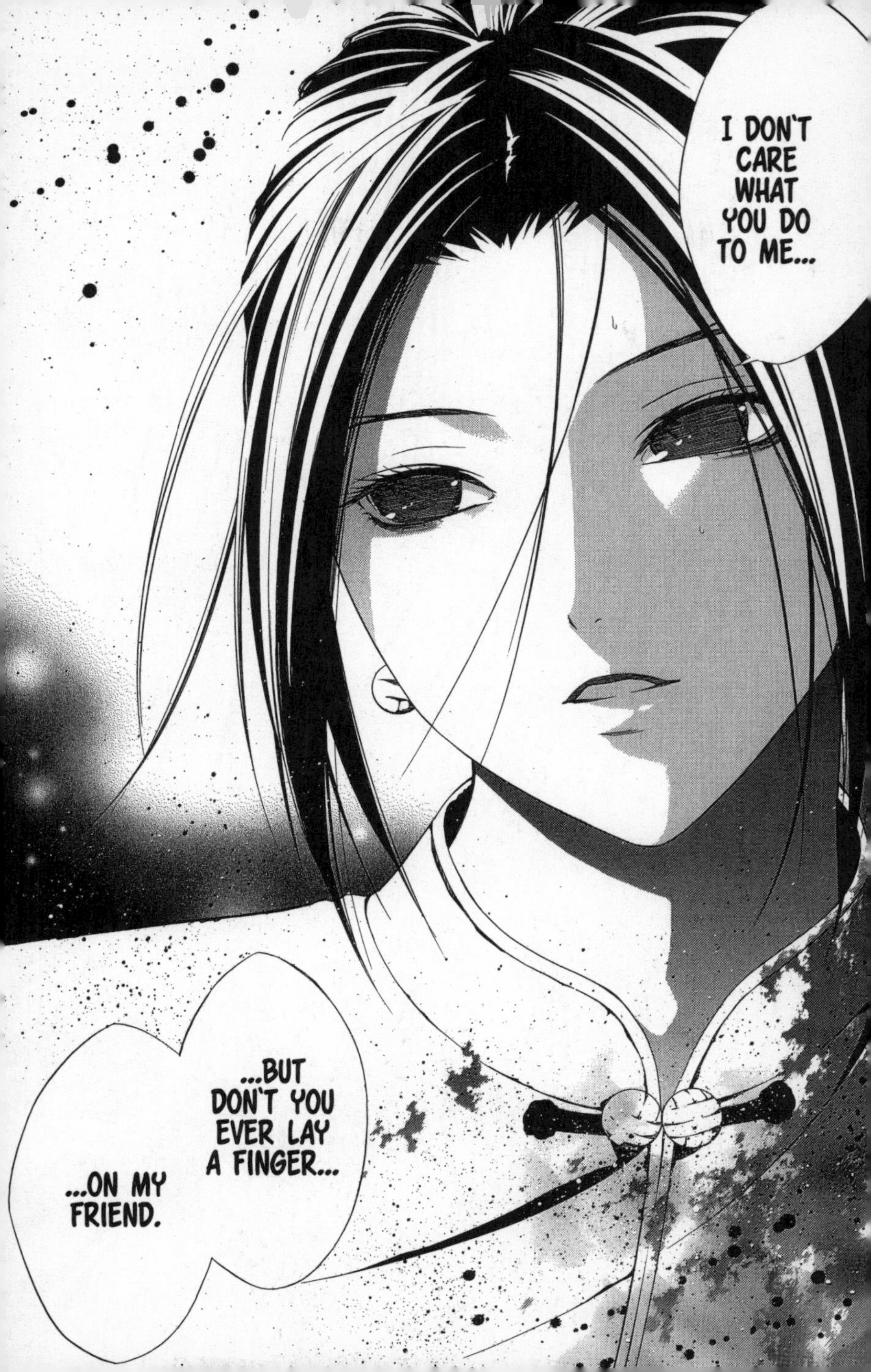
I DON'T CARE WHAT YOU DO TO ME...
...BUT DON'T YOU EVER LAY A FINGER...
...ON MY FRIEND.

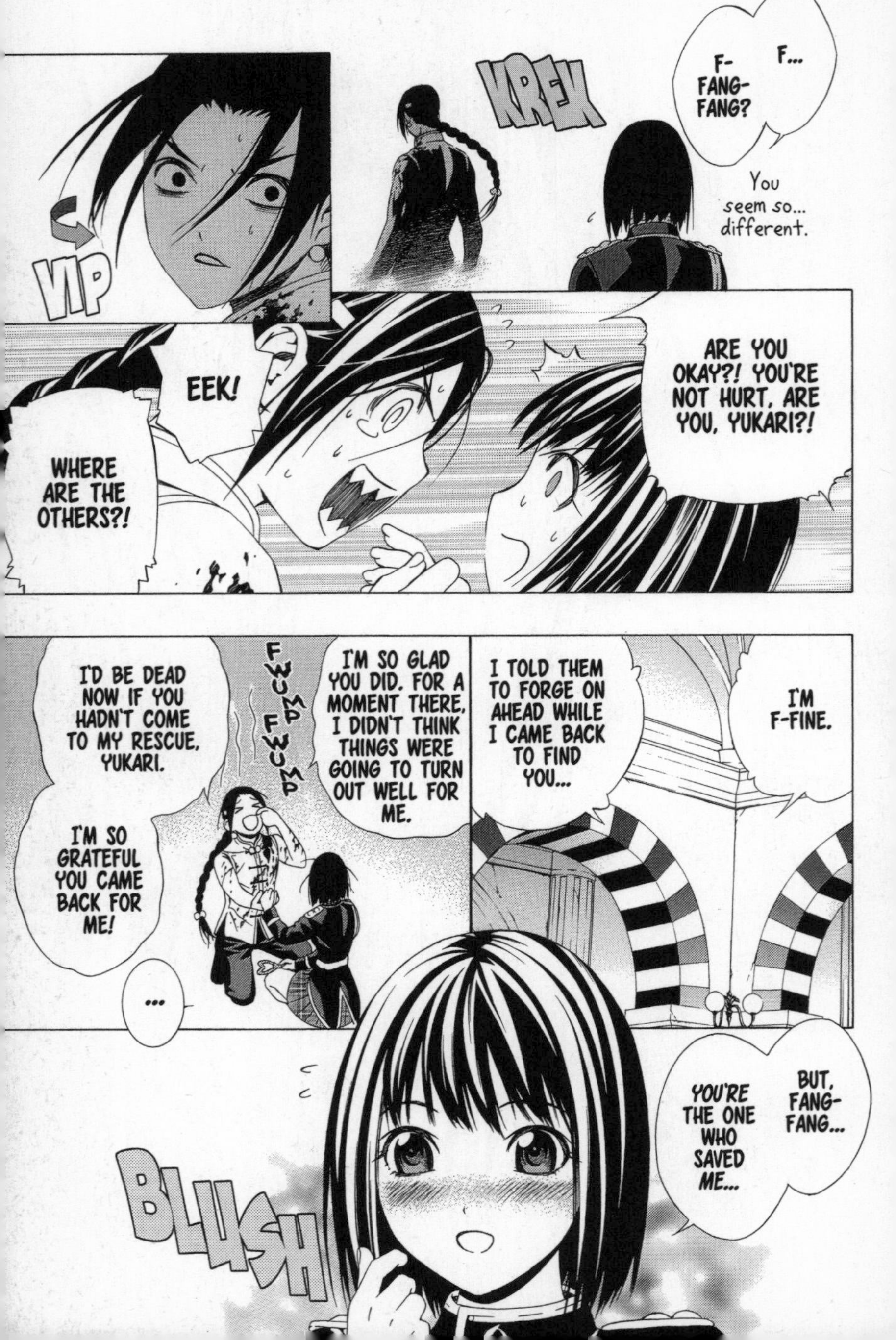
F...
F- FANG-FANG?
You seem so... different.
KREK
VIP
ARE YOU OKAY?! YOU'RE NOT HURT, ARE YOU, YUKARI?!
EEK!
WHERE ARE THE OTHERS?!
I'M F-FINE.
I TOLD THEM TO FORGE ON AHEAD WHILE I CAME BACK TO FIND YOU...
I'M SO GLAD YOU DID. FOR A MOMENT THERE, I DIDN'T THINK THINGS WERE GOING TO TURN OUT WELL FOR ME.
FWUMP FWUMP
I'D BE DEAD NOW IF YOU HADN'T COME TO MY RESCUE, YUKARI.
I'M SO GRATEFUL YOU CAME BACK FOR ME!
...
BUT, FANG-FANG...
YOU'RE THE ONE WHO SAVED ME...
BLUSH

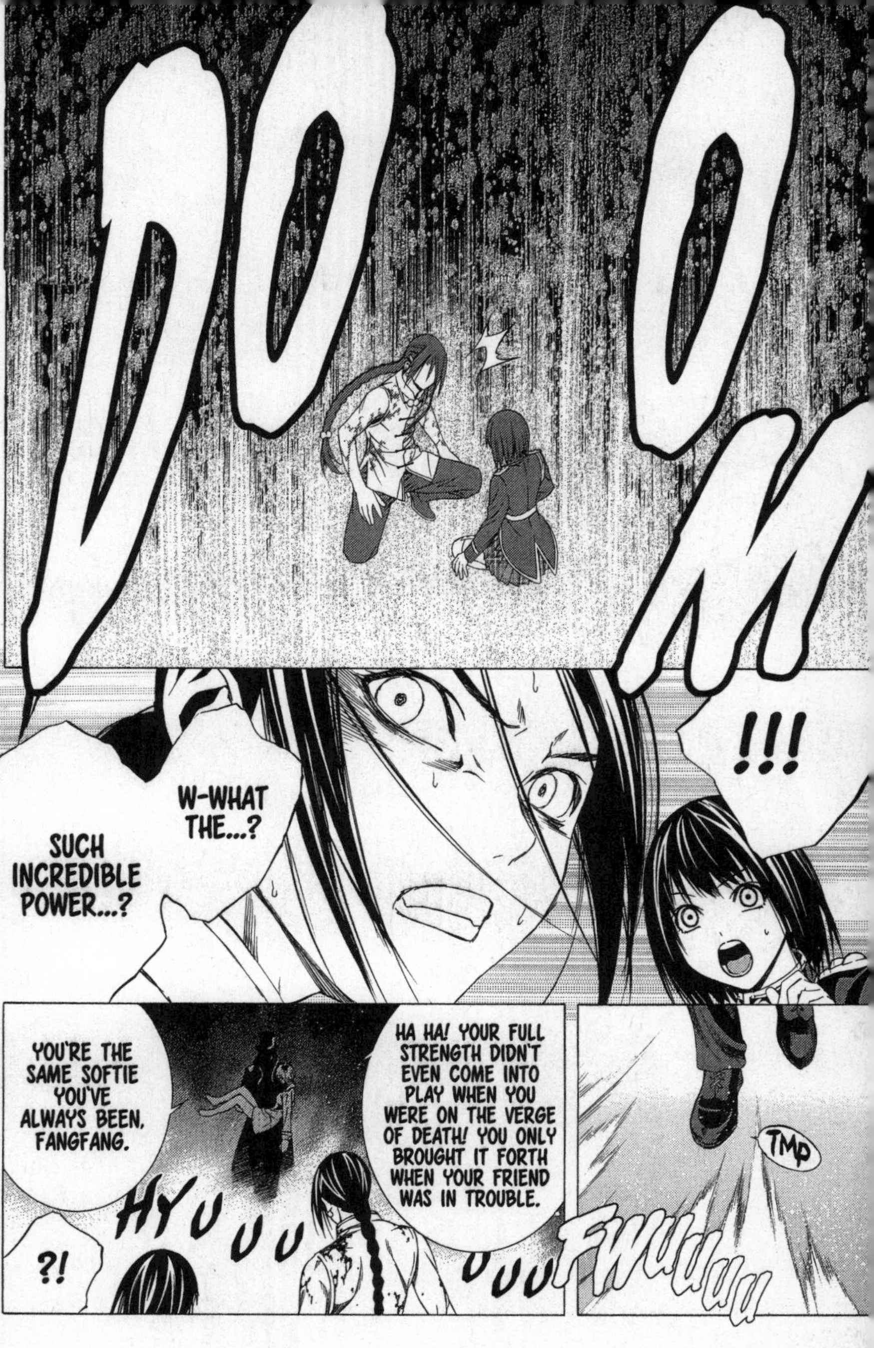
DOOM
!!!
W-WHAT THE...?
SUCH INCREDIBLE POWER...?
TMP
FWUUUUU
HA HA! YOUR FULL STRENGTH DIDN'T EVEN COME INTO PLAY WHEN YOU WERE ON THE VERGE OF DEATH! YOU ONLY BROUGHT IT FORTH WHEN YOUR FRIEND WAS IN TROUBLE.
YOU'RE THE SAME SOFTIE YOU'VE ALWAYS BEEN, FANGFANG.
HYUUUUUUU
?!

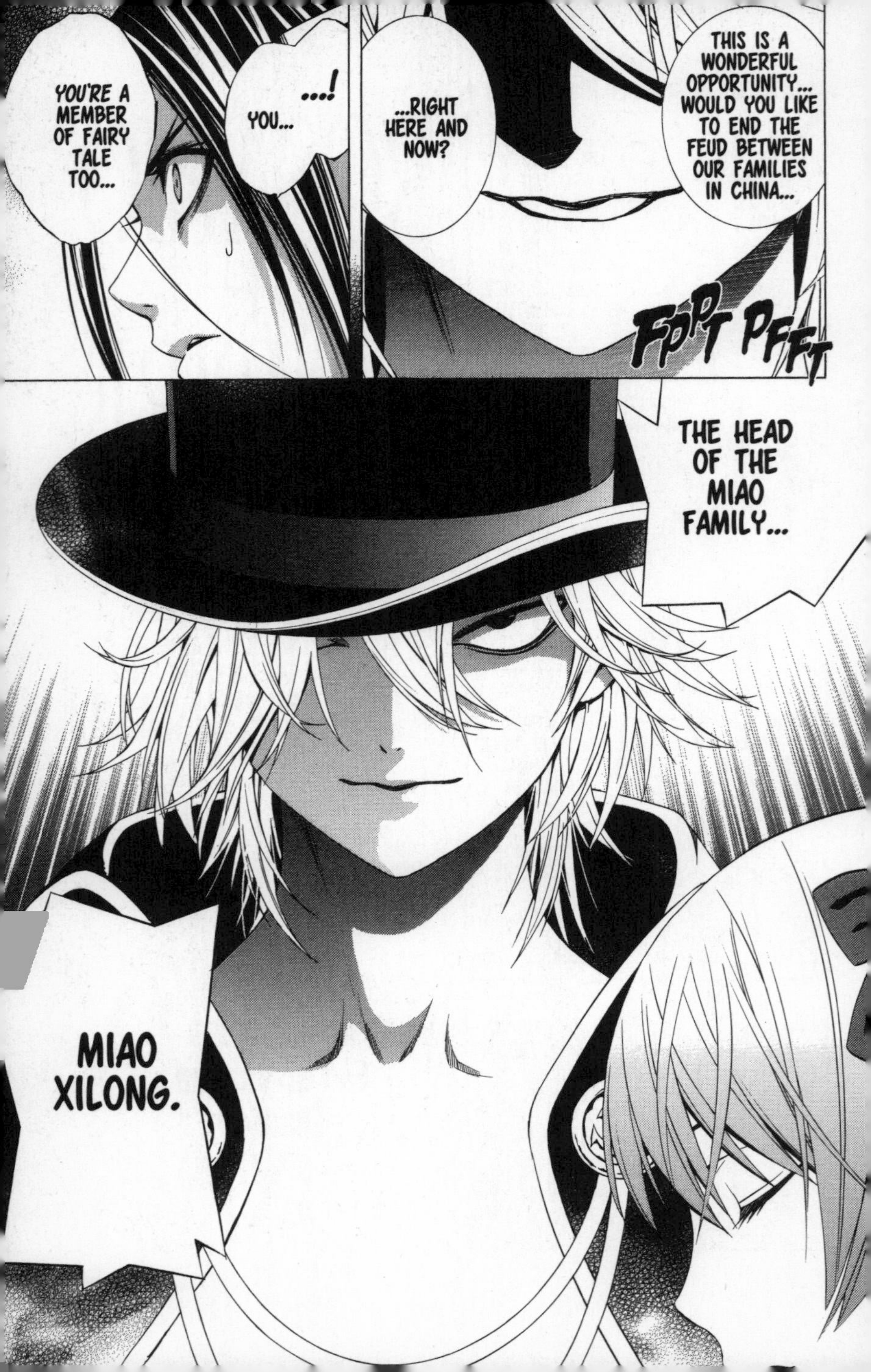
THIS IS A WONDERFUL OPPORTUNITY... WOULD YOU LIKE TO END THE FEUD BETWEEN OUR FAMILIES IN CHINA...
...RIGHT HERE AND NOW?
FPPT PFFT
...!
YOU...
YOU'RE A MEMBER OF FAIRY TALE TOO...
THE HEAD OF THE MIAO FAMILY...
MIAO XILONG.

ROSARIO + VAMPIRE

Season II

THIS VOLUME'S MEANINGLESS END-OF-VOLUME THEATER TAKES PLACE WHILE MOKA IS IMPRISONED IN THE HANGING GARDEN.

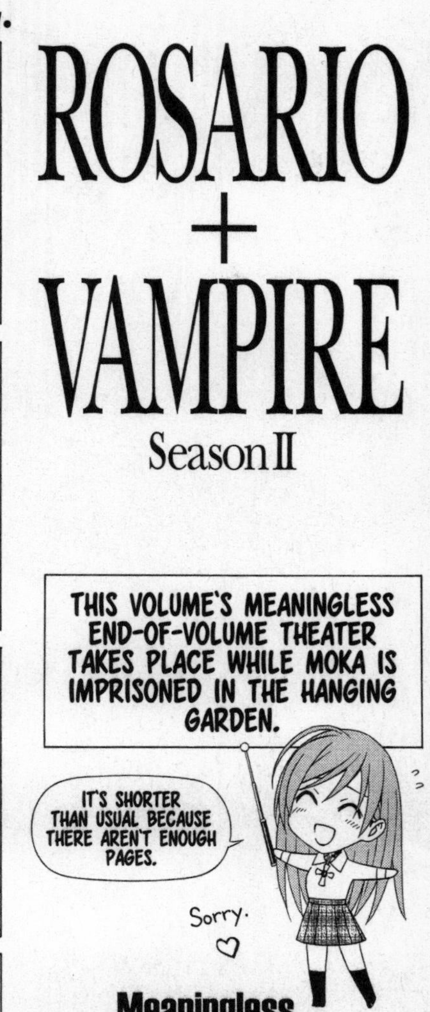
IT'S SHORTER THAN USUAL BECAUSE THERE AREN'T ENOUGH PAGES.
Sorry.

Meaningless End-of-Volume Theater

X

• Depressed-Depressed Moka's Diary •

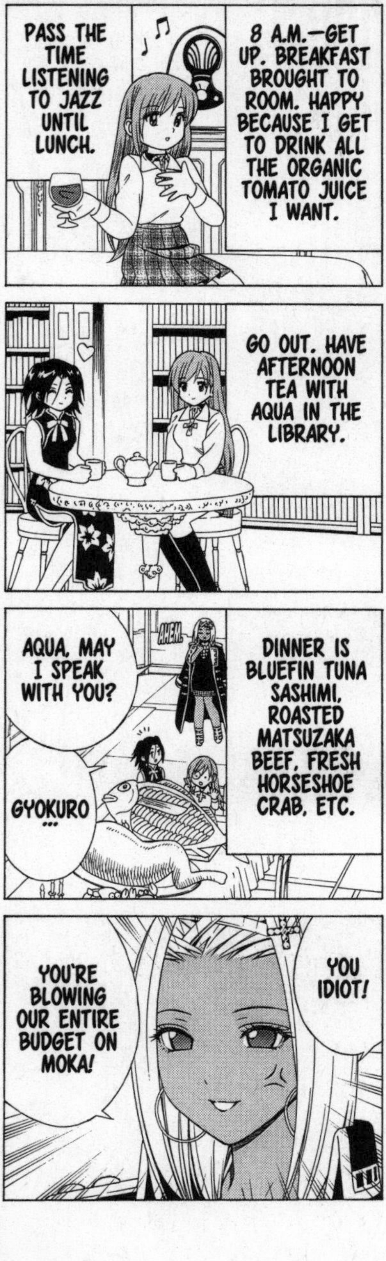
8 A.M.—GET UP. BREAKFAST BROUGHT TO ROOM. HAPPY BECAUSE I GET TO DRINK ALL THE ORGANIC TOMATO JUICE I WANT.
PASS THE TIME LISTENING TO JAZZ UNTIL LUNCH.
GO OUT. HAVE AFTERNOON TEA WITH AQUA IN THE LIBRARY.
DINNER IS BLUEFIN TUNA SASHIMI, ROASTED MATSUZAKA BEEF, FRESH HORSESHOE CRAB, ETC.
AHEM.
AQUA, MAY I SPEAK WITH YOU?
GYOKURO...
YOU IDIOT!
YOU'RE BLOWING OUR ENTIRE BUDGET ON MOKA!

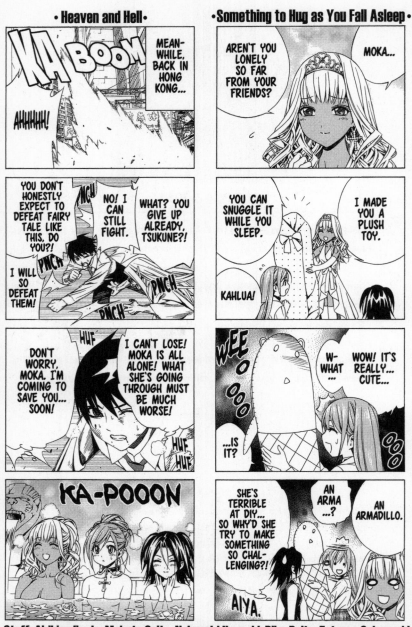

•Something to Hug as You Fall Asleep•

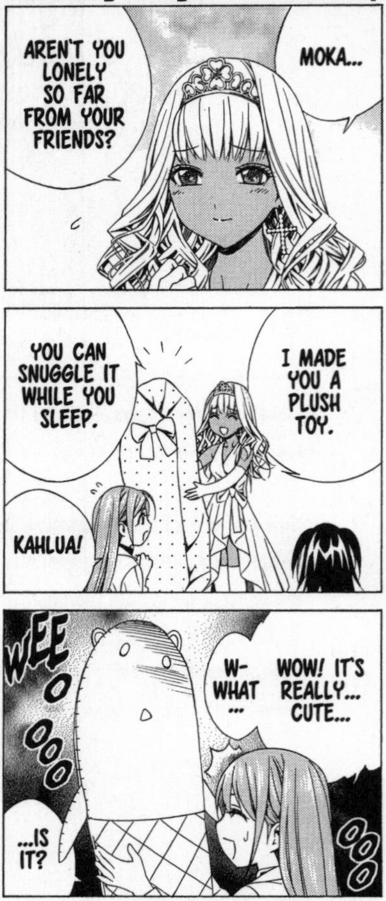
MOKA...
AREN'T YOU LONELY SO FAR FROM YOUR FRIENDS?
I MADE YOU A PLUSH TOY.
YOU CAN SNUGGLE IT WHILE YOU SLEEP.
KAHLUA!
OOO
WOW! IT'S REALLY... CUTE...
W-WHAT ...
WEE OOOOO
...IS IT?
AN ARMADILLO.
AN ARMA ...?
SHE'S TERRIBLE AT DIY... SO WHY'D SHE TRY TO MAKE SOMETHING SO CHAL-LENGING?!
AIYA.

•Heaven and Hell•

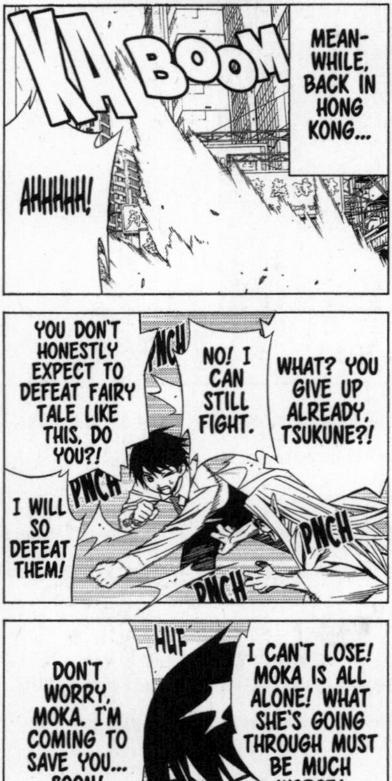
MEAN-WHILE, BACK IN HONG KONG...
KA BOOM
AHHHHH!
WHAT? YOU GIVE UP ALREADY, TSUKUNE?!
NO! I CAN STILL FIGHT.
PNCH
YOU DON'T HONESTLY EXPECT TO DEFEAT FAIRY TALE LIKE THIS, DO YOU?!
PNCH
PNCH
I WILL SO DEFEAT THEM!
PNCH
I CAN'T LOSE! MOKA IS ALL ALONE! WHAT SHE'S GOING THROUGH MUST BE MUCH WORSE!
HUF
DON'T WORRY, MOKA. I'M COMING TO SAVE YOU... SOON!
HUF HUF
KA-POOON

Staff: Akihisa Ikeda, Makoto Saito, Nobuyuki Hayashi, Rika Daita, Tatsuro Sakaguchi
CG: Takaharu Yoshizawa Editor: Junichi Tamada, Takuya Ogawa Comic: Kenju Noro

AKIHISA IKEDA

I love the *Sticky Fingers* album by The Rolling Stones. It's a perfect blend of rock, blues, soul, gospel—creating its own world. That's what gets me.

Now, this series isn't as grand as all that, but...the world I'm trying to create in Season II is something like it: a story that blends action, romantic comedy, fantasy... I even change the atmosphere in each volume.

Basically, what I'm trying to say is, to those who are expecting to see lots of romantic comedy and *moe*—consider yourself warned! Volume 10 is full of battle scenes!

Akihisa Ikeda was born in 1976 in Miyazaki. He debuted as a mangaka with the four-volume magical warrior fantasy series *Kiruto* in 2002, which was serialized in *Monthly Shonen Jump*. *Rosario+Vampire* debuted in *Monthly Shonen Jump* in March of 2004 and is continuing in the magazine *Jump Square (Jump SQ)* as *Rosario+Vampire: Season II*. In Japan, *Rosario+Vampire* is also available as a drama CD. In 2008, the story was released as an anime. Season II is also available as an anime now. And in Japan, there is a Nintendo DS game based on the series.

Ikeda has been a huge fan of vampires and monsters since he was a little kid. He says one of the perks of being a manga artist is being able to go for walks during the day when everybody else is stuck in the office.

ROSARIO+VAMPIRE: Season II
10

SHONEN JUMP ADVANCED Manga Edition

STORY & ART BY **AKIHISA IKEDA**

Translation/Kaori Inoue
English Adaptation/Annette Roman
Touch-up Art & Lettering/Stephen Dutro
Cover & Interior Design/Ronnie Casson
Editor/Annette Roman

ROSARIO + VAMPIRE SEASON II © 2007 by Akihisa Ikeda
All rights reserved. First published in Japan in 2007 by SHUEISHA Inc.,
Tokyo. English translation rights arranged by SHUEISHA Inc.

Printed in the U.S.A.

Published by VIZ Media, LLC
P.O. Box 77010
San Francisco, CA 94107

10 9 8 7 6 5 4 3 2 1
First printing, November 2012

www.viz.com

www.shonenjump.com

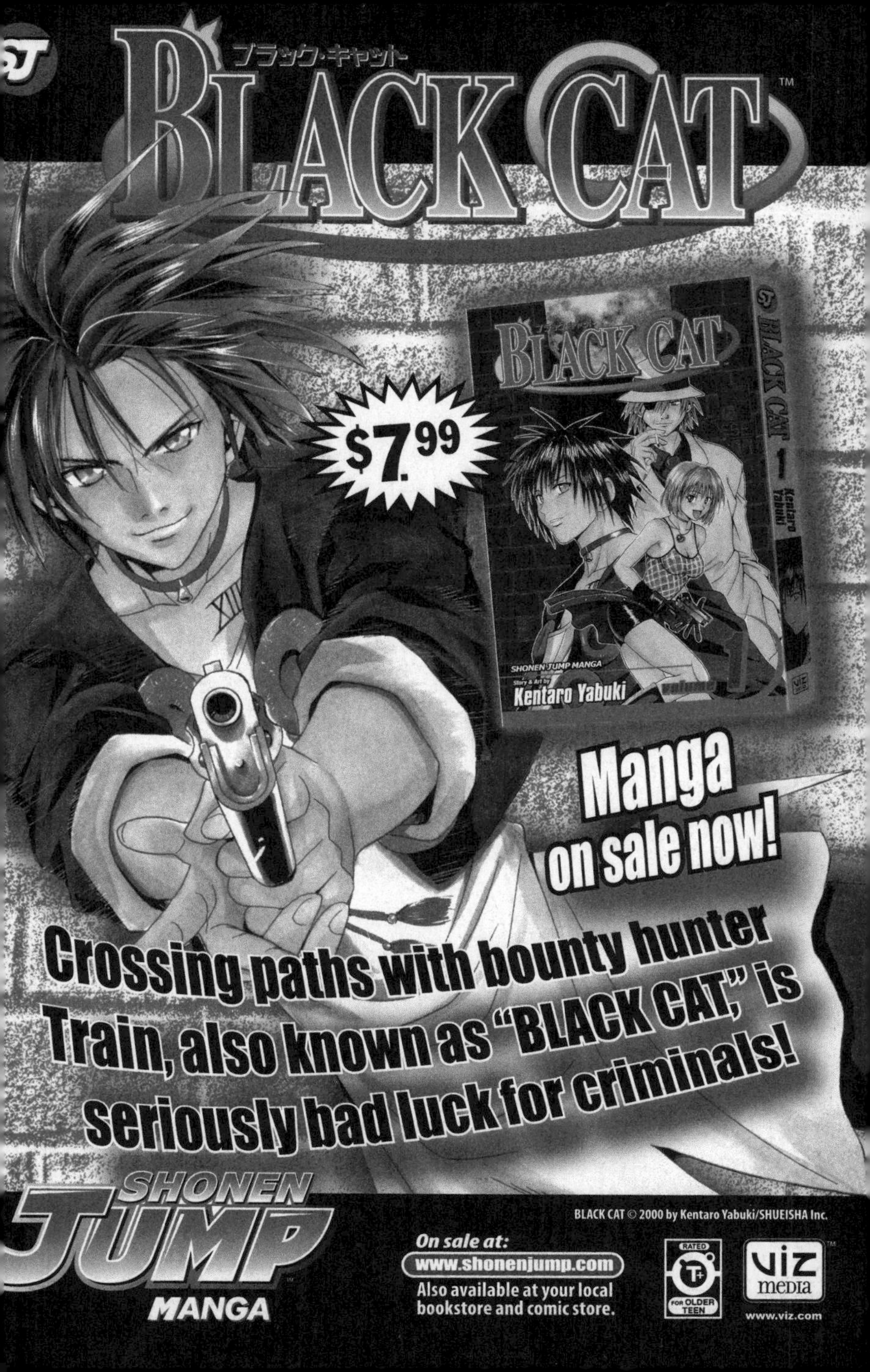
ブラック・キャット
BLACK CAT™
$7.99
BLACK CAT
SHONEN JUMP MANGA
Story & Art by
Kentaro Yabuki
BLACK CAT 1 Kentaro Yabuki
Manga on sale now!
Crossing paths with bounty hunter Train, also known as "BLACK CAT," is seriously bad luck for criminals!
SHONEN JUMP MANGA
BLACK CAT © 2000 by Kentaro Yabuki/SHUEISHA Inc.
On sale at:
www.shonenjump.com
Also available at your local bookstore and comic store.
RATED T+ FOR OLDER TEEN
VIZ media
www.viz.com

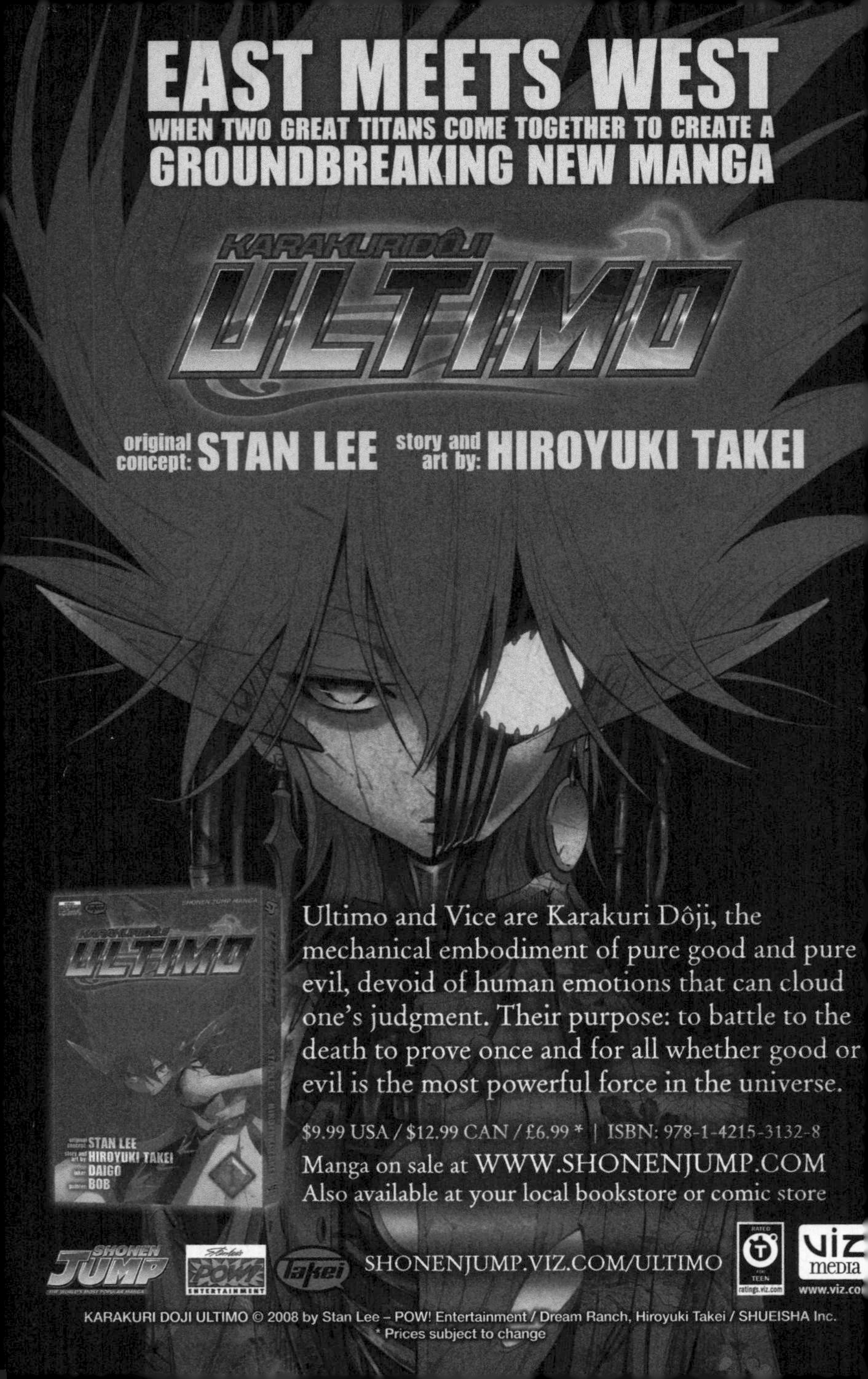
EAST MEETS WEST
WHEN TWO GREAT TITANS COME TOGETHER TO CREATE A
GROUNDBREAKING NEW MANGA
KARAKURIDÔJI
ULTIMO
original concept: STAN LEE
story and art by: HIROYUKI TAKEI
Ultimo and Vice are Karakuri Dôji, the mechanical embodiment of pure good and pure evil, devoid of human emotions that can cloud one's judgment. Their purpose: to battle to the death to prove once and for all whether good or evil is the most powerful force in the universe.
$9.99 USA / $12.99 CAN / £6.99 * | ISBN: 978-1-4215-3132-8
Manga on sale at WWW.SHONENJUMP.COM
Also available at your local bookstore or comic store
SHONEN JUMP
POW! ENTERTAINMENT
Takei
SHONENJUMP.VIZ.COM/ULTIMO
RATED T FOR TEEN
ratings.viz.com
viz media
www.viz.com
KARAKURI DOJI ULTIMO © 2008 by Stan Lee – POW! Entertainment / Dream Ranch, Hiroyuki Takei / SHUEISHA Inc.
* Prices subject to change

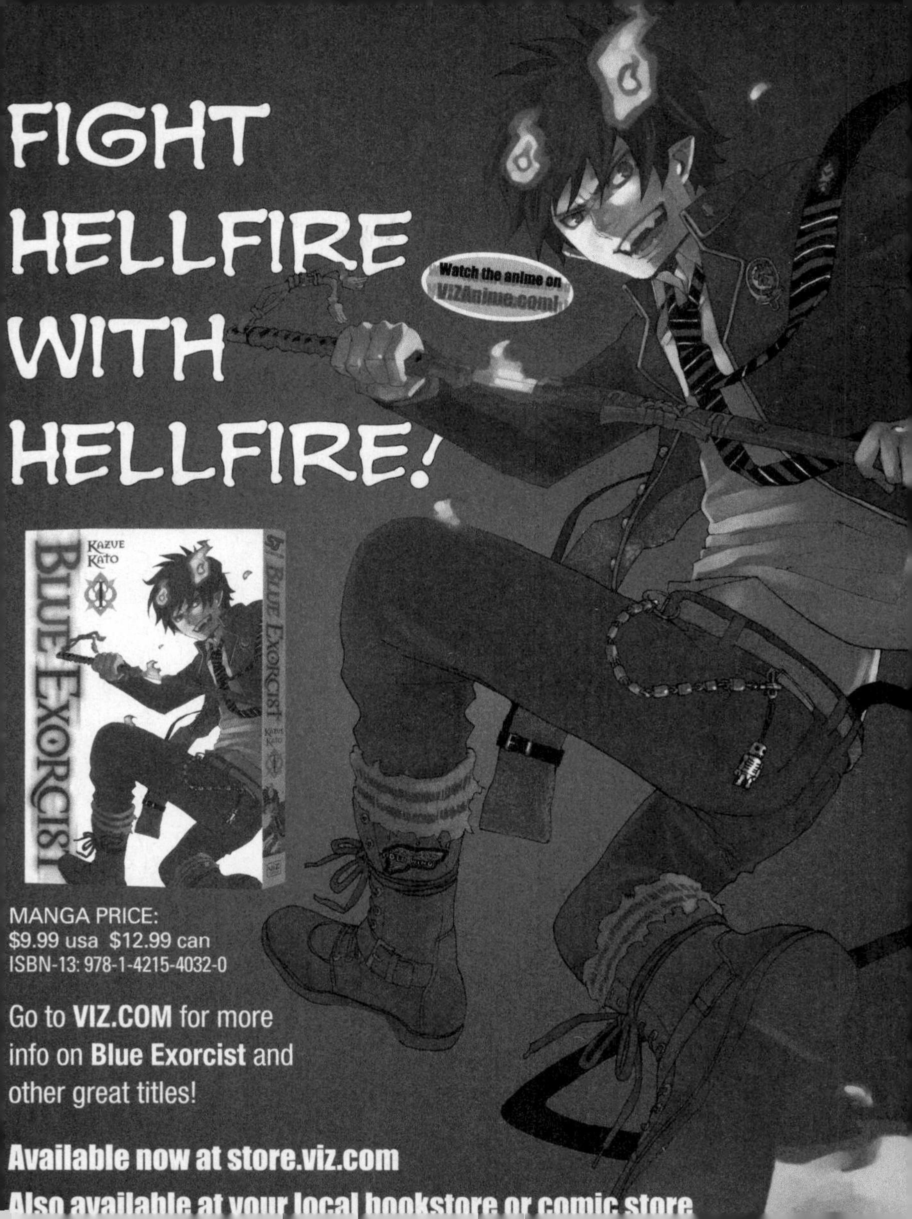
FIGHT HELLFIRE WITH HELLFIRE!
Watch the anime on VIZAnime.com!
KAZUE KATO
BLUE EXORCIST
MANGA PRICE:
$9.99 usa $12.99 can
ISBN-13: 978-1-4215-4032-0
Go to VIZ.COM for more info on Blue Exorcist and other great titles!
Available now at store.viz.com
Also available at your local bookstore or comic store

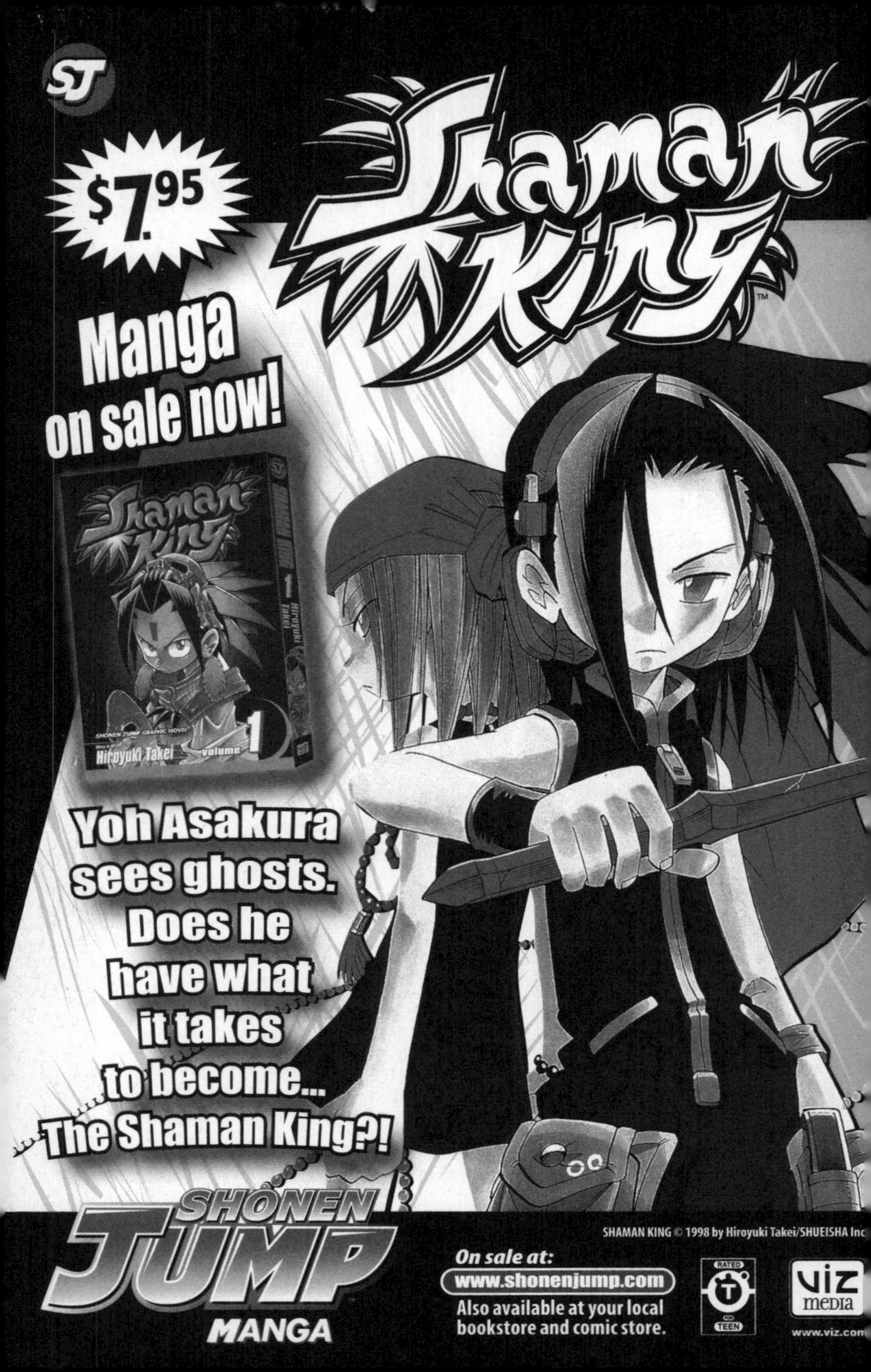
SJ
Shaman King™
$7.95
Manga on sale now!
Shaman King
SHONEN JUMP GRAPHIC NOVEL
Hiroyuki Takei
volume 1
Yoh Asakura sees ghosts. Does he have what it takes to become... The Shaman King?!
SHONEN JUMP MANGA
SHAMAN KING © 1998 by Hiroyuki Takei/SHUEISHA Inc
On sale at:
www.shonenjump.com
Also available at your local bookstore and comic store.
RATED T FOR TEEN
VIZ MEDIA
www.viz.com

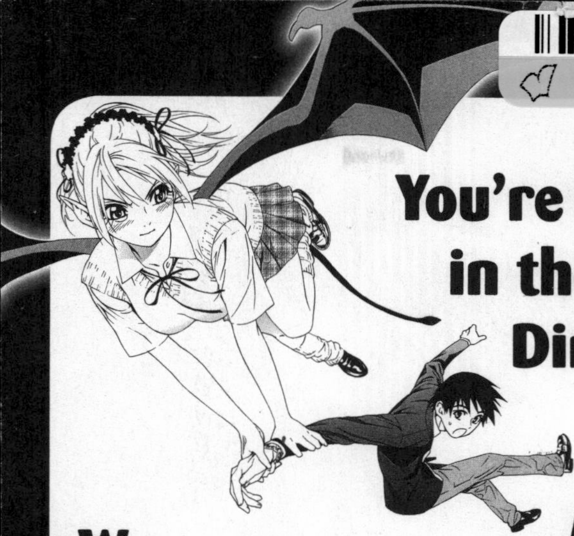

You're Reading in the Wrong Direction!!

Whoops! Guess what? You're starting at the wrong end of the comic!

...It's true! In keeping with the original Japanese format, **Rosario+Vampire** is meant to be read from right to left, starting in the upper-right corner.

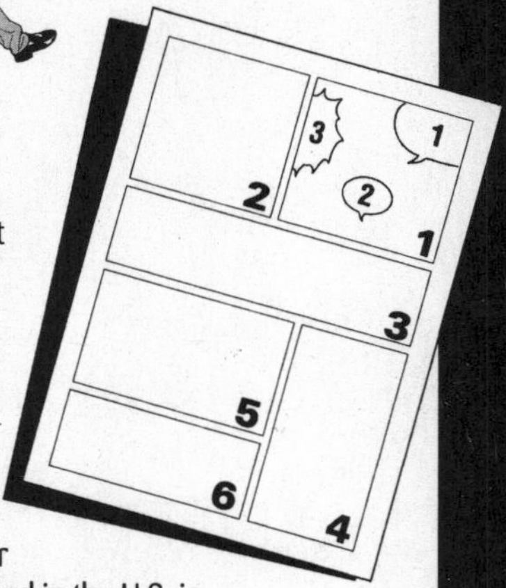
1
2
3
1
2
3
4
5
6

Unlike English, which is read from left to right, Japanese is read from right to left, meaning action, sound effects and word-balloon order are completely reversed... something which can make readers unfamiliar with Japanese feel pretty backwards themselves. For this reason, manga or Japanese comics published in the U.S. in English have sometimes been published "flopped"—that is, printed in exact reverse order, as though seen from the other side of a mirror.

By flopping pages, U.S. publishers can avoid confusing readers, but the compromise is not without its downside. For one thing, a character in a flopped manga series who once wore in the original Japanese version a T-shirt emblazoned with "M A Y" (as in "the merry month of") now wears one which reads "Y A M"! Additionally, many manga creators in Japan are themselves unhappy with the process, as some feel the mirror-imaging of their art skews their original intentions.

We are proud to bring you Akihisa Ikeda's **Rosario+Vampire** in the original unflopped format. For now, though, turn to the other side of the book and let the haunting begin...!

—Editor